LANGUAGES AND SILENCE
IN THE GERMAN-POLISH BORDERLAND

LANGUAGES AND SILENCE
IN THE
GERMAN-POLISH BORDERLAND

Elizabeth R. Vann

PIASA BOOKS
New York

Published by PIASA Books
The Polish Institute of Arts and Sciences of America
208 East 30th St., New York, NY 10016

ISBN 978-0-940962-74-3
Library of Congress Control Number: 2015952513

www.piasa.org/pb.html
Printed in the United States of America

This is for all victims of totalitarian regimes and ideologies,
most especially for those who,
in twentieth-century Europe,
experienced two

■◼■

Contents

CONTENTS

Preface

THE APPRENTICE AT AUSCHWITZ

For years, I thought that the story I am about to tell did not belong in this book at all. Very soon after I moved into the village I call Dobra, the principal of the local elementary school told me, quite unelicited, "You will never hear about what happened here after the war. That generation has died without talking about it to their own children." I understood that these two sentences did not quite align in 1992; many who experienced the Second World War and its aftermath were still alive. I took it as a warning about what not to ask, and really, I had no problem with that. I knew there had been terrible trauma, but I didn't see it as relating either to societal multilingualism or to ethnic and national identity. I was there to describe culture—to produce ethnography—with a focus on the connection between language and identity. What did the war have to do with that?

Besides my perception of its irrelevance, a rule of anthropological fieldwork I was taught as a college sophomore is that you conduct yourself in the field in a way that will make the people there happy to welcome any other anthropologist who might come after you. Anthropological ethics do not include asking questions that upset people, that feel to them like prying. It is different for journalists; they have limited time and an ethic of discovery. We anthropologists stay in the field for a long time and work with what we are offered, depending heavily on participant observation. We act as participants in whatever is going on, but observe as we're doing it and ask questions as appropriate. As anthropologist Elizabeth Traube puts it, our method is hanging out.

Contrary to prediction, survivors did tell me stories of the war and its aftermath. The principal was wrong. Several neighbors who had experienced the end of the war as adolescents poured out their stories to me as soon as they met me. I listened politely, out of a respect for elders that I shared with the people I was living with; I carefully wrote the stories down because I had been trained to take notes on everything. I was shaken by the intensity of the violent experiences. And then I shook it off and went on with what I saw as the "real work."

"Young people don't want to hear about these things." I think all the people who had trauma narratives to tell told me that. So yes, perhaps many of the war generation had never talked about their experiences, as the principal said; they had taken their stories to their graves. But people born after the war were apparently playing a role also. They didn't want to hear it. I could understand that very well. These are hard stories to listen to, and to be honest, I didn't want to hear them either. I did listen, but in my attitude toward listening, masked as what I saw as "research priorities," I also "went native." I felt about it as other members of my own, postwar, generation feel. Eventually, I saw this reluctance to listen as a kind of "conspiracy of silence." Later still, I saw that these silenced stories might actually be centrally related to survivors' German identity, and I started examining my own ethnography, by then "written up" as a dissertation, for other silences, and for what they might mean.

The story that follows—the memoir of a German-speaker from the bilingual borderland who found himself placed as an electrical apprentice at the heart of the Holocaust—was the most disturbing and disruptive story that I heard. Yet eventually, it was this story that taught me to hear so many other silences—me, the linguistic anthropologist, professionally trained and personally inclined to attend to what is said. I'm putting it first, frankly, because I've tried both middle and end, and readers have told me that, in the middle, it totally disrupts the flow of the narrative, or, at the end, it "seems to come out of nowhere." Ultimately, that's the point about repressed material; it is disruptive, and it does seem to come out of nowhere.

In the last months of 1942, three years into the Second World War, Anton Fischer was fourteen years old and in the eighth grade. The time had come for him to choose a trade and apply for an apprenticeship. He most wanted to go to Hamburg to the Merchant Marine, but the officials at the work assignment office told him that they were no longer accepting cadets because of air raids. Becoming an electrician was a second choice, and he was told that there was a place open for an electrical apprentice in Auschwitz, in the IG Farben chemical works there, about a hundred kilometers to the east of his family's home near the city then called Oppeln (after the war, when the region was transferred to Poland, it became known as Opole. The *e* is pronounced as an *uh* sound, by the way, with the accent on the second syllable.) He asked his parents, and they agreed, reasoning that Auschwitz was not very far from home. From Auschwitz, their son could come home by train on weekends.

He lived in barracks housing about 700–800 apprentices, mostly from the Auschwitz area. As in the area around Oppeln, people living near Auschwitz were bilingual, many having learned a dialect of Polish first, at home, and German later, at school. Under the racist ideology of Nazi Germany, this meant that their status as true, Aryan, Germans was suspect. However, the official policy was that they were Germans; Anton had been taught in school that his people were a "VOLKSSTAMM," that is, a branch of the race, and that the

Polish dialects constituted a form of contamination to be rooted out. The grocery store in his village of Dobra had a sign that said, "A German who speaks Polish is a traitor to his race," to remind people of this. Anton himself, at that time, was able to speak only German, although his parents were bilingual. The apprentices always and only spoke German, and no questions were asked.

They were taught different technical careers—to be chemists, smiths, electricians, welders; as Anton Fischer put it, "all the professions that IG Farben needed." After spending a year learning a variety of basic skills, they started the specialized part of their apprenticeships, in workshops, under supervision. "And some of us—not a lot, two or three of us—we were assigned to the Jews, you see? I was placed under the supervision of two Jews in the electrical workshop. The director told me they were called, 'Jop Jupiter,' and 'Prinz Eugene.'"

From the beginning of April to mid-December 1944, Mr. Fischer worked in an electrical workshop where, he remembered, 80 to 90 percent of the people were Jewish prisoners. The apprentices were given work uniforms, while the prisoners worked in their camp uniforms, with the blue-and-white stripes, and had triangles of different colors sewn to the pockets—red, green, other colors. "I asked about it, and the guy said, 'Yeah, that's because we're political prisoners, you see?' They had to be distinguished, the different kinds—the political prisoners were in a separate camp. Or criminals, or deserters, or black marketeers. Well, I had no idea about the camp, I just worked there."

He drew me a map of Auschwitz, showing the IG Farben factory, the barracks where the apprentices lived, the iron gate inscribed with "Arbeit Macht Frei," (the bitterly ironic statement that "Work makes [you] free") and behind it, he pointed out, a camp in which there were, "How many was it? What did Jop Jupiter tell me? I've looked for him, we wanted to find each other after the war, for certain reasons, because we became real friends . . . oh, yes! Ten thousand! There were ten thousand Jews in that camp. And they told me that they had an orchestra, which played in the mornings when they went out to work, and in the evenings when they came back."

The young Anton was told some things and he saw some things. On his map, fifty years later, he showed me a shortcut into town that he used to take. "It wasn't the case that people couldn't go out. Only the Jews couldn't." The shortcut passed by fields where he saw women working, guarded by women. "They lived in a separate camp," Mr. Fischer told me.

As for food, he said, "We didn't have it any better than the Jews, we were living in a camp just like they were, and we got cabbage soup, different things, we did not get great food, right? We got camp food!"

I pursued the matter: "So," I said, "You're fourteen years old, you've never been away from home, you're used to your mother's cooking, and here you are eating this camp food. What was that like for you?" He replied, "I used to take care of myself a little with stuff from home. When I came home, I ate a good dinner, and my mother would pack some food for me, some bacon, onions, garlic, because the, the, [he stammered] because that's what the Jews wanted! I would ask them what I should bring them from home, and they always said, 'Onions and garlic!' And so I had some extra food, and then, and, I'll tell you, I'm going to tell you what happened that made us friends!"

With this, he reversed himself; he got better food than the camp inmates because he was able to leave, to go home on the weekends as his parents had anticipated. He was not only relying himself on the food he was able to get from home, but also sharing it with Jewish colleagues who, as he knew, could not leave. And having admitted this much, it was as if he felt he might as well tell me his most significant story. As he spoke, tears came to his eyes. He had to wipe them away, but he did not break down.

"I was looking for something in the workshop, and I opened a drawer that was always locked. There was an arsenal of weapons in it. A weapons cache belonging to the Jews. As I began to stand up, I found myself surrounded by Jews. Four or five of them, standing close around me. What would you have done, as a German?"

He paused, and I asked, "When you found yourself surrounded like that, were you afraid?" Mr. Fischer replied, "No, I wasn't afraid. But I understood that I had to make a decision. Something rose up inside me, and I said, 'I didn't see anything.' Then they moved aside, and I went back to my bench. And everything was uneasy, because they didn't know what I was going to do after that, you know? I looked around, a little, and saw how they spirited the weapons off somewhere else. But I didn't say a word. Then, when I went home for the week-end, I asked my mother and my father whether what I had done was right. And they said, 'Son, you did the right thing, but don't you breathe a word about this to anyone! You'll wind up in the camp yourself, for not having reported it! Not a word, not to anyone!' So that's what I did."

On December 15, Auschwitz was bombed, and the apprentices were sent home, as they were told, "for Christmas." Mr. Fischer recalled that he went to his teachers, "And I said, 'Mr. Jupiter, Prinz Eugene, sir, I'm going home now, so I came to say good-bye.' And Prinz Eugene said to me, 'Anton, if we survive the war, we'll surely see each other again.'"

The apprentices had been told that if they were needed, they'd be informed. And after Christmas 1944, word indeed came that Anton was to return to Auschwitz. "But my father said, 'Son, let me get this straight: the Russians are in Cracow and you want to go to Auschwitz?!' [Cracow is about 50 kilometers east of Auschwitz.] Well, it was good advice. So that's how I got out of Auschwitz."

With the Soviet army rapidly advancing through Poland to eastern Germany, German civilians fled westward. To be in territories invaded from the west by American, French, and British forces was considered much safer than to remain in territory under Soviet military control. Mr. Fischer's father's experience in the First World War suggested to him that a large family fleeing together was an easy target. He split the family up and Anton and two of his sisters headed southwest towards the mountainous Czech border. His sisters decided to stay in a town by the border, and Anton crossed over into the Sudetenland, still under German control. There he was picked up by the military police, briefly assigned to another electrical workshop, and then, about a month before Germany's surrender on May 8, 1945, drafted. As German forces retreated, driven west by the advancing Soviet army, Anton was involved in various last-ditch battles. Ultimately, when the armies invading from the west met the Soviet forces, he was captured by American forces. Like most of the captured German army, he was held for about six weeks.

After his release, he ended up staying with a family in Vienna. The linguistic politics had reversed themselves; now, if he wanted to return home, he had to prove his Polish identity by demonstrating that he knew Polish. He found a few Polish language textbooks, studied, and did well enough on an exam to convince the officials that he was a Pole and therefore ought to be allowed to enter what was now Poland. As for Jop Jupiter and Prinz Eugene, he tried to find them, through the Red Cross, after the war, and he was trying again at the time of our interviews. Prinz Eugene, Anton Fischer told me, was not likely still to be alive; he was in his forties at the time of the war. But Jop Jupiter might be. He was only in his twenties. "But," he added resignedly, "I don't know whether either of them survived the war." Ultimately, Anton Fischer died without having learned more about the fate of his teachers.

———

Mr. Fischer told me this story in his kitchen in September 1995. I realized that he had tried to tell it to me the first time we had met, in December 1993. It may be that he would have told it to me when I saw him in November 1994, if I had signaled any willingness to listen. And even having listened, taken notes, and recorded, I promptly and thoroughly banished the interviews to an intellectual black box labeled "Do something with this when the dissertation is finished, maybe." That black box got dumped out for me after the massacre at Columbine High School. In the wave of grief and shock that engulfed the country—it was the first high casualty massacre of innocent people in a public place, and before 9/11, remember—the news stories essentially led: "Two teenage boys searched the internet for Nazi propaganda, wore swastikas, gave each other Nazi salutes, and, on Hitler's birthday, they killed twelve students, one teacher, injured twenty-one more, and then turned their weapons on themselves." (See, for example, *Time*, May 3, 1999). A counternarrative formed in my mind: "Teenage boy growing up in Nazi Germany, surrounded by Nazi propaganda, taught his own racial superiority in Nazi schools, sent to work in the most horrific death camp of the Holocaust, keeps deadly dangerous secret for Jewish teachers!" It was only then that I decided to include Anton Fischer's story in the dissertation. But I didn't really know how or why it was important.

The reflections that eventually changed the title of the dissertation, "Language, Ethnicity and Nationality in the German-Polish Borderland," to that of this book, *Languages and Silence in the German-Polish Borderland*, is not the story itself, but the way it was told, and not my retelling of this story, but the way I almost failed to hear it. I had to wonder, how did I miss this? And what else have I missed? The answer to the first question sheds some light on field research and the pitfalls of its methodology. It's the answer to the second question, however, that led me to believe that silence demands analysis and explication just as much as anything that is said. It is an ethnographic fact, and a social fact in Durkheim's terms.

How did I miss this? When Anton Fischer first told me that he'd been an apprentice at Auschwitz, I quite simply didn't believe him. Furthermore, I thought he had an agenda: to try to monopolize my attention and direct it away from the Slavic/Silesian aspects of the linguistic and cultural situation in front of me. Finally, as I've said, I didn't want to hear it because it is an upsetting story and I didn't want to be upset.

I didn't believe him. It was January 21, 1993, and I had been living and doing research in Mr. Fischer's village since November 1, 1992. The event was a Christmas party sponsored by the village's local Social and Cultural Society of the German Minority (in Poland, traditional Roman Catholic practice forbids parties during the penitential season of Advent; Christmas parties are held after December 25). The German consul was an honored guest, and only German was being spoken in the room. As things were starting to break up, Mr. Fischer pulled up a chair beside me, introduced himself, wondered aloud whether his life story would be interesting to me as a researcher, and started to tell it. He began with what, over the course of almost three months, I had come to expect from people who sought me out: that he and his parents and grandparents all the way back had always lived in this part of Silesia, that this was their HEIMAT (homeland), and that the language of this region was always German. He himself, he said, had spoken only German until the end of the war, and had had to learn Polish from scratch, from books, in order to get by. But then he went on: if we're going to tell the truth about Nazism, we should tell the whole truth. He himself had done his electrical apprenticeship in Auschwitz, had learned his trade there, living in barracks, and had been taught by Jews. So he knew what things had been like there.

Later that day, I recorded, "All this was said in even tones, while I wondered how to react. Finally I asked him if he'd been back there since the war, if he'd seen the museum. He said he had, he'd been there with his brother-in-law, and proceeded to give me the 'we didn't know' formulation. He said, we saw what was to the right and to the left. This told me, at least, that he didn't intend to deny the existence of the death camp, but rather was trying to give me 'the good side of Nazism,' that it gave him an apprenticeship." OK. It seemed evident that he had lied to me about the language of his family and the region; he had responded to my question, "Tell me, do you also speak Silesian?" by looking away and saying, "As our parents taught us, and as school taught us. School taught us German," but I heard him speaking Silesian in another room not twenty minutes later. Furthermore the assertion that German boys had been employed as apprentices in the most notorious concentration and death camp of the Holocaust went well beyond my knowledge base, and I found it incredible. I thought, "Auschwitz is a town, as well as a camp; perhaps he did his electrical apprenticeship 'in Auschwitz,' living in some sort of barrack environment." The Nazis were big on camps of all sorts, and a lot of German kids wound up in them; for example, the regime housed children evacuated from cities under Allied bombardment to camps run by the Party (Koehn 1977). (Readers familiar with *The Lion, the Witch and the Wardrobe* will know that the British, in contrast, relied on foster families in the countryside.) It made sense to me that there might have been camps for apprentices in various places, including the town of Auschwitz. I thought that having perhaps been near Auschwitz, he was extending a claim to know "what really happened."

I thought he had an agenda. The kinds of views Mr. Fischer seemed to be expressing were in flood in the Polish territories that had been German before 1945, especially those which retained a population that had lived there before the transfer of territories, like Opole Silesia. Opole Silesia was astir with right-wing, western-backed German-language publications, expounding the Germanness of all of Silesia and engaging in body-count justifications: endless downward revisions of the number of Holocaust victims and upward revisions of the number of victims of the Allies' atrocities, such as the carpet-bombing of Dresden, as if getting the math to work out in Germans' favor would absolve German fascism in the eyes of history. I was not only reading a lot of it, but several people in Dobra had sought me out to expound upon it in person.

Furthermore, I had known even before starting the field research that the people who were active in German Minority clubs constituted a minority, and a sort of elite, within broader Opole Silesian communities. They had established themselves as "point people" for the German journalists who were paying attention to the region as never before. And they spoke German, whereas the journalists, of course, did not speak Polish. This was early in my fieldwork. I knew where there is social division, a fieldworker must gain the trust of people on the down side first, and here, evidently, those who identified as "Silesian," rather than as "German," were the down side. This group—the German Minority—clearly had its "party line" in order, as they were all saying the same things to the journalists. I did not want to be perceived as being in their pocket. We had been warned in our training about the problem of anthropologists being "co-opted" by a subgroup of the society under study. This was another reason to stay away from Anton Fischer.

I didn't want to hear it. In addition to Mr. Fischer's story, I heard about surviving the complete destruction of Dresden by aerial bombardment, ethnic cleansing, the danger of rape by Soviet soldiers. The way I was spotlighted as the intended audience, while everyone else in the room was ignored, told me that it was the presence of an outsider that was triggering their talk. Even when I had no suspicions of lying or manipulation, being in the spotlight is no way for an anthropologist to work. I felt that if I did not establish myself as positively uninterested in the war, its aftermath, and the politics of Silesia-as-lost-German-territory, I might never hear anything else, and, since the language chosen for these narratives was almost always German (an interesting fact in and of itself), that I might never hear anything substantive said in any other language. I knew that setting my research agenda in the eyes of the people around me in such a way that all of them would be able to articulate their views, in whatever language they wished, whether they experienced the end of the war or not, and whether they were ideologically committed to the Germanness of Silesia or not, was important. So at all opportunities with everyone I met, I said that my interest was multilingualism, and I insisted on speaking Polish. I returned Polish when addressed in German. I listened politely to these trauma narratives but I did not follow up. And in those ways, I acted just like

people of my own age from the group I was working with—a form of co-op-
tation that I didn't think to guard against. They speak Polish, and, as the people
who chose me to talk to repeatedly told me, "young people don't want to hear
about these things." So it seems that some survivors enforced silence on themselves; others had help from their grown children. Yet I was an outsider; it can
be easier, sometimes, to talk to an outsider than to your own children.

I actually didn't know that I didn't want to hear it until I had come to believe that the story was possible. I had listened to quite a bit more right-wing
German nationalist quasi-Nazi opinionating from Anton Fischer before that
happened. I wanted to stay away from him, after that January encounter, but
I wasn't able to, simply because he was the only electrician in Dobra. Wiring
was old; it was inevitable that I would occasionally have an electrical problem.
And so, almost two years later (November 21, 1994), I listened to him as he
rewired the plug to my space heater. He told me at great length about a recent
article in the *Upper Silesian Gazette* about how the fourteenth-century Polish
monarch Casimir the Great had signed a treaty saying that Poland would leave
Silesia in peace forever, and thus Silesia came to Germany forever. He said
that Silesia is not Poland, that they are merely under Polish occupation, and,
most alarmingly, showed me a little calendar and business card of an organization in Hamburg describing itself as the "government in exile" of the "East
German territories of the German Reich"—a clear reference to the Nazi
regime, which described itself as the "Third Reich," or "empire"—and it was
printed entirely in the Gothic typeface used at that time.

Yet again, I listened to him several months after that when he came to
work on the overhead light in my bathroom (June 10, 1995). He quickly found
his favorite topic, and I quickly tuned him out. It was that day that I suddenly
realized that what he was saying no longer sounded like propaganda. Electri-
fied myself, I listened as he described the physical layout of the concentration
camp at Auschwitz with the detailed memory people have for lived experience.
He added, "and when they went out in the mornings to work, there was an orchestra playing! And they were greeted with music when they came back in
the evenings!"

My God, I thought. I know that because when I was in high school, I saw
Playing for Time with Vanessa Redgrave. They didn't show that movie here.
How does he know it?

I was too well-trained not to pursue the inquiry once I knew I wasn't being
used as an audience for political beliefs that I found offensive, nor being led by
the nose by someone hoping to unduly influence my research findings. So I called
Jud Newborn, an anthropologist who had written a book on the death camps, and

asked him whether it were possible for a German boy to have done an electrician's apprenticeship at Auschwitz. It was, he said. There was a massive chemical plant at Auschwitz, a branch of IG Farben, the fourth largest corporation in the world (Dwórk and van Pelt 1996: 198). Its location at Auschwitz resulted from the confluence of favorable geography, the need of the warring Nazi regime to increase German chemical production, and the nearby availability of slave labor. IG Farben was built by inmates of Auschwitz, many of whom were beaten to death in the process (231–32). Skilled construction workers and technicians were brought to Auschwitz from other concentration camps to work there (208). There would have been Jewish electricians. In addition, a civilian, German workforce also worked for IG Farben, imported as part of the effort to colonize and Germanize eastern Europe. In fact, the town of Auschwitz was singled out to become an exemplary German town on the Nazi model, and the IG Farben / SS complex engulfed it (209–11). And IG Farben employed apprentices.

I conducted two lengthy interviews that September, and the narrative version above is based on those interviews. And then I banished the completed interviews to some vague future project after graduate school.

In short, I employed the defensive tactics of the Silesian postwar generation not just for emotional, but also for practical reasons. They, too, of course, may have responded to their parents out of anxiety not to be entirely overwhelmed by a trauma that happened a few years before they were born.

So for a start, what else I had missed was all the other trauma narratives. I have only my notes on these. Only in Anton Fischer's case did I follow up with a tape recorder. Of course I did nothing with that, either. But having realized my mistake, I slowly came to understand that the silences are as important as the languages, and that the silences, no less than the languages, are key to the cultural analysis.

It was historian and theorist Ewa Domańska who suggested to me that the word is not "silence," but "repression." It was a step I was not ready to take when she said it, in 2008. I had some interest in psychological anthropology as an undergraduate, but the graduate program I chose—the University of Chicago—was not strong in this kind of anthropology, and I moved away from that interest with little regret. I have felt, then, less than qualified to frame the issue in such frankly psychoanalytic terms. However, that hesitation founders on the rock of a core principle of anthropological inquiry instilled in me as both an undergraduate major and a graduate student: deal with what you find in fieldwork. Happily, Janina Fenigsen, a sociocultural and linguistic anthropologist, steered me toward reading that puts me on ground a bit less wet and slippery: another linguistic anthropologist, Don Kulick, has worked with Billig's reformulation of the Freudian "repression" concept to explore the way that, "in conversing, we must also create silences" (Billig 1999: 261, quoted in Kulick and Schieffelin 2004: 357). I go into this reformulation in more depth in the introductory chapter.

There are two points for readers to carry into the book. First, if it really is repression, in a reformulated yet still psychoanalytic sense, then it is perhaps not surprising that I so quickly "went native" in this regard. True, I had methodological hesitations. And, by the time I entered the field, I identified entirely as a linguistic anthropologist, and I was trained to focus on what is said. Further, I was busy, delighted not only to find rich linguistic material to work on but Silesian colleagues who shared my passion.

But stories like this one are emotionally overwhelming. That's why they get repressed. I was no more immune to that than anybody else in the situation. That's an inevitable problem of a human researcher working with human subjects, the "Heisenberg uncertainty principle" of the human sciences. But ultimately, the "silence," or "repression," has to be in the book, and has to "come out of nowhere." It has to be in the book, because while eight chapters are enough to wrap up the sociology, the linguistics, and the shared cultural understandings of identity, it is the silence—the repression—that sheds light on the forcefulness and intensity with which some people express their identity—on its vehemence.

Further, the repressed material has to be, as Germans say, "ein Kapital für sich." The phrase means literally, "a chapter unto itself." In use, it commonly means "a whole separate story." But it can also mean "something kept to oneself" (Walter Kempowski used this double meaning in his novel of the same name, about women prisoners of war in what became East Berlin). Perhaps it can be stretched to mean, "something kept *from* oneself"—a rough and ready definition of repression. Be that as it may, the whole point is that it has been banished from social life. It seems to make sense—to make the book reflect its subject matter—to banish further consideration of it to the last chapter.

So forget the apprentice at Auschwitz. Don't worry about it. We're not going to come back to it until chapter 9. But just please don't completely forget this: without the trauma narratives, there's no insight into the vehemence of identity, and it's the insight into the vehemence of identity that I see as the most important comparative finding of the book. Without it, too, I don't think the book's attempted contribution to a revised and revitalized culture concept is worth much either.

———

Every anthropologist's most profound debt is to the people who welcome her in fieldwork. For reasons to be made plain in the book, we made the decision—a difficult and ambivalent one—that nobody would appear here under their real name. Politically, as Silesians say, these are not those times, and it is my hope that the decision can be revisited, discussed again, and that there will be another opportunity, in print and by name, to express my deep gratitude to the people whose generosity fills these pages.

By any standard, this book has been long in the cocoon. Beyond reiterating that the research was funded by the American Council of Learned Societies (which funded both initial language training and initial write-up), IREX, and Fulbright-Hays, I will not repeat the thanks and acknowledgments I offered when the dissertation was completed in 2000. You know who you are. Rather, I will take that completion as the starting point of this book. It has made many new friends since it began its metamorphosis.

The dissertation was given a "letter of intent" by Mouton de Gruyter's Language, Power and Social Process series. Monica Heller's comments on that version were invaluably insightful and encouraging; she identified potential directions that I had not seen. In the "Mouton years," I benefitted from sharing summer living quarters with Deborah Skok, of Hendrix College, also working on turning a dissertation into a book: my "pace boat," friend, and encourager, who also made sure I stopped to buy groceries, cook, and eat. We especially enjoyed house-sitting for Barbara Rossing, of the Lutheran School of Theology at Chicago, whose work room was an inspiring library for her own book, then recently published, *The Rapture Exposed: The Message of Hope in the Book of Revelation*. Its accessible style, its relevance to a wide audience, and its thorough scholarship were models I hope to have emulated.

Monica put wind in the wings that carried the manuscript far beyond the destination she had envisioned. Over the course of three years, with my writing time being extremely limited by my "day job" as an inner-city public school teacher, I slowly stopped writing for the primarily professional target audience of the Language, Power and Social Process series. I started writing for the students my students would be, in a few years. On some level, I had realized that, as a public school teacher, there was no reward for me in writing a book for a primarily professional academic audience; that the qualification for research grants is not, as I had thought, a PhD, but rather a university affiliation; that the persistent undercutting of funding for education at all levels meant that the sabbatical clause of our school district's contract will never again be honored—in short, that this may well be my first and last research-based book. I thought I might as well write the book I wanted to write. Too, in terms of writing for undergraduates, I have an advantage over my colleagues in colleges and universities: high school teachers spend a lot of time learning about how young adults read and comprehend. I thought I might as well put that knowledge to use.

The book evolved, then, from a dissertation in linguistic anthropology into a readable ethnography. The idea for making it an extended meditation on a reinvigorated culture concept came from the four authors of the articles in the 2004 *American Anthropologist* issue, "A New Boasian Anthropology: Theory for the 21st Century," Ira Bashkow, Matti Bunzl, Andrew Orta, and Daniel Rosenblatt. They have been among the book's closest interlocutors, and I thank them for many stimulating conversations over the years. With the manuscript's reworking, also, came a rare and precious experience: an intellectual convergence with George Stocking, historian of anthropology and mentor, both at the University of Chicago and beyond, to Ira, Matti, Andy, and Danny. George and I had only known each other when I was a graduate student from serving together on a couple of faculty/student committees. I asked him to make up the quorum for both my dissertation proposal hearing and the dissertation defense, but I considered it unfortunate that I had so little in common with him intellectually; I would have liked to work more with him, otherwise. I never had a class with him. There were no reasons to thank him in the acknowledgments of the dissertation. It is a different story in these acknowledgments. George and I started corresponding in earnest, and getting together during my summer writing sojourns, when I was still in the Mouton de Gruyter phase of manuscript development. When I became consciously aware of the choices that I had made, and that their consequence was that Mouton and I were going to part company, George took the matter in hand. He encouraged me to go ahead and submit it, saying that if, after all, it were accepted, I would be free to start the next book—and that I had nothing, really, to lose in letting Monica make the decision. Once I had written a new book proposal, he helped me revise it, and he promoted it. I found PIASA through other networks, but that does not diminish my gratitude for his support.

At a personal level, as I write this about a year after his death, I feel awe at his generosity. As difficult as I find it to imagine, he found the complicating and often conflicting demands of my commitments as a writer, anthropologist, inner-city teacher, and Christian actually interesting. He had the grace to tell me that I had become wrapped up in his semi-conscious thinking. Years earlier, in the context of committee work, he had said that when he noticed that happening, it marked the difference, for him, between "a student," and "my student." I took his "adopting" me, in that sense, years after I finished my degree and as an institutional outsider to the academe, as a great honor. I miss him enormously.

PREFACE

Being two blocks away from his Hyde Park home, as well as a block and a half from the University of Chicago's Regenstein Library, also did not hurt. Summers spent subletting rooms in Brent House, the Episcopal Center at the University of Chicago, allowed this work to continue, and have been a source of lasting friendships. In particular, Olivia Bustion has been an invaluable co-writer. During the summer of 2012, our books, manuscripts, and laptops completely colonized the entire dining room, with the blessing of the chaplain and director, Stacy Alan, who told us that the house was there to be used, and posted a picture of us writing on the Brent House website. And the model for the book's culture concept metaphor is the magnificent chestnut in the back-yard of Brent House.

Leila Monaghan read the entire manuscript and offered comments, connections, editorial alerts, and encouragement. So did my father, Richard Vann. The comments of both the outside reviewers for PIASA, Marysia Galbraith and Janina Fenigsen, were invaluable, and included the one compliment I most wanted to hear: "Pretty hard to put down." PIASA's editor, Kathleen Cioffi, has been a delight to work with. Years ago John Comaroff told me that no aspect of a publisher is as important as having an editor you work well with—I feel lucky to have found such an editor in Kathleen.

In the hectic last days before the contractual deadline, which overlapped with my first days in Cairo, Matthew and Leslie Kirby of the Modern English School made meeting that deadline a pleasure rather than a stress-fest: they invited me into their home while repairs and painting were done in my new apartment, enabling me to colonize their dining room table and get it done. The eight students of my twelfth grade Honors English seminar helped me give the book a more reader-friendly first chapter, and created an engaging and informative website for this book, www.languagesandsilence.weebly.com.

The book flies, or at least flutters by, because of the intellectual gifts it has received, and this is an incomplete accounting of them. Its flaws, of course, remain my own.

LANGUAGES AND SILENCE
IN THE GERMAN-POLISH BORDERLAND

Chapter 1
MAPS FOR THE BOOK

Think of this book as being like a computerized map, a Google Earth map, say, that allows you to zoom in and out. Think of the book as addressing two conceptual levels, one comparatively zoomed out, and the other comparatively zoomed in. At the more zoomed-out level the book relates to a relatively broad set of intellectual concerns. I might call that level "anthropology among the social sciences." The more zoomed-in level, on the other hand, I might call "this book within anthropology." Consider the following guiding question at the zoomed-out level: What good is the culture concept, the central conceptual contribution of anthropology, after the turn of the millennium, when the formative conditions of the discipline are the stuff of history and museums? And a guiding question for the second level: How is it that Europeans come to believe, and some come to believe so vehemently, that they belong to ethnic-national groups?

THIS BOOK AS A "NEO" ETHNOGRAPHY

This book's ambition is to be a positive first encounter with ethnography, of the kind that makes readers want to read other ethnographies, and other kinds of ethnography. It is an ethnography for a revitalized, neo-Boasian culture concept and for fieldwork that I consider both neo-Boasian and neo-Malinowskian.

Anthropologists tend to locate the beginning of the discipline about a century ago, in the development of the "culture concept" and in the "fieldwork revolution." Anthropologists learn the language of the people they are going to work with and they live with them for at least several months, and generally for more than a year, relying on "participant observation" as well as interviews, surveys, elicitation techniques, and other methods of investigation. It is "participant observation," in the context of long term fieldwork, that distinguishes

1

anthropology from the other social sciences. The intellectual leaders of this "revolution" were, in the United States, Franz Boas, and in Great Britain, Bronisław Malinowski.

For a long time, the books that anthropologists "wrote up" when they returned often had titles on the model The (Insert the Name of the People Here). For professional anthropologists reading this, it may be worth reminding ourselves that these ethnonym titles are not too far in the past: I was assigned both *The Netsilik Eskimo* (Balikci 1970) and *The Navaho* (Kluckohn and Leighton 1946) in my Introduction to Cultural Anthropology course in the early 1980s. The contents were all-encompassing. Here's an incomplete summary of what's covered by Kluckhohn and Leighton: "History," "Land and Livelihood," "What the People Look Like," seven sections on family, government, the supernatural, language, ethics. As for Balikci, although published a quarter of a century later, its contents read as even more old-fashioned. The book has four parts, for a total of twelve chapters: "Man and Environment," "Man and Society" ("social collaboration" and "social tensions"), and "Man and the Supernatural."

By now, this kind of ethnographic writing is history. It may be recent history, it may be very troubling history, but it is over. Anthropologists have stopped writing in this manner and now consult the old ethnographies with a certain professional modesty—useful sources for information but not suitable to present to students as exemplary models. This shift has resulted from widespread and repeated self-criticism within anthropology, on account of the perception, as Ira Bashkow explains, "that concepts of culture inappropriately posit stable and bounded 'islands' of cultural distinctiveness in an ever-changing world of transnational cultural 'flows.'" By placing the broad sweep of societal living and culture within the covers of one book, anthropologists themselves constructed the boundaries of cultures, while treating them as if they were "naturally bounded objects that exist in the world for us to discover." Among the critics who have made this point are Clifford and Marcus 1986, Gupta and Ferguson 1997, Handler 1988, Manganaro 2002, Marcus 1998, Moore 1999, and, earlier, Wagner 1975 and Wolf 1972 (Bashkow 2004: 443). The "old" ethnographies are now seen as problematic both for the way they implicitly conceptualize culture (a theoretical issue) and for the way they implicitly claim to know about it (a methodological and epistemological issue).

It may be that one of the drivers of this discredited tendency to see and present cultures as bounded and different is fieldwork itself, in its very "awayness." Consider the fate of the ethnographies of the American anthropologist Hortense Powdermaker (1900–1970). Her first project, Life in Lesu (1930) was typically holistic in its approach to describing this Papua New Guinean society and culture. As her autobiography makes clear, when she went to Lesu in 1929, it took her four months to get there from London: four sea voyages followed by a rough ride by truck (Powdermaker 1966: 49–59). In North America, many of Boas's students traveled west to work with Native Americans; Margaret Mead, famously, went to Samoa. The sheer distance anthropologists traveled in order to get to their fieldsites may well have contributed to the sense that what they found when they got there was "bounded." It's easy to see a journey as crossing a boundary when it takes several months and makes you "the first anthropologist and first white person to live there" (Powdermaker 1966: 49). Over the course of her career, Powdermaker did fieldwork in four locations, the later two of which were unusual choices for the time: Papua New Guinea, Rhodesia (now Zimbabwe), Mississippi, and Hollywood. The ethnographies she wrote are out of print and no longer assigned in college classes. But her autobiography, *Stranger and Friend: The Way of an Anthropologist*, which she organizes around the fieldwork experience, is still in print. The chapters that describe her four stints of field research, as an online search of undergraduate syllabi reveals, are still assigned in relevant undergraduate courses within and beyond anthropology departments—in film studies classes, for example. So there's a problem of representation that is somewhat independent of content. Old style ethnographies won't do, but the same material, presented differently, can still be of value. There's baby and bathwater here.

In trying to resolve this dilemma, anthropologists look to two founders of the field: Franz Boas—who was born in Minden, Germany, in 1858; educated in Kiel and Berlin, where he also began his academic career; and after 1886 spent most of his life working at Columbia University in New York—and Bronisław Malinowski—who was born in Cracow, then in the Austrian Partition of Poland, in 1884; educated in Cracow and Leipzig; and after 1910 spent most of his career at the London School of Economics. Both are closely associated with the "fieldwork revolution" and the development of the culture concept; the approach of each differed with regard to both the method and the theory.

At both the conceptual and the methodological/epistemological level, anthropologists have looked to the early years of Boasian anthropology in the United States for resolution of these dilemmas. In a now widely cited collection of articles published in 2004, Ira Bashkow, Matti Bunzl, Richard Handler, Andrew Orta, and Daniel Rosenblatt tackle various aspects of what it would take to form a "neo-Boasian" anthropology. For our purposes here, it is Bashkow's take on the "boundaries" issue and Bunzl's take on the fieldwork issue that are most relevant.

Anthropologists have forgotten the rich complexity of the Boasians' own conception of cultural boundaries, Bashkow argues. Boasians saw cultural boundaries as "porous and permeable," often interested in drawing boundaries around them precisely "to gauge the historical traffic across them" (Bashkow 2004: 445). Boasians posited multiple boundaries; if one sets out to make a map, the contrasted areas of the map will be different according to what specifically one chooses to show. A map showing the distribution of fired clay pottery among Native Americans will show different boundaries than a map showing differing social organizations, and be different again from maps showing any of the following: "archaeological findings, foods, technology, language, physical indices, kinship, and the environment" (446). And finally, none of these maps conceived by the analyst necessarily corresponds with the subjective consciousness of members concerning where their group lives as opposed to where other groups do, or what indeed distinguishes their group from other groups. Rather, those subjective maps are interesting in their own right; the correspondences with anthropologists' maps, and lack thereof, can themselves form objects of study (445–47). Seeing cultures as somehow "within" impervious lines on a map, whether a literal map on paper (or a screen) or a mental map, is indeed problematic.

Perhaps American anthropologists have continued to suffer the disjunction of Boas's emigration itself. Boas's own doctoral and postdoctoral training was in the academic field of geography, a field that does not have much presence in American academia. In the United States, it is usually found within the departments of social sciences other than anthropology. Ongoing, regular conversation with geographers in the European tradition might have spared American anthropologists some trouble, for geographers routinely talk about boundaries of many different kinds: boundaries that emerge where two different spaces meet, like national borders, or where one kind of thing stops and another starts, such as the line that would connect the points where Russian small-gauge rail lines meet European standard lines. These are boundaries that, indeed, mark what Bashkow distinguishes as "barriers"—they are all about regulated transfer across them, be that of people, rail cargo, goods, or abstractions. Geographers also distinguish the kind of border that emerges as a blank space between sets of points, whether the points mark distributions or endpoints of trajectories, and they further distinguish whether that space of nonconnection is a natural feature, like a body of water, or something human-made, and if the latter, made in what way. They distinguish degrees and kinds of permeability of boundaries. From a geographer's perspective, American anthropologists have truly been operating with a seriously impoverished analytic vocabulary.[1]

The implicit message of books titled with an ethnonym and with tables of contents like that of *The Navaho* is that these other cultures are really, really different—different in every way, in every realm of human living. The implication, never stated, is that the boundary between the Native American Navaho and the culture of its Euro-American author is one of the blank space kind, and the boundary between the Navaho, the Tewa, and the Hopi (their nearest neighbors) is a barrier. And it's these two kinds of boundaries, the thick line and the blank space, that bring concerns about the impoverished American anthropological vocabulary for boundaries and concerns about Malinowskian fieldwork together.

The point of ethnography has never been difference per se, but American anthropology has mistaken cultural difference for the engine that powers ethnographic insight. As Bunzl points out,

> In the dominant tradition of post-Malinowskian U.S. cultural anthropology, the epistemic division between ethnographic Self and native Other is simply doxic, articulated with particular clarity by such luminaries of interpretive/symbolic anthropology as Clifford Geertz and Roy Wagner. For Geertz, person, time, and conduct in Bali are worth studying because "from a Western perspective," they are "odd enough to bring to light some general relationships . . . that are hidden from us" (1973: 360–61). Wagner, for his part, is even more forceful, arguing that the production of all anthropological knowledge, which he glosses as the "Invention of Culture," rests on experiences of radical Otherness that can render culture visible. (Wagner 1981[1975]) (Bunzl 2004: 435)

Ethnography is about questioning, widening—at times overturning—the assumptions of the anthropologist's society and culture about how humans operate as social beings, about what is or can be considered "normal," as Ruth Benedict pointed out in 1934 in her influential article, "Anthropology and the Abnormal." In that sense, where there's no difference there's no point, nothing to research. Yet as Bunzl argues, the idea of that blank space of Otherness between the ethnographer and the "natives" carries a very unfortunate implication: that nobody can properly gain insight into their own culture. Thus, in American anthropology departments, for a long time it was all but required of anthropology graduate students that they go somewhere else for their doctoral fieldwork, which has been treated as the rite of passage that distinguishes anthropologists from all other academics. Those who didn't were consigned to the "abject construction of the 'native anthropologist'" (Bunzl 2004: 435).

By the late 1980s, when I started graduate training, the critique of this implication had been recognized to the extent that graduate students were allowed

5

both to study in their own cultures—to be "native anthropologists"—and to plan fieldwork in nontraditional areas, like European countries. Yet the perception that "native anthropologists" are seen as somehow poor relations is one I can attest to: there was, at the University of Chicago in the 1990s, a subtle hierarchy of fieldwork sites in which returning to one's home, in the case of international students, or working in the United States, in the case of Americans, was not quite as worthy as going far, far away. And in relation to nascent "Europeanists," like myself, the faculty were a bit confused. Several professors told me, "This is a fine idea, but who are you going to work with? None of us know anything about Europe, as anthropologists." What best illustrates that confusion, to me, is that I shared no advisory committee members with my closest colleague, in terms of "ethnographic area"—Daphne Berdahl, who worked in the German-German borderland in the immediate aftermath of the border's disappearance, that is, Germany's reunification. That would never have happened with two graduate students both working in one of the "traditional" ethnographic areas, which the department had "covered" in its hiring.

It is ironic that what Bunzl calls the "post-Malinowskian U.S. cultural anthropolog[ical attitude]" necessarily consigns all postwar Polish anthropologists to "poor relation" professional status. Under Communist rule, Polish citizens' travel was severely restricted. Fieldwork was conducted perforce in Poland, or at least behind the Iron Curtain. In that light, as well as the light shed by the experience of U.S.-trained "native anthropologists" (and perhaps also "Europeanists"), this particular interpretation of Malinowski's legacy really looks insupportable. It denigrates the "research subjects," certainly, but also a sizeable chunk of the researchers. It seems to be a covertly hierarchical way of thinking; Americans, proud of their egalitarianism, tend to have trouble acknowledging such thinking in themselves.

Rethinking is a clear necessity. According to Bunzl, a partial answer can be found in the critiques of such scholars as Kath Weston, Kirin Narayan, Akhil Gupta and James Ferguson, and James Clifford (Bunzl 2004: 435–36). Yet all of them stop somewhat short of "deconstruct[ing] the category of 'native anthropology' itself." For Weston, the denigration of the "native anthropologist" serves as a reminder to the profession of its own power relations, but she does not propose how to change them. Narayan and Clifford both seem to retain the valuation of cultural difference while making an "us too" argument for "native anthropologists." For Narayan, this move comes by way of emphasizing that "The very nature of researching what to others is taken-for-granted reality creates an uneasy distance" (Narayan 1993: 682, quoted in

Bunzl 2004: 435). Clifford emphasizes the professional training of the "native anthropologist" as providing him or her with the "distance" seen as necessary for successful fieldwork. And Gupta and Ferguson back off completely; Bunzl assesses that for them, "Cultural differences between the ethnographer and her people, it would seem, are still crucial to anthropological knowledge production, even in this rethought and revitalized form of fieldwork" (436).

For Bunzl, the way beyond this dilemma is historical, and lies through the investigation of an "originary condition of possibility." Michel Foucault, the French social theorist famous for, among other important works, *The History of Sexuality: An Introduction* (1978), for example, "refuses to draw analytic leverage from the reified distinction of sexual orientation." It is an approach similar to that of Boas and his students:

> Much like Boas, Foucault developed this approach to interrogate and overcome the fetishization of difference. . . . In disrupting a regime of power that abjected certain bodies in terms of their reified subject positions, Foucault was thus engaged in a project of epistemological democratization that directly paralleled the Boasian attempt to efface the constitutive Otherness of the contemporary "primitive." (2004: 440)

Where Foucauldian history stops short, Boasian anthropology can step in. Bunzl identifies "the ethnographic 'blind spot' of Foucauldian genealogy, which is conceived as a history of such present phenomena as the 'homosexual' but finds its realization in the account of 'his' historical invention." Anthropology remains an interpretation of the present, but not an interpretation of cultural difference per se. Rather, an anthropological account is a "history of the present."

My interpretation of the "reticence about names" that I found in Opole Silesia, discussed in chapter 3, is an example of such a "history of the present." It is clear that people's habitual refusal to answer the question "What is your name?" or "What is his/her name?" is, in Bashkow's terms, a barrier. It functions to keep knowledge that is important to everyday social interactions away from outsiders. One can take a functional approach to it; one can see it as a "boundary-maintaining mechanism," and stop there. I argue, however, that this practice has a history in the intrusive changing of names by the two totalitarian states, Nazi Germany and Communist Poland. I maintain that understanding this practice that way is a deeper and richer interpretation, one that opens onto other ethnographic views. That is an example of a "history of the present" in this book. In that sense my approach to "the data" is firmly neo-Boasian.

What about the sad distinction between the "native anthropologist" and the "real" one? The practices of Boas and his students are a model because rather than imagining cultural differences as a necessary condition of anthropological understanding, Boas considered simply that there are certain difficulties associated with researching a very unfamiliar society and other difficulties associated with researching a very familiar one. One example of the former is a difficulty in language learning: our brains attune themselves to the phonemic system of our own languages (Boas called this the problem of "alternating sounds"). To this day, I cannot hear the subtle difference between the Silesian pronunciation of the sound spelled in Polish with ń and the Polish pronunciation. In transcribing my tapes, if all the other "alternating sounds" are Silesian, I have italicized it, to show it as contrastively Silesian, and written it as Silesian, as -on or -an, and I hope I'm right—it is an instantly recognizable difference to native speakers. This is a linguistic issue but it has cultural analogies. It's hard to "see" phenomena that don't fit what one has been socialized to see. Overcoming such difficulties, Boas thought, was a matter of training. Similarly, it is difficult for insiders to overcome what Boas called, "'secondary explanations,' the 'rationalizations of customary behavior whose origins were lost in tradition, but that were highly charged with emotional value'" (Stocking 1992: 6). Boas continuously emphasized the presence of secondary explanations among all human groups, a situation that rendered an insider's information regarding the history of any given text or custom inherently untrustworthy. Anthropologists, be they insiders or outsiders, thus had to reach beyond secondary explanation in order to discern "true" history. Here, again, it is training that overcomes this difficulty:

> Insiders and outsiders were thus differentially positioned at the onset of the ethnographic project. What is central in the present context, however, is that Boasian ethnography not only did not rest on that distinction but also was designed to efface it. Guarding against alternating sounds, outsiders would produce the same ethnographic data as insiders; at the same time, the critical awareness of secondary explanation would guide insiders (and the anthropologists who derived their information from them) toward the actual histories of contemporary ethnic phenomena. Conceptually, this meant that insiders and outsiders would generate the same kind of data and attempt the same kinds of historical reconstructions. (Bunzl 2004: 439)

An example of overcoming one such "secondary explanation" in this book concerns the dowry and postmarital residency system analyzed in chapter 8. In this culture, most women stay in their parents' homes after marriage; their

husbands move in (anthropologists call this "uxorilocal postmarital residence" or "uxorilocality"). When I asked why that was so, I was consistently told, "A woman gets along with her own mother much better than she would with her mother-in-law." (Note that the couple's moving out on their own wasn't considered within the range of possibilities.) This may well be true, but it's a secondary explanation, and it ends inquiry. Pulling on that thread, as I had been trained to do when offered easy, inquiry-ending answers, I discovered that the richest members of society did not practice uxorilocality. Why was that? Ultimately, after further inquiry, I argue that postmarital residency has to do with the maintenance of the class structure. In this sense, too—that I was taught to look beyond secondary explanations—my fieldwork was Boasian.

All this said, I am unwilling to disclaim Malinowski's contribution to the "fieldwork revolution." Boas and his students worked mainly with Native Americans, and it was possible to work with them in an ongoing way. Malinowski and his students had oceans to cross. The people they worked with were often not speakers of English, and often not literate. It made a difference, in the early years of the twentieth century, to what kind of collaboration with "natives" was possible.

What makes a difference in the early years of the twenty-first century is this: you, readers, are already in relationship with the people I worked with, just as I was already in relationship with them before I arrived. My relationship was defined by a particularly stern barrier, the Iron Curtain, and it continues to be defined, in part, by that now defunct border. On some level, everyone knew this. In chapter 8, for example, I describe the conflict, then unresolved, between Marta and the brother of her recently deceased husband, Johann, over what to do with the house in Silesia that they had co-inherited. It was a conflict, among other things, over whether it was worthwhile to invest in renovating a house in Poland, and as a supporting point, Marta used my presence in Silesia: "I did not have to go away to meet Elizabeth," she told Johann. "She came to us." Such things had not happened for fifty years. The existence of such preexisting relationships is one of the meanings of "globalization." The need to take them into account, as for example Basso does in his *Portraits of the Whiteman* and Bashkow does in *The Meaning of Whitemen: Race and Modernity in the Orokaiva Cultural World,* is part of what makes recent ethnographies, like this one, "neo."

These ongoing relationships play out here in various ways. They play out in that I fully expect, eventually, that my "getting behind" the secondary explanation about postmarital residence will become the subject of reflection for the people who offered it. There is no reason, as Boas would have pointed out, that a "native" cannot step behind a secondary explanation as effectively as an outsider. I even hope eventually to have those transcripts checked for the accuracy of those ń sounds; with contemporary technology, I can convert the recordings to digital format and email them to a native speaker. Unlike Hortense Powdermaker, I was able to return to Dobra, dissertation in hand. For me, it was a reassuring experience; I saw people doing things with words that I had not recognized in the field, that my outsider's eye had only perceived in the process of spending hours with the field materials, back in Chicago. Józef, leafing through the dissertation, said to me, "Ela, I see here my son's pseudonym. Is there something about him in this chapter?" When I explained my interpretation of the interactions in the section, "Fear Undergirds Aesthetics," which had come to me only after leaving the field, he smiled and said, "Yes, you're right, that is exactly what was going on." These are the kinds of differences that our current situation, around the turn of the twenty-first century, makes.

Ultimately, I am not ready to accept that the self/Other divide that Bunzl so rightly criticizes as really Malinowski's fault. Bunzl carefully calls it, "the dominant tradition of post-Malinowskian U.S. cultural anthropology" (2004: 436), and I think the care may be warranted. The problem is fetishization of difference, not its existence; and this fetishization fits a little too closely with other tropes of American culture; I'm not comfortable attributing it to a Pole born in 1884. I think that fieldwork as "heroized journey into Otherness" (Stocking 1992, cited by Bunzl 2004: 436) may itself be a secondary explanation, a way of seeing fieldwork that accords too closely with other mythic ways of seeing in our culture. We Americans are socialized from a young age to see our history in terms of a blank-space boundary. I refer to our identity as a nation of immigrants. We have stories of "the old country" and we have stories that begin with arrival. The journey itself, the blank space of the Atlantic and Pacific oceans, is not part of those stories.

How do we conceive of boundaries without twisting them into preconceived American cultural categories? As Bashkow points out, as analysts we draw the boundaries according to what we want to understand. Difference is important when it is *relevant difference*—relevant to multilingualism, say, or to ethnic and national identity. And the kinds of differences that provide that "mirror" are actually about position within larger social structures ("globalization") and history as well as about "culture" as traditionally and narrowly defined.

An excellent example is how Nancy Dorian's 2010 book, *Investigating Variation,* undoes received assumptions about linguistic variation. Linguists have believed that small societies, homogeneous in terms of lifeways, also exhibit homogeneity in terms of language. Variation within the community has been pegged to social differentiation, with variants tied to different social groups:

> The possibility of acoustically salient but socially unweighted variation can be difficult for speakers of long-standardized languages to credit fully, since most of us are accustomed to making social distinctions on the basis not just of easily detectable grammatical alternates but also of small and subtle differences in pronunciation. Responding as strongly as we do to such phenomena, we are inclined to doubt that speakers of other languages might be either oblivious of blatant variation or indifferent to it if they should become aware of it. The evidence proves to be very strong, however, that where a community population is socioeconomically undifferentiated to a remarkable degree and few (if any) community-external norms are brought to bear on local usage, pervasive individual variation, in the phonemic realization of morphemes, the chief case to be discussed here, not only can flourish but can do so without linguistic variants developing social values. This flies in the face of widely accepted generalizations such as the following: "Perhaps the only real sociolinguistic universal introduced so far in this chapter is social differentiation. The claim underlying this universal is that there are always differences in speech communities and that those differences correlate with the existence of social groups within a community" (Southerland and Anshen 1989: 332). "It is a commonplace of linguistics . . . that variation in speech (aside from age and gender. . .) is a function of (a) region, (b) social group, and (c) situation" (Honey 1997: 92) (Dorian 2010).

But it's not true, despite being a "universal" and a "commonplace." Dorian's decades of work in the small, homogeneous, minority-language community of fisherfolk on the north coast of Scotland, in East Sutherland, shows a high degree of "personal pattern variation," from speaker to speaker, with no correlation to social groups and no social weighting, no positive or negative evaluations from other speakers. This lack of weighting is difference relevant to linguists' preexisting assumption about language, "relevant difference." Overturning such assumptions is what anthropological and linguistic anthropological research is about. And this assumption was overturned, as Dorian points out in her conclusion, without any of the "experiences of radical Otherness" that Wagner holds are necessary to "render culture visible":

> I emphasize the apparent ordinariness of Embo village to make the point that what might be deemed "exotic" findings can appear in settings that do not appear the least bit exotic. If unexpected linguistic findings can emerge from a village in present-day Scotland, squarely within the industrialized Western world, it seems

11

reasonable to suppose that there are other settings, some of them perhaps equally ordinary-seeming and some more obviously different from the settings most linguists are personally familiar with, that harbor equally unanticipated sociolinguistic phenomena. (Dorian 2010: 312)

You don't have to go to Bali to find relevant difference.

So this book works with the most long-standing definition of culture, that of Sir Edward Burnett Tylor in 1871: "capabilities and habits acquired by man as a member of society" (quoted in Lowie 1934: 3). However, not all capabilities and habits so acquired warrant attention in this book. Not everything provides relevant difference. I don't look for distinctive, autonomous culture in material culture, technology, or how people make a living; in those respects, there is no analytic reason to distinguish a cultural group. Similarly, if we were to look in ritual, religion, or mythology, we would recognize that Roman Catholicism in Opole Silesia, as in the rest of Poland, is as about as integrated and centrally positioned in Roman Catholicism's world system as it is possible to get. We could search for surviving practices of local folk Catholicism, and in Dobra we would find people able to name and describe these, but we would have to find some other village to actually see them. However, I have no reason to think that these practices would be relevant to reshaping any preexisting assumptions of mine or of my readers.

If we looked for shared behavioral norms, at social organization, at socialization practices—and looked hard (which I did)—then we might get somewhere in our search for a distinctive culture. So it's at this point that I will introduce an ethnonym, and tell readers that the people I worked with call themselves "Silesians," and that I will consistently call them "autochthonous Opole Silesians," for reasons explained in chapter 2. Autochthonous Opole Silesians wear mass-produced clothes, but women wear them in a way that is culturally distinctive from Poles, as I discuss in chapter 4. They have distinctive behavioral norms, certainly; for example, a more authoritarian attitude toward child-rearing than most Poles. There is awareness of these differences among both autochthonous Opole Silesians and Poles. Although we examine this smattering of "cultural difference," the differences do not seem to warrant a whole book.

But what does make autochthonous Opole Silesians worth a book is their rich multilingualism and its ramifications in cultural ideologies—ideologies that concern matters that are of interest, like "why do Europeans come to believe, and some come to believe so vehemently, that they belong to ethnic-national groups?" Yes, people speak the Silesian dialect of Polish, standard

Polish, and standard German, and you won't find that particular mix elsewhere. Yet multilingual culture goes far beyond what people are able to speak. It takes form not only in which language or languages people choose to speak, but in what people say and how they say it, in what circumstances and to what ends, thinking and believing what they think and believe about what language does, and about what they do with language. In the borderland, habits of language and linguistic capabilities acquired by people as members of their society form a central cultural focus. It is this multilingualism, this cultural focus, that distinguishes these speakers from the surrounding Poles, from Germans to the west, and from anyone else, for that matter. Researching and unraveling the complexities of Silesian multilingualism was a big job, and worthwhile in and of itself, I believe. Yet, as I indicated in the preface, the foundational dictum of training for fieldwork, "Deal with what you find," ultimately led me beyond language to silence, and from there, to an insight about the vehemence of identity, at least for some autochthonous Opole Silesians.

There is a specific aspect of how anthropologists have traditionally looked at cultures that is particularly useful here, and it is the cognitive one implicit in Tylor's assertion that culture is "acquired." Autochthonous Opole Silesian culture is bounded in that it takes local, culturally constituted knowledge and locally socialized skills to operate in a socially interpretable and acceptable manner within it. That's the kind of "boundary" that I mean when I say that there is an autonomous culture among autochthonous Opole Silesians. But there's an irony: Opole Silesia has been utterly pervaded by relations with the two oppressively powerful states within which it experienced twentieth-century totalitarianism. In that sense, one would think it would be an ideal example of what Bashkow characterizes as "an ever-changing world of transnational cultural 'flows'" (2004: 443), within which, according to critics, anthropologists "inappropriately posit stable and bounded 'islands' of cultural distinctiveness." It's my thesis that that distinctiveness exists—I didn't put it there—that "the culture" is bounded, and that it is perceptibly stable. But the "stuff" of the stability comes precisely from those relations with the two nation-states, Germany and Poland. The borderland culture is a culture of betweenness.

In that sense, the rich multilingual culture is merely a vestibule. Of course, the rich multilingualism is an integration of the region's political history ("integration" in Benedict's sense; see Rosenblatt 2004). But following the corridors of multilingual culture opens out on other rooms equally cultural, equally bounded in the sense delimited above, and yet resonant with the traditional purview of social and cultural anthropology. Thus, for example, we find that understanding how identity ascriptions function to express moral disapproval requires understanding shared cultural norms, how to "be a good person" in local terms, as I discuss in chapter 7. And that, in turn, requires understanding how the kinship system works, particularly with regard to marriage and residence (chapter 8). Indeed, understanding *The Gift*, in Mauss's classic sense of delayed reciprocal exchange, is indispensable to grasping what is being summarized and symbolized when people use the language of identity as a language of morality. Beyond the culture concept, then, there are a few other concepts to be recuperated here on the way to understanding this culture of betweenness, this coherence forged out of the "flows." All these "old chestnut" concepts, it emerges, are relevant to more contemporary concerns about identity, power, and locality in a global system.

The conceptually troubled distinction between "ethnicity" and "culture" can serve to summarize and extend this discussion. If "boundaries" have been the "recurring inflamed tendon" of the culture concept, they have been the chronic thrombosis of the concept of ethnicity. Since Fredrik Barth's collection appeared under the title *Ethnic Groups and Boundaries* (1969), studies of "ethnicity" have sought their object in boundaries and their maintenance. Beyond the "boundary," there is no necessity of any kind of cultural difference "enclosed." Ethnicity, broadly, has been generally conceived as having something to do with groups that people are born into, that have relationships to one another as groups, maintaining a conscious sense of distinctive origin. Think, here, about British boarding schools, which are traditionally divided into "houses." Actual differences in the "cultures" of the houses are unnecessary; their organizational structures are the same and they exist to provide students with a group smaller than the school to identify with and to create the possibility of intramural athletic competition. Ah, but Hogwarts! Over the course of the seven Harry Potter books readers slowly learn that there *are* differences in the character, the culture, of the four houses, and that these are potent throughout the society. Slytherin House is an alumni network of evil. Readers learn that assignments to houses are often inherited from wizard parents, as well as being based on individual characteristics ("Why aren't you in Ravenclaw?" Hermione is asked after a particular display of intelligence.) It's this kind of difference—not just the structural opposition—and these kinds of boundaries, that we tend to associate with the term "ethnicity." Ethnicity, that is, is defined by its edges, and what lies within is of secondary concern.

Take an actually existing example. In their book, *Nationalist Politics and Everyday Ethnicity* (2006), Brubaker et al. investigate ethnic consciousness in the city of Cluj, Hungary. In this case, while there was hyperbolic, over-the-top focus on issues of ethnic-national origin at a political level, the differences between the Hungarians and the Germans weren't actually terribly salient in everyday life. In short, the boundaries—what they are, what they are ideologically based on, how and whether they are salient, how and whether they are "defended"—is a matter for empirical investigation, for the kind of investigation that Brubaker and his colleagues conducted: long-term, in-depth, participant-observation–based research conducted in German and Hungarian. For fieldwork, in short.

By characterizing this book as an ethnography for a neo-Malinowskian fieldwork, as well as for a neo-Boasian culture concept, I am not actually claiming to have recuperated anything lost under an avalanche of criticism, in the way that Bashkow et al. see their project of Boasian recuperation. Rather, I hope to show that a continuing Malinowskian approach is being reorganized, not by but rather around the ears of anthropologists, by the changes in the world itself, and by the changes in the discipline. For me, the smack-between-the-eyes obvious starting point is that I did my fieldwork in Malinowski's native Poland and my point-of-entry into "the field" was his native city of Cracow. Powdermaker's, in contrast, was Sydney, then a vast cultural distance from the "late Stone Age" world of the village of Lesu on New Ireland. When I was in need of rejuvenation and inspiration, I could even take the train to Cracow and withdraw to a secluded table in the carefully preserved café where the ancestor himself, along with his artist and writer friends of the Polish Modernist movement, used to hang out—an option not available to Hortense Powdermaker when she was "in the field." But more subtle, and more important, is how the existence of the "native anthropologist" as well as the "Europeanists," and their fieldwork encounters, has altered the "flows" of the professional culture of anthropology. By the end of the book, I hope to show that anthropologists, too, are challenged by change and creative in the face of it, and I address this specifically in the conclusion. The humanistic value of fieldwork—fostering mutual understanding—remains.

Vehement Identity

This book has one contribution to the literature on "ethnic identity" or "national identity" that I consider to be novel: the interpretation I offer about why some autochthonous Opole Silesians assert their German identity with such emotional vehemence. Much of my analysis is not new, belonging squarely to the "constructivist" or "instrumentalist" camp. The analysis in chapter 3 of the German identity of the village of Ostrów is about nothing so much as impression management, the deployment of the resources of ideologies of identity to the perceived advantage of the village. In the early post-Communist era, ideologies of identity offered considerable resources, so I was not surprised to find people deploying them. But that is not about vehement, emotional identity; on the contrary, it seemed rather calculated. Ultimately it was the harnessing of a deeply felt identity to the purpose of impression management that I found most interesting about the German Minority as an organization.

To contextualize my approach, then: If we look across the spread of people writing about "identity," in this case especially ethnic and national identity, we notice a gap. In the ideology implicit in journalism, as Blommaert and Verscheuren discover in their investigation of European articles, humanity is taken as divided into "natural groups, the folk perception of which conceptualizes them in much the same way as species in the animal kingdom" (1998: 192). These are "nations," or "peoples," or, I would add, "ethnicities." Their membership is identifiable according to what Blommaert and Verschueren aptly call a "feature cluster," consisting of descent, history, culture, religion, and language. Among those, language takes the foreground, often being taken as predictive of the others: "If feathers are predictive of beaks, eggs, and an ability to fly, so is a specific language predictive of a distinct history and culture" (192). These groups, as Brubaker points out, are posited as actors—Serbs, Croats, Chechens, what-have-you—and presented as having acted in much the same way that individual politicians are characters in the news. According to Brubaker, in scholarship, too, this "groupism,"

> has proved surprisingly robust. It has managed to withstand a quarter century of constructivist theorizing in the social sciences, a sustained critique of reification in anthropology and other disciplines, the influential and destabilizing contributions of feminist, post-structuralist, post-modernist, and other theories, and even the widespread acknowledgment, in principle, that "cultures," "communities," "tribes," "races," "nations," and "ethnic groups" are not bounded wholes. (2004: 3)

The gap, then, persists between those who write as if groups can be taken as "fundamental units of analysis (and basic constituents of the social world)" (2) and those who focus on constructivism. Yet Brubaker takes "complacent and clichéd constructivism," to task as well:

> Social construction has been a fertile metaphor in recent decades, inspiring a large body of work that has enriched and transformed our understanding of ethnicity (and of many other phenomena). Yet by virtue of its very success, the constructivist idiom has grown "weary, stale, flat, and unprofitable." Once an insurgent

16

undertaking, a bracing challenge to entrenched ways of seeing, constructivism has become the epitome of academic respectability, even orthodoxy. It is not that the notion of social construction is wrong; it is rather that it is today too obviously right, too familiar, too readily taken for granted, to generate the friction, force, and freshness need to push arguments further and generate new insights. One symptom of this intellectual slackness is that one often finds constructivist and groupist language casually conjoined. (3)

In anthropology and linguistic anthropology, I would be at a loss to cite recent work that fits the "primordialist" bill. Rather, we seem to tend toward very strong constructivist statements, such as this one by Bucholtz and Hall in the definitively titled *A Companion to Linguistic Anthropology*:

> One of the greatest weaknesses of previous research on identity, in fact, is the assumption that identities are attributes of individuals or groups rather than of situations. . . . But identity inheres in actions, not in people. As the product of situated social action, identities may shift and recombine to meet new circumstances. This dynamic perspective contrasts with the traditional view of identities as unitary and enduring psychological states or social categories. (2004: 376)

In this statement, I see two strands of thought from which I would like to distance myself. First, the statement is antipsychological. In contrast, I would restrict the meaning of "identity" to being an aspect of consciousness. My starting assumption is that because actions and situations do not have consciousness, identity cannot inhere in them. Second, in the word "dynamic" contrasted with "traditional," I see an implicit celebration. But is the (re)placement of identity into "situations" dynamic and liberating, or is it unreliable and amoral? Remembering that "natives" as well as "analysts" engage in this kind of debate, I would align myself with the many critical assertions I heard from autochthonous Opole Silesians concerning people who, with apparent ease, segued from Communist Party membership to devout Catholicism to German Minority membership (which overall has a political right-wing orientation): "Those are rubber-band people," or "people who turn with the wind like a weather-vane." Autochthonous Opole Silesians would not accept Bucholtz and Hall's position.

There are cultures, as Kulick and Schieffelin point out, that "do not expect or demand sincerity. Whether or not a person 'really means' what she or he says is not a topic for speculation" (2004: 352). They are writing, here, about language socialization, and more specifically, about "how different kinds of culturally intelligible subjectivities come into being," (identification with a group, such as an ethnic or national group, would be one of these subjectivities.) It is

17

important to bear in mind, first, that Kulick and Schieffelin are right—not everyone, in every culture, assumes that a person has a socially accessible self-presentation that bears a relation of to an inner self, a person's "true colors," which may or may not be accessible to others. But autochthonous Opole Silesians are Westerners, Europeans, Christians, and Roman Catholics, and they do make this assumption. Kulick and Schieffelin tell us that, "This concern with surface and depth is a profoundly Western problematic, one that has arisen from a long history of meditation on supposedly fundamental binaries (presence versus absence, body versus soul, mind versus body, conscious versus unconscious, etc.)" (352). Autochthonous Opole Silesians are participants in this problematic. Most visibly, they take the act of taking Communion, which is visible to all present in church (thus, almost the entire community) as a public statement of the alignment of inner and outer selves. The most pointed summary statement of disapproval, as we will see in chapter 7, is "how can a person act like that and then take Communion?" A strong and celebratory constructivist approach is not a good fit with this particular culture.

Because the task here is not to try to universalize identity, but rather to examine it in a European context, I would align myself with Brubaker's approach. Rather than suggesting a "middle way," he suggests a third approach: a cognitive psychological one. Brubaker argues that this is but a small step from the recent constructivist and subjectivist focus on categorization, as an outgrowth of defining ethnicity "in terms of participants' beliefs, perceptions, understandings, and identifications (2004: 64). In "Ethnicity as Cognition," he summarizes a rapprochement between "the humanistic, interpretive, holistic, and antireductionist commitments that inform most sociological, anthropological, and historical work" and "the positivist, experimentalist, individualist, and reductionist commitments of cognitive science" (69). Note that the word "holistic" connects with the anthropological self-criticism "recurring inflamed tendon" of the "boundaries" (as Bashkow puts it). What are the boundaries around? The "whole." Just as anthropologists have come to question their received assumptions about what exists beyond and around the culture, so cognitive psychologists have come to question their received assumption that centers explanation within the individual. This allows for the use of the resources of cognitive psychology in ethnography, in examining "identity formation" in this western context. For this book, cognitive psychology is the way into the question of vehement identity.

Specifically, chapter 9 draws on the theory of "cognitive dissonance" as it relates to the formation of attachment to predefined groups. (Note that there is no implication of the groups being "primordial"; they need merely predate the individual.) "Cognitive dissonance" is a psychological theory that addresses the way that people look back on experiences and bring them into line with their beliefs and wishes: how they modify their own memories. Memories that cause people to engage in self-justification are one relevant realm: "Any time a person has information or an opinion which considered by itself would lead him not to engage in some action, then this information or opinion is dissonant with having engaged in the action. When such dissonance exists, the person will try to reduce it either by changing his actions or by changing his beliefs and opinions. If he cannot change the action, opinion change will ensue" (Festinger 1963: 18–19). Cognitive dissonance is uncomfortable. In psychological experimental research (Festinger and Carlsmith 1959), when people were asked to do a boring task and then, not knowing that the experiment had not ended, to talk positively about it to people waiting to do the same, a difference emerged between those who were paid a dollar for their little lie, and those who were paid twenty dollars. Those who were paid a dollar afterwards rated the task as more enjoyable than those who were paid twenty dollars. Why? The larger reward justified the lie; it did the work of reducing the cognitive dissonance between being an honest, truthful person and telling an untruth to an innocent unsuspecting experiment participant, about to spend an hour packing spools into a tray and dumping them out again. But a dollar isn't enough money to allow people to tell themselves, "Well, for 20 dollars, who wouldn't tell a harmless lie? I did, but anyone would. I'm still OK" (Mook 2004: 237). So it is the people who were only paid one dollar who had the more compelling motivation to modify their own memories; they were not able to admit to themselves that they had engaged in a mindless and boring task and were now lying by saying it had been interesting and fun. They had to convince *themselves* that it had been interesting and fun. They had to make the dollar a tip for telling the truth, since it was not enough money to be an understandable motivation for telling a lie. So the lie ended up being quite a bit bigger.

Mook points out that cognitive dissonance has a bearing on the dilemmas of life in a totalitarian state:

> Consider this case of dissonance: "I have hurt this person. That means that I, a kind and humane person, have done a cruel thing." Can we reconcile these conflicting ideas? Perhaps, if we can say, "I hurt this person, but he deserved it! In which case my hurting him was not such a bad thing after all. Maybe I ought to hurt him some more!" This process, which has been shown by direct experiment, may shed some light on the atrocities that occurred during World War II—and elsewhere. (2004: 237)

As it happens, my research did not encounter anyone justifying hurting others in the manner above. For our purposes, the central application of cognitive dissonance theory is not to self-justification of actions, but to identification: to "initiation effects." If you sacrifice a lot to join a group, anything you then see in it that you dislike is dissonant: "After everything I went through to join this group, I can't dislike it." You can resolve the dissonance either by denying what you dislike about the group or by denying what you went through to join it. If the initiation is severe, it is more difficult to deny what you went through, and easier to deny what you dislike about the group.

This was tested experimentally by offering college students membership in a discussion group, then presenting one-third of them with reading that was very embarrassing, one-third with reading that was mildly embarrassing, and the other group with no reading. The the two-thirds with the embarrassing reading were told that they had to read the material in order to join the group. After they had read, they "listened to a recording that appeared to be an ongoing discussion being conducted by the group. . . . Afterwards, subjects filled out a questionnaire evaluating the discussion and the participants. The results clearly verified the hypothesis. Subjects who underwent a severe initiation perceived the group as being significantly more attractive than did those who underwent a mild initiation or no initiation" (Aronson and Mills 1959: 180). Note that "denial" is akin to the Freudian concept of "repression." Repression, as Michael Billig explains it, is based on the idea of self-deceit: "If we have secrets from ourselves, then not only must we forget the secrets, but we must also forget that we have forgotten them. To use Freudian terminology, the secrets must be repressed: and the fact that we are repressing them must also be repressed" (Billig 1999: 13). In the instance of severe initiation effects, then, what one dislikes about the group is subject to being repressed. But how does repression actually occur? In his book, *Freudian Repression: Conversation Creating the Unconscious*, Billig explores how the "silence" of repressed material is created by speech, and by speech with others—by discourse. As Kulick and Schieffelin summarize it:

> Billig agrees with Freud that repression is a fundamental dimension of human existence. But he disagrees with the idea that the roots of repression lie in biologically inborn urges, as Freud thought. Instead, he argues that repression is demanded by language: "in conversing, we also create silences," says Billig (1999: 261). Thus, in learning to speak, children also learn what must remain unspoken and unspeakable. This means two things: first, that repression is not beyond or outside language; and second, that repression is an interactional achievement. (Kulick and Schieffelin 2004: 357)

MAPS FOR THE BOOK

The focus of Kulick and Schieffelin's article is the language socialization of children. For the purposes of this book, we need to broaden that focus to include the socialization that continues throughout the life span. Parents socialize children, but children (think about teenagers) also change their parents. When we enter new environments—moving to a new country, a new city, a new school—those environments change us. In the case of Silesia, changes in regime had profound socializing impacts on people of all ages.

It is this "discursive psychology," as Kulick and Schieffelin point out, that allows linguistic anthropology to tackle the questions of, "how do individuals come to perceive the subject positions that are available or possible in any given context? How is the taking up of particular positions enabled or blocked by relations of power? How do particular positions come to be known as intelligible and desirable, while others are inconceivable and undesirable?" (2004: 356–57) We can get at these questions by looking at language; we can get at these questions by looking at silences. Thus there can be a unity of analysis of various silences, not just the repression of wartime trauma narratives (I have a telling, specific example in the interview data that I withheld from the preface), but also other kinds of silencing: each regime silencing the other's language; in the signature campaign, grandparents silencing the differing identities of younger household members; "dead" metaphors like "This room is so messy it looks like the front came through here"; the way the professor in chapter 3 is silenced; "approving silence" in chapter 7; and there may be more in the book. So while this book analyzes ethnic-national identity assertions (when people state who they are) and ethnic-national identity ascriptions (when people state who somebody else is) and looks very carefully at the circumstances of such statements, I argue that identity is as much about silence as about what gets said.

This, then, is the more specific, more "zoomed in" aspect of the book.

To recap, simply: broadly, the book hopes to offer students a positive first encounter with the culture concept suited to the conditions of the twenty-first century. Second, it hopes to add a particular insight to thinking about identity formation and assertion: why do some Europeans believe with such vehemence that they belong to ethnic-national groups?

THE BOOK'S NARRATIVE ARC AND TOPICS CHAPTER BY CHAPTER

The narrative arc of this book can be seen as a deepening exploration of autonomous culture, followed by an explication of culture as inextricably entwined with structures of power: to use a spatial metaphor, five chapters of deepening understanding of autochthonous Opole Silesian culture that hinge

21

onto four chapters of deepening understanding of twentieth-century central Europe.

In chapter 2, I deal with locality—with the "whereness"—of the research site, which in the case of European borderlands is historically problematic. Opole Silesia, notwithstanding the 1991 affirmation of the current border in the Treaty of Good Neighborship and Friendly Cooperation between Poland and Germany, remains in important social ways betwixt and between (all but the last section of this chapter can safely be skimmed by readers familiar with the complicated history of shifting borders in Silesia). Chapter 3 concerns what may aptly be called "boundary mechanisms," how autochthonous Opole Silesians maintain barriers to outsiders' interaction with them and manage the impressions of outsiders; however, it does this in a way sensitized to history. Chapter 4 both treats aspects of autonomous culture more deeply while at the same time beginning to explore how these autonomous aspects depend inextricably on relationship with the two states: culture as "betweenly" constructed. Chapter 5 focuses specifically on what I argue is the most distinct characteristic of culture in Opole Silesia, linguistic culture: also, however, a linguistic culture of betweenness.

Chapter 6, then, starts at the turning point, with the admission that in my ethnography of autonomy, I have deliberately participated in a kind of "conspiracy of silence" by autochthonous Opole Silesians. The cultural aesthetics of appropriate choice of language turns out to have a dark side. Here, then, I take linguistic culture as a departure point for considering the power dynamics between autochthonous Opole Silesians and the two overpowering states they lived in between 1933 and 1989. In chapter 7, I further that exploration by explaining how and why, for autochthonous Opole Silesians, ascriptions of identity to other people function as a discourse of moral disapproval. In other words, if you are living an upstanding, good life, nobody will talk about you as a member of an ethnic-national group. Run afoul of your neighbors, and you're likely to be talked about as a German or as a Pole.

That being the case, chapters 8 and 9 return to the question of why some autochthonous Opole Silesians choose to identify and assert their own German identity. Chapter 8 locates a subjective sense of identity in historically developed, nuanced differences of sociological position within autochthonous Opole Silesian society. It is chapter 9, then, that deals with the issue of vehement identity specifically. The organization of the German Minority in the months following the end of Communism in Poland swamped these intrasocietal divisions, with people who had been quietly hostile to one another for decades suddenly coming together to present themselves to a briefly attentive outside world as all Germans together. The chapter locates a reason for that in psychology. The conclusion, finally, meditates on how this kind of cultural object of analysis affects how we, in general, think about culture.

There is another way that some readers may prefer to read this book, or parts of it: as a zipper. That is, depending on one's purposes for reading, the chapters may be read in pairs. The preface, introduction, and chapter 9 can be read together primarily to understand the psychological aspects of national identity. Chapters 2 and 7 can be read together to understand the relationship of Opole Silesia's position in a larger European context, over the last 150 years, with slowly developing class consciousness expressed as nationality. Chapters 3 and 6 can be read to understand aspects of "boundary mechanisms" and how these relate to autochthonous Opole Silesians' defensive position vis-à-vis totalitarian states. And finally, chapters 4 and 5 can be read, simply, as a contrast

Main Topics	Chapter
Opole Silesia in the context of central Europe's political history and geography	2
Historical consciousness; identity politics; essentialism; cultural practice analyzed with reference to history	3
Household structure, social organization, and community political organizing; cultural and lexical change (borrowing)	4
Linguistic ideological tension (tolerance and loyalty); lexical register and reference; lexical change (semanticization of register distinctions)	5
State hegemony; narrative register; linguistic ideology (socially acceptable and unacceptable use of Polish and German)	6
Shared cultural values; delayed reciprocal exchange and social networks; interethnic relations as constructed in discourse	7
The sociology of identity; aspiration vs. loyalty as values in conflict; marriage and kinship as constructors of class; local history and state policy; identity discourse as indexical of all of the above	8
The psychology of German identity: cognitive psychology, developmental psychology, repression, cognitive dissonance; identity discourse connected to psychology	9
Our changing culture concept and the challenge of globalization	10

between cultural-anthropological and linguistic-anthropological approaches to ethnography.

For the further convenience of those readers who may wish to relate this book to other readings, or to read parts of it, but not the whole, I offer the chart on the previous page, which locates each chapter in relation to more general concerns in anthropology and linguistics.

GUIDANCE ON THE USE OF FONTS TO REPRESENT SPEECH

Finally, in a book all about language mixing, readers who do not speak Silesian, Polish, and German must have a way to see what autochthonous Opole Silesians hear. Of note is that "particular linguistic forms are more often *seen now* not as belonging necessarily to either one code or another, but as fully participating in more than one linguistic system" (Woolard 2004: 83). I italicized "seen now" because Woolard's paragraph refers to how linguists now see contrasts of languages; I refer, in contrast, to how autochthonous Opole Silesians evaluate spoken language. I asked, "What were you speaking just now?" repeatedly, and recorded the answers until I learned the social norms. In fact, I learned to distinguish Silesian from Polish by the social rules that govern their use several months before I developed the knowledge to distinguish them linguistically.

I have used fonts as follows to indicate the linguistic affiliation of stretches of speech:

Speech transcribed identically to the book's narrative is both Silesian and Polish.
If it's italicized, it's contrastively Silesian, and helps to mark what's said as Silesian.
IF IT LOOKS LIKE THIS, IT'S CONTRASTIVELY GERMAN.
IF IT LOOKS LIKE THIS, IT'S A GERMAN LOAN WORD NOW RECOGNIZED AS SILESIAN.
IF IT LOOKS LIKE THIS, IT'S CONTRASTIVELY POLISH.
IF IT LOOKS LIKE THIS, IT'S A POLISH LOAN WORD NOW RECOGNIZED AS SILESIAN.
The symbol *[Ø]* indicates that what is contrastively Silesian is the absence of a sound required in Polish.

Thus, "bird": ptʌk, ptok. The Polish word is "ptak," and the Silesian word is "ptok." The German word is VOGEL. It might be useful to bookmark this page, and refer back to it when trying to decipher the font changes.

Chapter 2

OPOLE SILESIA, BETWIXT AND BETWEEN

When we ask ourselves where a place is, we are asking with respect to something else. This is true whether we're aware of it or not, and it's true whether it's a physical place or a metaphorical one. We need landmarks. The answer I've given in the title—betwixt and between—implies a key question for any ethnography: where was the research for this book done? The book's title says, "in the German-Polish borderland," which is all right as far as it goes. We know we're between Germany and Poland. But "betwixt and between," means, according to *Merriam Webster*, "in a midway position, neither one thing nor another." The maps we're used to don't allow for this; there's no blank space between countries. One country extends all the way up to a line where the next begins. Yet in this case, it's fair to say that the research was done in a place negatively defined with respect to Germany and Poland, a neither/nor space. The aim of the chapter is not only to explain where the book takes place, but what it means that many kinds of maps give only a partial answer to that question. Chapters, having "aims," also have trajectories, or journeys; so do anthropologists in getting to the field. In Silesia, all these journeys, literal and metaphorical, overlay one another. Once we have a basic sense of place and history, we will see that the map that can get us to all these partial answers, and provide a sense of location for the book, is the railway map.

SOME BASICS ABOUT THE RESEARCH SITE

The primary site of this study is a village, to be called here Dobra (in Polish it means "good"; some villages in Poland do have this name), within the ethnically mixed Opole Province, Poland. Opole Province lies just west of the German-Polish border of 1921–39 (see maps 1 and 3). Within Opole Province, commonly called Opole Silesia, lie about four hundred villages to the east of the city of Opole in which, overall, more than 80 percent of the population is "autochthonous" (see map 2). "Autochthonous" is the word used to describe them in Polish sociological sources, and it means that these are people, or the descendants of people, who have lived in the region since before the Second World War ended in 1945. Opole Silesia has another population, that Polish sociology calls the "resettled" or "immigrant" population, consisting of those who moved there after 1945 from the eastern territories of Poland, which had been transferred, in accordance with the Potsdam Accords, to the Soviet Union. Silesia, for its part, was among the territories transferred in 1945 from Germany to Poland (see map 1).

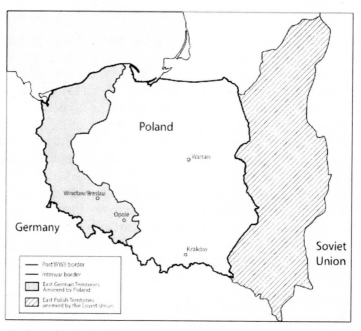

Map 1. Borders of Poland, 1921–present. The borders of the Polish state, reconstituted after the First World War, were changed after the Second World War.

The changes in sovereignty in 1945 were far from the first. Four dates mark previous changes of sovereignty: 1163, 1339, 1526, and 1742. For the most part, the ancestors of the "autochthonous" population have lived there since before 1163, when the first Kingdom of Poland fragmented, and since before 1339, when Polish King Casimir the Great, pulling it together again, agreed to an arrangement whereby the Bohemian (Czech) sovereign, John of Luxembourg, renounced claim to Poland and Mazovia in exchange for the entire region in which this ethnic enclave now lies, as well as 400,000 silver

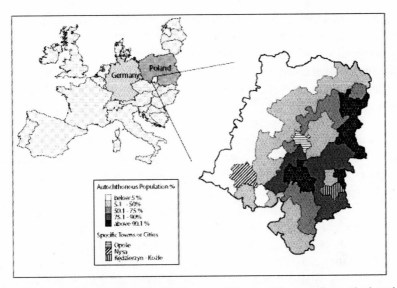

Map 2. Opole Province, Poland, in the context of Europe. The map shows the location of the province, as well as its ethnic demography.

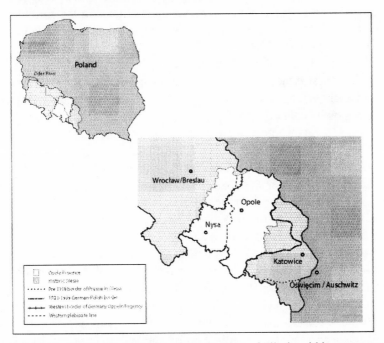

Map 3. Historic Silesia. The map shows the location of Silesia within contemporary Poland as well as the interrelationships of historical borders.

groats (Davies 1982: 95). Thus sovereignty over Silesia passed from Polish to Czech princes. Later, in 1526, it passed to Austria, with the accession of the Austrian Archduke Ferdinand to the Czech crown. This was a matter of inheritance; in contrast, in 1742, Frederick II of Prussia wrested Silesia from Maria-Theresa in the War of the Austrian Succession (he wanted Silesia's mining and textile industries). Silesia, then, has always been intimately connected with both the German-speaking and Polish-speaking lands, and to a lesser extent to the Czech-speaking lands. But it experienced the development of the nation-state as a German province; Silesia was the first Prussian acquisition in the process that eventually brought German principalities together in a unified Germany.

Opole Province is one of three Polish provinces that make up the region historically known as Silesia (Polish Śląsk, German Schlesien). Polish sources commonly refer to Opole Province as Opole Silesia (Polish Śląsk Opolski or Opolszczyzna), between Lower Silesia (Dolny Śląsk) to the west and Upper Silesia (Górny Śląsk) to the east. German sources, on the other hand, divide Silesia into two regions, Niederschlesien (Lower) and Oberschlesien (Upper) with Opole Silesia as the western part of Upper Silesia. The difference is historically constituted. The Polish usage is more attuned to the current, post–Second World War status of the area, as well as to local consciousness, and it is this usage that I adopt here.

The population pattern evident in map 2 has its roots in the Middle Ages. The Polish Piast princes who ruled it, or subdivisions of it, in the centuries before Czech rule, encouraged immigration from German lands, and German speakers slowly replaced the indigenous Slavs from the west eastward (Davies 1982: 49, 82). Yet this process stopped near Opole, where the River Oder (Polish Odra), which runs through all of Silesia, bends to make a short south to north line before resuming its southeast to northwest course (Rose 1935: 19). The soil east of the Oder was too sandy to make for easy farming; Slavs stuck it out, but Germans stayed on the more fertile soil west of the Oder. Prussia likewise tried but failed to settle many Germans there.

The autochthonous population consists of the descendants of these Slavs who stuck it out. The so-called "resettled" or "immigrant" population arrived after the Second World War from what had been, before the war changed Poland's borders, eastern Poland. Poland's borders were revised in the west and the east, so eastern Germany suddenly became western Poland, and eastern Poland was added to the western Soviet Union (Davies 1982: 489). The arrangement encouraged 1.5 million Polish nationals to leave the former eastern territories of Poland (Pogonowski 1996: 172; Mach 1989: 163). It also forced 3.5 to 4 million German nationals to leave the former eastern territories of Germany (Pogonowski 1996: 172 [3.5 million]; DeZayas 1977: 124; Kaps 1952/53: 83–84 [4 million]). These eastern Poles were resettled in the homes, farms, villages, towns, and cities that had been emptied of their German inhabitants.

The railway was indispensable to the postwar "population transfers," as it had been for transporting victims of the Holocaust. The railways were not built to transport people, though; the Prussian state built them primarily to move coal, steel, and machinery from their Upper Silesian sources to factories in the Ruhrgebiet in western Germany, and from there to port cities and markets. Map 4 shows the number of daily trains with proportionally thick lines. A sense of how dense, and tight, the rail network built by Prussia is in Silesia can be seen in map 5. Seven lines can be seen to converge at Opole, and nine at Wrocław (German Breslau). And every Polish seventh grader learns to recognize what social scientists have recently called a "phantom border." If you look at a map of Poland during the time when the country was partitioned among Prussia, Austria, and Russia (1795–1918), and you mark where dense rail lines become much less dense, and then connect those marks with a line, that line bears a remarkable resemblance to a map of the area during the Partitions of Poland, 1795–1918 (search "Phantomgrenzen in Ostmitteleuropa"). This was the time when Poland did not exist as a country at all, having been divided up among three great northern European empires of the time: Prussia, the Austro-Hungarian Empire, and Russia. Russia and Austria did not build a great many railway lines; Prussia did. This is only one of many ways that the history of Partition affects contemporary Poland: maps of phenomena as disparate as voting patterns and drinking habits (beer vs. vodka) continue to trace the Partition borders, ghosts of a political reality that ended after the First World War.

So the railway was of central importance in the social and economic development of this Prussian periphery, this "internal colony" (Hechter 1975), Silesia. It remains important for transport, though the industrial age in Silesia has ended, and cars and buses have become the primary mode of transportation for people. For this book, it is also vitally important because the railway works not only as an object of description and analysis, but also as a metaphor, and as a narrative device. As a metaphor, maps 4 and 5 position the research site in relation to Europe, and with that, in relation to anthropological understandings of locality. Literally, for Dobra, it was the laying of tracks through the village, in about 1860, that created space in which a German-identified bourgeois class could develop. As a narrative device, rail journeys to Dobra are

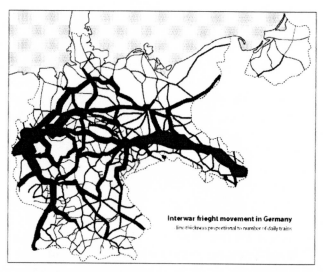

Map 4. Interwar freight movements in Europe. The map shows the frequency of shipments of freight by rail to and from Silesia, then in Germany, during the period 1921–39.

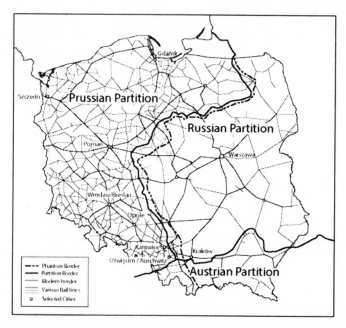

Map 5. Poland's railway phantom border. The map illustrates how the rail lines built by the Prussian state, in contrast to the lack of building in the Austrian and Prussian Partitions, continue to constitute a visible "phantom border" in the map of contemporary Poland.

useful for locating Opole Silesia within a mental, not just visual, framework. And from the east, the narrative train grinds to a useful halt, as travel across its two-dimensional x y Cartesian map encounters a z-axis: the historical dimension of contested territory and shifting national boundaries. Understanding Opole Silesia's position in relation to the tracks—in space and in historical time—leads to an understanding of its position in the "map" of ethnic and national identity. And that understanding is needed to shed light on the complexities of locality, complexities so overwhelming that I locate Dobra "betwixt and between," and Dobrans themselves refer to their place simply as "here."

OPOLE SILESIA IN THE WORLD SYSTEM

Take (another) look at map 4. This thematic map makes it very clear that the rail lines between Silesia and the Ruhrgebiet fit the definition of "arteries" as defined for transportation: "a large road, river, railroad line, etc." (*Merriam Webster*). They almost look, here, like a drawing of arteries in the physiological, circulatory system sense, with a heart in the west. Now in contrast, consider anthropologist Andrew Orta's description of his first arrival in the region of Jesús de Machaqa, Ingavi Province, Bolivia:

> In November of 1990 Ingrid and I traveled with Father Jan and Sister Marta. Snug in a late-model Toyota Landrover, we whizzed down the highway on our way to the parish of Peñas, a colonial town tucked in the foothills that rise into the Cordillera Real east of the altiplano. . . . With the assistance of Marta, Jan found the turnoff to Peñas and we left the highway for a rutted dirt road that put the Landrover to good use as we bounced and turned our way into the foothills. (Orta 2004: 27)

It's a remote locality. It's difficult to get to, both in terms of the poor condition of the road and in terms of navigating roads that are not marked. It invites a metaphor that Orta uses for this place in terms of its relationship with the Roman Catholic Church (14, 83, and 197) and in relation to global processes more generally (11): it's at the capillaries. With that, Orta not only captures the insularity of the place—the capillaries are the part of the circulatory system furthest from the pumping heart—but also affirms that as far as Jesús de Machaqa is from Rome, from the capital La Paz, from any center of industrial production, it nevertheless participates in world systems, of institutional religion, of politics, of economics.

Opole Silesia, in contrast, is easy to get to by motor vehicle, or by train. As a result of its proximity to Upper Silesia, very few Opole Silesian villages lie far from a rail line. They're on the arteries. In many ways, the region is extremely integrated. Its inhabitants, autochthonous and resettled, are Roman Catholics who feel closely tied to Rome through identification with the Polish Pope John Paul II, and, in the case of autochthonous Opole Silesians, the German Pope Benedict XVI as well: "Now," a woman told me happily during the summer of 2010, "I have a blessing in my house from both the Polish pope and the German pope." Politically, it is in Europe; it is not a former colony of Europe. Economically, it is next to one of the heartbeats of European industrialization, Upper Silesia.

But the question is, why would one go there? The city of Opole lies along a curve of railway that extends from Odessa on the Black Sea to Szczecin on the Baltic. It lies between two major hubs, less than 200 kilometers apart, at Wrocław, where nine major lines converge, and Katowice, the heart (note the metaphor) of the densest part of the rail network. From Odessa, then, one can travel (or send freight) through Opole Silesia to the Baltic port city of Szczecin, or to Leipzig, Berlin, Munich, Prague, or Vienna. The rail lines through Silesia connect Warsaw, Gdańsk, and St. Petersburg with Vienna, Rome, and Prague, to name only a few. In short, Opole Silesia is not the kind of place people go to. It's the kind of place people go through. Being on the arteries is not the same thing as being at the heart.

Poles go through Opole Silesia. When I traveled, as I often did, from Cracow to Opole, I found that at Katowice, most of the people in the train got out. The people traveling west from central or Eastern Poland were going there or to another destination which required them to change there. Experience showed it to happen the same way going from Opole to Cracow. Boarding a train at Opole headed for Cracow, one entered a crowded train which few were getting out of, and it remained crowded until Katowice, at which point many people got out. The eastbound intercity trains were used by those coming from Lower Silesia to get *through* Opole Silesia to their destinations in central and eastern Poland beyond.

For their part, in the 1990s, before widespread car ownership, the 37.6 percent of the province's population who are autochthonous (Rauziński 1992) traveled less within Poland than the Polish population. They are not socially tied to the rest of Poland in ways that necessitate much interregional train travel. The low interethnic marriage rate, of about 9 percent, contributes to this: family members are in Opole Silesia or in Germany. Further, the rate of migration from villages to cities is low among the autochthonous population compared to the resettled group (Berlińska 1990: 113). Like other Polish Catholics, they regularly visit pilgrimage shrines; however, they are renowned for visiting St. Anne's Mountain, near Opole, with the regularity and devotion that Poles reserve for the Black Madonna of Częstochowa. So neither familial nor religious obligations make them frequent travelers on the intercity trains. They rely much more heavily on the local trains that travel from Opole to the villages than they do on intercity trains.

In the 1990s, when autochthonous Opole Silesians traveled outside the province, they were generally going to Germany. Bus tickets to various German cities were (and still are) for sale not only in Opole, but also in many of the villages, where small businesses are contracted as vendors. The owner of one such bus company told me that about a third of their business came from Wrocław, a third from Opole, and a third from the villages around Opole. One can infer that villagers' travel to Germany was as habitual and frequent as their travel within Poland was (and is) rare. This is how that math works: the population of Wrocław, essentially entirely resettled from territory formerly in eastern Poland, was almost ten times that of Opole (1,128,800 vs. 126,404), and about three times that of the entire autochthonous population of Opole Province in 1977 (it would be less now, due to emigration, and there would be some overlap as this figure includes residents of Opole). If both groups were traveling with equal frequency to Germany, one would expect that three times the number of tickets would go to Wrocław as to the villages around Opole. Instead, the same number of tickets was being sold in both places. So it seems that autochthonous Opole Silesians bought bus tickets to Germany at three times the rate of the population whose roots are in what was once eastern Poland (see Rauziński and Szczygielski 1992: 74–83).

And autochthonous Silesians differed, and still differ, in the destination of their labor migration and emigration. In the 1990s, I never met a Pole who did not have relatives in North America, and I never met a Silesian who did. When I heard from Poles who had gone to another country to work for a while, I never heard about any other countries than the United States and Canada, and I never heard Silesians talk about any country other than Germany. When I returned after Poland joined the European Union in 2004, I found that the United Kingdom had become a destination of choice for Poles, whereas Opole was plastered with advertising for agencies arranging labor migration to the Netherlands (this for reasons to be explained below, when we discuss citizenship). In 2007, even the risers of the main stairs in the Opole train station had been painted, in a repeating pattern, with the name of such an agency. There were also billboards all over Opole to catch the attention of drivers, but the advertiser apparently calculated that the autochthonous use of intraregional trains was strong enough to warrant publicity in the train station.

One thing to notice about Opole Silesia in the world economic system: all of Opole Province, indeed all of Poland and beyond that all of the former Soviet bloc countries have found themselves integrated as a vast reserve of labor for western European countries. People are pulled along those transport arteries by the need for work and wages. The extraction of coal and steel westward has been replaced by extraction of workers. Since one of the defining features of the colonial situation is extraction, the essential position remains that of an internal colony.

So Opole Silesia is not a destination. In terms of the Roman Catholic world system, go on through to Rome. In terms of the political world system, there are direct rail connections to both Berlin and Warsaw. In terms of "high" culture, try Cracow, Prague, or Vienna. Economically, people migrate from there, not to there. It's not a place to go to—unless you happen to be interested in multilingual societies or issues of ethnic and national identity.

OPOLE SILESIA AS A RESEARCH DESTINATION

Finding a mystery to solve is a good starting place in taking one's skills from a master's degree to a Ph.D. In my case, I was eager to use my German, which I had learned as a teenager, and to gain another language along the way (little did I know how much easier German is than Polish). History cooperated: six months after I had decided on "a German minority in Eastern Europe," the Communist government of Poland fell (June 1989). Soon after the fall of the Berlin Wall, on November 9, I had my mystery.

The *Chicago Tribune* headline read, "German-Polish Mass is the Latest Sign of Change":

> WARSAW – West German Chancellor Helmut Kohl, visiting a shrine of German resistance against the Nazis, prayed Sunday for true reconciliation between Poles and Germans 50 years after Hitler swept through Poland and ignited World War II. Kohl, accompanied by Polish Prime Minister Tadeusz Mazowiecki, also prayed for a peaceful future for all of Europe, in turmoil as East European nations break with postwar communism and edge uncertainly toward a new order. (Butturini 1989)

A few weeks earlier, when he had visited St. Anne's Mountain, Kohl had been greeted with a banner that read, "Helmut you are our chancellor also" (Butturini 1989). I later learned that the "German Minority," as political party and organized "social club" or "society," emerged quickly in Opole Silesia. By August 1989, German Minority organizers had gathered 200,000 signatures on letters declaring that the signers considered themselves to be German

(Berlińska 1989: 11). By early 1990, when the unexpected death of a senator necessitated a by-election, the Social and Cultural Society of the German Minority (which was, by then, its official name) was able to oppose Solidarity, fielding a candidate who won the seat in an election campaign marred by anti-German and anti-Polish graffiti and other incidents (Harden 1990).

Self-assertion by ethnic-national groups (the existence of which had been denied by Communist governments) was happening all over Eastern Europe. What was mysterious in Opole Silesia was that, as far as I could understand from afar, these self-professed Germans of 1989 were the direct descendants of the self-professed Poles of 1919. Reading the western, and especially German, press coverage on Silesia (and journalists had apparently descended on the region in droves), it became evident that the German Minority consists almost entirely of village dwellers, living in the villages to the north, south, and east of Opole (see, for example, Kifner 1990; Schneider 1990). And yet, I knew from Rose's 1935 work, *The Drama of Upper Silesia*, that the inhabitants of these villages were classified as Poles in the German census of 1910. And it was village dwellers who were the constituency of the Polish nationalist movement that followed World War I, which campaigned for the annexation of southeastern Silesia to Poland, and staged three armed Silesian uprisings in anticipation of the 1921 plebiscite (Rose 1935: 165–79). It was the city dwellers, on the other hand, who were classified as Germans, and who, in large part, seem to have identified as such. Now, the city dwellers are Poles. I knew, before my first visit to Opole Silesia, that during the massive post–World War II population movements, forced by various degrees of violence, one thing that had *not* happened was a migration of German city dwellers out to the villages. Village dwellers were autochthonous; their ancestors had been there before the German population just as they had been there before the Polish population that replaced the Germans after the Second World War. How, then, did the Polish villages of 1910 become the bastions of the German Minority in the 1990s?

That is the question that I sought an answer to, boarding a train for Opole for the first time, in 1991. Underneath it lies the question I stated in the introduction: how do people come to see themselves as members of ethnic-national groups at all?

I also suspected that these autochthonous Opole Silesians were going to be great people for a linguistic anthropologist to work with. The people quoted in the western press kept saying that the reason German was no longer spoken in their communities was that the Polish Communist government had suppressed it, but I knew that could not be true. I was familiar with Dorian's work on Scottish Gaelic (Dorian 1981, 1985); the English state tried to extirpate Gaelic with sustained effort for hundreds of years, but never with complete success—how could the Polish state have managed it in a few decades? No, there had to be more to this picture than met my faraway eye.

If anything I underestimated the interest of Opole Silesia as a research site on both counts. As we will see when we arrive in Dobra at the beginning of chapter 3, identity turned out to be a topic at the very surface of social life, as well as one having depths to be plumbed. As for language, it wasn't necessary even to get as far as Dobra. The Opole train station was far enough. When I had extra time, waiting for trains, I used to go to the public phones area and amuse myself with a game of "Guess the Identity." The point was to try to guess from appearance whether a caller was Silesian or Polish and then wait until the call went through to find out. Appearance might or might not provide a clue, but the give-away was the voice. Would the person sound Silesian, or Polish? I didn't have to hear the words to tell the difference.

The trains themselves were predominantly Silesian-speaking environments. Not only that, but language was a topic of conversation, for example, while waiting for one. On July 26, 1993, for example, two family groups were talking about other people, specific other people, in a cheerful and positive tone, and talking about their language abilities, especially about the competencies of the children. One, it was said, doesn't speak X (I did not catch whether the language was Polish or German—it could have been either, depending on whether the child was growing up in Silesia or in Germany in an emigrant Silesian family), but he understands everything. This they agreed was good; it's a good thing if he understands everything. Yet however cheerfully they spoke, the implication was that it would be better if he also spoke.

It's a commonly expressed value. Silesia is a place where, if you want to strike up a conversation in a tavern, you can say, "It's a good thing, don't you think, for a person to speak more than one language?" (Notes, March 26, 1993—I was not the addressee, nor did the speaker know me). Or, you could comment on the prettiness of the German lyrics to the popular music being played (which, in an autochthonous village, was almost sure to be German), and draw your interlocutor into a series of evaluations of various languages: German is pretty, Polish is hard to pronounce, Silesian is easier. (Notes, May 1, 1993—I was the interlocutor). In my first few weeks of fieldwork, the most frequent question asked of me was what languages I spoke. And within weeks of beginning fieldwork I found myself listening to a factory administrator's son with a high school education tell me things about Icelandic, as an example of historical linguistic process, which I had learned in college (Notes, January

26, 1993). It's not just the phenomenon of the train station telephones: that language is to Silesians as skin color is to Americans, a means of categorizing people socially. Autochthonous Opole Silesians play with language, manipulate language, talk about language, make multilingual puns, value the learning of languages—in short, treat language as a preoccupation of central cultural importance. Language is to autochthonous Opole Silesians as E. E. Evans-Pritchard said that cows are to the southern Sudanese Nuer: "[Nuer] are always talking about their beasts. I used sometimes to despair that I never discussed anything with the young men but livestock and girls, and even the subject of girls led inevitably to that of cattle" (1940: 18–19). And while I don't think Evans-Pritchard was as interested in cows as the Nuer are, I had the good fortune to be as passionately interested in language as autochthonous Opole Silesians are. It was a good match.

"GREEN SILESIA" AND THE POSTINDUSTRIAL MEGALOPOLIS

Why is there a linguistic and cultural "there" there, as Orta puts it (borrowing from Gertrude Stein)? We have talked about Opole Silesia as a place that trains run through, rather than to. I called it "negatively defined in relation to Germany and Poland." Then I said it's fieldworker's gold for a linguistic anthropologist. What kind of social/cultural/linguistic space is this?

It is, once again, in movement that we can find the answer. Let's start with movement across physical, topographical landscape: movement that can be described very quickly and pleasantly, and movement that can't be. If you approach Opole Silesia from Berlin, from the northwest, you travel along the 350-kilometer long expanse of the Oder River Valley as it defines Silesia, that is, southeast of its sharp bend to the north at its confluence with the Lusatian Neisse, the geographical underlay of the Oder-Neisse line, the post–Second World War German-Polish border. Bucolic green fields and gentle hills characterize the whole valley. The same is true of the approach from the northeast, from Warsaw. The train route from the capital takes one straight through rural areas of Poland, so the view is of gentle hills, woods, and fields all the way. Villages in Opole Silesia are only a few kilometers apart, and the Warsaw line passes through many of them, so that in daylight (which lasts in midsummer until after 10 p.m.) the view is broken by church spires and village streets and houses (after dark, however, in the 1990s, one saw nothing, because streets in Polish villages were so poorly lit).

From the south, from Vienna or Prague, the beautiful, tourist-destination mountains begin to hint more strongly of the overlay of politics on geography.

These mountains are part of the Sudeten range, one of several which cross central Europe more or less parallel to the equator; Hitler's appropriation of the Sudetenland from Czechoslovakia in 1938 was his first major expansionist move. The Oder originates in the mountain passes between the Sudeten and the Carpathian mountains, just as another great river, the Elbe, originates between the Sudeten and the range just west of them, the Ore Mountains (Hamburg, Germany, is near the port at the mouth of the Elbe). The Sudeten themselves run northwest/southeast, and the Oder winds down their southeastern limit in a backwards C until it reaches the great plain which forms not only Poland but also northern Europe west to the North Sea and east to the Urals. From there the river parallels the mountain range. Traveling from the south, most of your time in the Sudeten Mountains will be spent on the southern, Czech side, for they fall off much more steeply on the northern side than on the southern side. On the Czech side, elevations as much as 100 kilometers away from the 1,500-meter-high peaks of the Sudetens are still 700–1,000 meters above sea level, whereas on the northern, Polish side, the Oder has an elevation of less than 200 meters for most of its length; yet it is, at every point, less than 150 km from the peaks. (Alas, poor Poland, the name of the country comes from the word meaning "field"; Poland is a plain crossed by rivers, and, too easily, by armies.)

But it is the route from the east, from Cracow, that most reveals the human geography and history of Silesia. This route passes through Upper Silesia on its way to Opole. Cracow is about 75 kilometers east of Katowice, the heart of the industrial Upper Silesian megalopolis. The route goes through cities set close together: Zabierzów, Rudawa, Krzeszowice, Trzebinia. The rhythm and bump of the train measure out a view of thin, straight trees, in copses, not woods, never alone in the field of vision, sharing it with pylons, spaced across the landscape, more than one line of them at any moment, receding from the tracks at various diagonals, wide and squat. There are buildings, enormously square, with enclosed conveyor belts slanting down, high-perched spoked wheels like huge pulleys; these buildings are often painted baby blue, but a thick coat of dirt obscures most color. Settlements look like several-storied boxes laid on end, all alike, set at close angles to one another, with windows and balconies for drying laundry. And then, more cities, bigger ones: Mysłowice, Katowice, Zabrze, Gliwice. Large, old buildings, of several stories and elaborate decayed facades and steep roofs. They, too, are end on end, along streets that parallel or recede from the train tracks. Their ceilings were built high, and their windows are tall, divided into quadrants, with small panes atop long panes, so that, once, I caught an evening glimpse of a man washing windows inside, standing on a chair, backlit, looking as if he were crucified against the window frame.

In Upper Silesian cities in the 1990s there was no paint, so there was no color. The cityscape was grey and brown against the sky, which in the evening was red with the fumes of dying industry. Sometimes the air inside the train stank. Upper Silesia was a place where buildings fall in on themselves, sinking into the mine shafts below, which were never properly reinforced. At the time of publication, the industry is all but dead and the air no longer stinks. Upper Silesia is no longer a region so valuable that it confounds diplomats or sparks international violence.

And then, further west, the copses give way to woods, and fields, and the view opens out. The cities are much smaller—as grimy, but less gargantuan. Some call Opole Silesia "green Silesia," in contrast to the urban decay of Upper Silesia. It's back to the bucolic views of the approaches from the northwest and northeast.

That's what you can see from the train.

LINES ON THE LAND, SPACES OF RACE, AND DESTINATIONS OF VIOLENCE

More important is what you can't see from the train. Depart, mentally, from Cracow again. The train takes you across lines which are invisible to the eye but inscribed in the minds of those who natively navigate the terrain with the indelibility of violence: the political boundaries drawn by victors after the First and Second World Wars. They are invisible on the ground, no longer marked by the ritual of border crossing, but in order to understand the locality of Opole Silesia, it is essential to understand them.

It is between Trzebinia and Mysłowice that, unnoticed, the line is crossed between what was once Austria and what was once Prussia. Just there, at this juncture, a rail line, which hugs the 1795–1918 Partition border just within Austria, intersects ours. Change for a southbound train, then, at Trzebinia, and you will get to Oświęcim, or Auschwitz, about 20 kilometers farther on (about 50 km from Cracow). In fact, four rail lines converge in this border town, where the logic of defending ethnic boundaries was taken to its genocidal extreme.

Boundaries have multiple meanings: the border just crossed, the historic border between the Austrian and Prussian Partitions, took on a meaning during the three years following the First World War critical to the construction of ethnicity and nationality. The Partition of Poland ended with the First World War, on November 11, 1918. So this line became the border between the newly resurrected Poland and . . . what? Woodrow Wilson's ideals for Europe after the First World War were that members of different nations, as defined by language and culture, ought to have political autonomy; they ought to form states. But these Wilsonian ideals of nation-statehood were challenged in areas where people of different languages and cultures lived in close physical and social proximity, such as southeastern Silesia. To award territory east and north of Silesia to the new Poland was easy; it had been Polish before the Partitions. Silesia had not been Polish since 1163; yet the posterity of those twelfth-century Poles still lived there, mainly in villages, though Germans formed the majority of town dwellers. Furthermore, argued the Polish delegation to the Peace Treaty convention,

> Upper Silesia . . . was essentially Polish, since the proportion of the Polish-speaking population exceeded 90 per cent in many of its districts. Historically, it was an ancient Polish province (even called Old Poland); nationally, it was Polish, the Germans constituting only a small percentage of the population; geographically, it belonged to Poland and represented an indispensable link between Poland and Czechoslovakia; economically, the Silesian coal basin would give Poland's industrial development a solid foundation. (Kaeckenbeeck 1942: 3)

Initially, the Allies agreed, and unconditionally ceded the whole of southeastern Silesia to Poland. However,

> No point of the first draft of the Peace Treaty brought a more emphatic protest from Germany than the cession of Upper Silesia to Poland. In the remarks of the German delegation it constituted an absolutely unjustified inroad into the geographical and economic structure of the German Reich. Since 1163 Upper Silesia had had no political connexion whatever with Poland. There were no Polish national traditions in Upper Silesia, no memory of Polish history; nor had Upper Silesia participated in the liberation struggle. Germany further denied that Upper Silesia was inhabited by a clearly Polish population. . . . Nor did the Upper Silesians speak literary Polish, but a Polish dialect, a mixture of German and Polish, which was not used for literary purposes. In particular, this dialect constituted no characteristic of nationality and was not incompatible with German national consciousness. Besides, the whole development, intellectual and material, of Upper Silesia was due to German work. . . . Nor was its cession to Poland in the interest of peace, for Germany could not reconcile herself to the loss [emotionally], [a loss] which would make her unable to fulfil her obligations arising out of the war [financially, i.e., reparations].[1] (Kaeckenbeeck 1942: 4–5)

The solution was to involve the inhabitants in the decision as to whether the region ought to belong to Poland or Germany by means of plebiscite, a popular vote: Germany? Or Poland? This was both a way to pass the buck and an assertion of faith in Wilsonian ideals, in the existence of essential national identity within individuals. If that's true, if people have an essential national identity, then they can be counted on to vote their identity. Logically, then, plebiscite follows the principle of self-determination.

A train from Cracow crossing the border just east of Mysłowice in 1919, then, crossed into a region of officially indeterminate nationality. Ethnic-nationalist principles ensured that it had to be undefined. Linguistic maps of the region at the time look like maps of island chains, and the only kind of island that nationalism can tolerate is a real island. This is because a national border must constitute "a defensive zone [standing] opposed to the linear boundary or line of demarcation separating two jurisdictions or territories" (Sahlins 1989: 6). You can't place a small area of another ethnic nationality within a different ethnic nationality's state.

Add to that the problem of the railway, and the economic value of the industrial region it served. No, "the peacemakers acknowledged that when the language line crossed a vital railway five times in twenty-six miles, ethnicity had to yield to economics" (Marks 1976: 22). Frontiers based on ethnic lines "proved impossible of realisation" (21). There could be no border drawn to enclose the Poles and exclude the Germans; the fate of the area would have to be decided by democratic majority.

So, it was an easy call to place Silesia east of the old Partition line in Poland. West of it was indeterminacy as far as the imagined line marking where mixed ethnic habitation gave way to entirely German settlement. And where would that be, officially? The line was drawn from a toelike bend in the border river with Czechoslovakia near Neustadt (Polish: Prudnik), due north until township boundaries became convenient underlays, and then followed these until the boundary between the German regencies centered on Oppeln (Opole) and Breslau (Wrocław) became convenient, paralleling this line to the west a little at the north end. Regency boundaries were, of course, also district boundaries, since a district was a subunit of a regency. In the context of contestation, borders generally do not disappear. Rather, the level of their administrative significance changes (see map 3).

This, then, was the region. There is an entire scholarly literature about this violent and propaganda-ridden plebiscite: for example, I refer readers to Tooley for a general history of the plebiscite, to Kaeckenbeeck for a discussion of the international legal aspects of the division, to Marks for contextualization within a larger European context; Dotts Paul provides an extensive annotated bibliography of books and articles (1994: 50–54). The details of the history of the plebiscite are beyond the scope of this project: briefly, the campaign was characterized by propaganda, pressure, and violence. An organized pro-Polish movement staged three Polish nationalist uprisings, in 1919, 1920, and 1921, the last and bloodiest of which followed the voting and did result in the revision of an initial border to Poland's advantage (Rose 1935: 173). The nationalist campaigns polarized villages; they polarized families. Issues of class were deeply implicated, with the German side warning of a dire economic future under "POLNISCHE WIRTSCHAFT" (Polish economy), a term used derogatorily to imply "disorganized, inefficient, and poor." The Polish side, for its part, promised salvation from German bourgeois oppression of the Silesian Polish-speaking industrial and agricultural working class (Tooley 1997: 136–71).

In terms of absolute numbers, Germany got about 60% of the vote, but discounting emigrants not resident at the time, only 53%. If one further discounts the residents of the two westernmost districts, which, according to Rose, were so solidly German that they should never have been included in the plebiscite area at all, then votes for Poland exceeded those for Germany by 30,000—in practical terms, a fifty-fifty result. The border then drawn followed the lines of district boundaries except through the few kilometers which involved the division of the industrial region. Most of that went to Poland. Rose states that this border "has been called the most curious, most difficult, and worst in Europe," (Rose 1935: 181–82). This difficult border lasted until the Nazi invasion of Poland on September 1, 1939, at which point Upper Silesia was reincorporated into the German state, with a slice beyond, including Auschwitz, pasted onto the new "East Upper Silesia" for good measure.

It is at this point that these historical lines on the land shed light on why, after Poland joined the European Union in 2004, "Work in Holland" was inscribed on every riser of the main stairs in the Opole train station. It is because the government of the Netherlands had not opened its labor market to holders of Polish passports. You needed a German passport to work in the Netherlands. That was clever move on the part of this small country. There may have been as many as 450,000 Poles in the United Kingdom by summer 2007; that would have been too many people for the Netherlands to cope with. Of course, the population of Germany is almost twice that of Poland, but the German economy supports its population within its own borders and provides work to migrants; Germans generally don't engage in labor migration. And most German citizens live within its borders. But not those whose citizenship depends on where borders used to be.

In German constitutional law, all individuals who were themselves born, or whose parents or grandparents were born, within the 1937 borders of the German state (prior to the Nazi regime's appropriation of Czechoslovak lands; the last year of internationally legal German borders until the end of the Second World War) are defined as Germans. Germany, like Communist Poland, employs a racial definition of being German (*ius sanguinis*). But for descendants of citizens of that Germany, ethnicity is assumed, not interrogated; nothing further than place of residence need be proven. This distinguishes autochthonous Opole Silesians from Upper Silesians, who live east of the interwar border. Upper Silesians are not subject to this civil definition; they must prove that they are *ethnic* Germans. Like other German minorities in eastern Europe, they may rely on cultural activity: children's attendance at German-language schools or supplemental instructional programs, membership in cultural organizations, German-language religious activity, and so on (cf. Verdery 1985 on Transylvania). Alternatively, they can rely on the Nazis: their lists are a legal way to prove ethnicity to the German government. In 1940, Hannan tells us,

> The Nazis introduced the VOLKSLIST, a document in which individuals identified their ethnicity according to one of four different categories. Germans were assigned to the first two categories, the third was for "Ślązaks," [Silesians] and the fourth was for ethnic Slavs. . . . The Nazis recognized as Polish only those individuals who declared themselves Poles. When most of the population resisted the Volkslist registration, the Nazis used force to compel compliance. (Hannan 1996: 52)

But autochthonous Opole Silesians don't have to worry about any of this. They can be granted German citizenship by presenting parents' or grandparents' birth certificates, conscription papers, death certificates—anything that shows citizenship. It is not difficult for them to become dual citizens of Poland and Germany. And as German citizens, they could work in the Netherlands. This created, for Holland, a manageably sized labor pool at least until May 2007, when work permits were no longer required for Polish workers.

Back in the train, we cross the interwar border just beyond Katowice. Let's stop the train with its engine west of this line and its last carriage to the east of it, so as to focus on the z-axis of history. Until the end of the First World War, a train stopped at this spot would have been entirely in Germany. Until the border was drawn in 1921, it would have been entirely in the plebiscite region. Until the Nazi invasion of Poland, it would have been half in Germany, half in Poland. Until the end of the Second World War, entirely in Germany. And, soon after the Second World War ended, in 1946, a train traveling on these same tracks would have had its engine in a region where nationality was once again indeterminate—but its last carriage would have been undeniably in Poland.

Chapter 2

History repeated itself. After the First World War, the Allies had assumed the Polishness of territory which had been Polish before the Partitions; after the Second, they assumed the Polishness of the territory which had been Polish before the Nazi invasion, that is, east of the interwar border, where we've stopped the last carriage of our train. Likewise, they assumed the Germanness of the territory west of the old World War I–plebiscite line. This time, however, the relevance was not for drawing borders, but for moving people. West of the western plebiscite boundary, the entire population was expelled to the occupied zones of Germany, town by village, in a set of military operations. East of the interwar border, officials targeted people as Germans selectively. But between those two lines, a policy of "verification" was adopted. People were considered German until proven Polish, but those who could prove themselves Polish were allowed to stay. Such proof was linguistic in nature—one could prove one's Polishness by being able to speak Silesian Polish, or even being able merely to recite the Lord's Prayer in Polish.

This was the result of reversing the post–World War I logic that attempted to address the inevitable minority problems built into the idea of the ethnic-national state. After the First World War, the Allies attempted to draw borders around ethnic groups. After the Second, they decided to draw the borders, then move the people to the appropriate place. What followed was what the Potsdam accords called the "orderly and humane transfer of populations," or in a more accurate evaluation, "By the end of the 1940s up to 10.5 million Germans had either fled or been expelled from the post-war territory of [Poland and Czechoslovakia], some 7.5 million from Poland and slightly over 3 million from Czechoslovakia" (Ahonen et al. 2008: 87). The Poles whose homes were now located in the Soviet Union (about 1.5 million of them) technically had the choice to stay, but most did not. (For discussion of forced population movements in Europe during and after the Second World War, I recommend Mazower, Reinish, and Feldman 2011 in addition to Ahonen et al; articles in Vardy and Tooley 2003 treat the entire twentieth century.)

As an example of the role language played in this process, let me offer the reminiscence of an elderly nun whom I interviewed. After the war, members of her order were targeted for deportation to Siberia. They were carried by train, first, to the southern mountains of Poland, near the town of Zakopane. There they were brought out of the train. By prior agreement, the monolingual German speakers among them kept quiet, while the bilingual sisters chatted as vociferously in Silesian as ever they could. The officials who had received the train were dismayed: "My God!" they exclaimed, "They told us they were sending us a trainload of Germans, and all we've got here are Poles!" The

44

train was stopped; the nuns were held in that area for three years, and then allowed to return to Opole Silesia (Notes, November 20, 1994).

In order to be allowed to stay, Opole Silesians also had to sign a loyalty oath, which read in part,

> After the destruction of the Third Reich I would like to accept Poland as my fatherland. I ask the Polish authorities to forgive me and accept me into the family of the greater Polish people. I promise to be a true and obedient citizen of the Polish Republic and to break off forever all connection with Germans and Germandom, to uproot thoroughly feelings for Germandom, to raise my children in the Polish spirit and to light in their hearts the love of Poland, fatherland of my ancestors. (quoted in Urban 1994: 68–69)

Speaking German became illegal, punishable by fine or imprisonment, only a few months after speaking Polish ceased to be illegal. All cultural organizations previously incorporated by the Nazi government were incorporated by the Stalinist Communist government, and all German cultural elements were expurgated from them. Even using German loan words in Silesian was punishable, as recalled on a special broadcast of Radio Opole, "Po Prostu Ślązak," ("Simply a Silesian," March 12, 1995). The raconteur had led a folksinging group of autochthonous Opole Silesians after the Second World War. He remembered that although he repeatedly urged his singers to censor their speech when in the presence of Poles, they were unable to avoid German loans entirely, and fines were sometimes imposed.

Thus, what created an "autochthonous" population in Opole Silesia was the way that the post–World War I and post–World War II ascription of ethnic indeterminacy to the region allowed some of the region's inhabitants to survive the expulsions in situ. The borders of Opole Province bear a logical relationship to, but are not the same as, the administrative boundaries that predate them. They follow the western border of the German Oppeln regency except that two districts were added, while the eastern boundary follows the interwar border except that the districts containing major industrial cities were added to Katowice Province (see map 3). The effect was to create two provinces distinct in economic base— an entirely industrially based Katowice Province, and a mixed industrial and agricultural Opole Province. This is the historical basis for the fact that German sources divide Silesia into two, Lower and Upper, with Opole Silesia as the western part of Upper Silesia; Polish sources follow this history more closely, dividing Silesia into three: Lower Silesia, Opole Silesia, and Upper Silesia.

In terms of ethnic consciousness, too, the division is potent, as I mentioned above, for Opole Silesians talk about Upper Silesians as "Silesians too, but different." The next comment is usually, "they talk [i.e., speak Silesian] differently." Indeed, contact between Upper Silesians and Opole Silesians comes mainly through army service and networks in Germany. A pirated cassette of an Upper Silesian comedy and music troupe circulated widely in Dobra; villagers' relatives in Germany had gotten hold of it from Upper Silesian connections there, and, indeed, the people who gave it to me were not able to understand all the words. As another example, I once witnessed an Upper Silesian associate of a neighbor, acquainted through work in Germany, attempt to exclude a Polish guest at a social gathering by telling an ethnic joke derogatory of Poles; the joke fell flat because none of the Opole Silesians present understood a key Upper Silesian word (Notes, July 31, 1995). An introduction to a joke (discussed further in chapter 4), told by a man in his twenties, can serve to sum up the relationship. He explained that despite the hostility toward Silesians rampant in army life, the soldiers in his unit were able to band together: "It turned out that there were a whole lot of people from Strzelce, from Gogolin, from Krapkowice [towns in Opole Silesia] and from various villages, *not to mention people from Katowice, Zabrze, Gliwice, and so on.*" (Emphasis mine; Notes, October 25, 1994).[2] In remembering his army unit, he thought first of all the places in Opole Silesia that his fellow soldiers came from, and then added the places in Upper Silesia, as if to say, "Not only did I find people who were Opole Silesians like myself, but also many of that other kind of Silesians, Upper Silesians."

Beyond the interwar border, in Opole Silesia, in the plebiscite area, the landscape is much more pleasant, with much healthier air, but it, too, partakes of the history of violence which has repeatedly engulfed southeastern Silesia. It goes beyond ethnic cleansing. If we were to change trains at Kędzierzyn-Koźle, and take a bus from Nysa,[3] it would only be about a hundred kilometers to the town of Łambinowice (Lamsdorf), which has sometimes—falsely—been set beside Auschwitz as an example of atrocity. It was an old POW camp, established for French prisoners during the Franco-Prussian war of 1871, and it was used again in both world wars: "When the Red Army liberated Lamsdorf [from the Nazis] in March, 1945, they found there mountains of corpses and half-starved prisoners" (Bździach 1995a: 452, my translation). Under Soviet-backed Polish administration, the camp's tradition continued: it was used as an internment camp for people from the area who were awaiting expulsion to Germany, or who resisted it. Placards informed the populace that "All Germans who ignore this command [to leave] or who try to destroy, damage, or hide any of their belongings or property will be immediately incarcerated in the camp at Łambinowice" (455). It is estimated that between several hundred and a thousand people perished—perhaps 75% of all internees. (Esser, reported by Urban 1995: 453) Esser's report was widely circulated both in West Germany and in Silesia in the 1950s (Nowak 1995: 453). Most of the internees were monolingual speakers of German, but some bilingual. One woman recalled on an interview on the Radio Opole cultural program "Nasz Heimat" (May 12, 1995) that she was released from the camp when her aunt signed the loyalty oath discussed above.

So when we've crossed the interwar border but not reached the western line of the plebiscite area, where are we? Consulting the map, we can note that we are in the ethnic enclave depicted in map 2, for its boundaries are almost determined by the interwar border on the east, the Czech border on the south, the western boundary of the plebiscite region, and the ancient northern border of Silesia (compare maps 2 and 3). We are betwixt and between.

Or as autochthonous Opole Silesians say, we are "here." Of course they understand the term "Opole Silesia," but they tend to avoid defining their place as a participant in the region/territorial state hierarchy. Their place is defined with respect to them, not with reference to the nation-state.

The following interactions illustrate this equivocation:

1. I came into the tavern to find a stranger in his late forties sitting across from my housemate, disheveled and clearly drunk. A neighbor of ours came in, and the stranger began a conversation with the three of us which quickly became heated; he was set on determining "how German" Dobra was. At one point he asked who the head of the local German Minority was, and on being told the name, asked "Is he a German?" Our neighbor replied impatiently, "He was born in Germany and he stayed here." ["Germany" moved; "here" is ambiguously contrasted with it.] (March 26, 1993)

2. The breakfast that followed a memorial mass, a year after the death of my housemate Marta's husband, brought the deceased's aunt into conversation with Marta's mother. Over several simultaneous conversations in the group of eight adults, I heard my housemate's mother say to the aunt, "[I asked] where he came from and he said, more from Poland." ["bardziej z Polski"] The aunt replied, "And he came here?" ["Here" is contrasted with a place considered "more," or to a greater extent, to be Poland.] (July 21, 1993)

3. Of people who decided not to emigrate to West Germany although given the opportunity, especially her father-in-law, Marta often said, "He felt that his place was here." She phrased the statement this way, using "here," even during a conversation which might have called for "there," since it took place in Germany. [The use of "here" becomes frozen in this kind of context; it comes to refer to a person's place even when the conversation takes place elsewhere.] (inter al. March 1993)

4. A friend and I made an arrangement by which she helped me with Silesian and generally served as "informant" in exchange for my helping her eleven-year-old daughter with English. One day she was showing me some Easter eggs, explaining to me how they are decorated "here," when her husband broke in, wanting to gloss the word. She snapped at him: "Elizabeth is already aware of what we mean by 'here'!" [Again, the use of "here" is frozen, a cultural stereotype, a usage an anthropologist learns as part of socialization.] (March 23, 1993)

These usages illustrate an incorporation of the sense that Opole Silesia is negatively defined with respect to Germany and Poland. No one wants to identify it definitively as a subdivision of either Germany or Poland. All that is certain is that it is the place of the people who refer to it that way.[4]

All that remains, then, is to bring the sense of where "here" is to the primary site of the research, Dobra. For while I attended festivals, visited, and interviewed in other villages, Dobra is the place where I lived from November 1992 to August 1993, from October to December 1994, and from March to October 1995 (twenty months, in all). It is where I went to church, visited school twice a week during the 1992–93 school year, spent many evenings talking in the tavern, conducted all my structured linguistic research, gathered genealogies, and developed intensive research relationships with eight households. And now, after twenty years and several return visits, Dobra is home to me in Silesia. So, what kind of a village is it?

How the Railway Changed Dobra Forever

No Opole Silesian village is far from railway tracks. But the railway runs through Dobra; Dobra has a station. As we will see, this fact has deeply influenced its social and sociolinguistic structure. I had come to Dobra on the advice of Danuta Berlińska, a sociologist at the Silesian Institute in Opole, who had seen (and enjoyed) a performance by the women of Dobra's German Friendship Circle (as the local clubs of the Social and Cultural Society of the German Minority in Poland called themselves). She thus had the impression that the German Friendship Circle was active in Dobra, and that the village was worth checking out as a possible fieldsite. That Dobra had a cabaret for Berlińska to experience in 1990 has everything to do with its having gotten a railway station in about 1860.

A look at satellite imagery of Opole Silesia shows that most villages have become roadside settlements. That is, their buildings are laid out along roads that lead to other places. However, the original settlement pattern in Opole Silesia, as elsewhere in Europe, was a radial layout around a church. The church, as the community's defense against war and flood, was built on the highest ground available. (Because the river valley is very flat, flooding is a real concern, with the Oder having inundated Silesia as recently as 1997.) This was true, also, of Dobra, where the oldest streets are those near the church, on the opposite side from the railway (see map 6). The streets on the other side of the church, which run parallel and perpendicular to the tracks, were laid after the railway.

The tracks are about half a kilometer from the church, more or less parallel to its front door, such that from a train, one watches the church in the distance swing into direct view as one approaches Dobra, and from the plaza in front of the church, one's view of the village ends at the railway crossing. Thus, after the coming of the railway, the radial pattern of streets was overlaid by a pattern centered on a $\perp$ with the vertical line being the main road, and the double horizontal lines being the railway tracks.

People call this the village center. The church marks the northern edge of it, the wide main road and the buildings on it define it, and the railway tracks mark its southern edge. At Corpus Christi, when the sacrament is carried in a procession from the church to outdoor altars, the altars mark the corners of this space. The center of Dobra extends from the church to the railway tracks. And standing at the tracks looking toward the church gives a very different view of Dobra than looking away from it.

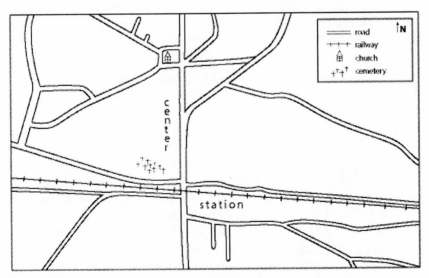

Map 6. Dobra, the field site. The map shows a schematic diagram of Dobra's village center, which is focused on the church and the railway line.

If we stand on the road with our backs to the tracks and facing the church, looking straight down the road, we see a line of houses. If we look to the sides, but away from the village center, we see an expanse of fields intermittently marked off by a line of houses. This is true regardless of where one stands in Dobra, unless one is facing the village center, because houses are built along the branching roads (many of which, in the 1990s, were unpaved) with fields in back. (If you compare this aerial view with one of the American midwest, with farm buildings at the corners of huge fields, isolated from one another, you realize how different rural Silesia is from the American rural landscape.) Houses are of brick or cinderblock construction. In the early post-Communist period, most were plastered over; now, almost all are. Most houses have peaked roofs; some of the newer ones have flat ones; the bigger, more opulent ones have dormer windows. Plots have fences in front and back. On most streets, we can see a solid row of fences: picket giving way to brown metal to green metal. The impression of privacy is strengthened by the fact that Silesian houses do not have doors on the street side, but at the back or side, and that every house has a dog, kept in a cage, which barks whenever anyone comes through the gate.

The village center makes a very different impression. Between the tracks and the church, the road is wider and tree-lined, and on the left side a low hedge divides it from a broad lane which fronts buildings. The sidewalk, on the right side only, was put in toward the end of my fieldwork, during the spring of 1995. The previous sidewalk had decayed almost beyond recognition. The buildings, which are on both sides of the road, are larger than most of the houses in Dobra. Most are three-story, many-roomed buildings. One, for example (the house of the former Schraft family tavern), has a very large room, two smaller rooms, a kitchen, and a small bathroom on the first floor, five rooms including a kitchen on the second floor, and at least four finished attic rooms on the third floor. They are impressive buildings. They also clearly show signs of neglect: they are un-painted, with outer plaster cracked in many places, especially under windows. They date from the first decades of the twentieth century, the oldest of them from 1890. Little has been done to maintain them since 1945, for reasons that will be explored in chapter 8, and the impression of decay is well-founded: engineers inspecting a house (in spring 1993), prior to a planned renovation, reported that it would be cheaper to raze it and build new than renovate it, and the possible sale of one building fell through, in the 1980s, when the buyers saw the state of the property and the fungi growing in many of the long-abandoned rooms.

Still, there are businesses in the village center. On both sides of the road, the buildings, though underutilized, do house businesses: three grocery stores, a store selling household supplies, two clothing stores, a store selling news-papers and cleaning supplies (the usual combination in Poland), a tavern ori-ented toward family business, and a bar oriented solely toward men and drinking. But it is obvious to everyone that the center was built to accommo-date more businesses than are currently in operation. Its decline since 1945, the reasons for it, and prevailing attitudes about it are key to understanding why some Dobrans assert German identity, and will also be considered in depth in chapter 8. For now, bear in mind that there are more businesses in Dobra than in most autochthonous Opole Silesian villages.

If we walk along the main street beyond the tracks, continuing away from the center, we quickly come to woods. Dobra ends here, and the road leads on to the next village, less than three kilometers away—a typical distance between Opole Silesian villages. The woods are of mixed deciduous and coniferous trees, here as elsewhere, for the "ethnic enclave" area of Opole Province is more heavily wooded than the western crescent ("Lasy Opolszczyzny" 1995). Besides the sandy soil, this is one of the reasons that German settlement did not take hold here during the Middle Ages. As Rose states, "The Polish histo-rian Zemkowicz has drawn attention to the far-reaching influence in particular of the heavy forest belt that stretched across the Oderland just below Oppeln as a veritable *silva liminaris*" (Rose 1935: 19). Dobra is a village within this forest belt.

From the woods, then, fields were cleared and villages established, and eventually registered. A veritable spate of such "first mentions" date to the end of the thirteenth century; this was very convenient for an anthropologist con-ducting research at the end of the twentieth, since these "first mentions" are considered the birthdays of villages, and a seven-hundred-year birthday must, of course, be marked with celebration. These celebrations inevitably included a narrative which cites the date of first building and rebuildings of the village church, the founding of the school, and, if relevant, the coming of the railroad.

For villages on the rail lines the dates when the tracks came through are important because, as Kaeckenbeeck's states, "The great advance of Upper Silesia in the nineteenth and twentieth centuries was primarily due to the de-velopment of the railways" (Kaeckenbeeck 1942: 434). And in his book *Peas-ants into Frenchmen*, Eugen Weber specifies three elements as essential to the development of national consciousness in nineteenth-century France: military service, schooling, and rail travel (Weber 1976). Dobra already had the first two; the railway gave it the third. And this, in turn, sheds light on the fact that the German Minority is more active here than in other, smaller, more isolated, and more socially homogeneous villages. Their activity ensures that the inhabitants of Dobra in the 1990s had to think actively about issues of language, ethnicity, and nationality; the historical reasons for it mean that they had had to do so for a long time.

Kaeckenbeeck is referring to economic growth, but for our purposes, it is important to understand that the space that the railway created, between the tracks and the church, is the social space of German national identity in Dobra. The center became the "business district" of a village which began to develop socioeconomic differentiation and hierarchy within its bounds. It developed as the richest part of Dobra, so ultimately, the railway came to define a social space of class: a center-periphery distinction. In turn, ethnic and national consciousness have always been deeply related to class in Silesia, so the village center developed as rich, bourgeois, and German.

Its center, with its comparatively many businesses, is not the only respect in which Dobra is unusual. In population, it is much bigger than average. In 1989 it was one of the twenty largest of the 921 villages in Opole Province. Its population was listed as about 2,100; the Province average was 538, and villages of over 1,000 made up only 12% of the total number (Heffner 1993: 75 ff). Not only is it the seat of a parish church, but it also has an elementary school, a forestry office, and a German Friendship Circle. Not every village has these institutions. Roughly half the villages have schools and parish churches; about three-fourths have GFCs. Dobra has one of only eight administrative forestry offices ("Lasy Opolszczyzny" 1995).

All these characteristics—the large population, the many local institutions present, and the extent of nonagricultural nature of Dobrans' labor—make this an unusual village in the Opole Silesian context. However, in Opole Silesia, as we discuss in chapter 8, it is social stratification that heightens ethnic and national consciousness. In Dobra these differences of social class have long been present. This makes it an excellent site for a study based on intensive ethnographic and linguistic fieldwork. And the force that drove the development of that social stratification is precisely what brought us there: the railway.

A final note about what Dobra was and was not, in the context of the immediate post-Communist era. It was a time when ethnic-national tensions in eastern Europe were making headlines all over the world, and beginning to explode into war and ethnic cleansing in the former Yugoslavia. In fact, I had waited for months for autochthonous Opole Silesians to appear on the front page of the *Chicago Tribune*, figuring that if these people did indeed exist as a self-conscious group, the times were such that they were sure to make international headlines eventually—it seemed as if everybody else had. Within Poland, Silesia was the center of a veritable print journalism storm at the time.

I can attest to that; before researchers had internet search engines, there were clipping services that employed readers to find newspaper articles related to topics that clients specified; you would receive the articles in the mail. From 1992 to 1994, I employed such a service, based in Warsaw, for the Polish press. I received over five hundred articles about Opole Silesia. It was new that the press was free to write even about the existence of ethnic minorities in Poland; the Communist government had denied that there were any. It was a time when the atrocities of the Second World War could be discussed openly, and articles about the newly discovered "German minority in Poland" became a focus for this discussion. Commentary articles had headlines like "Germans: Is Our Fear Exaggerated?" or, sympathetically, "Having the Courage To Be Oneself." Considerations included political inflections, financing, ways to ensure adequate representation in the Polish parliament, dual citizenship, and the political activities of the TSKMN party, the Social and Cultural Society of the German Minority. There were articles discussing issues of economy, of autonomy (mainly in Upper Silesia), of culture, and the reintroduction of instruction in German with the support of the German government as well as articles summarizing sets of other articles. Furthermore, journalists covered issues of conflict. The anti-German and anti-Polish graffiti of the by-election continued. There were lively discussions about village names, with German Minority members wanting to return to the names they remembered from childhood, which the distressed Poles viewed as Nazi-imposed names; about welcome signs (whether they should be bilingual); and about war memorials as, for the first time, Wehrmacht veterans were emboldened to demand recognition of fallen comrades. And one village, Dziewkowice, had a village chair who inflamed tensions not only by insisting that the village's name be changed back to the one it had had in the Nazi era, Frauenfeld (before then it had been called Schewkowitz), but by inviting a group of West German skinhead neo-Nazis to use the village as a base of operations in Poland.

"This is just *way* overblown," opined the assistant whom I employed to index all these articles for me, shaking her head. Indeed, there was only one Dziewkowice, and Dobra is not Dziewkowice. As I describe in chapter 7, the tensions I observed in interactions between autochthonous Opole Silesians and Poles in Dobra never went beyond words. In general in Opole Silesian villages, the primary sites of everyday outbursts of tension were generally considered to be grocery stores and schools, but as it happened, in Dobra, these institutions were run by autochthonous Opole Silesians. The low percentage of inhabitants of central and eastern Polish origin in Dobra led to the situation described in chapter 7; Poles who could not get along, for whatever reason, were isolated, without support from other Poles who might share their negative feelings about the local village society. A study sited primarily in a village with a 50-50 ethnic split might look very different from this one; on the other hand, Silesian Institute sociologists Danuta Berlińska and Franciszek Jonderko think that I might have had considerable difficulty "crossing the line," that is, establishing research relationships with members of both groups, so it might have proved impossible to center research in such a village.

In short, there are two characteristics that make Dobra different. There is its comparatively large size and its history of a differentiated class structure. This heightens ethnic and national consciousness. And there is its relative ethnic homogeneity. This may have contributed, in the early post-Communist period, to keeping tensions relatively calm.

Yet it is well to bear the tensions of the times in mind. It was not considered impossible that Silesia might explode. At a meeting of the Dobra German Friendship Circle on May 6, 1993, a representative of the German consulate told the assembly, "You have to realize that depending on what you do now, History will, or will not, write: 'because of these people, there was a war in Silesia after Communism fell.' I don't think any of you really want that written about you."

The room was silent, chastened; one woman affirmed on behalf of everybody, "Nobody wants that."

Chapter 3
SILENT MEMORY AND IDENTITY TALK

Practically speaking, my first task when I arrived in Opole Silesia was to find a place to live in a village that I thought would make a good primary site for my research. It was October 1992; as I discussed in chapter 2, ethnic-national tension was all over the newspapers. I read; I started taking trains and buses to various villages for a look around.

In any Polish village, conducting extended research requires the approval of the priest, so I set up an interview with the rector of the Dobra parish. If all went well, our talk might lead to an opportunity to say, eventually, "Oh by the way would you mind if I moved to Dobra for a year or two and researched a dissertation about multilingualism?"

Even on the short walk from the train station to the rectory, signs of ethnic nationalism were in evidence. I noticed a copy of *DIE SCHLESISCHE NACHRICHTEN* (The Silesian News) in the back of a car. It is a paper published in Germany by a right-wing German political organization that takes a special interest in the territories transferred to Poland after the war and those who were expelled from them. This interest, over the years, has taken the form of hoping for the restoration of preexisting national borders; in September 1990, for example, it published a map of Silesia's pre-1921 borders under the caption: "Silesia remains our future in the Europe of free peoples." About halfway between the railway tracks and the church, I noticed two bulletin boards, side by side. One was exposed to the weather and showed signs of wear; it displayed two notices. The other was enclosed in glass, and it was crammed with notices relating to the German Friendship Circle: in Polish, a notice about a German language course; in Polish, a notice about possibilities for work in Germany, as builders, roadworkers, and so forth; in Polish, a longer article, the topic of which I did not write down. In German, however, there was an article of more ideological orientation, wondering about when Silesian autonomy would finally come: "All over eastern Europe people are reorganizing themselves into their natural nation-states. In Yugoslavia it's happening with violence. . . . People long to throw off the unnatural borders that Stalin forced on them." And, finally there was a page of local news from, again, *DIE SCHLESISCHE NACHRICHTEN*.

The priest, when I met him, turned out to be an older gentleman. Because he specifically mentioned that he had never spoken Polish before 1945, when he was fifteen years old, I knew that he was precisely sixty-two. I played the role of an attentive listener as he explained to me, at length, that Silesia is German. It was Saint Jadwiga, who came from Bavaria (in German her name is Hedwig), who established the orientation of Silesia in that direction. The people here didn't feel Polish, they felt (here he hesitated) German. Those who felt Polish left and went east to Poland after the border was drawn (he seemed to have the interwar border in mind). And after the war, many left. Nobody thought that these territories would remain "under Polish administration," otherwise everybody would have left—except then the borders were closed and they couldn't leave. In recent years, many people have left for Germany, for "purely nationalistic" reasons and also because there are no prospects here.

At great length, he explained that the fact that people in Silesia do not speak German was the fault of Polish Communist suppression of the language, in the form of disallowing the study of the language in schools and universities. "There were no schools, there were no teachers. It was not possible to study German. In Wrocław, yes, in Warsaw, yes, but not here. Older people can speak, write, and read German; they went to German school. But younger people cannot." He explained that it was only that very year that, for the first time, a German teacher had come from Berlin to teach German in the Dobra elementary school (part of a group of teachers sent, as I later discovered, by the German government). Personally, he said, he felt himself to be a German. "A person who is Polish is Polish, but . . ." he shrugged.

By this point, I was conscious of the fact that I was in danger of missing my train back to the city. The end of the interview was dragging on a bit, complicated by his asking me whether I spoke German, and his surprise when I told him I spoke it better than I spoke Polish. His look seemed to say, "Then why have we been speaking Polish?" although all he said was, "We can speak German then" (in German). He completed pleasantries in German, and invited me back, telling me he could ask another autochthonous man to talk to me, which was a good, and bad, sign for my possibly choosing Dobra as a fieldsite—and I missed my train. Anthropologists never rush people through their good-byes.

I said it was a good, and bad, sign, because while I had to find a village where the priest was willing to have me, I also had to find one where I could take an unbiased approach to the research, and it was clear, as I wrote in my notes, that, "This priest is going to lead me straight to the German Minority." I fully expected the "other autochthonous man" to share the priest's German identity, and, as it turned out, I was right. Bringing Saint Jadwiga into it was a special, Roman Catholic twist; other than that, he had told me nothing that I had not been reading since 1989 in the German press about Silesia. One impressive aspect of the quick organization of the German Minority was their ability to present a seamless picture of their community as German to western journalists, and, although a researcher, I was clearly being treated as a journalist. It was not a category that I particularly wanted to be in. I knew there were other stories in Silesia. I was also aware that powerful groups within the societies where anthropologists work often attempt to co-opt their research to their own ends, and, furthermore, that the relatively disempowered are unlikely to be willing to work intensively with an anthropologist who is perceived as "in the pocket" of the local power elite. Luckily, missing my train led me to a much more productive entré into Dobran society: not the rectory, but the bar.

The next train wasn't for three hours. I was hungry. I went into one of the little grocery stores on the main street, and asked if there were a restaurant in Dobra, and while I was told that there was not, I was led to a small "baro-kawiarnia," or "café-bar" (in this book, I usually call it the "tavern"). It is a place where men go for beer or vodka but where couples, women, and children also go; there is something to eat or drink for everyone there. I ordered a small pizza. The waitress turned out also to be the owner, Marta, a young widow who, a few weeks later, invited me to live with her (this was my enormous good fortune). But at that point, of course, I knew nothing about her except that she was about my age, around thirty, and was wearing black, the significance of which I failed to understand (Polish Catholics wear black for a year following the death of a spouse or parent). I introduced myself, told her where I was from and that I was in Silesia to do research on language, and I took the opportunity to chat, in a researchy kind of way.

"They told me in Opole that there's a cabaret here," I said.

"Not that I know of," she replied.

"Oh."

"Well . . . Maybe there is. We have the German Minority here. Maybe they organize something."

"But you don't know?"

"I stay away from that! I consider myself to be Silesian!"

At the next table, one rather drunken man was speaking seriously to another as follows: "'BITTE,' to 'PROSZĘ,' a 'DANKE,' to 'DZIĘKUJĘ!'" ("Bitte" is "please," and "danke" is "thank you!")

Marta made her identity assertion surrounded by German in written as well as spoken form. Autochthonous Opole Silesians had connections with Germany throughout the Communist period; Marta had used these to supply her business with wares not yet available on the Polish market. The tavern was a small room, meagerly furnished by Western standards, as Marta was painfully aware. Against the back wall a bar accommodated three stools, and behind it, a display case offered fourteen varieties of Polish beer, eight varieties of vodka, several cheap wines and other liquors, German-produced juices in cardboard cartons, chips, and the German-made chocolate eggs which have a toy inside, called ÜBERRASCHUNGSEIER (surprise eggs). Next to the bar, a poster hung offering the wares of Schöller brand ice-cream; next to that hung a crucifix. "It's been there the whole time," Marta later told me proudly (April 26, 1993). "One time members of the Communist Party even held a meeting at the table under it. How I wished I had a camera!" Against the opposite wall was mounted a coin-operated electronic game of chance, labeled entirely in German but for a few words, like "fun!" and "happy!" in English. In the front window a placard declared the establishment, in Polish, as a sales point for bus tickets to Germany; round-trip fares to various Ruhrgebiet destinations of high autochthonous Silesian population density appeared below. On this late October afternoon (October 19, 1992), it was already dark and cold; a wood fire burned in a fireplace behind our table, heating the room directly as well as sending hot water through a radiator attached to the back wall. German popular music emanated from speakers behind the bar.

Within a few hours, then, I had seen an article asserting Silesia's status as "nation-state" on public display, been offered a lecture on the historical reasons that Silesia and Silesians are really German, heard a vehement assertion of Silesian identity, observed a couple of drunks showing off their very minimal command of the German language to each other, and noticed a preponderant presence of the German language in the form of commercial products in Dobra's tavern. At that point I realized that this kind of identity was clearly a topic of discourse at the very surface of social life. It was not long before I also encountered unfamiliar cultural norms. I did not know Marta's name until I had already agreed to move in with her. Marta was, in other words, less sensitive about offering to let me live in her house, and far less sensitive about sharing her sense of Silesianness, than she was about telling me her first name. I soon discovered that this reticence about names was something she shared with other Dobrans, and that names were not the only matter about which my new acquaintances were reticent. These were my first experiences of languages and silence. What to make of this silence, and this loquacity?

SILENT MEMORY: RETICENCE ABOUT NAMES

Fieldnotes, March 23, 1993: "I asked Marta who somebody was today and she told me where the person lived." I was used to it by March. A fieldworker's training had saved me from asking Marta her name before she was ready to tell me. I quickly learned that asking anyone's name would elicit a blank stare, where the person lived, or who the person was related to. "It makes it kind of hard to take notes," I commented on November 24, 1992, after a month in Dobra. I began to learn how to learn names:

> November 26, 1992: Names I now know: Justyna's mother is Karolina. I found this out because Justyna called her by name and Marta reprimanded her, told her to say, "Mama." Marta's sister is Magda. I found this out because Marta said, "with my sister, with Magda." As for Marta's regular customers, one of the drunks is Jan—I've heard him so addressed. Same way I know Piotr's name. I've heard Sonja and Agata both referred to and called by name.

I learned that reticence about names is a cultural characteristic of autochthonous Opole Silesians:

> When we were in Opole we went to see a colleague of Marta's. When she was in the kitchen making coffee I asked Marta if she were from the east [the territories transferred from Poland to the Soviet Union after the Second World War]. Marta said she was. Later she asked me how I knew. I said firstly because Marta spoke Polish to her [rather than Silesian]. Secondly because she immediately told me what her name was. Thirdly because her house was furnished/decorated differently than Silesian houses. And finally because she lives in Opole. Marta didn't quibble with any of these indices. (November 26, 1992)

> November 27, 1992: Marta explained that one of the things that makes Silesians different is their attitude toward giving their names. For example, yesterday when we visited her friend, she immediately gave her name. Marta stopped doing that a long time ago. "If I meet someone new, I don't know if there will be further contact or not." Knowing someone's name seems to belong to having an ongoing relationship.

Chapter 3

Others agreed:

> May 13, 1995: I asked Adam about my impression that, compared to Poles, Silesians are reticent about giving their first names. He confirmed this, comparing the customs he sees "out there" when he's on business, with how he himself behaves, and with what he observes here.

As time went on, I learned names by going to school. School is a place governed by class lists and calling on students by name; perhaps this is why young people of school age are much more ready to share their names, as Marta said that she herself used to be. When I met Angelika Stanik, whom we will meet again in chapter 6, and two of her friends, they told me their names immediately; they were in eighth grade at the time. Learning the names of children put me in a position to "dig" for names. I could jump into conversations in which children were discussed with questions such as, "Your granddaughter was in the school play? I saw that play! Which one is your granddaughter?" People would answer that kind of question, because the question signaled that I had an ongoing relationship with people in Dobra. Not so the direct question:

> June 2, 1993: In the tavern this afternoon, Marta asked if I would drink coffee with Alicja and . . . she trailed off. I said, who? She said, you'll see. So over coffee I asked him what his name was. Although he's seen me several times now, and was with his girlfriend, whom I know, and at Marta's, where he has often been with us, he hesitated considerably and was prodded by Alicja before he answered.

Gradually I was able to expand my knowledge of names. Eventually, I realized that autochthonous Opole Silesians themselves learn names in the same way that I had learned to learn them: by overhearing someone who already knows the name address the person. On June 22, 1993, a beautiful day, I passed a fence where a woman in her sixties, a distant cousin of Marta, Maria Rataja, was chatting with another woman of about the same age, whom I didn't know. This is an opportunity that a good ethnographer does not pass up. When I came up, Mrs. Rataja asked me if I had been visiting Iwona, her daughter, and said that her husband, whom I had run into on my way there, had told her: PANI ELŻBIETA (Miss Elizabeth) went by. At that point the other woman said, "PANI ELŻBIETA? PANI ELŻBIETA. ELISABETH." I said, as was my habit, "The English is nearer to the German, but it doesn't matter to me: ELŻBIETA, ELISABETH, Elizabeth." Then she introduced herself: "You probably don't know me. I am the mother of Franek Sattler." In short, Mrs. Sattler heard my name, then repeated it a couple of times and translated it, as if to memorize it, and then she introduced herself. But, as is typical for an adult, she did it by means of a family relationship; she knew that I knew her son, who has three children in the school.

Years later, as I have been reading my fieldnotes and writing this section, I have opened a file that has, simply, a list of autochthonous Opole Silesian first and last names, telephone book style, and I have been changing the names. I have been feeling conflicted about it. Pseudonyms have been a matter of controversy in anthropology. "Credit where credit is due," Bonnie Urciuoli states, explaining her decision to use the real names of the "informants" of her study of issues of race and ethnicity among New York Puerto Ricans (Urciuoli 1996: 13). I agree, and, when the dissertation was completed and I returned to Dobra to show it off, I met mixed reactions to the changed names. Marta did not want her name changed. "I am not afraid," she said. "You can leave my name." She was the only one to put it like that, but many of the people I worked most closely with were ambivalent. They are proud of their work on this book. For my part, I was increasingly aware that name-changing has unfortunate historical resonances. On the other hand, I can't escape the fact that, as I established rapport and began my work, many people agreed to work with me based in part on my assurance that I would protect their identities; some demanded that assurance; and some young adults who appear in this book as children asked for it later. Anyway, without specifically asking the permission of every named person in this book, I can't change the policy now.

On the other hand, there are a couple of good reasons to use pseudonyms. For me, one of them is this: the people in this book are not the people I know. I have done my best, as a writer, to do justice to them. Everything I report here was said, and said by specific people who have specific pseudonyms. But no real human being is defined by what they said on various occasions during only three years of their life. I have created no more than a shadow. Yet taking seriously the idea that the characters here are, at least, shadows of real people, we can see the use of pseudonyms as reflecting autochthonous Opole Silesians' reticence about sharing names. If this book establishes a relationship between readers and the people in its pages (and I hope it does), then we must acknowledge that the relationship is not an intimate, trusting one. Silesians' practice of keeping their names private would thus pertain. Since my own neighbors in Dobra would not introduce me by name to their visiting friends from another village, why would I introduce them by name to utterly unknown readers? Their cultural practices deserve respect.

My job is to explicate why their sensitivities make sense.

Chapter 3

Why are autochthonous Opole Silesians reticent about sharing their names? As it happens, exploring the trouble with pseudonyms gives the answer to this question. Understanding why my changing names echoes uncomfortably with Silesians' experiences between two states shows why they are reluctant to tell me, or other outsiders, their names in the first place.

Names in a book help readers keep track of a cast of characters; names in real life carry other kinds of social information. In the case of Silesia, the spread of names in use reflects the diversity of the region. And so, I have adopted the policy of trying to follow the linguistic origin of the individual's name in choosing a pseudonym: German names of people and places are changed into other German names, Silesian names into other Silesian names, Polish names into other Polish names, and for a surname that occurs in Polish, German, and Dutch but most frequently in French, I chose a French name, Garant.

Mr. Garant is the staunchly German-identifying school principal whose memoirs I draw on in chapter 8. He may be descended from one of the soldiers of many nationalities who marched through Silesia, and sometimes stayed there, at various points in history. That his name cannot be definitively identified with any one European nationality underlines that there is no necessary relationship between the linguistic origins of names and who people think they are in an ethnic or national sense. In the twentieth century, unfortunately, both Germany and Poland have made a link between names and identity, made the essentialist claim that Silesians and Silesia are their own, believed that names should reflect essence, and acted on that belief by doing in the real world of society what I, with the best of intentions, am doing in the narrative world: changing people's and places' names. That is the unfortunate resonance of using pseudonyms.

Silesian Names and their "Purification"

Silesian has developed, for centuries, borrowing liberally from both Polish and German. The historical development of place names places this in high relief. Understanding this history provides a baseline for considering the "purification" efforts of German and Polish mid-twentieth-century totalitarianisms. And that understanding, in turn, provides our first example of silence as creative culture.

The history of Silesian place names is well described in an article entitled "Changes in place and personal names in Silesia before and after the Second

World War" (1995). Authors Monika Choroś and Łucja Jarczak begin by distinguishing three periods of Polonization and Germanization: (1) from the beginnings of German settlement in Silesia to the transfer from Austria to Prussia (dated from the invitation to German settlers which followed the Battle of LEIGNITZ / LEGNICKI POL in 1241 to the mid-eighteenth century); (2) from the development of the modern nation-state to the end of German sovereignty over Silesia (mid-eighteenth century to 1945), during which period the Nazi era deserves special attention; and (3) the postwar era. During the latter two periods, names were changed by official acts of agents of central governments, whereas in the first, the process was "spontaneous," the result of language contact between indigenous Slavs and German settlers.

According to Choroś and Jarczak, as German settlers founded villages and moved into villages already established by Slavs, and as, slowly, German became the governing language, names became Germanized through a number of processes. Some Slavic place names were phonologically assimilated into German: "In this way, Brzeg became Brieg, Bytom → Beuthen, Leśnica → Leschnitz, Dębnik → Damnik." In other words, phonetic elements and combinations which do not exist in German were altered. The process also occurred in the other linguistic direction; names of villages and towns founded by Germans were phonologically Polonized: "Kreuzburg → Krucibork → Klucbork → Kluczbork." Similarly, Polish toponymic suffixes, -ice, -ici, or -wice (the subjects/people of) and -in, were replaced with German -dorf, -wasser, -burg, -haus(en), or -thal (village, water, castle, house, valley), and the Polish toponymic suffixes were also added to German patronyms, yielding such forms as "Ocyci" (Otto + ici), "the subjects of Otto." There were numerous loan translations: "Izbicko (1324) → Stubendorf (1688) [room village]; Stara Wieś → Altdorf [old village]; Pokrzywnica → Nesselwitz [place of nettles]." Some villages were known under two names, one German and the other Polish, until one or the other name prevailed; "in some cases the double names persisted for a longer time, for example: Falkenberg/Niemodlin, Olesno/Rosenberg, Georgenberg/Miasteczko, and Breslau/Wrocław." Personal names were similarly affected, Polonized and Germanicized. "Czudaj" was Germanized to "Schudaj," and "Kołoczek" → "Kollotzek," but, in the other direction, "Döring" became "Durynek," "Vier" → "Fiera," "Thiel" → "Tyl," "Götze" → "Giecka," and "Gutman" → "Gutmanek" (Choroś and Jarczak 1995: 458–59).

I have replaced Silesian names with other Silesian names; sometimes these can be distinguished from Polish names by the distinctive phonology of the dialect: the name that translates as "cooper" differs only in one vowel,

Bednorz vs. BednArz; the same is true of "Black," Czorniczek vs. CzArniczek. But many Silesian names are Silesian in the sense that they are an ancient mix.

The legacy of the early medieval social field was reminiscent, in some ways, of that of England after the Norman conquest, as English and French influenced one another. On the other hand, unlike Silesia, England is an island, defended by water, raided by seafaring Vikings, invaded by Caesar, by William of Normandy, and by nobody else. Who, living in or visiting the south of England, still recognizes the name of the village of "Three Chimneys" as a phonological assimilation and folk etymology of the Norman French word for "road" (French "chemin")? Does the surname "Corbett" sound French to anyone now? English incorporated a French influence that became historical and unnoticed, a matter for schools and scholars to bring to consciousness. But in Silesia, a borderland, consciousness of language contact was never able to lapse. The process of German settlement was ongoing, and since in southeastern Silesia the indigenous population continued to speak its own language, processes of language contact were ongoing as well. They were intensified after Frederick II wrested Silesia from Maria Theresa of Austria in the 1740–42 War of Austrian Succession, as he wanted to encourage further German settlement in Silesia. Many new villages and towns were founded; their names underwent the same variety of alteration processes described above. Yet increasingly, in the modern era, names remained linguistically distinctive, and ancestors of the people in this study came to carry names that remain easily recognizable as German, Polish, Silesian, or perhaps even French.

Frederick was concerned with people, not languages; he is famously remembered to have said that he spoke German "only to horses." But when nineteenth-century nationalism brought the link between language and nation, the ongoing consciousness of linguistic origin affected how people perceived these names. Villages with names like Schewkowitz evoked concern from the German state in a way that the village of Three Chimneys, whose French origin was lost to consciousness, could not. The official project of Germanization of place names began in 1873 (Choroś and Jarczak 1995: 461), but with the triumph of the concept of nation-state after the First World War, it intensified. The newly re-created Poland polonized place names, and German authorities reacted in kind, reciprocally, by Germanicizing Slavic place names. Yet beyond providing a straightforward way for nation-states to assert their hegemony, an ideology of "utility" and "purity" also came to play a role. In 1930, an article entitled "The Purification of Our Place Names," by Walter Krause, described the motivation for Germanization as follows:

Moreover, the alteration of useless old Slavic place names is justified and necessary. Place names which are unpronounceable or difficult to pronounce (and also linguistically corrupted), like Chmiellowitz, Chronstau, Chrzowitz, Laskarzowka, Rzetzitz, Wierchlescha and others inhibit communication and therefore require purification. No people of the world has exhibited the same kind of conservatism toward such useless names as we Germans! . . . The first principle will have to remain that old German names [replaced by Polish alternates] and names later assimilated should be restored. Foreign names which allow for easy translation should be translated, *so as to avoid making identification unnecessarily difficult* (like Brzezina = Birkenau, Birken). We can go ahead and accept folk etymologies. In many cases so-called assimilation will prove practical (Chobie → Koben). Where neologism is necessary, they should not be arbitrary, but must be undertaken with reference to local realities (quoted in Choroś and Jarczak 1995: 462, emphasis mine; my translation).

This argument, incidentally, provides a good example of implicit silencing about something. Imagine you are an "eastern German." Don't be anxious! This purification is not going to cause you confusion and difficulty! We'll change Polish names to German ones that mean the same thing. So if you see "Birkenau," or "Birken," you'll know that that's the village that used to be called, "Brzezina." Why are we doing this? Because "Brzezina" inhibits communication.

However, do readers who do not know Polish and German find translating "Brzezina" to "Birkenau" or "Birken" helpful? I doubt it. This would only help a person who understands all three words (which mean "birch trees"). But if you understand all three words, then "Brzezina" didn't inhibit your communication in the first place. So the "something" that gets silenced here is widespread bilingualism in Silesia. It's a "German only" perspective that finds Polish place names useless, difficult, and impure.

Three years later, Hitler overturned German democracy. Few place names had been changed before then, and until 1935 they were changed at the request of local governing councils. But between 1936 and 1939 the Nazi regime changed all Polish-sounding place names to German ones. The campaign was extended to personal names. Starting in 1934, parents (especially mothers) were pressured to give newborns German names; they were threatened with the denial of state social support (Choroś and Jarczak 1995: 464–65). And in 1938 the regime established the "law on the alteration of first and family names." The campaign to change personal names was supported by the NATIONALSOZIALISTISCHE VOLKSWOHLFAHRT (Nazi People's Welfare) and the BUND DEUTSCHER OSTEN (League of the German East), which exhorted the inhabitants of the borderlands as follows:

> Dear Countryman!
> As you already know, it is the goal of the leadership of the BDO to make our beloved borderland purely German in an external, as well as in an internal sense. Attached please find a sheet which will provide information on the legal regulations concerning the Germanization of names.
> And now, which name will you choose?
> First, consider your genealogy. Does your wife, mother, grandmother or other relative have a pure German name? In this case you should, if possible, take this German name. If this is not possible, or if, for some reason, you prefer not to choose this name, you must try to translate your foreign-sounding name. In this you need not be narrow-minded. It is not necessary for a Kupczak to become a Kaufmann; he can also be a Krämer, Kramer, Kremer, Köppke, Köpeke, Kubert, Kuschel, or Küster. It is not necessary for a Kluska to become a Nudel; he can also become a Klaus, Klose, Kluge, Kessler, Körner, Klesse, Krohner or Kruse.
> (quoted in Choroś and Jarczak 1995: 464)

One can only marvel at such generosity, to offer the range of German dialectal variants as a palette of choice in accomplishing this purely aesthetic alteration, aimed solely at making names a true reflection of the real, internal, essential Germanness of the Kupczaks and Kluskas, itself simply assumed. Such was the dilemma for autochthonous Opole Silesians in the Nazi regime: they were offered inclusion in the German VOLK, with all that implied in terms of safety from persecution, at the mere price of forgetting why every previous regime had considered and classified them as a Polish minority. "Repress that memory!" they were told without words. "Silence it! We'll save our persecution for the real Poles to the east! (And for the Jews, of course.)"

Between 1945 and 1950, all place names in Silesia were Polonized according to exactly the same linguistic ideologies and principles by which they had previously been Germanicized. Personal names, too, were altered: "The alteration of personal names was supposed to follow the wish of the individual, but in fact happened primarily on official initiative, often without the permission of the affected party" (Choroś and Jarczak 1995: 467). This is the way it is invariably remembered by the people I did research among; as Marta's father, Norbert Nicholaus, told me, "I received a letter informing me that 'Norbert' had been removed from my name and 'Nicholaus' changed to 'Mikołaj,'" its Polish equivalent. The letter came from the local administration; the names of all the students in his school had been examined for proper Polishness (March 27, 1993).

It is important to understand, however, that personal names were not Polonized so severely that all distinction between a Silesian surname and a Polish one was erased. Autochthonous Opole Silesians report fighting in registry offices over names, both over first names they wished to give their children and over Silesian characteristics such as the medial *o* instead of A. But forms such as Bednorz persisted. German names were sometimes, also, modified in orthography only: Schmidt → Szmit, Schild → Szyld. And medieval Polonizations such as Durynek, Fiera, and Tyl were not subjected to further alteration.

More recently, diplomatic agreements between Germany and Poland in 1986 and 1988 established laws allowing individuals to change personal names. Between 1989 and 1991, 941 applications were received, of which 714 were petitions for the restoration of German names (Choroś and Jarczak 1995: 468). In an autochthonous population of about 300,000, that's about 0.003%. The low percentage tends to give a false impression about the politicization of names in Silesia. Rather than assuming that the changing of names is not an important issue to people, I believe it is more realistic to assume that few people are willing to file an official request for a name change precisely because the issue has been so extremely politicized (one should note that there is also a fee to have it done). They are exercising the same caution that keeps most autochthonous Opole Silesians away from organized politics in general. Their rate of Communist Party membership was lower than that of the Polish population in general (Danuta Berlińska, personal communication), and in some cases their reluctance has been the bitter fruit of experience with the Nazi regime. In one family, the father, an adult in the 1930s, advised his sons, "As long as you live in a borderland, don't join *any* political party. You never know what may happen." He had succumbed to pressure to join the Nazi party, and had spent the ten years following the war in hiding, until an amnesty was declared (June 4, 1995).

Remember the issue here: the state is asserting that the right to safety (in the Nazi state) or the right to live within the country (in the Polish Communist state)—in short, the right to all the protections and benefits of citizenship—is essentially based on race, and that language and the linguistics of names reflects that essential identity. If the names aren't doing that reflecting, it has to be because they've been corrupted, and that corruption ought to be purified. Yet, as we saw above, many Silesian surnames are Silesian in the sense that they are an ancient mix, Slavicized German, or Germanized Polish. There is no way, in strict linguistic terms, to classify them as belonging exclusively to one or the other language, unless one arbitrarily decides that whatever came first is for that reason "more real."

Besides, on a personal level, there is no natural link of name to self-experienced identity. Consider the following story: a father of young children told me that, as a child, he had often listened to his father argue issues of nationality with a friend named Stanisław, a very typical Polish name. His father, he said, when his emotions were up, used to rant and shout, "JESTEM NIEMCEM !" ("I'm a German!" in Polish). Stanisław was much more self-controlled, quiet. They were both well-read, articulate, so in those ways it was an even match. As a child, however, it seemed to him that the neighbor was the wiser of the two. He promised himself that when he grew up and had a son, he would name him Stanisław after this man. And he did; his first son's name is Mateus Stanisław. His in-laws weren't entirely pleased about this Polish name, but they allowed it. But his second son is Stefan, after his father. "Now tell me," he concluded, "Of these two Silesian boys, is the one going to think more German and the other more Polish?" I asked how long we'd have to wait to find out. He said that the younger one was two, at the time of the conversation, June 21, 1993. When I asked him about it during the summer of 2006, he laughed and reported that both boys think like Silesian teenagers. A name by itself doesn't influence how people think; only a name in the context of a culture can do that.

The German and Polish states usurped personal, familial, and cultural autonomy by changing personal names. People younger than Norbert experienced this usurpation. A man born in the 1950s told me that his wife was from Dobra, and her name is Inge; in school some of the teachers used to call her "Irena," because Inge is a German name (July 31, 1995). That reminded me that in the school variety show that I had seen at the end of the 1993 school year, the kids scripted an exchange in which a teacher asked, "What is your name?"

The answer: "Fritz."
"Yes, but what is your name in school?"

The variety show was supposed to be funny. The days when teachers actually behaved this way in the Dobra school were past. Yet the kids remembered the experiences of their elders, and put them in their play.

"I would have just kept signing my name Norbert, forget it," said Norbert's wife, hearing her husband tell me this story. And in contexts that were exclusively autochthonous Opole Silesian, people could do that. Is it any wonder, then, that in Dobra, knowing someone's name is a privilege of trust? Potentially, a stranger, in the bad old days, could have reported that So-and-so was using a name not approved by the state.

I have replaced Silesian names with Silesian names, German with German, Polish with Polish, but I have tried to do so in a way that helps readers remember that knowing names is a privilege of a trusting relationship. In deciding which Silesian names to choose as pseudonyms, I considered what kinds of names readers could imagine having a trusting relationship with. "Małgorzata," for example, could be read by an anglophone reader as "Malgor-za-ta" (this is an incorrect pronunciation of the Polish, but at least it's possible). But few people reading this book could actually have a trusting relationship with someone named that. Inventing a pronounciation is a long step from looking at the word and thinking, "Right, I know people called 'Margaret'." That's the equivalent, in English, of "Małgorzata." I chose actual Silesian names like Klaudia or Franz, which are readable for anglophone readers. To make translated conversation sound authentic, also, when I am addressed by name, I translate what was actually said from Elżbieta, the full form of my name, to Ela, one of my nicknames—unless the person used the German form, Elisabeth. I have always found it difficult to follow a narrative filled with names of people and places which evoke no sound image for me. I find them difficult to remember, and difficult to imagine real relationships among people who have such strange names. As Gaston Dorren has argued (2014: 288), "names originating in unfamiliar languages are harder to remember, and the unfortunate consequence is that we, as humans, experience less sympathy for the people so named."

The strangeness, the exoticism, of unreadable foreign names is perhaps doubly undesirable in a book centrally concerned with oppression. Reading that people had to fight to be registered under the name, "Bednorz" rather than "BednArz" does not have quite the same impact as imagining a situation in which the government insists a family change its name from "Cowper" to "Cooper" (the Polish word "bednArz" means "cooper," a barrel-maker, as does its Silesian cognate, and "cowper" is an old, alternate spelling.) Reading that the state changed people's names from "Nicholaus" to "Mikołaj" is, perhaps, not quite as shocking as imagining the state changing someone's name from "Marie" to "Mary." The unfamiliarity of the names may mask the fact that they are, indeed, *personal* names, and mask the totalitarianism of changing them.

So I chose pseudonyms that English speakers can read. I concede a point to Krause insofar as I've avoided multiconsonant clusters and diacritics. Barred l's (ł) may be read by anglophones as l's; in fact they indicate the sound "w." I have not been able to avoid "sz" or "si" but readers may as well learn now that both are roughly equivalent to the sound represented in English by "sh": "Kasia" is \kashuh\, and Urszula Krysiak is \urshoola krishak\. The "sz" sound also figures very centrally in chapter 4, because Silesians say "s" where Poles say "sh." Perhaps—I hope—if I were starting my research now, when Poland is already a member of the European Union, I would not have to assure people that I would protect their identities. Ethnic tensions were much more acute when I began the research in 1992 even than when I finished it in 1995, and by 2006, they were even more attenuated (although they had not disappeared). But it may be just as well to remember, in this book, a time when people had such fears.

What's in a name? Not ethnic identity, not an essential link to one's nation, but certainly a link to one's family, one's community, and one's personal history and psychological identity. Autochthonous Opole Silesians have woven their history, their relationships, and their shared memories of oppression, into a cultural practice: reticence about names. They have turned silencing into silence.

In the reticence about names, we have an example of how paying attention to what people are reluctant to say to outsiders can shed light on autochthonous Opole Silesian culture and history. In the next section, we turn to what people are eager to say to outsiders.

CONSTITUTIONAL CITIZENSHIP AND CONFLICTING IDEOLOGIES OF NATIONAL IDENTITY

What is it that Marta was so quick to tell me that she "stays away from," on the grounds that she "consider[s herself] to be Silesian?" Her vehemence, her readiness to share this information, has complex roots, and we will return to them repeatedly in the book. The answer that we need to explore at this point, is this: the German Minority is a political party as well as a social club. Insofar as it is a political party, Marta doesn't like its politics. Insofar as it is a social club, she doesn't like the company. The issue is one of authenticity, of honesty. As we will see—and this was especially intensely true in the era immediately after the fall of Communism—German Minority clubs found themselves having to convince financial patrons of the "Germanness" of their villages. In this, they elided the complexity of that identity for themselves as individuals as well as assuming the right to represent others. It was a highly contested situation.

At the level of the regional political party, the German Minority has to be highly sensitive to how Silesia is seen by various powerful audiences to the west, on which it depends for financial and political backing: the German state, its voting citizens, and nongovernmental groups interested in giving money. Of such groups, those associated with the West German League of Expellees play a special role. The League of Expellees is a West German association which represents those expelled from the territories transferred from Germany to Poland after the Second World War. Its position in the German political spectrum is right of center. The League of Expellees maintained hopes that the borders might once again be revised in Germany's favor right up until those hopes were completely crushed by the "Treaty between the Federal Republic of Germany and the Republic of Poland on the confirmation of the borders existing between them," of November 14, 1990.

The organizational structure of the German Minority in Poland exactly copies that of the League of Expellees: both consist of an umbrella organization with a political role and small member clubs dedicated to the preservation of the music, dance, cuisine, dress, folktales, and so forth. In the case of League of Expellee clubs, the culture in question is that of the various formerly German regions that members come from, mainly Silesia, the Sudetenland, and East Prussia. The result of this dual structure is that support for the German Minority in Poland comes from the League of Expellees in three forms: umbrella organization to umbrella organization, umbrella organization to individual clubs, or club to club.

At the level of the umbrella organization, all the money that the League has is tax money. According to a representative of the League of Expellees who visited Dobra at the time of a summer festival (July 18, 1993), the money that the League has invested in Silesia comes from a fund earmarked "for the use of Germans in the Oder-Neisse territories" (as they used to be called—he pointed out that the phrase has been officially replaced with "Poland"). The League of Expellees is one of several intermediary organizations (VERMITTLUNGSOR-GANISATIONEN) entrusted with distributing the funds, along with, among others, the Red Cross and the Roman Catholic Charities organization, Caritas. Because of their intermediary position, their funding is subject to the vagaries of German politics. During the round of budgeting prior to the summer of 1993, the League of Expellees, alone among these intermediary organizations, had taken a 60% cut. Enemies of its right-wing politics had had the upper hand. The chair of Dobra's German Friendship Circle was actively lobbying this representative to get some of this money for Dobra during his visit. Importantly, the federal nature of the funding assures that the word "German" is defined constitutionally, that is, all progeny of citizens of the German Reich within its 1937 borders count. This is also true of federal German money that comes by way of other entrusted organizations, or by way of the German consulate.

There are competing ideologies of the right to citizenship, of "national identity" within the German constitution. The legal language that states that all progeny of citizens of the German Reich within its 1937 borders count is civil in nature; people are citizens by virtue of living their lives in the German state, regardless of their "ethnicity." The German constitution also grants citizenship rights to, for example, the Volga Germans, descendants of Germans who immigrated to Russia in response to an invitation from Catherine the Great. This is a group that has lived in the Russian state for generations; it is their ethnicity that qualifies them for German citizenship. The same ideology, until changes introduced in 2000, excluded the grandchildren of Turkish immigrants to Germany, children who were born in Germany to parents also born in Germany, from ever becoming German citizens.

This is an old, widespread way of thinking: the right to citizenship proceeds from nationality, nationality proceeds from ethnicity, and the primary sign of ethnicity, in Europe, is native language. This ideology has its roots in the broadly influential intellectual movement of German Romanticism. In the early nineteenth century, Wilhelm von Humboldt asserted "that the structure of languages in the human race is different because and insofar as language is the spiritual distinctiveness of the nations themselves" (Humboldt 1830–35, 7:43, quoted in Coulmas 1985: 11; my translation). As Bucholtz and Hall have put it, "The scholarly tradition of Romanticism, motivated by the emergence of nationalism, indelibly linked language to ethnicity in a quasi-biological fashion" (2004: 374). As the many principalities in which German dialects were spoken united politically and became the nineteenth-century Prussian nation-state (a process essentially completed at the end of the Franco-Prussian war in 1871), Germans were encouraged to see their allegiance to their local region (and dialect) as a subset of their natural bond with the German nation.

The local region, or homeland, is called HEIMAT in German, and state-funded education was used to instill love of HEIMAT and nation, for example, through many children's songs glorifying emotional bonds with idyllic streams, rivers, windmills, coastal flats, hills, forests, and so on, depending on local geography.

But never mind; autochthonous Opole Silesians have German citizenship rights under the German constitution; and they cannot be denied aid that comes from tax money that is earmarked for "Germans." However, when a local German Friendship Circle pursues financial support from a local League of Expellees club, that money comes from private donations, and that particular club must be convinced that the village is a worthy recipient of the voluntary donations of its members. And most members of League of Expellee clubs define "German" the way that von Humboldt did. It is inescapably obvious that the postwar generation of autochthonous Opole Silesians, by and large, do not speak German. Why, then, would local German Minority clubs have sought this particular kind of support, since it requires them to twist the nature of their claim to German identity?

The reason that the League of Expellees played a special role in supporting autochthonous Opole Silesian villages is that they got in first. They had already positioned themselves to play a special role before the fall of Communism. While the changes of 1989 precipitated a wave of interest by various organizations and municipalities, it took some time for these contacts to develop. In contrast, the League of Expellees had always had an irredentist interest in the territories "under Polish administration," and this interest had already led them to develop contacts with local village political elites (which, in Communist Poland, necessarily meant members of the Communist Party), before 1989. Thus it was the League of Expellees who actively supported the initial organization of the Social and Cultural Society of the German Minority.

It seems likely that part of that support consisted in suggesting that the German Minority adopt its organizational structure. Their political interest in Silesia was that the remaining autochthonous population made Silesia an exemplar of their slogan, "Silesia remains German." The leadership stuck to the "borders of 1937" definition because it was not in the political interest of either the League of Expellees umbrella organization or the Silesian German Minority to apply the "quasi-biological definition." But it was ideologically inconsistent not to do so, and their membership was not consulted. After Communism fell, it became possible for members of League of Expellee clubs, as well as German journalists, to visit Silesia and check things out for themselves. It then fell to the leadership and members of local German Minority clubs to manage their visitors' impressions.

Recall that in my first conversation with the priest in Dobra, he made a great point of blaming the postwar generation's inability to speak German on the lack of opportunity for learning German in schools in Silesia. It was a point consistently made to outsiders. It was usually also pointed out that Silesians were fined and imprisoned for speaking German in the Stalinist years that immediately followed World War II. The image that the German Minority was projecting in the early and mid-1990s was that Opole Silesia had been a monolingual German-speaking society until 1945, when the German language was immediately, severely, and entirely effectively suppressed, at which point, save for the memories of older speakers, it became a Polish-speaking society. The Silesian dialect, together with the ethnohistorical fact that autochthonous Opole Silesians descend from Slavic peoples, is hidden from view. When I asked, and when I observed other outsiders asking about the Silesian dialect, people implied that Silesian is a German dialect. Communicating these partial truths could be a delicate task.

I never heard anyone admit that the leadership of the German Minority had given its membership actual instruction as to how to handle outsiders who ask awkward questions about language, but when I was perceived as an outsider, the uniformity of my handling had the whiff of a "party line." The first German Minority member I met (the man the priest, as he had promised, introduced me to) stated:

> People settled here from Germany . . . and that's why we have real German names here. But as in all borderlands, the people spoke bilingually. . . . For example in Alsace-Lorraine, . . . the people also have their own dialect. And therefore our language . . . is not real Polish. Nobody could really speak Polish here. . . . [I]t's its own dialect, . . . exactly like in Germany, the Bavarians also have their dialect, right? (Notes, October 19, 1992).

Without lying, he encouraged me to think of Silesian as a German dialect. Had I been so inclined, his comments would have enabled me to believe, or continue to believe, that this was a German-speaking area, and that everyone learned Polish after the war from the Poles who moved in.

This kind of response was not confined to Dobra. When I asked questions about Silesian of the chair of the German Friendship Circle in a village that I call Rybna, he claimed not to know what I meant by the term. In Opole Silesia, he told me, German had been spoken until 1945, and then, perforce, Polish had begun to be spoken (September 25, 1995). And the chair of the German Friendship Circle in another village, that I call Grabina (Julia Kunisch, who figures also in chapters 4 and 9), showed me a recently published dictionary called *SO SPRICHT MAN IN O/S* (How they speak in Upper Silesia) (May 1, 1995). She'd gotten it from the German Minority; it had been privately published in Germany. The introduction read in part:

> In [this] brochure the vocabulary of our Upper Silesian homeland [HEIMAT] is presented. . . . This work should provide proof that the Upper Silesian house dialect has very little to do with the Polish language. The assertion of the Poles, that our homeland is an originally Polish land, is thereby disproved. The strong Polonization of the last decades has not succeeded in destroying Upper Silesian linguistic elements.

There are strategic spaces of veracity and untruth between the statements, "Silesian is not Polish," which is true enough, and "Silesian has very little to do with Polish," which is linguistically unacceptable, and then the next extreme, which I never heard actually stated, "Silesian is a dialect of German." That is an outright lie. To my knowledge, it was only ever propagated during the Nazi era: "W. Mak 'proved' in 1933 ([published in] "DER OBERSCHLE-SIER," Opole) that the Silesian dialect is completely separate, having nothing to do with Polonica, being connected rather to the German dialects" (Rospond 1959: 340).

As I said, the game that I observed was obfuscation rather than misrepresentation. The patronage relationships in play—the money—made the stakes high. It was, on occasion, a suspenseful game.

IDENTITY POLITICS IN THE VILLAGE OF OSTRÓW

The most acute such encounter that I observed occurred at the 700th year anniversary celebrations of a village I call Ostrów (May 29, 1993). The German Friendship Circle, which controlled the village council, had established a patronage relationship with a local club affiliated with the League of Expellees, quite early after the fall of Communism, in 1990. In the process, the chairman of the village council had told this League of Expellees group that "80% of Ostrów is German." This is undeniably true in the legal terms of the German constitution, in which, remember, all individuals who were themselves born, or whose parents or grandparents were born, within the 1937 borders of the German state are defined as Germans and entitled to German citizenship. However, the chairman of the village council must have known that people whose native language was a Polish dialect would not be accepted as truly German by members of the League of Expellees. Managing this discrepancy became difficult when this village chairman invited members of this group to come to the celebrations.

Their bus trundled up just after the morning event, the dedication of a monument stone memorializing the hollow in the woods where the priest and villagers had hidden from the invading Swedes during the Thirty Years War, called the "priest-hole." I had been invited by a historian I knew from the Silesian Institute, a man in his sixties, a native of the village. He had been asked to give a lecture that afternoon. His father had fought on the Polish side in the Silesian Uprisings that followed the First World War and an uncle was later killed in Auschwitz as a Polish nationalist. He is among the few autochthonous Opole Silesians who definitively identify as Poles; he accepts the nationalist ideology of native language and culture indicating nationality, and the logical conclusion is that by this measure, Silesians are Poles (although he understands the historical complexities which have led some to reach different conclusions). Also present was another native of the village, also in his sixties, a much less highly educated man who, unlike the professor, still lives there and is very grounded in local life. He, it emerged, spoke about issues of identity much as the German Minority members quoted above do.

From the bus emerged a group of German men and women, mostly in their fifties or older, and a group of girls dressed in the traditional costume of *western* Silesia (Lower Silesia)—that is, of the Silesia that had been monolingually German-speaking—the Silesia that founders of the League of Expellees were expelled from. They explained that they had been specially invited. The girls were going to dance that afternoon. They wanted to know what was going on, and, told that a memorial had just been dedicated, they wanted to see it. The professor and the local man offered to show them the monument stone. As autochthonous Opole Silesians educated before 1945, they were able to converse fluently with the monolingual Germans. When we reached it, one of the men in the group looked at the inscription, and asked belligerently, "Why is this written only in Polish? They spoke only German here!"

With that statement, the monument stone, dedicated to Ostrovians forced to hide from political struggles long past, suddenly became a focal point for a political struggle actively playing itself out in the present. Implicitly, the forty-minute conversation that followed was an interrogation of whether the village was really as German as the guests had been led to believe. Were Ostrovians legitimate participants in the national community that the Germans represented? The issue was particularly acute in that their participation was as worthy recipients of financial support—support that these particular Germans, as one of them made clear to me that afternoon, intended for fellow Germans only ("It's right to help them out. After all, they are Germans like us.") During this free-for-all of a discussion, the professor tried to present the historical facts of language use in this region of Silesia, the local man tried to keep the visitors from concluding that these facts mean that autochthonous Opole Silesians are not really Germans, and the visitors tried to sort it all out, while one of them repeatedly paraphrased a fundamental question: "I don't understand how it can be that the villagers here could be Germans when Germans were expelled after the war, and it was Poles who were allowed to remain."

Given the essentialist link between native language and national identity, what hope was there for the man from Ostrów, who has a pressing interest in presenting the village as German? Short of flatly contradicting the professor, that is, lying outright, what could the local man do? Well, he manipulated the terms of nationalist linguistic ideology. Although "native language" is important, language has another role in nationalist ideology, and the local man emphasizes that in one aspect, the village conforms to expectations, while diverting attention from the problematic issue of "native language." Let us consider the beginning of the conversation.[1]

> MAN FROM LEAGUE OF EXPELLEES GROUP: Why is there only Polish here? They only spoke German here.
>
> PROFESSOR: I can't really completely support that. In the, um, POPULATION LIST, that is, at the end of the nineteenth century there were still, that is, in the school there were eleven pupils who came from German families, and, then, there were over a hundred and eighty from Polish families. Yes, so it was . . .
>
> M, LE: But that was when they had immigrated, when the Prussians had let them in, but not before that.
>
> P: No, before that there were, ah, Slavic inhabitants, that is, the place names and everything is, is, Polish, so one didn't say a, ah, a, a "Priesterloch" [priesthole] or something like that, one said, until today one says "KSIĘŻAdól" or "FARLEdól" [where "Farle" is a German loan blended with Slavic "dól"], so the whole region it was Polish and also the, ah, name "Ostrów" and not "Austrau," "Austrau" doesn't occur until the eighteenth century, that is in the archives.
>
> M, LE: Yeah?
>
> LOCAL MAN: But that's looking back on it. One can't, because we don't exactly know either, so . . . but anyway, the name, well, there was a German priest here, right? [He reads the name of the priest who hid his congregation in the "priest-hole" from the stone's inscription.]
>
> P: Yes, but the priest came from Berlin. He had been here for three . . .
>
> LM: A person can argue about whether only, whether only Polish was spoken, back then, right? It's hard to tell [this sentence exhibited Polish syntactic interference]. At any rate there were here, this and that kind of people were here, right?
>
> M, LE: Well, yeah, but . . .

The local man's strategy here is historical equivocation. He softens any fact that the historian presents by asserting that the truth is unknown, which, if true, would allow the visitors to believe whatever they want. Yet this is not his only strategy. As the conversation progresses, he plays on the complexity of nationalist linguistic ideology.

Nationalist ideology makes a two-fold demand of language. This correlates with the German constitutional definition of citizenship rights, which also has two strands. Recall that according to the German constitution, there are two categories of eastern Europeans who may be granted citizenship. Autochthonous Opole Silesians fall into one category: descendants of citizens of Germany in its 1937 borders. When the League of Expellees cites autochthonous Opole Silesians as privileged examples of "Silesia remains German," they are either ignoring/ignorant of the linguistic facts or alluding to this aspect of the definition of "German." On the other hand, Upper Silesians, as well as other inhabitants of Poland, the Czech Republic, Romania, Russia, and other eastern European countries where German-speakers settled over the centuries, may or may not have rights to citizenship depending on whether they can demonstrate, not only descent, but also an active commitment to their German heritage in the form of continued use of the German language and maintenance of German cultural practices.

These two categorizations reflect different strands of European definitions of citizenship. The first is civil, based on an assumption of common political identity, more or less independent of ancestry, language, or culture (the question of "more" vs. "less" seems always problematic). This is the model of citizenship that was found in the multi-ethnic Austro-Hungarian and Prussian empires that collapsed at the end of the First World War, and is still found in the United States and Canada, in the Netherlands, and in the secular French state. The second is racial, with culture and language as important expressions of ancestry. This is the model of citizenship exemplified by Israel, which, like Germany, has a "right of return" based on ancestry—and also found in the right-wing politics of the nations mentioned above. The German constitution recognizes both strands.

The civil definition of citizenship also makes demands on language to allow one to participate fully in the national community. The imagination of the modern national community, as Benedict Anderson has pointed out, depends on a "national print language" which allows all members of a nation to read and listen to a national media. In this sense of having the ability to participate, by virtue of their fluency in the national language, the older generation of autochthonous Opole Silesians are fully German. The local man points this out repeatedly.

Ancestry, conceived racially, does not come into this definition. The inner, psychological sense of identity, however, does. Civic participation has its own emotional valence. Deep associations with a language do not have to come from one's earliest childhood, from one's mother, as the phrase "mother tongue" may imply. A man of this generation describes this particularly well, explaining that he and his wife are "of German heritage." Having learned German culture in school, he said, he can't be easily reoriented toward Polish culture. For example, what is the Polish poet Adam Mickiewicz to him? The

German poet Friedrich Schiller is closer to his heart; he feels familiar with Schiller's poetry, which he read as a schoolboy; he has a relationship with it. His wife added that it's different—legitimately different—for younger people, whose schooling was Polish. "Heritage," the artistic culture of literature and music, is important, and the "heritage" of prewar Silesians is that of German national culture.

Anderson's point, then, allows us to understand the two-fold demand of nationalist ideology on language. The language people use should be a psychological link to, and pragmatic index of, commonality with the nation's past, and also allow full participation in the nation's present. For individuals, then, the linguistic identity which most straightforwardly establishes a claim to national identity is that exemplified by the German visitors to Ostrów: monolinguals in the state language. A native speaker of the state language has the hearth-and-home link to the historic development of the nation and the ability to participate fully in the civic life of the nation—not to mention being able to read Schiller.

No other linguistic identity is quite as good. Domestic speakers of a dialect of a national language have the link to historicity, because the nation is held to have grown out of its own past "folk culture," and the standard language, out of its once fragmented dialects. But dialect speakers will have to acquire the standard language in order to participate, or risk being stigmatized, tellingly, as "backward"—as if they had somehow stepped straight out of the fourteenth century, before German became standardized. Immigrants fare even worse, since their language serves neither historicity nor participation: the national language must be acquired, and maintaining the immigrant language underlines foreignness. German-identified Opole Silesians have a specifically borderland form of the problem: they are domestic speakers of a dialect of the wrong language.

This is the reality that the local man needed to silence.

The Germans in the woods near Ostrów that morning were not interested in civic definitions of national identity. Their comments clearly revealed that they believed that one person can have only one, unambiguous national identity and that language is its outward manifestation. We can see this in their repeated questioning throughout the day: "How many inhabitants does this village have, and how many of them are Germans?" Before the start of the ceremony to dedicate the monument stone, I recorded a conversation to this effect between a German free-lance journalist and an Ostrovian, and this conversation also emerged at the end of the argument. Furthermore, it was posed later in the day in such a way as to foreground it extremely: at the formal ceremonies, those at which the professor gave his lecture and at which the German girls performed their folk dances, and at which various awards were bestowed. One of the high officials of the central administration of the German Minority called this question out to the village council during a question-and-answer session. That he posed it in German, while the language of the proceedings was Polish, reveals the intended audience: this answer was expected to be meaningful to the visitors. Yet in a society in which individuals do not necessarily identify with only one nation-state, or with any nation-state, a simple, numerical answer cannot be exactly "true."

The ideology of the German visitors was also revealed by their comments during the argument at the monument stone. One man said, "I would disagree [with the inscription being only in Polish] because we've got to do here with the German people, and not the Polish people, right? The Thirty Years' War was a war with the Germans, and not with the Poles. And they've got that turned around here." Yet the Thirty Years' War was not simply a war with the German people in the sense of modern nation-state warfare. Ostrów was in Austria at the time. And the Austrian state was multi-ethnic.

Another thrust of the conversation underlines that the League of Expellees group viewed language, especially in public, written-literally-in-stone use, as a primary symbol of identity. They spent some time discussing why a predominantly German village would have allowed such a monument to be inscribed only in Polish. Their conclusion was one often offered by the German Minority: that the Polish authorities must not have allowed it. But most autochthonous Opole Silesians see written Polish as a common language, a lingua franca, that is appropriate for public use and does not symbolize identity.

All three of these assumptions reflect the image of a culturally and linguistically monolithic nation-state which can only accommodate two possibilities of individual national identity: either one is a member of the nation-state nationality, or one is a member of a national minority. Such membership is established on the basis of native language and cultural practice. Neither historical assimilation or "civilization," so important to the French model of nationality, nor "multi-culturalism," that important if problematic feature of the American model, counts.

The local man, then, is faced with the task of obfuscating the reality of his village's history in face of the professor's attempts to clarify. As I said, one of his strategies is historical equivocation, yet this is not his only strategy. Immediately following the exchange quoted in full above, the local man brings out the German Minority linguistic trump card:

MAN FROM THE LEAGUE OF EXPELLEES: Well, yeah, but . . .

LOCAL MAN: We didn't know the Polish language at all. It was a Silesian laguage, right? It was . . .

M, LE: A dialect, right?

WOMAN FROM LEAGUE OF EXPELLEES GROUP: Water Polish, Water Polish, yes? [WASSERPOLNISCH is a derogatory name for Silesian Polish. The term "water" was also prefixed to the names of other languages spoken within Germany.]

LM: Water Polish, yes? One speaks it, there are a lot of expressions. . . .

2ND MAN FROM LEAGUE OF EXPELLEES GROUP: A mixture of German and Polish. LM (overlapping): German expressions are, and then these other . . . not like the Polish. We didn't know the Polish language at all.

M, LE: No.

LM: When the Russians arrived, we had to look in books first, what it was in Polish. We knew the Silesian language, right? But not the Polish. And that's connected to it, one can't tell, today, how it really was. At any rate, the people were here, then, Germans and there were also, that is, Polish, the people here are that too, right?

The point is clear: Silesian is not Polish. We did not speak Polish. Therefore, because language is a primary index of national identity, we cannot be considered Poles. On the other hand, we did speak German. Therefore, surely, we can be considered German. The local man is echoing a sentiment I heard often from older autochthonous Opole Silesians, who don't consider that an unwritten language with no literature really counts as a language. Remember the man who shared his feelings about Schiller: "Our *language* was German." And if that means something different to us than to our visitors, well . . .

Also, it is perfectly true that in the immediate aftermath of the war, Silesians were often forced to use dictionaries to express themselves comprehensibly to Poles. Even if the first word to come to a speaker's mind was Silesian, since Silesian is not a written language, the speaker would have to think of the German translation before looking it up. The only dictionaries were German-Polish ones.

In the following excerpt, the Local Man finds some sympathy from one of the German women, who echoes his point, although her doing so gives the Professor the opportunity to counter it. Yet, as mentioned, most of the League of Expellee group seem quite determined to continue to believe that Opole Silesians are German, and yet another woman helps out again by coming down firmly on the side of the value and nobility of the literary language. Here is the exchange:

WOMAN FROM THE LEAGUE OF EXPELLEES: And that's the case, and this German, um, Polish can't have been the Cong-, how do we say, the Congress Kingdom Polish, as they have it now, as they speak it now, they must have also had this other, as we say, well, we say "Water Polish." [The woman has sensitively repeated the Local Man's argument; she also seems to be sensitive to the fact that "Water Polish" is a derogatory term.]

OTHERS: Water Polish, yes, Water Polish

PROFESSOR: Well, but, but . . . (others continue to mull over this term, Water Polish)

W, LE: And that is a, Water Polish is a dialect.

P: Is a dialect, but there's a dialect also among Cracovians or in Zakopane or, for example, in other regions, the people did not speak literary Polish or German.

ANOTHER WOMAN FROM THE LEAGUE OF EXPELLEES: No, we also have this dialect.

P: . . . but rather their dialect.

M, LE: It's the same in German! In Bavaria we have . . . (he is drowned out)

P: But here it was . . . the German language as official language, and the school language and at work, so one didn't, let's say, develop a German dialect like in Lower Silesia. It was the literary, it was the German language of the stage, that is, our people spoke High German.

W, LE: Yes, yes, yes.

P: At home they spoke Polish, in dialect form, and, and when they got into jobs, in school they spoke High German such that you could understand it all over Germany, and not like in Bavaria or wherever.

M, W, LE: Yes, yes.

P: There, you see! [This is the longest speech the Professor has been allowed to make.]

OTHER W, LE: Yes, that's right. The Upper Silesian, we always said, speaks a pure, High German.

P: Yes, but that was because it came from school! (laughs)

It is true: eastern Silesians, whether autochthonous Opole Silesians or Upper Silesians,[2] spoke standard German. Their ability to participate linguistically in the national community cannot be questioned. All that can be questioned is their historical link to a racially conceived nation where standard German, it is held, grew out of German dialects. Autochthonous Opole Silesians who identify as German manage to present themselves, and their communities, as German by emphasizing the "participation in a national community" aspect, and obfuscating the "authentic link with the history of the nation" aspect.

But that is not the only ace in their hand. It's true that the German visitors are privileged in many ways. In terms of identity, they are monolingual German speakers and life-long residents of the territory of the German state, even if some of them were militarily expropriated and forced to move in order to stay within it. They also have more money, generally speaking, which puts them in a strong position in practical politics (what Germans call "REALPOLITIK"). In the final analysis, the most important ability of Opole Silesians to "finesse the situation" may not lie in the obfuscating emphasis on standard, literary language. During formal, indoor proceedings, the professor got his chance to give the historical lecture which had so often been interrupted in the woods that morning. He traced the village's original settlement by Slavs, the development of bilingualism, and concluded by saying, "It is thus evident that this is a Polish village."

The League of Expellees group were all present in the lecture hall, seated in a row. Seated in a row also were various officials of the German Minority: the council chairman who had invited the Germans was there, and the official who had asked how many Germans lived in Ostrów was too. They heard this concluding remark with utterly impassive expressions. But, then, why should these bilinguals worry about this view being presented? This part of the celebrations was under official auspices of Ostrów, a unit of the Polish state. The professor gave his lecture in Polish, and none of the Germans understood it.

It is a great aid to this strategic self-presentation that the distinction between Silesian and Polish is inaccessible to Germans. If you don't know Polish, you cannot hear the difference between Polish and Silesian, and then you can believe that the only Polish spoken in Silesia is imported from east of the old German border. You don't even have to grapple with the existence of "Water Polish." On the other hand, when the "party line" is not given in German, it can betray itself. For example, consider one interview in which I and the interviewee each spoke our own Polish, and the interviewee (predictably) asserted that before the war, "practically only German was spoken. . . . After the front came through, they told us that those who had been going to school had to keep going to school. We didn't speak Polish here, practically not at all. People say Polish was spoken here; that's not true, it's nonsense."

I asked, "How did you learn Polish then, after the war?"

The woman replied, "Z koleżank*oma*!" (With friends!)

OK. That inflectional ending, *-oma*, is contrastively Silesian. In standard Polish, it would have to be -AMI. So let's assume that it's true that this woman spoke only German before 1945, that it was the language of her family as it was, at the time, the language of public life. If that were true of every family, then the only "friends" with whom she could have learned Polish would have been Polish friends who had moved in from the east. Friends who say "z koleżankAMI." But that's not how she learned to speak. Her speech betrays the fact that she learned "Polish" from autochthonous Opole Silesians.

What we see in this German Minority "party line" is strategic management of how important outsiders see the community, in a situation where outsiders often have purse-string importance for the community. As a hint that such factors are in play, consider that after seventeen months of fieldwork, I had a very different conversation with the man who had compared Silesian to Bavarian for me, back on that second visit to the priest's house. He told me that the neighboring village of Nowa Studnia, which I knew had been founded under Frederick II's settlement policies, with the name Neubrunnen, had been settled by Slavic Silesians; the first, German, settlers had quickly abandoned the sandy soil. I expressed surprise; I hadn't realized that. "Oh, come on," he scolded. "You should have been able to figure that out from the surnames there! 'Skowron,' 'Krawiec,' 'Stanik,'—these are Slavic names!!" (Notes, June 27, 1995). The man who had once seemed to want the outsider to believe that Silesian is a German dialect was now reprimanding the linguistic anthropologist for failing to draw the correct conclusion.

And maybe it wasn't so important, anymore, that outsiders see Silesia as German. By then, the reaffirmation of the borders, as well as the "Treaty . . . on Good Neighborliness and Friendly Cooperation" of July 17, 1991 had greatly increased the ability of Opole Silesian villages to establish positive working and patronage relationships with a range of Western German municipalities and civic organizations. Many more recently established relationships allow Opole Silesians to be open and honest about their cultural practices and historical experiences. Indeed, Berlińska argues that overall, what drives German interest in helping communities in Poland is the borderland experience itself: a large proportion of such relationships are established between communities in the historical western and northern borderlands of Germany and communities in the former German eastern territories, whether now inhabited by an indigenous or an immigrant Polish population (Berlińska: personal communication). On the other hand, perhaps the other part of the formula had also changed, and I was no longer being treated as an outsider.

IN FROM THE EDGES

After the German visitors had climbed back into their bus, ready to go on to the center of the village, and the professor, the local man and I had gotten back into the car, the local man said to me, "Not all Silesians identify as German."

"I know," I said, "I've been here since November." After all, I had met one who does and one who does not on my first day in Dobra.

This chapter began with introductions and has ended with inside knowledge. It both began and has ended with people's eagerness to introduce themselves to outsiders in terms of ethnic national identity, but with a change in orientation: at the beginning, I was the one whose impressions were being managed, while by the time I was invited to Ostrów, I was watching others' impressions managed. In between, one small item of autochthonous Opole Silesian culture formed a juxtaposition, and that was the shared, cultural reluctance to share personal names with outsiders.

In the discussion of "boundaries" in the first chapter, I noted that all humans draw boundaries. So, where are the edges of German identity in Opole Silesia? Is this a German village? Who gets to see that boundary, and who gets to define it, and using what criteria? All identity assertions point to boundaries. But the edges aren't enclosing empty space, or something that is just the same within as beyond, like a cookie cutter on rolled-out dough. The instrumentalist claim, that identity is a matter of practical advantage, is inadequate in Opole Silesia. The political, practical, and financial advantages by no means do justice to the motivations of German-identifying autochthonous Opole Silesians, although they have a rough and ready relevance, as far as they go. Nor are those who assert Silesian identity moved solely by reaction to their German-identified neighbors. If we are to understand these assertions, we need to focus on what is inside the edges. Assertions *of* identity are made *from* identity. Understanding the widespread reluctance to share personal names is only a minimal beginning, in that regard.

Chapter 4

FINDING CULTURE

I offer the following metaphor for beginning to understand autonomous autochthonous Opole Silesian culture: coming inside. By the end of chapter 2, we had gotten to Dobra, as seen from the train, and from its central street—in short, from the outdoors. We spent much of chapter 3 outdoors also, in the woods near Ostrów. We have gone inside into public spaces: the priest's reception room and a village tavern. We have yet to see the inside of anyone's home. To understand vehement identity, to understand autochthonous Opole Silesian culture—simply even to understand how the German Minority managed to organize itself so quickly, so soon after the fall of Communism—we need to examine the fruits of autochthonous Opole Silesians' kind invitations to let me get to know them in their homes. Houses, in autochthonous Opole Silesia, are powerhouses—places of power (cf. Jonderko 2007).

A large house of brick or cinder-block construction, with a high fence between it and the road, standing in a row of similar houses, with a door at the side or the back, and a dog in the yard: that is the appearance of most autochthonous Opole Silesian houses. Either recently or not so recently, an autochthonous Opole Silesian man took the lead role in building the house. He used his skills as a bricklayer, or plumber, or electrician, or carpenter, or more than one of those skills, and, with the key help of his wife, he mobilized friends, neighbors, and relatives in the work of building a house. Typically, the land was a gift from his wife's parents; typically, the young couple had been living with the wife's parents since their marriage. Their moving out may have made room for the new husband of one of the wife's sisters. This, at least, was the pattern that persisted through the 1980s and that I found during the 1990s. And in building the house, the couple anticipated a time when one of their daughters would be living in it with them, and with her husband and their young children. Parents expect a daughter, or, less frequently, a son, to stay in the parental home. People of my parents' age, on learning that I have no siblings, were often shocked that I was away in Silesia doing research rather than living with my parents. When my parents visited me in Dobra in 1993, I asked my father to let it be known, in his limited German, that I had their approval.

Some houses are divided horizontally. Marta's sister, Magda, for example, lives with her husband and three children on the bottom floor of a two-story house built by her parents on land given to them by her grandparents—her mother's parents. They had a kitchen, a bathroom, and two other rooms: a *KINDERZIMMER*, where the children play, watch satellite TV, and sleep at night on sofa beds, and another room, which also has a TV, where adult gatherings, such as their birthday celebrations, are held, and where she and her husband sleep on sofa beds. Her parents lived upstairs. Other houses are divided in another pattern, but with the same effect: from top to bottom. One enters and faces a stairway and two internal doors on either side. These doors, not the outside ones, often carry metal plaques inscribed with the surname of the family residing on that side. That these plaques are common goes along with the preference for postmarital uxorilocality: the young family will have a different surname, because it is the daughter who stays, and she takes her husband's name. Whether divided horizontally or vertically, the house has two of everything: two kitchens, two chimneys, two satellite dishes clinging to the outer walls.

And often, speaking of division, two identities. "Not all Silesians identify as German," the local man told me in the car, after the debate in the woods near Ostrów. In fact, generally, not all Silesians within a single household identify in like manner. Not far into the introduction I hinted that the quick organization of the German Minority, as both political party and network of social clubs, was the work of the generation of autochthonous Opole Silesians born when Opole Silesia was within German borders. We have had some further hint of the generational correlates of dissent over "who we are," at least insofar as all the German-identifying autochthonous Opole Silesians encountered have indeed been of the generation born "in German times"—though we should note that the professor is also of this generation—while Marta is about thirty years younger. Her parents, by the way, consider themselves to be Germans. Furthermore, they consider Marta to be German.

This ethnographic observation parallels the findings of sociological, survey-based research. In 1990 and again in 1993, Danuta Berlińska and Franciszek Jonderko, sociologists who work in the Silesian Institute in Opole, conducted survey work in which they asked people, "Who are you? Who do you feel yourself to be? How would you describe yourself?" As possible responses, they offered and a palette of choices: "a Pole," "more a Pole than a Silesian," "more a Silesian than a Pole," "a Silesian," "more a Silesian than a German," "more a German than a Silesian," or "a German." Those questions and possible answers make sense because identity in Europe forms both a contrast set and a nested hierarchy. The contrastive aspect of identity assigns a single, or at least dominant and distinctive identity: if you are Spanish, you are not French. The nested hierarchical aspect of identity allows for multiple identities as long as they are ordered: a Liverpudlian is not a Londoner (contrastive identity), but both are English; most European "national" identities subsume "regional" identities in this way. At a higher level, however, neither the Liverpudlian nor the Londoner is French.

Not all Silesians identify as German. That statement presupposes that the local identity, the category of "Silesians," or, more carefully, autochthonous Opole Silesians, grounds and centers national identity. Because of its borderland history, Opole Silesia is a region that is not definitively subsumed to one national identity, the way that Paris is to France or London to England. Instead, it is like other borderland regions—the Cerdanya, between Spain and France; Alsace-Lorraine, between France and Germany; Schleswig-Holstein, between Germany and Denmark—all European borders have their nationally ambiguous borderlands. Berlińska and Jonderko did not give respondents the options "more a Pole than a German" or "more a German than a Pole," because, although logically possible, those options do not make cultural sense within the nested hierarchy. On the same level, the two are mutually exclusive. Rather, the questions targeted the degree and strength of ethnic identity—"being Silesian"—and the question of which of two, mutually exclusive, higher order identities people might, or might not, select to go with it.

The results of Berlińska and Jonderko's research are schematized in Figure 1. As we see, not all Silesians identify as German; in fact, almost 50% of respondents stated that they consider themselves neither Poles nor Germans but simply "Silesian." Another 15% considered themselves "more a Silesian than . . ." either a German or a Pole. Polish-oriented responses, both equivocal and unequivocal ("a Pole," or "more a Pole than a Silesian"), account for about 20% of the total, and German-oriented responses for about 15%, though Berlińska and Jonderko warn that this result may be deflated by respondents' fears of admitting to German identity, suppressed in Communist Poland. They state that if all those who replied positively to the statements, "Today in Silesia it is not possible / not completely possible to show that one is a German comfortably and without fear" were added to those who considered themselves

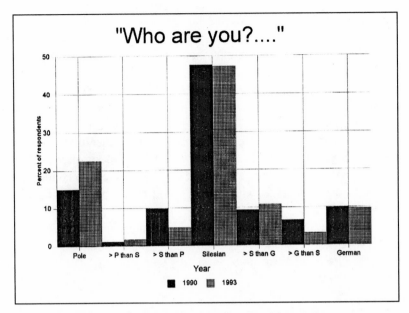

Figure 1. Autochthonous Opole Silesians' responses to the survey question "Who are you?"

German, then the percentage of German-oriented responses would rise to 36.1% (Berlińska and Jonderko 1993: 36–37). I would likewise suspect underrepresentation of German identification; in Dobra, I never heard anybody assert Polish identity, while there were many people who asserted German identity.

Of statistical correlates with other aspects of social identity, the most important is age. 72.2% of those declaring the German option were born before 1937. In contrast, 57.1% of those who chose the Polish option were born after 1953 (the year of the Stalin's death). Almost 40% of these respondents had a Polish spouse (Berlińska and Jonderko 1993: 36), an interesting point, considering an intermarriage rate of less than 10% (Berlińska 1989: 8, 1990: 111). We will return to this point at the beginning of chapter 7, when we consider why having a Polish spouse fosters Polish identity; this opens out onto power relations between the ethnic-national groups. Here, our concern is power relations within autochthonous Opole Silesian society, between generations.

The number of autochthonous Opole Silesians who signed declarations that they consider themselves German, by August 1989, was 200,000. If the more generous estimate of German-identifying respondents is, in fact, valid for the entire autochthonous Opole Silesian population, that percent would equal about 108,000 persons. Where did the German Minority get the other approximately 92,000 signatures? They were, I discovered, the work of 72% of 36% of the autochthonous population; in other words, of the approximately 77,760 German-identifying autochthonous Opole Silesians who were born before 1937. The youngest of this group were fifty-two in 1989. Old enough to have grown children, perhaps a daughter, living in the house with her husband and their children.

The house that I described, built to house three generations, is a house that looks forward to power. In autochthonous Opole Silesia, gerontocracy is a fact of social life. The height of power in the life cycle is to be the parents of a grown married daughter with growing children, the heads of a three-generation household.

This is something that the leaders of the signature campaign knew. They gave very specific instructions about how the signatures were to be gathered. As Julia Kunitsch, who was involved in this process in the village that I call Grabina, explained it,

> We kept hearing, in this village, in that village, all the Germans are signing a letter declaring their nationality. Sometimes people brought the news from work, sometimes at a party, wherever people got together. At first I didn't believe it, but when the news got to my husband he was on fire. We're going there! At any rate after a while we found out that we were supposed to go to Gogolin [a town where the regional headquarters of the German Minority still is], and we went there to get a model letter. How they wrote the letters, what we were supposed to write on it, I've got it somewhere still, put away at home. And people from our village came by our house to sign the letter. But we'd been told to bring it to Gogolin as soon as possible. So that Gogolin would know how many of us there were in the different places. Once we had the names, we got in the car and took the letter to Gogolin.

Or, consider what I was told in Rybna, by the chair of that village's German Friendship Circle: he and a friend had approached other, trusted people, and they divided up the village and went door to door. They carried a form divided into columns, and for every signature the organizer wrote the name, address, date of birth, the nationality the person considered him or herself to belong to (i.e., German) and left the rightmost column for the signature. Furthermore, in telling me this story, the chair pulled out his copies of the original signature forms and showed them to me in all their five-column glory. Household members appeared together, which makes sense, as the signatures had been gathered door to door. But they were not merely grouped together: the signatures of every family member were written in one hand, or alternatively, the first signature was in one hand, the second in another, and all the others in the first. I surmise that in those cases, the male head of household deferred to his nearest social equal, his wife, before signing the names of their subordinates. Checking the conveniently specified birthdates of the household members, I noted that the signatures were listed in approximate order of age, oldest to youngest; it was the grandfather who did the signing; in some cases, the grandmother signed her own name. And the people whose names had been signed for them, I found, were not only children, but people of my generation, with birthdays as early as the early 1960s—people in their late twenties at the time of the signature campaign.

Here it is that we see that the social structure of the household and family, and the cultural knowledge of the leaders of the German Minority, bear directly on the mystery that started us on our journey in chapter 2: this region of Poland is inhabited by a self-professed German national minority; when it was in Germany, the same region was inhabited by a self-professed Polish national minority, and the former seem to be, in many cases, the direct descendants of the latter. This is true because in both cases—that of the self-professed Polish minority after the First World War, and that of the self-professed German minority after the fall of Communism—it was not the entire group doing the self-professing. In the older instance, those actively engaged in the Polish nationalist movement that followed World War I, including the Silesian Uprisings, were a subset of the population, and in the latter case, those who actually signed declarations of German nationality were also a subset. But they were a powerful subset. For while it is true, as Berlińska and Jonderko found, that a majority of young Silesians identify with their ethnic group more strongly than with German nationality, it is also true that in Silesia, it's not very important what you think until you become a head of household—until you build a house of your own, or until your parents, or your wife's parents, cede control of the property to you. This is a culturally recognized moment known as *Wycug*, in Silesian, or AUSZUG in German ("moving out"—yet another model of division can be that the parents move to a smaller house on the property).

In short, the extra approximately 92,000 signatures came from those among the 77,760 autochthonous Opole Silesians born before 1937 who signed the names of their household subordinates. This is easily within their authority. And indeed, in two years of fieldwork I met no one of my own generation who had signed his or her own name—and, with the exception of Marta, who objected to her parents vociferously, I met no one whose name had not been signed.

Once, after several months of fieldwork (on May 6, 1993), I asked Marta's father a question I almost never asked anyone explicitly: what do you consider yourself to be?

"German," he said. "I went to German school for five years."

"And if you hadn't?" I pursued.

"I was born in Germany. I learned German. The language here was German."

My notes state, "His attitude here was: Silesian is Polish and unworthy. Silesian is half Polish, half German, and people here thought it up. But the *language* here was German."

"What about your children?" I continued.

"They are also German because my wife and I are German."

People consistently offered this kind of terse, categorical statement, always making the exact same three points. That is why I so rarely felt the need to ask this question myself. People who were born in Germany, who went to German school, and who consider their language to be German, use these three criteria to justify their German identity. People who were born after 1945, and therefore were not born in Germany, did not go to German school, and who do not speak German, use these same criteria to explain their sense of themselves as Silesian. In Dobra, nobody ever talked about being Polish—only, occasionally, about *not* being Polish.

On one level, that is the discourse of identity in autochthonous Opole Silesia. And yet, as Berlińska notes, it is not only Marta's generation, the postwar generation that came of age in the 1970s and 1980s, that largely does not identify as German. It is also true of that generation's grandparents. According to Berlińska, the national identity of the prewar generation was

> labile, of a nominalistic character, that is, there existed no deep feeling of connectedness with German national culture. The following response illustrates this position best: "My parents considered themselves whatever the situation warranted. But not so much Germans, because the pure Germans were on the other side of the river" [i.e., farther west, across the Oder]. (Berlińska 1989: 6; cf. Bjork 2008)

There are generations of identity in Opole Silesia, and differences among generations. These differences go back a long way. German identity, as manifested in the immediate post-Communist era of the 1990s, was closely associated with the generation born before 1937. They came of age, then, between about 1920 and 1953, during the interwar period, the Nazi era, and the Stalinist era.

FINDING CULTURE

The Generation of Identity: Clothes and Words

An assertion *of* identity has to be made *from* identity. There has to be a social actor making the statement for some set of subjectively experienced reasons— reasons that are interpretable. Those reasons bring us into the realm of cultural analysis. In the third chapter, we found a historical answer to the question of why autochthonous Opole Silesians are hesitant about sharing personal names. In the last section, we examined the question of how the German Minority managed to present 200,000 signatures of people asserting German identity within a few months, despite the fact that sociological research would indicate that only about 100,000 would be likely to do so. We found an answer in the structure of the family and household, a social structural answer.

At this point, on our way to understanding vehement identity, we begin to find answers in culture. Cultural answers, for a start, relate both to beliefs and ideology and to practices and socially patterned behavior. Such answers come from observing, and from conversing. To understand more deeply what people mean specifically when they assert an identity, we need to know more about what people mean more generally: in what they say, in what they believe, and in what they do.

For example, what does what people wear mean in relation to their identity? The patterned behavior of wearing certain kinds of clothes is, in part, a conscious choice that is believed to symbolize autochthonous Opole Silesian identity. This is a matter of ideology. Certain clothing choices—women's clothing choices, as it happens, at certain events—have the same function as a verbal identity assertion, just like saying explicitly, "I consider myself to be German, Silesian, or Polish." However, in another sense, women's clothing choices are not about the contrast among identities. They are about the contrast among generations within the community. And what is true of clothes is true also, it turns out, of a certain kind of words.

Throughout Europe, East and West, festivals dedicated to the celebration of "culture" give a central role to women's clothes. Usually, these festivals focus on regions; usually, they involve both music and dance, and the "traditional dress" of the region that the performers come from—or the region whose dances and music they perform—is the costume of performance. Most of this "traditional dress," is derived from nineteenth-century peasant garb, as this was prettied up for liturgical celebration of life-cycle rituals. It is not only emblematic of a "culture" which must now be self-consciously promoted, but nostalgic for a time conceived as more culturally pure, before forces of integration and homogenization overtook the continent.

93

The Polish Communist state, like other European nation-states, encouraged Polish citizens to see their local region as a subset of the Polish nation. The state actively promoted the concept of regional variation with national integration through, for example, museums devoted to regional culture. The Roman Catholic Church, too, continues to encourage the wearing of "traditional" regional dress by participants in important events, such as the processions of pilgrims. Thus it is that one could buy a doll decked out in the regional dress of any region of Poland in a "Cepelia," or folk art store, and also see women in that dress in procession at various pilgrimage sites. When women wear "traditional dress," they are participating in a nonverbal identity assertion. What they wear makes a statement of self-consciousness of contrastive identity: "My dress shows that I am Silesian rather than Cracovian. I have a bodice with a sash rather than an embroidered black vest."

In Dobra in the 1990s, one saw the oldest women wearing the kind of dress in church that women wear in processions at St. Anne's Mountain, the pilgrimage shrine of Silesia. In doing this, they take on the role of visibly asserting Silesian identity in public. Their dress is traditional; it has historical depth. Yet this same generation of women, when they were young in the 1920s and 1930s, asserted their identity in a much different way: by becoming the first generation of Silesians who did *not* wear traditional dress in the normal round of their lives' activities.

Autochthonous Opole Silesians wear mass-produced clothes of the same materials, brands, and styles as other Europeans and North Americans. But they wear them in a distinctive way, a way that is unremarked, probably semiconscious or unconscious, but that nonetheless distinguishes autochthonous Opole Silesian culture. Old women's dress in church in Dobra seems to constitute the contrastive outer edge of a cultural system of dress which is not, in its entirety, caught up in such self-conscious contrast. The system is much more centrally concerned with relations within the autochthonous Opole Silesian community, in culturally autonomous disregard of contrastive identity. That it is grandmothers whose dress constitutes this nonverbal identity statement fits entirely with what we have learned about the role of the grandparental generation in presenting verbal identity statements, in their five-columned glory. That it is grandmothers', rather than grandfathers', dress, that plays this role fits the larger cultural scene: female dress, throughout Europe, is a site of symbolic display to a greater degree than male dress.

Old photographs show us that this culturally distinctive system of dress has been created within living memory and that the generation that now includes the oldest women in Dobra had a major role in creating it. It is a system that reflects the power of men over women, and of the older generation over the younger. And it is a system which implicates words, in the form of loans from German, as well as dress.

In church, of course, we see not only the traditional dress of the oldest women but also the dress of people of all ages. Traditional practices of rural Polish Roman Catholicism, still observed in the 1990s, aid us in seeing those of Silesian culture, for the highly structured social space of the church organizes the congregation not, as in American Protestantism, into nuclear family groups, but according to age and gender. Children sit in the first few pews, boys on the pulpit side, girls on the left. Teenagers sit behind them. While some women do sit on the right side, men do not sit on the left side. The church, then, divides people into three age groups intersected by gender, and when the congregation is encouraged to hear special instructional sermons, in preparation for Holy Week and Christmas, each group comes at a different time to hear a different sermon: one for children, one for youth, one for men, and one for women.

Women who sit on the right side are usually sitting with their husbands, and both the separation and its breach are reflections of a gender hierarchy. The pulpit is on the right side of the church: on a practical level, it is easier to concentrate on a performance unfolding directly to the front than off to one side. On a symbolic level, this organization of the congregation communicates that the men's ease of concentration is more important than the women's. The gender separation in church resonates with other realms of Silesian life, where men take the active role in courting, men continue to work for wages after children are born, men make financial decisions, men are figures of final authority in regulating the behavior of dependent children, men decide whether or not to emigrate to Germany, and only men are active in organized politics.[1] Priests, figures of great power in Poland, speak first and foremost to men. If women sat with their husbands, they could be understood as behaving congruently with their familial and religious role, as showing solidarity with the "head of the family." Men have no such license, and before my return trip to Silesia in 2000, I never saw a man sit on the left side in church.[2] Yet it will become increasingly clear that when women created an age-graded system of sartorial symbolics, in the first decades of the twentieth century, they were acting a role of "essentializers of identity" which is culturally appropriate to their gender and which is, in its own way, a powerful role.

In general, clothes worn to church, especially by youth and adults in their twenties and thirties, are opulent. One sees many leather jackets on men, and leather skirts on women. Materials hold creases well and fit well. In talking about dress, people refer to the standard set by western magazines; adults who have emigrated to Germany sometimes feel pressure to "dress well" when they are in Silesia, and are sometimes criticized for dressing so well as to be showing off. The standard is a German one, yet observing women's dress in church closely, you can see that there is something about it that doesn't come from western magazines: six generational cohorts that dress distinctively from one another: girls, teenagers, young women to about forty, women from about forty to about sixty, women older than sixty, and the special, small group of the oldest women in the village.

Only the oldest women do not wear mass-produced clothes. Girls wear frills with store-bought bows in their hair (generally kept long, although between 1993 and 1995 a noticeable number of girls cut their hair short). Among teenage girls, the frills and bows disappear, and jeans appear. However, hair is still brushed smooth and held back. In Opole, too, when high schools let out and the streets teem with teenagers, you can tell which girls are autochthonous Opole Silesian by the neat appearance of their hair and clothes. Girls with loose, unbrushed hair, carefully ripped jeans, untucked shirts, and jackets that are shorter than the shirt are Polish. Silesian teenage girls reject the look of studied scruffiness popular among their urban Polish counterparts.

Women who have finished school, started to work, and married cut their hair. "They no longer have time for it," I have been told. Make-up is used by teenagers and young women, but not widely. Women of this age group dress for church in strong colors with gathered sleeves, lacy collars, draped bodices, and the like. In winter, they wear jackets or coats of nylon. Women from about forty to about sixty wear felt coats in the winter with knitted berets; a few wear felt hats. They often perm their hair, but, strikingly, they do not dye it, nor do they ever wear make-up. Because Polish women of this age do do these things, women of the two groups look more different from each other at this time of their lives than men, or younger women, ever do.

Comparing the dress of the oldest three generational cohorts of women, we find that the dress of women from forty to sixty consists of conservative sets consisting of skirt, blouse, and jacket, or tailored dresses. Among the next oldest group, dresses are not colorful. They are either blue or black. A triangular scarf is worn around the head or shoulders. Shoes are low-heeled and dark in color. These clothes are old.

The dress of the very oldest women consists of a collarless, straight black jacket over a long, straight, black skirt with an apron. Around their shoulders they may wear a large triangular fringed scarf. They may wear a lacy, triangular scarf over their head. These are the clothes recognized as traditional Silesian dress. They are home-sewn.

Notice, then, that women have taken fashions from beyond their community and fitted them to their own sense of fashion appropriate to age. There is nothing in particular about this that asserts Silesian identity. It's "just culture," so to speak. Only the culminating point of the age-grading has a place in a contrast set of the various traditional dresses of Europe, and thereby asserts identity. That contrast set hides its history; cultural festivals present local culture as timeless. But the symbolic system of age-graded dress dates, at least in its broad outlines, from the 1920s and 1930s, and it was young women who mainly shaped it. And what was done with clothes was also done with words.

We can compare dress for church in the late 1980s with dress for church in the 1940s by looking at how people were dressed in a group wedding picture from each of these decades. In the forties, as in the eighties, one can see that younger women wore tailored dresses with gathered sleeves, lacy collars, draped bodices, and the like. Women between forty and sixty wore blouses and skirts, though not jackets. Older women wore "traditional dress." Looking at older photographs, one sees younger women, and more of them, wearing "traditional dress." Some wedding pictures from the 1910s and 1920s show very young women in "modern" dress while all the older women are in some form of "traditional" dress. One particularly telling photograph shows a girl and boy, aged around six, wearing the sailor suits which both Europeans and Americans so strongly associate with the first decades of the twentieth century. The girl is leaning against the knees of an old woman in traditional dress. In the second row a man is filling the shot glass of a young woman wearing a dress with shoulder pads, a collar, and V-shaped pleats. A symbolic system was being created in which "traditional" dress became more and more rare, the province of older and older women, while younger women wore "modern" dress in ways particular to their community (see figure 2).

The first three decades of the century, then, were a time of change, led by young women. The changes these women introduced then became entrenched. Although the oldest women in Dobra now would have been of an age in 1920 to abandon their collarless black jackets and long black skirts, their aprons and scarves, for colorful dresses and shorter skirts, their elders did not. These same women, now that they are old, find it appropriate to wear these clothes to church. Women who were young before 1937 now wear the very traditional dress their generation once threw off. And although mass-produced clothes have gradually become more pervasive, and fashions have changed somewhat (and especially changed for young people), succeeding generations of younger Silesian women, too, have moved along in a symbolic system set then.

Figure 2. Top, a wedding picture from 1949, showing the generational pattern of dress that had, by then, become established. Bottom left and right: A Silesian mother photographed in traditional dress in 1935, and her daughter, photographed in modern dress, in 1939. The difference of only five years supports the inference that young women took the lead in adopting wider European norms of dress.

This is a symbolic system of autochthonous Opole Silesian culture, and no one now thinks of the dress of the younger women as flouting norms. But in the first three decades of the century, wearing "modern" dress did constitute an act of looking beyond the norms of the ethnic group. Then, discarding "traditional dress" represented change. The "modern" dress that now seems simply normal once seemed metropolitan, perhaps even daring.

So much for clothes. Words, also, followed the arc of this trajectory. Matuschek describes the massive Germanization of the Silesian lexicon during the 1920s as follows:

> [D]uring the interwar period the Silesian village awakened from lethargy and threw off many traditions. Young women stopped dressing *po chłopsku* [à la peasant] (*jupa, mazelońka, lajbik,* etc.) and started dressing *po pańsku* [à la nation-state], which meant in practice à la city (*KLEJT, ROK, PYMSKI, HALTER, BUBIKOPF, DAUERWELA . . .*). (Matuschek 1994: 60)

Note how German loan words replaced their Silesian predecessors. Relexification not only affected the vocabulary of clothing. Matuschek describes the scope of it as follows:

> *FOTER, FATER* <VATER, ojciec, "father"; *MUTER* <MUTTER, matka, "mother," *BANA*<BAHN, kolej, "railway"; *GESZYNK*<GESCHENK, prezent, "gift"; *BEZUCH*<BESUCH, odwiedziny, "visit"; and words for clothing, cork, suit, inheritance, teacup, butterfly, herring, button, teacher, suitcase, ice skates, eyeglasses, socks, young lady, cemetary [*KIERHOF*—see below], handkerchief, and many others. Further, the entire administrative vocabulary, household terms, clothes and accessories, kinship, names of months, health, agriculture, all parts of a bicycle, names of sports. (41–43)

The words had a different fate than the clothes. Mass-produced clothes were incorporated permanently into a meaningful cultural system. But, many of these words did not remain a common part of Silesian parlance after the war. In part, this is doubtless a function of external pressures: during the Stalinist period using German loan words could subject speakers to fines, whereas economic changes discouraged people from continuing to sew clothes at home. In part, it may because "switching out" one source language for another was not difficult in a culture lacking an ideology of linguistic purity. However, there is one similarity: both the clothes and the words are involved in an intergenerational dynamic within autochthonous Opole Silesian culture. When the young people of the 1920s started using these words, they were incorporating material taken from the nation-state into Silesian life. Their use reflected a cosmopolitan outlook. When the young people of the 1990s use them, on the other hand, they are the special symbols of a specifically Silesian identity.

For, although they are not used in daily parlance, these words remain available to young speakers in certain ways. For example:

> April 28, 1995—I took the train from Opole to Dobra that takes a great many high school students home from high school. A group of girls was seated in facing seats, talking and laughing. As the train passed a cemetery, one of the girls made a show of looking attentively out the window. "*KIERHOF*," she said solemnly, and all the girls collapsed back in their seats, helpless with laughter. . . . Inhabiting their elders' voices was highly amusing to them.

Knowing this German loan word, in addition to the Polish loan that they would be likely themselves to use, CMENTARZ, added humor to their conversation. But the use of German loans goes beyond humor. I once asked a group of fourteen-year-olds whether it was possible to talk about speaking "pure Silesian," the way they talk about "pure Polish." They said yes, that meant to speak using only Silesian words *and the ones taken from German*. I pursued the issue: "You mean like *KARTOFLE* [potatoes] and *HAVAFLOKI* [oatmeal]?" The teenagers assented.

"And for you, are those German words, or Silesian?"

"Silesian," they said. But about their own, less "clean" speech they had said, "We know when we're speaking which, but we're aware that we bring in stuff from Polish" (Notes, March 30, 1993). In other words, importing from Polish is importing from Polish, but the importing from German that their grandparents had done, well, those words are, as I once heard it put, "*RICHTIG* Slonski"—real Silesian.

A similar sensibility emerged during one of my elicitation techniques, an exercise in which I asked people to look at a series of pictures which told a story, without text, and to tell me the story either in Polish or in Silesian. I was recording the six-year-old nephew of my housemate Marta as he told, in Silesian, the story of a picture of a grown-up and a child placing a package in the trunk of a car. I asked him to make his story as Silesian as possible, and his mother, Magda, and aunt, Marta, helped him to do this by offering him German loans:

> BOY: *Dziolcha* stoj*a* i *pakuja* do *auta* . . . [Girl stands and packs into car. . .]
> AUNT: *GESZYNK*! Jad*a* na *URODZINY*! [present! (She) goes to (a) birthday!]
> MOTHER: Na *GEBURTSTAG*! No! [to (a) birthday! That's it!]

In the good-natured competition to produce Silesian, Marta topped her nephew and his mother topped her sister, making the story more Silesian by the use of German loans. Incidentally, the women also introduced an association of the story being told with a frequent and important event of Silesian social life: birthday celebrations.

Again, what once seemed metropolitan now seems merely Silesian. And this, in turn, resonates with the statistics that identify 72.2% of people who declare themselves "German" as born before 1937. Once, when people born before 1937 were young, wearing "modern" clothes and importing words from German meant a lifestyle *po pańsku*, in the fashion of the state: the German state. But unlike the interwar period, the Communist period was not a time when Silesians took in customs from the outside, reworked them, and made them their own. And now, for younger people, looking to the German brought in during the first decades of the century no longer constitutes looking out from the ethnic group, to the state beyond it. On the contrary, it constitutes looking back in time to a historical connection with Germany which had in the 1990s become an integral part of Silesian—as opposed to Polish—cultural tradition. So we can wonder whether older people's assertions of German identity summarizes a sense that "I grew up at a time when our community looked beyond itself to the nation it was a part of, before our community closed in on itself."

So what is "Silesian" emerges, indeed, as inherently relational. If young people think of German loans as "real Silesian," then they think that the relationship with Germany is normal, natural, nonthreatening, and part of Silesian life. The grandparents, on the other hand, may be achieving this effect somewhat in spite of themselves. They, after all, disproportionately take "being German" as an important aspect of their identity. They might prefer their grandchildren to take their German loans as German, rather than as Silesian.

A complicated scenario. Tokens of identity are valorized in the exercise of power between genders and generations. Elders valorize these tokens, because they have the power to do so, but even the relationship of their intentions and the interpretations made by younger people is not entirely straightforward. "Culture" shades through age-grading from practices which are distinctive, but not valorized as contrastive (e.g., the distinctive generational pattern of women's fashion), into those valorized as contrastive (e.g., the traditional dress of the oldest women), and all the "stuff of culture" is taken from a "culture" larger than, and in some sense encompassing, autochthonous Opole Silesia. And yet, this culture of mass-produced clothes and borrowed words is focused not only on intergroup relations, but also on intragroup dynamics; it has a focus of inward orientation, away from the edges where the contrast between what is Silesian and what is Polish is marked.

FINDING CULTURE IN MULTILINGUAL JOKES

Paradoxically, then, Silesian culture is not only relational, but also autonomous; not only discernable in its contrast with what lies beyond its edges, but also in its own creative complexity. We are beginning to take the measure of that complexity, as it has been formed in history, as it is manifested in social structure, in habitual practices, and language usage.

A joke encompasses all these aspects of culture. It relies on shared knowledge that develops over the course of history; its characters reflect a social structure; telling jokes is a social habit and a linguistic one. As Seizer points out, "In the [1970s and 1980s] anthropologists have joined linguists and folklorists in significantly extending the study of speech acts and their contexts under the rubric of verbal performance. . . . Joke texts and contexts are now recognized as worthy of anthropological attention," notwithstanding earlier neglect, for "while multiple generations of anthropologists diligently collected the 'stories, sayings and songs' they heard in the field and readily recognized these as 'integral element[s] of culture' . . . , they left the joke to languish where it lived" (1997: 62). Bearing this in mind, then, if we can identify a distinctive "Silesian sense of humor," surely, we've found "culture."

The "Silesian sense of humor" is an example of culture that is autonomous not because it is disconnected or separate, behind some kind of boundary, but because the way the humor is constructed is unique. This is not a stock repertory of jokes that are "Silesian," the way that the Grimm Brothers presented the fairytales they collected as "German" (though in fact, versions of them are found widely in Europe). Rather, this is a sense of humor deeply embedded in power relations between autochthonous Opole Silesians, on the one hand, and Poles and/or Germans, on the other; these are jokes that take shape in the context of domination by two nation-states. And what better place to begin to understand this humor than the one place, in autochthonous villages, where such power relations are played out every day: school.

In school, whenever a teacher holds up a picture, draws a picture on the board, or refers to a picture in the textbook, and asks, "What is this?" there is almost always someone in the class who gives the answer in Silesian, and the kids think that's very funny; everybody laughs.

I observed this kind of humor, experienced it myself, and saw how two classes included it in their end-of-year skits satirizing their school experience.

I first observed it in a science lesson. A third grader was asked to identify what was in a picture in their textbook, and when he said, "insects," in Silesian, everybody laughed. The teacher smiled and, as usual, said the standard Polish word. When I, myself, was asked to speak to a seventh-grade class about "life in America," I used an aerial photograph of Los Angeles to start a discussion of urban sprawl, the stress of commuting, and air pollution, hoping to make the point that the United States is not utopia. I started out, of course, by showing them the picture and asking, "What are these?" "*Chałpki!*" (Houses!) came the answer, with due accompanying laughter (March 30, 1993).

Once, also, I was asked to stand in for the German teacher with the second grade, and I decided to focus on the spelling of the sound called in English "long i," which is spelled "ei" in German and "aj" in Polish. The word for egg is a felicitous illustration, since it is EI in German and jAJko, in Polish. Accordingly, I drew a large oval on the blackboard and asked, "What's this?" "Jujko!" came the response, with laughter (May 4, 1993).

But the most dramatic—literally—instance of this form of school humor was its central place in an annual ritual of reversal. On April 23, 1993, grades 5, 6, and the two seventh-grade classes presented dramatic skits to grades 1, 2, 3, and 4, and their teachers. While the imaginative fifth grade presented a version of "Little Red Riding Hood" called "Little Blue Jeans" every other class presented parodies of classroom situations. "All on the same subject," the history teacher commented later, in a tone of voice which suggested that this was the usual subject, year in and year out. Two of the classes used the same joke: a teacher points to a picture of a bird and says, "What's this?" The answer: "Ptok!" And then, in an aggrieved tone of voice, the teacher says, "But one doesn't say, 'ptok,' one says, 'ptAk!'" In this situation, it was the audience who laughed.

The linguistic norm was far from the only one the kids presented themselves as breaking. In their skits, they dressed badly: mismatched socks, cut-off jeans, jeans jackets without shirts, and the girls' hair in particular was sloppily parted and sloppily put in pony tails. They wore overdone, sloppy stage make-up, freckles, black eyes, and so on. They threw paper around, came in late, ate chips in class. In other words, they broke all the rules; having to answer in Polish was one of the rules.

Actually doing that in class, then, is a subversive practice, even though, in the 1990s, it is merely funny and the teachers don't really mind. However, a closer examination reveals much about the chasm of power between two kinds of groups which, in school, happen to be overlaid: there is a power differential between children and teachers, and there is a power differential between autochthonous Opole Silesians and Poles. In autochthonous villages, all the children are autochthonous and almost all the teachers are Poles. To understand why breaking this important linguistic rule is subversive humor, it is necessary to understand the context: how language is dealt with in school.

The first grade is the place where socialization to school begins, and happens most explicitly. In the first grade classroom in Dobra, children usually sit very still. They sit in same-sex pairs at tables arranged in rows, their attention following the teacher as she moves around the classroom. Their teacher is empathetic, commenting in January that it is a time of year when many children get sick, which is a very, very bad thing, and in May that it is very upsetting when children bring animals home from the forest, and, as often happens, they die, so that although animals are very interesting and cute, it is really better to enjoy them outdoors. In her lessons, she tells stories: family life stories, counting stories, cautionary tales. She pauses frequently, leaving openings for the children to fill. When she does, every hand goes up. She smiles often. When she rejects an answer, she says, "Well, maybe. Does anyone else have another idea?" As she moves, she watches the children. No child sits for more than a few minutes at a time without finding her behind him, smoothing his hair, placing her hands on his shoulders, touching his cheeks. She seldom raises her voice, rarely scolds, never punishes. She praises their stillness, reminds those who talk or slouch, frequently repeating that this is the way we do it, this is good, this is right. The classroom is quiet. The children have a ten-minute recess, away from the classroom, every hour. Recesses are loud.

One morning (January 15, 1993), she announced, "Today, we are going to learn about the sounds 'SZ' and 'CZ'" (/sh/ and /ch/). She asks the children to offer words beginning with these sounds. All hands go up; we get "szanować" (to value, take care of), "szalik" (scarf), "szosa" (highway), and "szafa" (cupboard). A girl offers "sukienka" (dress). Perhaps she has been hearing the sounds through Silesian ears: Polish sz corresponds to Silesian s. The teacher asks the girl to repeat the word. She carefully repeats the other words the children have offered, and then, turning to the class, she asks if they hear the sound of "sz" in the word "sukienka." "No," they chorus. She turns to the girl and says, "They don't hear it. Can you hear that 'sukienka' doesn't have the sound of 'sz'?" The girl nods.

She reminds them that "szkoła" (school) also begins with "sz." Then she asks the children to stand. She asks them, altogether, to make a sound like a train letting out steam, "Shhh . . . ," then like a train moving, "Ch!" Everyone, teacher included, moves their arms like the pistons of a train: "szzzz . . . , cz! szzzz . . . , cz! szzzz . . . , cz! szzzz. . . , cz!" She tells them to place their hands in front of their mouths, so they can feel the steady expulsion of air in "SZ," and the plosive quality of "CZ." The sounds often appear in conjunction; next she asks them to make the train say the word "jeSZCZe" (still, yet).

She then reminds them that the word "CZApka" (hat) begins with "cz," and asks first one side of the center aisle to repeat that word, then the other; then the boys, then the girls. "In school," she says, "We don't say 'skoła' for 'szkoła,' and for 'CZApka' . . . what do children say for 'CZApka?'" A child raises her hand, and offers the Silesian equivalent: "*cołpka*." "Yes. In school we say 'CZApka,' and not '*cołpka*.'" She asks each child to say the word in turn. Then she asks who wears hats? Children offer policemen, Santa Claus. When a child calls out, "chimney sweep," giving the word its Silesian pronounciation, "kominiorz," she repeats the word in its standard Polish pronounciation, "kominiArz."

Next, she asks the children to take out their reading books. They have already read the story at home. "What is it about?" she asks. "A mother and a daughter *ARE KNITTING*," a child offers.

"Yes, that's right! In school, though, we don't say '*TO KNIT*,' we say 'WE ARE KNITTING.' [Not '*STRIKOWAĆ*' but 'ROBIMY NA DRUTACH.'] Can we all say that together?" Everyone does. Three children then come to the front, and each reads a part in the story: the mother, the daughter, the narrator.

I was reminded of that day several months later (May 8, 1993), when I found myself among a group of university student pilgrims at the shrine of the Black Madonna of Częstochowa, all singing from their hearts, "Madonna, O Black Madonna, how good it is to be your child!" (Madonno, Czarna Madonno, jak dobrze twym dzieckiem być!) Because the Black Madonna is considered the Queen of Poland, it was a powerful expression of the goodness of being both Roman Catholic and Polish. For me, singing along but actually neither, it was an experience of alienation that reminded me of the "we" I'd seen created that day in school. Both were instances of the construction of identity in discursive practice; the difference between them was that the song presupposed an identity already formed among its singers, while the lesson helped discursively create a new identity.

It did this in the way the teacher used and transformed the artificiality of the story for these autochthonous Opole Silesian children. Most of the children in the class don't speak Polish at home; don't refer to the activity being described as KNITTING. Autochthonous Opole Silesian girls and women knit, but they don't talk about it like that. The story was about a domestic scene which was, to the children, as hypothetical as the word problem presented in their math lesson that day: "Jadwiga has 7 złoty . . ." One is about as likely to meet a Jadwiga in an autochthonous Opole Silesian village as to meet a Hedwig outside the pages of a Harry Potter novel: it is a typically Polish girl's name. (Interestingly, the Polish translation of Harry Potter preserves the German/English form of the name for Harry's owl: Hedwiga—would Jadwiga not be exotic enough for the world of wizardry?) Similarly unrealistic, for these children, was the idea of having 7 złoty. As a result of the hyperinflation of the first months after Communism ended, the smallest unit of currency circulating at the time was the 100 złoty note. It was was worth about a third of a cent.

The teacher had no choice about whether or not to read the story; curriculum is standard across Poland. She transformed the alienation of it by discursively creating a separate social space for the use of Polish, a linguistic *domain*, as Fishman called it (1972) and at the very moment of creation, by marking it as the domain of the class, of a "school 'we'" as implicitly opposed to a "home 'we.'" It was a step that took her usual practices of distinguishing a realm of formal classroom speech to a new level.

On this day as on all days, she repeated anything said in Silesian in its standard Polish form. Following, and supporting, the policy of the school's principal, she makes no attempt to regulate children's speech to each other during recesses; in class, of course, speech among children in any form is not allowed. (In public places as well, and when adult guests are present at home, Silesian children do not speak without express permission.) But in interactions with her that are not centrally a part of the performance of a lesson, such as children's requests that she clarify directions, she responds to Silesian without bothering to repeat what was said in standard Polish. That is her way of marking out a domain of formal, standard, classroom speech. On this day, however, she raised that practice to the level of a rite of passage, the components and processes of which conform beautifully to the classic analysis laid out by Van Gennep in 1908. The teacher discursively created a metaphorical train ride through the terrain of linguistic markers of identity.

She started by taking the children into a space where the usually unconscious phonological level of speech became highly alienated, an object of conscious examination, in asking for words with the sound of "sz." She took this alienation a step further by leading them in imagining the sounds of speech as the sounds of a train. Finally, when they were all completely enraptured by the train they had collectively created, she had them give it a voice, make it talk, say the standard Polish form of the word "je*sce*." And then, she led them out of this liminal space of pretend, and now they found themselves as children who, able to make the train say the word "jeSZCZe," are also able to say that word themselves. It only remained to define this ability in terms of the social identity of "we here in school." The grammatical first person plural was pressed into the service of this redefinition several times, most dramatically in the treatment of *STRIKUJON*, "they are knitting." The teacher could have repeated the exact form of the Silesian that the girl had said. Instead, she transformed it into the impersonal infinitive, while the desired, Polish, word was expressed, like everything else, in the first person plural, "we," form. The lesson was brilliant pedagogy.

However, like most of education, it was at once liberating and oppressive. Most Silesians value their ability to speak standard Polish, and believe that it is the job of schools to teach children to speak it. This is an old attitude in Opole Silesia, where people also believed, and still believe, that it is the job of the schools to teach German. In that sense, then, learning to speak standard Polish is liberating in the way that acquiring all useful skills is liberating: it increases a person's capacity for autonomous action. On the other hand, there can be no question that not all children unambivalently enjoy the tight discipline of the classroom and the controls placed on speech within it. If the lesson described is a kind of rite of passage, the question of its efficacy arises: to what extent do children psychologically accept the "school 'we'" into which they have, as innocent six-year-olds, been led? The question is all the more compelling considering that the linguistic policies and practices current in the Dobra school in the 1990s are incredibly liberal and sensitive when compared to those experienced by these children's parents. The principal of the Dobra school, exceptionally, is himself autochthonous, as well as being a wonderfully gifted educator. The old attitude may be summarized as "You are Poles and we will punish any sign you give of being anything else."

In this light, we can begin to understand that the fact that answering the question "What is this?" in Silesian is humorous does indeed suggest that the psychological acceptance of the school identity is less than complete. So why do kids do it? Well, ask a stupid question . . .

The practice is subversive because it takes advantage of the vulnerability of the teacher at the moment of asking. The question, "What is this?" is purely rhetorical, having the sole function of "getting the students involved." Usually the answer is incredibly obvious. Answering in Silesian exploits the students' being given the stage, however briefly, to break the rules of school discourse. It does so in a way that simultaneously plays on the stereotype of autochthonous Opole Silesians and Silesian speech as backward, awkward, or stupid and, in the telling—in exercising the power momentarily to disrupt the lesson—gives Silesians the last laugh. In laughing, the children give the lie to an implicit insult: that they are so stupid that teachers have to check whether they can really identify a bird, an egg, an insect, houses. It is self-deprecating laughter, but it is the laughter of insight, trickster laughter, laughter of having played the stereotype and, in doing so self-consciously, subverted it. And that trickster character is the essence of other manifestations of Silesian humor as well.

Silesian humor is so culturally specific that you can tell the non-Silesians in a room by the fact that they're not laughing. And yet, it is deeply relational in that the reason they're not laughing is that they don't understand the Silesian position in intergroup dynamics; this is what animates the humor. Take, for example, Marta's niece's aunt through marriage: when Marta's extended family got together to celebrate Eva's First Communion, I knew that her uncle's wife had to be Polish. I had not met them before: Marta is Eva's *mother's* sister, whereas the aunt is her *father's* brother's wife. Only a major celebration would bring the two sides of the family together. Eva's father's grandmother was also there, and it was an interaction with this matriarch that clinched my impression of the in-law aunt's probable Polishness. "D*ej* mi t*a TASZKA!*" (Give me that purse!), the matriarch instructed her imperiously. Her granddaughter-in-law could easily interpret the requested action, that she give her something, because the Silesian is so similar to the Polish, "D*AJ* mi t*Ą* . . . " But she had trouble knowing what to hand over. She reached uncertainly for the purse the old woman seemed to be pointing to, asking, "*TASZKA* to TORBA?" ("*TASZKA* is purse?" Notes, May 30, 1993).

And when somebody told the story about the cat in the Dutch oven, she not only had to be told what the cross-linguistic pun was, but (and this was what I most noticed), she really didn't think it was funny. Everyone else thought it was hilarious.

It was a good moment for that joke, about the cat in the Dutch oven, because only these more distant relatives hadn't heard it. It was a story about my own linguistic socialization. I told it first privately to Marta, having caught on to the zest autochthonous Opole Silesians have for multilingual punning of all sorts. But, as sometimes happened to me in the field (and would that it only happened in the field), I didn't completely understand what I was doing. If I had understood, I wouldn't have been disappointed by the fact that she didn't laugh at all. I would have understood that a joke only comes into its own in the gatherings of small groups of Silesians (in my experience invariably fifteen or fewer), related by familial ties or ties of acquaintance, who gather for food and drink to celebrate birthdays (always) and various other occasions. That's the place for jokes, and at such gatherings Marta told this story many times. Here it is: at one of my first Sunday dinners at Marta's parents' house, when I really did not know anything about anything, I heard Marta's mother making some comment, as she stood by the Dutch oven on the coal stove, about the "ka*c*ka" (pronounced "katska") within. I already knew that Silesian assimilates words from German by adding "-ka" to the German word, like *TASZKA* from German TASCHE, "purse," or *FLASZKA*, from FLASCHE, bottle. Working backward got me to KATZE, "cat." I was not yet as familiar with the fact that /s/, spelled "*c*", is the Silesian phonological equivalent of Polish /ch/, spelled "cz" (remember the hat, *col*pka, CZApka). Ka*c*zka is the Polish word for "duck." So for a moment I did wonder which animal I was eating.

Marta's many repetitions of this story (though I categorically deny that I was ever in any real doubt or that I surreptitiously looked into the pot) proved that the experience fit a cultural joke-telling type. Eva's Polish aunt didn't get it—her lack of response was one indication that this genre is specific to autochthonous Opole Silesian culture.

Here are some other examples of jokes of this genre. Note that some of them don't sound like anyone's actual experience (numbers 1, 2, and perhaps 3). Some of them could well be someone's actual experience, passed on orally (perhaps number 3, and 4, and 5). Some of them are personal experiences remembered and retold over many years (numbers 6 and 7). And some of them are new, like the "cat in the Dutch oven" (number 8). In short, this is a live oral genre. Jokes of this sort are generated on an ongoing basis.

1. The German says: "Po obiedzie *biera* BUCH UND LESE" [After dinner I take a book and read]. The Silesian replies, "A *jol GENAU* tak samo: *buch* i le*za*" [And I exactly the same: collapse on a bed and lie there].This plays on the difference between the German words for "book" and "read" and their Silesian homophones. (January 13, 1993).

2. Two Silesian girls go to work in Opole. They decide they're really going to be Polish, so they put on make-up and everything, and one of them says, "OK, girls, now we're going to speak Polish." Later another says, "JA ZABIŁAM siedem ćmów" [I killed seven moths]. Another corrects her; in Polish it should be "CIEM," because ów is not the genitive plural ending of feminine nouns in Polish (numerals higher than four take the genitive in both). She answers, "Czym? [With what?] *LACZEM*! [With a slipper!]." She mistook the soft "ci" for a hard "cz." (August 1, 1995).

3. Women are standing in a line in a produce store in German times, and one of them says to the others, "Girls, just tell me again what the f*** the German word for *TOMATE* is?" It's TOMATE, loaned into Silesian; the Polish word is POMIDOR (Notes, July 31, 1993).

4. Grandma comes back after her first Christmas Mass after the war, where she hears the Polish Christmas carol, "Lulajże, Jezuniu, lulajże, lulaj." [Hush, little Jesus], In Silesian unfortunately "lul*ej*" means not "hush," but "go wee-wee." She says, "Oh! These Poles, they are without shame, that they sing such things in church!" (Notes, July 31, 1993).

5. Grandpa, on learning that the Polish word for "cup," Silesian *SIOŁLKA*, is FIL-IŻANKA, cracked, "That's because there's such poverty in Poland that they even lick out cups!" The pun turns on -anka being an ending that can nominalize a verb, and on the similarity of FILIŻ with the stem of WYLIŻAĆ, "to lick out" (June 25, 1995).

6. In the tavern in the late evening (November 24, 1992), all dozen or so people in the room got into a long interaction with much joking, most of it linguistic in some respect, some of it sexual. There was a pun made on the word ELF (eleven) and the word SECHS (six). I thought it was a double entendre with "sex," but it was later explained that the sexual content had to do with somebody's having these numbers of children, and should there be more. A woman in her thirties took the role of saying "This talk has gone far enough" at a couple of points; for example, "It's a good thing there are no children here." In the midst of this there was a great deal of laughter over somebody's relating a linguistic experience from schooldays. He was trying to communicate the word "butterfly," without success, so boldly, he had guessed at the Polish word. Instead of saying the Silesian "*SZMETELOŁK*" he said, "szmetelaczek." The Polish word is MOTYL. Cross-linguistic punning is as funny as sex, it seems.

7. Franz Skorupka, who, in chapter 1, reported that when he entered the army he found himself in a unit with many other Silesians, recalled that one of the Poles, trying to be friendly, told them that he, too, knew a little Silesian. "OK," they said, "Tell us what a *CUG* is." (*CUG* < ZUG, train). "Oh," he said, "That's a train" (POCIĄG). "Very good," they said. "Now tell us what an *ANCUG* is." (*ANCUG* < ANZUG, "suit"). "Hmm, *ANCUG*. I guess that must be an express train." (October 25, 1994)

8. Another thing that happened that got retold and laughed over: Marta said to me, "Brr! Pada deszcz!" (Brr! It's raining!) I replied, "Yuk!" She understood my intent, but punned: "Jak? No, jak zwykle, z góry na dól! [How? Why, the usual way, down from above!]" "J" spells the English /y/ sound in Polish. (January 20, 1993).

These jokes are all trickster jokes, but the trickster is not a stock character, such as in the German folk genre called SCHWANK, where the main character, Till Eulenspiegel, always plays a trick on another character; the listeners identify with the trickster, and throughout the joke, they, like him, see through the trick. The trickster and the audience together are as wise as an owl (EULE), and hold the mirror (SPIEGEL) of truth. But in these autochthonous Opole Silesian jokes, the trickster is not a character. The trickster is language itself. It doesn't seem to matter on whom the trick is being played. Sometimes, it's being played on a Pole or a German. But often, it's being played on a Silesian. The autochthonous Opole Silesian listeners see through the trick because they, unlike the characters in the joke, know all the languages in play. These are not ethnic jokes in the sense that they target another group. They are cultural jokes in the sense that it is members of the group who know how to appreciate them.

Consider the joke about the word for "butterfly" (#6). This is a first-person joke, told by the person who experienced the situation himself. But there is a critical difference between the protagonist of the joke and the person telling it, even though they are "the same person." The child protagonist of the joke was tricked by language. The grown-up teller of the joke was not. That is the heart of the humor. These are jokes about people being tricked by language, whoever they may be, told by, and to, people who are not being tricked by language. The reason these jokes are not funny if you're not autochthonous Silesian is that in order to inhabit the role of the insightful, amused listener, you have to be multilingual in Silesian, Polish, and German; this kind of knowledge is a characteristic of being autochthonous Opole Silesian.

But, as the humor in school illustrated, they are in-group jokes whose humor derives, also, from a social field fraught with relations of unequal power among groups. Consider the "trickster" element in the following joke (it was told, in Silesian, by a stand-up comic who performed at the Dobra German Friendship Circle's celebration of "Mothers' and Fathers' Day," May 14, 1995). The protagonist of this and many other jokes is, ostensibly, the comic's brother, Peter:

> He went to Germany, right? Couldn't find work as a welder, so he was ready to take the train home from Cologne; he didn't get work so he wanted to come back from Cologne, and he was already at the train station, but he looks, and across from the train station there's a zoo, and written on the fence of the zoo it says, "Seventeen marks an hour," so he says "I'll go ask." He went to ask and the supervisor speaks really good Polish because he missed the bus back in '45, right? "Sir," [and the supervisor's speech is rendered in a very formal and now somewhat archaic-sounding Silesian] "We've got a very particular job. One of our gorillas died, and we've tanned the skin, and we'd like you to dress up in the skin and if you would, to jump around a little in that cage you see there." Of course Peter says, "Hey, for seventeen

111

marks an hour I can jump around all day." So he starts jumping around, and the people like it! More people come along, a crowd gathers, and Peter jumps more and more, and then he jumps up and grabs hold of this branch they've got in the cage, he wants to swing on the branch, but it breaks and Peter falls right into the tiger cage below!! He starts yelling, "Help! Help! Save me! The tiger's gonna get me!" and the tiger says [in Silesian], "Will you shut up?! They'll fire us both!!"

The teller speaks Silesian, Peter speaks Silesian, the zoo supervisor speaks Silesian, and, in the punch line, the tiger speaks Silesian too. Who are Silesians in this joke? Peter, like practically all Silesian men, goes to Germany looking for work, and he's willing to do something so silly and humiliating as pretending to be a gorilla in a cage for a wage. Peter is taken in, in a sense—he is surprised that the zoo supervisor is, after all, a Silesian, and he's doubly surprised that the tiger is also, like him, a Silesian. His surprise is the audience's surprise, his revelation, the punch line of the joke. In that sense, as well as in the fact that he does something so common to the Silesian experience as to look for work in Germany, Peter is the image of the Silesian. At one level, the image of the Silesian is that of a person being tricked.

But at another level, the picture of Silesians is almost the inverse: not the fool, but the wise owl holding the mirror of truth. The joke shows Silesians as being everywhere, where you'd least expect them, and in the final analysis, the people being taken in are not so much Peter, but the people gawking at the purported gorilla. The revelation at the end reveals to the joke's hearers the depth of the deception perpetrated on the zoo's visitors: they are not only being deceived today, now, in the matter of the gorilla, but they are being deceived on an ongoing basis, regularly, gorilla and tiger and who knows what other animals, by a conspiracy of Silesian zoo supervisor and Silesian workers. In that sense, the joke's on the Germans.

This is a joke that turns the tables, an instance of a genre of humor that depends on the audience's understanding of the tables that are there to be turned. The Silesian sense of humor, then, can be seen as an "integral element of culture," but "culture" inheres in insight and understanding of the power dynamics in play *between* groups. In that sense, "culture" is defined by what surrounds it; defined by its contrast with the harsh oppressive power of the nation-state societies with which Silesian is inextricably entangled.

In that light—though not blinded by it, shading our eyes a bit—consider a joke that reveals these power relations even more clearly. It comes from the same routine as the one about Peter, except that here, the person tricked is a Pole. The Pole is a woman, and, though not presented as a teacher, she certainly acts like one. The setting is not a school, but rather another common point of contact between autochthonous Opole Silesians and immigrant Poles, a grocery store:

> A Silesian girl comes into a store and says, "*I would* like *COOKIES* and *CHOCO-LATE*." The Polish clerk replies, "DEAR, one doesn't TALK that way. One SAYS 'COOKIES' and 'CHOCOLATE.'" The Silesian girl repeats herself: "*YES*, but *I would* like *COOKIES* and *CHOCOLATE*." The clerk tries again: "But DEAR, that's not the right way. You HAVE TO SAY, 'I WOULD like COOKIES and CHOCOLATE.'" The Silesian girl repeats herself in Silesian again. Finally the clerk says, "Look, I'll show you how you're supposed to talk. Here, let's trade places. You come behind the counter and pretend to be the clerk, and I'll go out and come in and pretend to be the customer." So the little girl comes behind the counter and the clerk goes out, and when she comes in she says in perfect Polish, "PLEASE MADAM, I WOULD LIKE COOKIES and CHOCOLATE." The little girl says, "We don't serve *chadziajów* [Polacks] here."

This word, *chadziajów*, is even more harsh than the word "Polack" sounds in English. It is said to derive from the Ukrainian word for "farmer"; it refers to the fact that most of the Poles who arrived in Silesia after the war came from present-day Ukraine, from what Silesians saw as the uncivilized East. It means every negative stereotype that autochthonous Opole Silesians hold about Poles: that they are dirty, disorganized, and lazy.

The word was in pretty common use in Dobra in the 1990s, and people usually didn't remark on it. But they often betrayed some anxiety about it by asking me whether I knew what it meant, and I saw them do the same thing with the other outsider in the village, the German teacher. And occasionally someone tapped the stereotypes (which readers may have found familiar), and made an explicit analogy with American race: soon after I arrived (December 19, 1992), so soon that I didn't know the word yet, my tavern notes say, "[The man] was drunk, a fact evident from his flushed cheeks and his wife's comments. He had some derogatory name for eastern Poles. He told me that they were like blacks in America. That they wanted to get paid for no work. That they were always striking. That was the gist of it." Five months later, (May 3, 1993), again over drinks in the tavern, Brigitte, who helped a lot with the next chapter, shut down a similar commentary from one of her cousins. She had repeatedly told him to stop using the word *chadziaj*. When he persisted, telling me that Poles are like American blacks and that he approves of the KKK, Brigitte glared at him and told him he had it backwards: it's not Poles who are like American blacks, but Silesians, because Silesians are the ones who are oppressed, and "You wouldn't want somebody burning a cross on *your* lawn, would you?!" If Brigitte was worried that her cousin was offending someone she had recently befriended, me, she was right.

Out of the tavern, back to the shop: the joke above plays to both Brigitte's view and her cousin's: Silesians are oppressed, and Poles are, well, I don't quite want to say "stupid," but... let's say that while this woman is tricked by the child, she is also tricked by her own lack of awareness. She seems blind to the fact that she is acting offensively, that her behavior is oppressive. If she knew she were, she wouldn't walk straight into the trap. Powdermaker pointed out long ago that understanding the way that oppression really plays out is much easier for the oppressed than the oppressors (1966: 188). Poles, like some white Americans faced with the Civil Rights movement, claim with some frequency that Silesians and Poles got along splendidly until the activists of the German Minority came along and created problems where before, everyone had been perfectly content with their place in the social order. I heard this view from a priest and from one of Marta's suppliers; I also heard the opinion indirectly, for example, passed on by the school principal, who commented, "They certainly had no problem when they were locking people up for singing German songs."

The Polish woman in this joke doesn't really know what she is suggesting when she says, "Let's trade places." She doesn't know what life is like in that place: the place in the social order where autochthonous Opole Silesians have been placed. The child gave her a quick, sharp lesson. That joke got the biggest laugh of any in the routine, and when I repeated it to an acquaintance who has been the only autochthonous Opole Silesian in an entirely Polish workplace for many years, he laughed so hard he cried.

So here is what we've found in finding culture in autochthonous Opole Silesia: it's about language; it's about power; and if we are going to "get it,"— and now I mean more than just the jokes—we need insight into life in that place in its delicately different shades, gradations, and nuances.

Chapter 5
A CULTURE OF LANGUAGE

In chapter 3, words appeared in the form of names. In chapter 4, they appeared as German loan words valued as especially Silesian and as jokes. In this chapter, we discover how it is that something as small as choosing a word for "chair" can express identity.

It's not that choosing the word *stolik* over the word KRZESŁO and over the word STUHL asserts that one is Silesian rather than Polish or German the way that wearing a bodice with a sash rather than an embroidered black vest asserts that one is Silesian rather than Cracovian. It is much more than a simple matter of contrast. Silesian is a multilingual language, and it is the aspect of autochthonous Opole Silesian life that is most culturally distinctive. In this chapter we find out what that means.

KASIA AND THE SHOVEL

Kasia was really upset at the suggestion that she was habitually using a Polish word for "shovel," and not a Silesian one. In the spring of 1993 (April 23), Kasia was ten, and she and I had a close relationship (she is Marta's niece). We were exploring the grounds of an old house, and we came across an old, broken shovel. She called it "łopata" and I said, "szufelka." She said, "Right, *łopata* is Silesian and SZUFELKA is Polish." Going on what I'd heard, as well as the obvious German origin of the word, I argued: "No, ŁOPATA is Polish and *SZUFELKA* is Silesian." She insisted. I said, "Well, we'll go ask Grandpa."

Grandpa backed me up. Kasia wailed, "But I always say 'łopata'! I don't even know what 'szufelka' is!!" Her grandfather, visibly impatient with the outburst, responded, "You can say whatever you want to. You can even sing if you want."

Why did Kasia get so upset at the idea that she was unknowingly using a Polish word instead of a Silesian one? (By the way, other Silesian speakers told me that *łopata* did sound more Silesian to them; Polish too, after all, has a lot of German loan words.) The way she wailed, the way she distanced herself from what she felt was the Polish word ("I don't even know what it is!"), suggests that the matter touched her at her core, that it was a matter of identity. Autochthonous Opole Silesians learn Polish and German in school and from the media, but they learn Silesian from their own community. It is theirs in a way that the standard languages are not; Silesian is the language that most reveals their minds. Kasia felt like her unknowing use of a Polish word somehow made her different than what she feels herself to be. Kasia is a Silesian. She's not a Pole. It was a matter of contrast.

But it is not simply a matter of contrast. She might have gotten more sympathy from Grandpa, if it were. There's a lot more at stake here. Two axes of tension suspend these kinds of minute linguistic choices, and these axes, these tensions, structure the complexity of Silesian speech. The first concerns how people think about language: it is a matter of linguistic ideology. The second has to do with how people make meaning with language: it is a matter of using language, of linguistic pragmatics. In the final analysis, the two intersect one another.

Linguistic Ideology: Tolerance vs. Loyalty

Silesian is a multilingual language, drawing on multiple linguistic sources to accomplish its communicative tasks. It is highly permeable to Polish and German. It has an enormous number of loan words. People switch among languages easily. What people define as "Silesian" can vary widely: from speech that is almost linguistically indistinguishable from standard Polish to speech that a Polish speaker would not be able to understand, as well as from speech that is entirely free of German influence to speech that is thick with German words and phrases. For people used to thinking of "a language" as something standardized by institutions of education, business, and media, this degree of variation can seem bewildering. It is not bewildering to autochthonous Opole Silesians, nor is their situation unusual in the overall spread of global languages. As Suzanne Romaine has pointed out, "Membership in a community may be established and maintained primarily in terms of interactional rather than language norms" (1994: 23). In other words, being a competent speaker of Silesian means knowing the social rules by which people use the historical resources of Silesian *and* German *and* Polish.

When Kasia's grandfather rebuked her with the words "You can say whatever you want to. You can even sing if you want," he was reminding her that autochthonous Opole Silesians value this permeability. In this sense, autochthonous Opole Silesians are much more like the East Sutherland Gaelic-speaking fisherfolk, with their "socially unweighted variation" (Dorian 2010) than like members of minority language groups engaged in processes of language reclamation that involve "purity," such as Catalan. Autochthonous Opole Silesians do not make Silesian the object of an ideology of linguistic purity. They are loyal to it; that's why Kasia got upset. But they value linguistic tolerance. That's why her grandfather got annoyed with her.

In the spring of 1995, after almost two years' experience in Dobra, I had established rapport to the level that I knew people would be willing to answer my direct questions. This enabled me to employ structured linguistic elicitation techniques, which are analyzed later in the chapter, and it allowed me to conduct a small-scale survey of language attitudes. I kept it with me and pulled it out, asking people to participate as opportunity presented itself. Ultimately, I gathered responses from sixteen respondents, some of whom I spoke with together with spouses, others singly. Although the number of respondents was small, consensus emerged on a number of points, showing that I had been "on to something" in the questions I asked. I was after responses in several realms. First, how do people think about what language it is that they speak in various situations? Responses to prompts concerning which language people think they're speaking supported the impression that they define their social milieu as Silesian-speaking. People have a strong sense that they know what they're doing when they speak. To the statement "I usually speak Silesian among Silesians," twelve out of fifteen respondents gave an unequivocal "yes." One respondent replied, "You feel it out, usually talk to older people in Silesian, other than that you accommodate the other person," (accomodation, note, is a form of tolerance). The other naysayers were the German Minority leaders I discussed in chapter 3; they were managing my impressions. In other words, only people juggling the particular contradictions of being a German-identified autochthonous Opole Silesian talking to an outsider said anything other than that they spoke Silesian among Silesians. And to the statement, "I speak 'this way/that way' [a Silesian idiom for code-switching], but I always know what is in Polish and what is in Silesian," *everyone* said "yes."

So much for knowing what you're doing, but what about preferences? To the statement "I can speak Polish, but I prefer to speak Silesian," eleven people agreed, while three said it depended on the situation. Two protested that I hadn't offered German as a first-choice option, but both of them nevertheless ranked Silesian above Polish. One woman expressed her discomfort with Polish as follows: "Because I speak five words in Polish, and with the sixth I'm a goner." Furthermore, thirteen respondents agreed that Silesians should pass on the Silesian dialect to the next generation, while one said it didn't matter and one equivocated.

In general then, a widespread sense of purposeful speaking of Silesian and a high valuation of the language, as we would expect in any linguistic minority in Europe. And speaking Silesian is wrapped up with a sense of being Silesian in a way we would also expect in language-symbolizes-culture Europe (as discussed in chapter 3). Nine respondents agreed that a person who stops speaking Silesian stops being 100 percent Silesian. The chair of the Dobra German Friendship Circle and his wife disagreed; interestingly, since their Silesian was almost indistinguishable from Polish at that age, so did Kasia and her sister Eva. One respondent, Urszula Krysiak, followed the logic of the statement to its conclusion: the problem with Silesians who stop speaking Silesian is precisely that they *do* remain Silesian. For Silesians, speaking Polish in a Silesian-speaking environment is showing off, whereas for Poles to speak Polish is fine, wherever they are. If Silesians who stopped speaking Silesian also stopped *being* Silesian, it would be fine for them too.

The particular experience of having a language associated with one's own group, while experiencing other languages as well, leads to a particular form of attachment. To the statement "Silesian is prettier than Polish," the nearest thing to disagreement that I was offered was the assertion that you just can't compare them. Five respondents agreed unequivocally and without commentary. However, this statement brought the value of tolerance into play: "For us, yes, but that's a personal matter. I couldn't speak clean Polish with my neighbors, and you have to hold to the traditions of your birthplace." And, "For me, it's pretty. Maybe it disturbs others. But every dialect has its own sound, and I would not be disturbed by the sound of other dialects." And, "It *is* pretty. But I also like the sound of Polish when I hear it on the radio or TV." One respondent said that it depended; that, for example, he did not like Polish swear words. Polish swear words are "sharp," whereas Silesian swear words are "more funny." This is a particularly clear projection of attitudes about people onto language: when Poles swear, they mean to hurt, but when Silesians swear, on some level they're only kidding.

Franz Skorupka, Brigitte's husband, also mentioned humor: Silesian is prettier and funny.

"Why funny?" I asked. "You mean all the *WICE* [Silesian jokes]?"

"Yes, but just the words are funny. Like the verb, '*wylonać*,' from '*lon*.'

['*Łon*,' the third-person masculine pronoun, also means 'the whatsit.'] Or, take *żdżiebko* [a little bit—in Polish, TROSZECZKA]. *Żdżiebko* is a funny word. Polish is a serious language. 'Ciekawy jeSTEM KTÓRA jeST teraz godzina' [I am curious what hour it is now] is a serious-sounding sentence.[1] Or take *chadziel* [outhouse]. If I say to a Pole, '*kaj san* jes*[Ø] chadziel*' [where is the outhouse here], he won't know what that is and he'll follow me in!"

Franz is an accomplished teller of stories and jokes and the most linguistically sensitive person I worked with in Silesia (as well as a gifted woodcarver). He was pointing out innovativeness, onomatopeioa[2] and informality—all of which he appreciates in Silesian, but not in Polish. Quite simply, he can do more with Silesian. Silesian reveals his creative mind; Polish merely communicates.

"I speak to my children in Silesian," Franz Skorupka once told me, "because I am Silesian" (October 25, 1994). Pride in the group equates to pride in the language, here as elsewhere in Europe. But this pride exists within a field of creative tension. In our very first discussion of language, when Marta's second cousin Iwona invited me to meet Franz and Brigitte at her house because she considers them among the best Silesian speakers in Dobra (April 24, 1993), Franz announced,

"Bo JA też MOGĘ MÓWIĆ, *ino* lepiej mi *sie gołdać*."

[Because I also can speak, but better for me to speak.]

That is, idiomatically, "I can speak Polish, but I like speaking Silesian better." It was a neat linguistic trick, turning on the fact that the word MÓWIĆ, "speak," is both a Polish word and not a Polish word at the same time. There are boundaries between languages, and we "translate" (carry across) between languages; that's what I did when I used the word "speak" to translate MÓWIĆ. *Gołdać* is a Silesian word, and MÓWIĆ is a Polish word; they both translate to "speak" in English. That's how it works when you think about languages as clearly bounded, and Silesians can appreciate the apparent silliness—how can one prefer speaking to speaking? On the other hand, for autochthonous Opole Silesians *gołdać* specifically means "to speak Silesian," and MÓWIĆ means "to speak Polish." That's what gives the statement its idiomatic, actual meaning—that Franz prefers speaking Silesian. And because that meaning of MÓWIĆ—"to speak Polish"—exists only for Silesians, MÓWIĆ, becomes a Silesian word, *MÓWIĆ*. That's the kind of subtle, playful meaning-making that is possible with an ideology of language that allows speakers to intermix.

It is the potential for these wonderfully subtle kinds of wordplay that would be sacrificed if people were to get too hung up on what is Silesian and what is not Silesian. It's an appreciation of that possible loss that leads grandfathers to tell growing children, sing if you want, but don't get upset about what's the real Silesian word for this or that. Besides, two totalitarian regimes took an attitude of linguistic purity—toward German and then toward Polish—and autochthonous Opole Silesians suffered because of it. The community value is not to do that with their own language, Silesian. That's what was at stake in the little family kerfuffle over the word for shovel.

Yet, tension remains. If tolerance always trumps loyalty, if everyone can say whatever they want, couldn't that mean the end of Silesian entirely? Why speak Silesian at all? And if the community gave up Silesian entirely, it would no longer have a language of its own on the basis of which to distinguish its linguistic values from the totalitarian ideology of linguistic purity.

This question of whether the boundaries among languages matter or not, and of what is at stake in a "yes" or "no" answer, is the field of creative tension within which pride in Silesian exists. This tension is not something I ever heard autochthonous Opole Silesians discuss directly. What they state is the value of tolerance. My statement "It's impolite to correct somebody's speech. As long as you can understand, let them talk as they want" evoked strong agreement from all respondents. Comments included, "Different people speak Silesian differently," "Poles get on our nerves by taking it on themselves to teach us Polish," "It's uncivilized," "If someone corrects you, you feel stupid. It's like he's saying he's better than you. No, you should listen and be quiet," and "I can't even imagine correcting someone's speech; it's so tactless." Yet as we continue, in this chapter, to explore the rich creativity of the Silesian culture of language, bear in mind that both horns of the linguistic ideology dilemma reflect Silesia's place between. They have the language loyalty typical of Europeans, and expectable of Europeans in a multilingual speech environment. On the other hand, their community has a value of linguistic tolerance which, itself, can be seen as cognizant of their group's linguistically oppressed position. As we continue to explore the cultural creativity that permeates the question of how one maintains a sense that one is speaking Silesian, of what "Silesian," after all, is, keep this tension in mind. We will return to it in the last section of this chapter.

MAKING MEANING: REGISTER VS. REFERENCE

Grandpa was also, of course, essentially correct. If everyone knows the words in all three languages, any one of them will convey meaning; if everybody understands all lexical alternates similarly at a nitty-gritty Saussurean linguistic level of "sound-image referencing concept," then it doesn't matter whether you use one sound-image or another.

A CULTURE OF LANGUAGE

I have heard it remarked that "DZBANEK, *KONEFKA*, KANNE, to jedno i to samo." It almost rhymes. "PITCHER, *PITCHER*, PITCHER, it is one and the same." Indeed. At the level of semantics, or reference, it doesn't matter. Yet precisely because it doesn't matter referentially, the contrast of linguistic alternates is able to carry kinds of meaning that have nothing to do with shovelness, or pitcher-ness. With referential function taken care of, pragmatic function can come to the fore.

Recall the situation in school, where a teacher's question, "What's this?" draws an answer in Silesian which makes everybody laugh. Another dimension of the humor is that the kids are poking fun at the teacherly insistence that it matters whether the answer is given in Silesian or in Polish, when on a semantic, referential level, it doesn't—as long as everyone knows what both words mean. In this sense, it is a move of demystification, as in "The Emperor's New Clothes." It matters socially, pragmatically, only, because Silesian words don't belong in the culture of "us as people in school." This is a tension—it matters / it doesn't matter—that is different from the loyalty/tolerance tension, because this one operates in all languages by virtue of the availability, in all languages, of alternate ways of accomplishing semantically equivalent reference, or "saying the same thing." Stated differently, autochthonous Opole Silesians' languages function as registers with respect to one another, where "registers" are described as follows:

> Language users often employ labels like "polite language," "informal speech," "upper-class speech," "women's speech," "literary usage," "scientific term," "religious language," "slang," and others, to describe differences among speech forms. Metalinguistic labels of this kind link speech repertoires to enactable pragmatic effects, including images of the person speaking (woman, upper-class person), the relationship of speaker to interlocutor (formality, politeness), the conduct of social practices (religious, literary, or scientific activity); they hint at the existence of cultural models of speech—a metapragmatic classification of discourse types—*linking speech repertoires to typifications of actor, relationship, and conduct*. This is the space of register variation conceived in intuitive terms. (Agha 2004: 23, emphasis mine)

The different registers in anyone's language, or languages, can be played with, manipulated, used to make strategic communicative choices, by everyone; it can be done in "all speech communities that have more than one 'way of speaking' (i.e., all, as far as we know)." (Woolard 2004: 74) That's why the tension, "it matters / it doesn't matter," is universal, while the tension between loyalty and tolerance depends on historical experience. However, the two tensions do intersect, otherwise the same anecdote about Kasia would not be able to illustrate both; this is what we will return to at the end of the chapter.

All kinds of linguistic alternates are capable of carrying nonreferential contrasting meaning: those of sound (phonological), of words (lexical), of grammar (syntactic), of intonation or accent (prosodic), and others. But for our immediate purposes, we need only add one item to Agha's list of "typifications," and explore how autochthonous Opole Silesians link speech repertoires to typifications of the contexts of experience of objects. In other words, we need only consider lexical alternates: PITCHER, *PITCHER*, PITCHER; nouns which "mean the same thing," but picture them in different realms of experience to see what speech repertoires the pictures evoke. In their difference from one another, the "same things" have meanings that have nothing to do with what they specify in the material world.

For referentially, that is what nouns do: they specify. DZBANEK, *KONEFKA*, KANNE, it's the thing you pour milk from. Lexical reference specifies this object in a field of material reality, gives it a name based on perceivable characteristics. What perceivable characteristics "count" in this specification varies by language; Saussure's point that different languages conceptually partition the world differently is apropos here: for example, in writing this, I have been puzzling over my translation, knowing that "pitcher" has given readers an image of ceramics and dining tables, while the referent that I know of all three Silesian alternates is a metal thing that does not come indoors, but rather travels back and forth from entryway to cow stall. The next stop for the milk is the pan in which it is boiled, and is the ceramic or glass thing on the table also DZBANEK, *KONEFKA*, KANNE? At that point it was not "Please pass the pitcher," but "Please pass the milk." It is a question of what perceivable characteristics are salient in this instance of naming, of the specifics of specifying, of how Silesian referentially partitions the world. In English I would say "pitcher" whether it's metal or ceramic, whether it's used outdoors or indoors, but is that the same in Silesia? I'm not sure.

Register, on the other hand, is not a matter of picking something out of a field of material reality (denotation), but rather of placing it into a field of social experience (connotation). The field is different, for while reference partitions the world according to perceivable characteristics, register operates among various social contexts. And the order of these various social contexts, in turn, is not an order of arbitrary agreement on whether what you pour from on the table should be called by a different name than what you pour from outside, but a different kind of cultural order: not an ordering of community perception, but an ordering of community experience. Consider, for example, the word "decant." Its definition reads, "gradually pour (wine, port or another liquid) from one container into another, typically in order to separate out sediment" (Oxford dictionaries). More generally, however, you pour milk; you decant wine. The only other use of "decant" that I've ever heard occurred in a recent argument with airport security. At issue was a bottle of medicinal lotion, bigger than 100 ml. We hadn't brought a doctor's note. After some minutes of argument, the officer told me that I could go buy a 100 ml plastic bottle in the secure area of the airport, return to security, and decant some of the lotion. Apparently "pour" didn't fit the gravity of the situation.

Just as the ordering of community perception differs cross-linguistically, so does this ordering of community experience. The discussion of the last few pages can be resolved into an ethnographic question about autochthonous Opole Silesia: what cultural orders of experience are tied through lexical register to the contrast among lexical alternates in circulation in the community? How do lexical alternates originating in Silesian, Polish, and German form enregistered alternate sets in which a choice of one or another alternate invokes one or another culturally specified context? How is autochthonous Opole Silesian culture expressed in such choices: for example, in choosing a word for "chair"?

Lexical Register as a Cultural Map of Space and Time

The answers to these questions, it emerges, also depend on an understanding of Silesia's historical and continuing position between Germany and Poland. I hypothesized that this would be the case, and constructed an elicitation technique to explore the hypothesis. Here's how I investigated it: I chose seven objects from common experience: bicycles, eggs, buttons, houses, girls, chairs, and gates ("chairs" finishes this exploration; "gates" takes us beyond it). These objects, I knew, could be referred to, at least, either with a Polish- or a Silesian-origin word, and both alternates were widely known and used in the community. I knew that German-origin and German words were also likely to be invoked. The respondent's word choice was to be guided by contextual cues of the referent in question as shown in different pictures. The contextual clues evoked a local vs. a nonlocal context, and the present vs. the past.

It is very important to note that I did *not* in any way guide respondents as to "what language" to use in responding. I spoke Polish, respondents spoke Silesian in some degree of standardization or lack thereof. Any word they knew that could refer to the target object in the picture was fair game, and I did not ask them to evaluate whether the words they had given me were "Polish" or "Silesian" or "German." I did not want to seem to be asking, "In which language do you feel it appropriate to refer to this object as pictured this way?" I wanted people to have the freedom of their own vocabularies, knowing myself, as they know, that the words that make them up come from different languages, and are, in the case of German and Polish, incorporated into Silesian speech to different degrees. In assigning fonts to the responses, then, I depended on knowledge of local evaluation of linguistic origins that I had gained in participant observation.

A verbal description of the pictures precedes discussion of results for each. Responses to all the objects proved revelatory, though not always in the way I expected. Pictures of bicycles, eggs, buttons, houses, and girls worked well. There was trouble with "gate" because I failed to make a semantic distinction between a vehicle-sized gate and a pedestrian-sized gate. (In English we have the word "wicket," which refers to particular type of pedestrian-sized gate that's next to a larger gate, but this word is uncommon in the United States.) But working through my confusion with consultants opened my mind to how differences of register can become, with time, semantic distinctions, which will be discussed at the end of the chapter. Of all the words chosen, however, it was the choices of words for "chair" that most beautifully illustrated the workings of register and the particular culture of register in Silesia.

As stated above, the contextual cues contrasted in two ways: by proximity in time, and by proximity in social/cultural space. Respondents could recognize, in other words, that something was modern, or that it was archaic; that it was something local, or something distant. Previous research suggests that the alternate drawn from the "more intimate" language of the repertoire would be chosen to name the more culturally proximate objects (see the conclusion to this section). What is interesting in this case, however, is that the inclusion of that second axis of contrast, and the availability of material drawn from not two but three linguistic sources, allows us to see something much more nuanced.

Seventeen speakers gave me responses to these prompts, though not everyone gave responses to all of them. Most were interviewed individually, while two couples were interviewed together, one in the presence of their two young sons, one of whom offered some responses; and one respondent's adult daughter came along and offered some responses. Eleven respondents were female, and six were male, which reflects the difficulty of finding men at home in Silesia. Respondents ranged in age from under ten to over seventy. Two had acquired Polish first, eight Silesian, and seven German.

Which alternate, I asked, "fit better" with which picture? For the sake of clarity, I always began with bicycle, because the contrast between Silesian *koło* ("wheel"—a translation of German RAD, from FAHRRAD) and Polish ROWER is a common and widespread linguistic stereotype brought up almost always by both Silesians and Poles, in conversations about the Silesian dialect (even, on one occasion, by a four-year-old child, November 11, 1994). Thus the bicycle offered a culturally available example of there being "different words for the same thing," and a good frame for my saying, "if you had to choose one of the words to go with one of the pictures, which word would you choose for which picture?"

One definition will be necessary here. When two ways of saying something convey the same referential meaning, but one implies for speakers that the referent is remarkable in some way, linguists call that alternate "marked." For example, the questions "How tall is he?" and "How short is he?" both mean the same thing, and both get an answer in feet and inches. But the first is "unmarked," the second, "marked," because it implies for speakers that "he" is extraordinary, remarkable: short beyond expectation. In the same way, when more than one word for the same thing circulates in a community, one of them may express the speaker's impression that a particular thing is extraordinary.

BICYCLE

One picture, taken from a magazine advertisement, pictures a cyclist riding down a hill covered with golden autumn leaves, toward the viewer's right. The cyclist is wearing cycling clothes, most notably a helmet and tight shorts, and the bicycle is a mountain bike.

The other picture is a photograph taken locally, showing a large-wheeled bicycle leaning against a fence. The bicycle is painted black and shows some rust. It is equipped with a white wire basket on a frame attached to the rear wheel. It is a woman's bicycle, and the frame between the seat and the handlebars is curved, rather than straight, which marks it as an old bicycle in local knowledge. In fact, the brand label on the shaft of the handlebars says "Wanderer," which means that the bicycle is of German, hence pre-1945, construction. This label is not visible in the picture, but the bicycle is a clear instance of a local type.

The following tables list all the words that any respondent gave for each picture, and the number of total responses. They do not specify how each person responded to the prompt pictures. It will be necessary to do that only for "girl" and "chair."

125

For all respondents, the contrast between referents was obvious and obviously corresponded to the contrast between Silesian- and Polish-origin lexemes. ROWER was chosen by eight respondents; the German words by two. Even people unable to give an explanation for their choice, including a six-year-old boy, made it. With the exception of two respondents who cited the technical term ROWER GÓRSKI ("mountain bike") discussed briefly below, the choice was always explained in terms of cultural and temporal proximity:

> ". . . traditional, looks like something seen in a village."
> "This is 'ROWER GÓRSKI', and this is '*koło* nasze'" [i.e., "This is a 'mountain bike' and "this is 'our kind of a bike.'"]
> "[The old local bicycle] is associated with childhood, whereas the new one is different, not everyday."
> ". . . a village bicycle, right here [u nas] in Silesia, whereas [the magazine ad bicycle] is 'extra.'"
> "Because this one looks Silesian, and old, like grandmothers ride. ROWER is a new generation, a mountain bike, it's more Polish, everyone rides that kind, whereas—yes!—this is a bicycle that only Silesians ride."

For some older speakers, however, the newness and foreignness of the mountain bike were associated with German, rather than Polish: the two German responses came from speakers over sixty. Importantly, this suggests a contrast of Silesian with *either* standard language. The choice of which standard language to use in contrast to Silesian seems to depend on age. The commentary by a woman in her seventies on the picture of the mountain bike deserves consideration in this regard: the bike was being ridden by

TABLE 5.1
Responses for "Bicycle"

old local (snapshot)	new (magazine ad)
koło	ROWER
	FAHRRAD
	RENNRAD

(10 responses)

A CULTURE OF LANGUAGE

SPORTOWIEC, jakiś RENNFAHRER
[an athlete, some sort of racing cyclist]

This woman did not use German to name the racing bike; the response she offered was ROWER. However, it is clear that Polish and German both serve to symbolize the contrast with Silesian. The rider was young (the respondent pointed out), and a specialist. In contrast the old local bike "might be ridden either by a young person or an old one, because you could take it to do grocery shopping, for any occasion."

Two uses of standard language overlay one another here. First, the Polish symbolizes the foreignness of the bicycle. Second, the German is used as the finale, the finishing touch. This is a very common use of German among autochthonous Opole Silesians. It is of a piece with the following examples:

1. Two men, age about sixty, were hanging radiators in a house. After completing the installation of a metal hook, one of the men tapped it with a tool and remarked with satisfaction to the other: "Helmut, ES KLINGELT" [It rings!] (Notes, December 2, 1992)

2. The following conversation took place in the tavern, between a customer who had ordered coffee and the server. The customer said, "Proszę też mleko i cukier na to [Please also milk and sugar for that]." The server replied, "Cukier jest, nie ma mleka [There's sugar, but there is no milk]." Customer: "To SAHNE! [Then cream!]." Server: "Też nie ma [None of that either]." "Ale ma być mleko! [But there should be milk!]." "Mamy cukier, proszę pana, ale nie mamy mleka [We have sugar, if you please sir, but we do not have milk]." "ABER OHNE MILCH SCHMECKT DER KAFFEE NICHT! [But the coffee does not taste good without milk!]." (Fulbright Interim Report, February 1993)

3. A "Sound of Music" exit: After an afternoon gathering in the tavern, it came time for Magda's family to go home. Their father brought the car to the front, while their mother encouraged the three children into winter outerwear. As is customary, the children were encouraged to drink some juice before leaving. Nine-year-old Kasia drank, adjusted her scarf, went to the door, turned, and said, "Dobranoc!" [Good night!] to the assembled company. Her seven-year-old sister Eva followed her exactly, a moment later. But when five-year-old Łukaś, the youngest and last, got to the door, he turned and said, "Dobranoc! GUTE NACHT!" The remaining adults laughed in an "isn't he cute" kind of way (Notes, November 26, 1992).

EGG

Three snapshots: One shows a single egg in a straw-filled metal box of the kind Silesians give hens to nest in. The second shows several eggs in a trans-

127

parent plastic jar on shelves displaying other dairy products: the typical presentation of eggs in a store. There was a third snapshot, which simply shows an egg against a dark background, but this did not capture most respondents' attention.

TABLE 5.2
Responses for "Egg"

nest	uncontextualized	store
je*jc*o, ja*jc*o (dialectal variants)	jAJKo, EI	jAJKo, EI

(four responses. The other respondents had only one word, jajko, in their speech.)

Silesian for the egg in the nest, Polish *or* German for the egg in the store. "Because in a store, you say JAJKO for *jajco*," and "because that's what shop assistants say," were the reasons given for assigning the Polish alternative to the store display eggs. The woman who assigned the German word said that the eggs were surrounded by products with German labels; thus she was making it "fit," in a common move of linguistic aesthetics. (Although it was not a "German egg," and the photo was taken in a local store, she may have been right about the labels, since there are a lot of German products on the market in Poland). The woman who assigned EI to the uncontextualized egg may have wanted to give each picture a different word.

BUTTON

One shows a tall man, leaning slightly backward in the picture, dressed in a suit of a dark blue or black, consisting of trousers, white shirt, tie, vest and jacket. The jacket is unbuttoned, and buttons are visible on the vest, which is done up.

The other picture shows a green felt jacket without cuffs, lapels, or flaps over the pockets. Next to it is a green oblong cap, coming to a point in front and back, with a furrow down the middle and feather on one side. There is no person in this picture.

TABLE 5.3
Responses for "Button"

suit vest	green felt jacket
GUZIK	*KNEFLIK, KNEFLE* (a variant)
	GUZIK (with commentary)

(eight responses.)

Explanations for assigning the Silesian-origin word to the vest clustered around issues of cultural proximity and temporality. The suit was described as "international," "elegant," and "for a wedding, holiday, or church," whereas the vest was "old," "old-fashioned," "associated with childhood," "like a TRACHTENKLEID [regional traditional dress]," "regional," "more sporty—for an occasion on the sports field,[3] or singing—not for church."

This consensus ranged across age and gender. However, two women in their twenties, while commenting that *KNEFLIK* is appropriate to the vest and that "older people" or "my grandmother" say *KNEFLIK*, stated that they themselves use *GUZIK* in their Silesian.

A seventeen-year-old girl, in fact, wanted to choose *KNEFLIK*, but needed help to do so: it did not belong to her active vocabulary. I saw her struggling and asked, "Are you trying to remember the word *KNEFLIK*?" She said she was.

HOUSE

Three pictures, two snapshots: One shows a small, square, grey-plastered house with sloped roof and one brick chimney, with fence in front and door at the side. It is a typical Silesian village house of postwar construction. It is in Dobra; one or two respondents recognized which house it was. A second shows a large, elaborate house, intricately decorated with porches, porticoes and columns set far back from the fence. It is one of several houses on the main road to Opole reputed to have been built by people known as "Gypsies" or "new rich" within the last five years. (I do not know whether they are actually Roma or are simply so identified because of the stereotypical association of "Gypsies" with ostentation.) And the third picture was taken from a booklet by the outdoor Museum of the Opole Silesian Village. It shows a collection of restored buildings mainly from the eighteenth century: two wood-plank houses with terrace-thatch roofs, one seen from the side, one from the end, with part of the roof of a third visible at the left of the picture, and a crowd of people in modern dress talking in small groups or examining something displayed at little wooden booths in front of the houses. Some people guessed the origin of the pictures taken from this booklet.

TABLE 5.4
Responses for "House"

local contemporary	archaic Silesian	contemporary foreign
DOM	*chałpa*	BUDYNEK (building)
chałpa	*chałpka*	BUDYNEK MIESZKALNY
	DOMEK (diminutized)	(residential building)

TABLE 5.4 *(CONT.)*
Responses for "House"

SKANSEN (a term the respondent had heard on the radio for such old houses)	PAŁAC (palace) VILLA ZAMEK (castle) GMACH (edifice) DOM

(nine responses.)

Five respondents called the contemporary house DOM, while four called it *chałpa*. This suggests that both words are in fairly wide circulation. For some, *chałpa* has taken on associations of archaism, but not for all. One person chose DOM for the local house because it's "contemporary," yet another said "*chałpa, chałpa* normalna." On the archaic house, one person commented, "*Chałpa* fits better, just like in Polish it would be CHAŁUPA." The wife of the chair of the German Minority repeated the earlier comment that the archaic house has associations "with childhood, when we used to speak Silesian more." (She and her husband have abandoned the dialect as much as possible). The woman who gave us the assessment of the cyclist, above, reached for Polish to explain that while both were *chałpa*, one was DOM MIESZKALNY (a residential house) and the other DOM ZABITKOWY (a historical house). (Here we see the standard language called upon when greater specificity is desired, an issue which will be discussed further in chapter 8.)

It's interesting that the contemporary house could be called by the unmarked Polish word for "house," whereas the archaic one could not. These are the response pairs respondents came up with: contemporary, DOM: archaic, *chałpa* (4); *chałpa*: *chałpa* (2); *chałpa*: *chałpka* or SKANSEN; *chałpa*: DOMEK; DOM: DOMEK. In seven cases, the extraordinariness of the archaic prompt was expressed using marked pairs, but the marked pairs were different: Polish : Silesian, unmarked : diminutized (a common mechanism for creating markedness pairs in Polish), and unmarked : special register. *Chałpka* and DOMEK are diminutives. SKANSEN is a word the respondent heard used in reference to such houses on the radio, a special word. What is important about this is that it points out that for respondents, the contrast among source languages is one *among* ways of symbolizing contrasts. It functions, in this case, in the same way as diminutization functions, and in the same way that calling on a special word functions. It is a register modality among register modalities.

With "bicycle," "button," and "egg," it was often the Polish term that seemed marked. With "house," we see that Silesian can also convey extraordinariness. Once a speaker assimilates a Polish word, its Silesian alternate becomes marked.

I included the fancy new house more or less as a joke; it elicited a number of synonyms, all drawn from Polish.

GIRLS

Three pictures: One picture, from a magazine, shows a small girl seated at a low table, set with doll-size plates and teacups. She is evidently about three or four years old. She is dressed up in a light-blue patterned dress. She has long blond hair tied with a ribbon. On her right is seated a teddy bear, on her left a doll dressed in an old-fashioned dress. She is leaning toward the teddy bear with the doll teapot in her hand, pouring him imaginary tea. A second picture (in black and white, xeroxed) shows a gymnasium scene in which several rows of teenage girls are engaged in calisthenics. In some rows, the girls have their arms straight out to the side at shoulder-height; in others, they are squatting. The gymnasium has a balcony; ropes hang from the walls, where there are also vertical climbing bars. The girls are dressed in below-the-knee loose-fitting shorts and sailor blouses. It is easy to see that the scene is of pre–World War I vintage (1910, as it happens). The third picture is a photograph of a girl of about ten on a large, rusty swing, with fields in the background. She is dressed in a nylon jacket and jeans. Her dress, the scene, and the fact of the picture being a snapshot identify her as local; in fact, a few respondents recognized her.

Because respondents had three pictures to work with, they were able to make two discriminations, and, if they wanted, discriminations along both axes. The second discrimination, inevitably, was constrained by whatever choice the person had already made. Because of this, it is useful to consider the responses of each respondent individually:

TABLE 5.5
Responses for "Girl"

	magazine	local	1910
Respondent 1	DZIEWCZYNKA	*dziołcha*	PANIENKA
R2	DZIEWCZYNKA	*dziołcha*	DZIEWCZYNKA
R3	—	*dziołcha*	DZIEWCZYNKA, *dziejwecka*
R4	*dziołcha,*	*dziołcha*	DZIEWCZYNKA

TABLE 5.5 *(CONT.)*
Responses for "Girl"

	DZIECKO		
R5	DZIECKO	DZIEWCZYNA	*dziołcha*
R6	*dziołska*	MÄDCHEN	*FRELKA*

One would expect the local pre-adolescent girl to be called *dziołcha* in four of six responses, because "girl" in Silesia is used as a term of address. Even I, then around thirty, was called "*dziołcha*" by people of my parents' age with whom I had close relationships. One respondent, recognizing the girl, said, laughing,

> To jest *dziołcha*, bo to jest *dziołcha* Stankowa!!
> That is *girl*, because that is *girl* Stanik [+adj. ending]
> "That's a *girl*, because that's the Stanik *girl*!!"

That being the case, it's the exceptions that require explanation. The grandmother who said MÄDCHEN for the local girl commented, "because it could be [my granddaughter]." In her three-generation family, the children are being raised trilingually, spoken to only in Polish by their father, only in Silesian by their grandfather, and only in German by her, while their mother speaks all three with them. This strategy earns them the respect of neighbors, but the family is exceptional. Few Silesian girls get called MÄDCHEN on a regular basis in everyday life.

The respondent who said DZIEWCZYNA to this picture, exceptionally, had gravitated first toward the 1910 picture, saying they were *dziołchy* because they "look folklorey." Emphasizing the temporal axis may then have led her to use Polish for the modern pictures in contrast. It was young respondents who chose a high-register Polish word (PANIENKA) to express archaism and the associations of institutional context, and two older respondents who used an archaic Silesian word, *dziejwecka* and a German loan (*FRELKA*<FRÄULEIN).

As for the little girl in the magazine picture, her appellation seemed to turn on that of the other two. Respondent 1, as mentioned, was forming a contrast of the modern pictures with the archaic; she used Polish for both contemporary girls. Respondents 2 and 3 contrasted the cultural proximity of the "Stanik girl," to the cultural distance of the tea-party magazine girl and gave her her unmarked Polish appellation. However, she was awfully cute, and one respondent, interviewed when there happened to be a four-year-old girl in the room, said with a warm smile that she was *dziołcha* or "dziecko," "like Agata here." Respondent 6 is a special case in that her intimate relationship with a girl is a German-speaking one: for her, exceptionally, *dziołska* is a comparatively emotionally distant term.

So far, we've seen that the contrast among words originating in the three languages serves to index the context of referents in several ways: Silesian for the familiar, Silesian bicycle, Polish for the egg pictured in a context in which Polish would be spoken, Silesian for the archaic vest button recognized as worn in Silesia, as opposed to Polish for the fancy suit button not worn by autochthonous Opole Silesians. In the case of "house," the fact that, for some speakers, *chałpa* has been replaced by DOM allowed us to see how speakers used a variety of strategies to symbolize a contrast between an archaic Silesian house and a contemporary Silesian house. "Girl" further illustrated this; while Silesian is called upon to symbolize cultural closeness, respondents used linguistic resources in various creative ways. But, as I said above, the pictures of chairs worked best, perhaps because with chair, I had four pictures, enough to cover all possibilities of two axes of differentiation: culturally and temporally proximate, culturally distant but temporally proximate, culturally proximate but temporally distant, and culturally and temporally distant.

Chair

One picture, from a catalog, shows a modern kitchen chair in light wood with a slightly shaped seat, round-top back of frame and spokes, with no arms. A second shows an upholstered upright chair in dark wood, with turned legs, and a straight, carved back, set against a background of wooden panelling. A third, from the museum booklet, shows a simple chair with a flat, uncushioned seat, and a one-piece back with a heart shape cut into it. The chair is next to a wooden table covered by a striped cloth, and is bathed in the light from a small, uncurtained window below which there is an intricately painted chest. The picture is dominated by the beamed ceiling of the room and by an elaborate loom against the wall perpendicular to that near the chair. A fourth shows a simple upholstered chair, of wood, with no arms, set under a table with a reading lamp, behind which one can see racks displaying academic journals.

One observation that we can make is that the more remarkable presentations got more marked responses, including two word explanations like BIUROWE KRZESŁO, BÜROSTUHL. The linguistically mixed response is a first example of something we will explore further: calling on Polish to add specificity to information, a function emphasized by positioning in the phrase, "*STOLIK*

POKOJOWY w *izbie*," "A sitting room chair in a sitting room." This is because in Polish, adjectives follow nouns when they emphasize partition, "this specific kind of something." So both the position of the word and the language chosen for it emphasize what particular kind of chair it is.

TABLE 5.6
Responses for "Chair"

modern wooden (magazine) (culturally and temporally proximate)	archaic fancy upholstered (culturally and temporally distant)	library chair (culturally distant, temporally proximate)	museum (culturally proximate, temporally distant)
STOLIK, STOŁEK (variants)	*STOLIK, STOŁEK*	*STOLIK, STOŁEK*	*STOLIK, STOŁEK*
KRZESŁO	KRZESŁO	KRZESŁO	*siedzyjnie*
STUHL	STOLIK POKOJOWY W *izbie* (a sitting room chair in a sitting room)	STUHL	BIUROWE KRZESŁO (office chair)
HOCKER	POSTROWANY *stolik* (an embellished chair) STUHL	SESSEL	KÜCHENSTUHL
	SESSEL	BÜROSTUHL (office chair)	

(eight responses.)

At first glance, however, these results seem to indicate nothing specific, only that speakers have a spread of choices in responding to the tasks. Words originating in all three languages could be used for *every* prompt—except one. Luckily, the exception is highly telling. The spread of responses reflects the spread of choices speakers have. In the apparent lack of order, it reveals the ordering of experience.

So which picture is missing a language? If you look at the fonts, you'll see *SILESIAN*, POLISH, and GERMAN for every chair except the one from the museum.

And why? The answer becomes clearer when we look at responses for each respondent individually.

The first three responses came from one interview. The first was offered by a woman in her seventies, the second by her daughter, in her forties, and the third, again, by the older woman. In response 1a, German is used for distance, while the contrast between Polish and Silesian is used to express the contrast between contemporary (Polish) and archaic (Silesian). For R2, the contrast between Polish and Silesian is used to express the contrast in cultural distance (Polish "distant"). Archaism is left out of it. R2, the daughter, born after 1945, cannot draw on German to work in the archaic/contemporary contrast. The second set of responses by her mother don't manipulate either axis of difference, and this probably reflects on the discourse position: what's in play here is that the standard languages—both of them—are used for further explanation and specification. This is done twice by means of whole phrase switching from the matrix Silesian and once by means of a typical intraphrasal switching pattern.

For respondent 3, a teenager, German is contrasted with Polish *and* Silesian as modern vs. archaic. The choice of German expresses modernity and

TABLE 5.7
Responses for "Chair" by Individual Respondent

	modern local	modern distant	archaic proximate	archaic distant
R1a	KRZESŁO	STUHL	*STOLIK*	STUHL
R2	*STOLIK*	KRZESŁO	*STOLIK*	KRZESŁO
R1b	—	BÜROSTUHL, BIUROWE KRZESŁO	KÜCHENSTUHL	*stoliki* POKOJOWE W *izbie*
R3	STUHL	SESSEL	*STOŁEK*	KRZESŁO
R4	KRZESŁO	—	*STOLIK*	*STOLIK,* SESSEL, POSTROWANY *STOLIK*
R5	KRZESŁO	KRZESŁO	*STOLIK, siedzyjnie*	KRZESŁO
R6	*STOLIK*	*STOLIK*	*STOLIK*	KRZESŁO
R7	*STOLIK*	STUHL	HOCKER	KRZESŁO

(eight responses.)

modern comfort: "STUHL, because this looks typically German," and "SES-SEL, because SESSEL is more comfortable and these are padded." Within the Slavic system, the contrast is of cultural proximity: "KRZESŁO, because this reminds me of a royal castle," and "*Stołek*, because it looks traditional, old Silesian."

For respondent 4, the Polish/Silesian distinction expresses modern vs. archaic, while within archaism, both Polish and German express distance.

Respondent 5 is highly educated (a surgeon), and of the postwar generation, hence does not know German. For him, the contrast between Polish and Silesian, as expressing archaism, goes along with the DOM: *chałpa* strategy, one instance of which was also his. *Siedzyjnie* looks like an attempt to Silesianize the comparatively technical Polish "seat," SIEDZENIE, but the term may be an archaic Silesian word in its own right.

For respondent 6, Polish expressed fanciness as opposed to plainness.

For respondent 7, Silesian represented the most proximal presentation of "chair," and Polish the most distant, with different German words occupying the intermediate positions:

culturally AND temporally proximate	culturally proximate BUT temporally distant:	culturally distant BUT temporally proximate:	culturally AND temporally distant:
Silesian	German	German	Polish

Nobody chose a Polish word for the museum chair. The conjunction of archaism and cultural proximity precludes the use of Polish. Why?

Here is where we clearly see a temporal-spatial mental geography, which one could gloss, "back then, here, they didn't call things in Polish." The archaic culturally distant fancy chair, on the other hand, could have been found either in Germany or in Poland. As for the archaic proximate chair being called in either German or Silesian, one can note that factually, of course, the museum chair may date to a time before widespread Silesian/German bilingualism, but the prevalent ideology is that "we have always been bilingual." One can imagine great-great-great-Grandma calling that thing KÜCHENSTUHL.

Evaluations of cultural and temporal distance are ideologically embedded in the choice of words originating in the three languages; we have seen this also with the other words. We have seen too, that the languages can be pressed into service in various ways. What "chair" most neatly illustrates, however, is how community experience constrains linguistic choices. These constraints are broadly expressed in the following list:

If . . .	Then . . .	As if to say . . .
+temporally distant, +culturally proximal	NO POLISH	"Back then, here, they didn't use Polish"
+culturally distant, temporally either distant or proximal	STANDARD PREFERRED	"This is not a Silesian thing, but it can be associated with either Polish or German."
+temporally proximal, +culturally proximal	SLAVIC PREFERRED	"These days, around here, we usually use Silesian and Polish."

What is different in the Silesian situation is that we're not dealing with bilingualism, but rather with trilingualism. In deploying word choice onto a map of ethnic space, an "our kind of object" vs. a "their kind of object," "their" is two different groups, and the language of either can symbolize the distinction. However, in the other direction, the distinction is not drawn so boldly: responses to the culturally and temporally proximal prompt were distinguished by the absence of German, not by an overwhelming preponderance of Silesian responses. There is an interesting contrast here between the fact that Polish is kept out of "our past", whereas German is all but kept out of "our present." This is of course consonant with historical events. Choices, then, did not so much reflect a generic sense of ethnic distinctiveness as inflect a shared cultural map of space and time. Consciousness of Silesia's place between, and the history of that betweenness, guided responses to this exercise. Thus, this European case supports the conclusions of comparative work both within and beyond Europe:

> Rather than arising as an automatic response to social structural factors, however, the practice of codeswitching is mediated by speakers' own understanding of their position in that structure. . . . It is ultimately not any objective positioning of value of a language, but rather speakers' ideological interpretation of and response to that value, that are mobilized in codeswitching. Because of this, codeswitching and related translingual phenomena can provide a window on social and political consciousness, as both Hill (1985) and Gal (1987) have argued. (Woolard 2004: 82)

So there it is, then. It's a small thing, choosing a word for "chair," when you have several lexemes, drawn from three different languages. It's not an identity assertion; it doesn't say, "I am Silesian." But it is an expression of identity, in that people's choices follow the contours of their own autonomous culture; they reflect the ideological ordering of their community's experience. Autochthonous Opole Silesians have a culture of register—put more broadly, a culture of language. And there's more to it than this.

Autochthonous Opole Silesians' shared sense of time and space also guided choices in natural discourse, at a broader level than choice of nouns: specifically, in one of the ways that autochthonous Opole Silesians use German.

We have already discussed two uses of German: there are many German loan words in Silesian, used especially by older speakers, that are considered particularly Silesian—*RICHTIG* Sl*o*nski. Silesians also use German as a stylistic finale (an "escalation switch") as exemplified in the three examples given under "bicycle." Now we will discuss two more: in another kind of escalation switch, autochthonous Opole Silesians use German stylistically for emotional intensity, as the following examples attest:

1. I was visiting Franz Skorupka's family to conduct an elicitation technique whereby I showed people a set of pictures that tell a story and asked them to tell the story both in Polish and in Silesian, when the family's six-year-old son decided to have a go at it. From his father's lap, he produced first a Silesian version and then attempted a Polish version: "Tata *PAKUJE* do *AUTA* . . . [The daddy is packing into the car . .]." Franz was exasperated at his son's failure to produce "clean Polish;" he interrupted with sarcasm dense with affectively intense German loans: "*JA, 'PAKUJE, 'GENAU* to je*[Ø]* po polsku! [*SURE, 'IS PACKING' EXACTLY* that is in Polish!]." (Tapes, November 30, 1994).

2. When autochthonous Silesians warn a small child that something is hot, they say "HEISS!" not "GORĄCO!" For example, Diana Osa used this word to warn her toddler son away from my coal stove (October 22, 1994). This is a widespread practice. Diana, and another person from another village, explained that they do this because it is easier for a child to grasp the situation if you say, "HEISS!" (Notes, January 18, 1993, February 3, 1993). Yet on another day (December 18, 1994), I heard Diana hand a cup of tea to her son and say, nonchalantly, "GORĄCO." In the context of prevailing switching patterns, apparently, "GORĄCO" needs to be said in even tones; truly threatening heat requires "HEISS!"

3. One of the examples given above is both an example of German as the finale, or finishing touch, and German as a language of emotional intensity: the one where the customer wanted milk in his coffee and couldn't get it, and said,

"ABER OHNE MILCH SCHMECKT DER KAFFEE NICHT! [But the coffee does not taste good without milk!]."

In this kind of usage, German seems to be a language of power, something to draw on to communicate intensity (perhaps especially, as in these examples, to people whose power is less).

There is one other regular appearance of German, besides its enregisterment by the space/time map: the Slavic system of forming verbs of motion indicating specific direction has been blended, and sometimes replaced, by a calque (an overlay or translation) of the German system. In Polish, such verbs are prefixed by prepositions to form directional verbs, for example:

iść – to go by foot
wejść – to enter
wyjść – to exit
dojść – to arrive (there)
przyjść – to arrive (here)

rzucić – to throw
wrzucić – to throw into
wyrzucić – to throw out

jechać – to drive or to go by a vehicle
wjechać – to drive in
wyjechać – to drive out
dojechać – to arrive (there)
przyjechać – to arrive (here)

nosić – to carry
wnosić – to carry in
przynosić – to bring

German, on the other hand, like English, places prepositions at the end of the clause. Silesian follows this German practice. Sometimes these replace the Slavic prefixed prepositions; sometimes both are present. Here are some examples:

W*ciepnij* to *REIN*!
[In]throw that in!
Throw that in!

Chapter 5

D*ej* to *RAUF*!
Give that on!
Put that on [there]!

This is a calque that follows the logic of using German as the finishing touch, as well as using standard language to make information more specific.

Let's return to the space/time map. Consider the following two code switches to German. While driving in a car with two women in their sixties, one of them pointed out to me a castle by the roadside:

Tam mie*skoł* GRAF. EIN GRAF HAT DORT GEWOHNT.
There lived count. A count has there lived.

And the other woman affirmed, "JA, EIN GRAF HAT DORT GEWOHNT" (August 15, 1995). Second, in early March 1993, Marta drove her sister, Magda, Magda's son Łukaś (Marta's nephew), and me to visit their brother, his wife, and their children in Bochum, Germany. The mother of Marta and Magda's sister-in-law lives nearby, and she was in the apartment when Magda's husband called from work to see how things were going (there were no telephones in Dobra until 1996). He gave a weather report. Later, the mother commented, to no one in particular:

W Polsce pada śnieg. A tu deszcz. ES REGNET UND REGNET.
In Poland falls snow. And here rain. It rains and rains.

The count, of course, spoke German, and lived in Opole Silesia at the time when Opole Silesia was in Germany. The women symbolized that through code choice. As for the snow and rain, the contrast between them and the contrast between the places of their falling was symbolized by a contrast of languages.

An instance of this, particularly interesting for me, capped an anecdote told during this visit by Marta's brother about his family's experience of a conversation with the man who was soon to become their elementary school principal. Their son Henryk was to enter first grade in the fall, and the principal conducted interviews with all the families of children entering from non-monolingual German homes. The interview was pleasant; while the parents felt that their bilingualism was being tested, they also knew that their own and their son's German would pass muster. At the end, the father related, the principal asked their son what he wished for the summer, to which the child replied, "To have a fun vacation in Silesia and then come back and go to school." The principal replied that he, too, wished for that, but that "[the student] needed to have a better shirt." (He

140

was wearing a tank top.) The parents reassured the principal that they would send him to school in a white button-down shirt with collar and the interview ended pleasantly. The only German word in the narrative was "shirt." In using the word HEMD, the young father relied on the stylistic appropriateness of naming in German the item of clothing to be worn to school in Germany. The linguistic incorporation of the German word neatly mirrored his son's coming incorporation in German school. The appropriateness of this stylistic choice created an iconic echo: the principal, too, was talking about appropriateness.

In these examples, aspects of the social context of speech invoke the orders of community experience which make the contrast of languages culturally meaningful. The women in the car know, and are telling me, that this is an old castle which housed German nobility during German times. In Bochum, we had all been present for the phone call and heard the news that it was snowing in Poland. And as we listened to the story of the school interview, we knew, of course, that we were in Germany and that Marta and Magda's nephew would go to school there.

It is particularly interesting that the context—a shared sense of position in the space/time map—is necessary. Without the context, this sentence, "The principal said that the student needed to have a better SHIRT," sounds weird to autochthonous Opole Silesians; they don't like it, they think the sentence sounds better with "shirt" in Polish. I know this because, during my last months in Dobra, I conducted a structured linguistic elicitation technique designed to check out whether there are, in fact, constraints on permissable language mixing—whether it's true, so to speak, that you can say whatever you want, even sing if you want to. I presented respondents with two possible versions of sentences meaning the same thing, and told them that in each case, one sentence was one that I had actually heard in the community, while the other(s) I had changed a little bit. Which version, I asked, sounded realistic? I attempted to engage phonological, syntactic, and lexical issues in the exercise. I found what I was looking for: the same grammatical constraints on codeswitching that others have found in other multilingual situations. In brief, language mixing is possible within constraints that operate at the level of syntax, the language system that governs how words can be combined into sentences. In multilingual societies, switches occur at junctures where the change of languages does not violate the syntax of either language (Poplack 1980, 1988). Speakers reject switches that occur within phrases that are highly syntactically cohesive, such as verbal phrases; Silesians are no exception in this regard. It's important, before we turn to the cultural and ideological subtleties encoded in codeswitches, that we first set the baseline: in Silesia, as in other multilingual situations, some kinds of mixing simply sound weird.

I had included switches that were not within highly syntactically cohesive phrases in order to catch whatever contrast might emerge. But in looking for syntax I found a couple of other things, too: language loyalty, for one, and the space/time map, for another. Consider the following results for the seventh sentence in the elicitation technique:

Sentence 7:
Dyrektor *gołdoł, że synek* musi mieć lepszy HEMD / *KOSZULA*.
The principal says that the boy must have a better shirt.

Number of respondents who chose the . . .

switched version	unswitched version	either
1	16	1

One respondent, who chose "unswitched," and had not heard the story of the interview, put her finger on the issue precisely by commenting that only the unswitched alternative would do "unless the principal was in Germany." Having been interested in whether other, similar sentences would get whatever reaction that one might get (which, as we've seen, turned out to be negative), I had included, also, two other sentences designed to probe the acceptibility of German within Silesian/Polish. One of them I simply made up: "I was IN THE STORE and I bought bananas." The other one occurred as the answer to a question: "Who will do it? The ones FROM NEUBRUNNEN." The spread of responses was as follows:

Sentence 6:
Byłach IN GESCHÄFT i kupiłach banany. OR Byłach w sklepie. . . .
I was in the store and I bought bananas.

Number of respondents who chose the . . .

switched version	unswitched version	either
1	15	3

Sentence 11:
"Kto to zrobi?' [Who will do that?]
"Ci AUS NEUBRUNNEN" / "Ci z Nowej Studnii" [The ones from Nowa Studnia (a neighboring village)]

Number of respondents who chose the . . .

switched version	unswitched version	either
1	14	3

A CULTURE OF LANGUAGE

In real life, "Ci AUS NEUBRUNNEN," was uttered at a meeting of the German Minority by a woman in her sixties. Every respondent commented that "we don't say NEUBRUNNEN, we say 'z Nowej Studnii,'" the Polish name for the village. Evidently only an active older member of the German Minority, in a meeting of same, would say this, thereby indexing self-identity, context, and perhaps an attitude that "it is, after all, a German village." The switched version of sentence 6 was not said, and "I was in the store and I bought bananas" is a banal statement generated by me. Here, respondents reached to explain it. One woman, old enough to have shopped during German times, who chose "either" at first, rejected it because it would have to be incorporated, i.e., "w *GESCHÄFCIE*" (the -cie is a Slavic ending for nouns expressing location). But then she relented. A woman in her fifties who chose the unswitched one commented that the first sounded like something that monolingual German speakers who had to learn Polish after the war would have said; the comment put her finger precisely on the situation of another older woman who chose "either." A teenage girl said the first one sounded like something someone might say to show off some knowledge of German, however minimal, behavior which is a salient part of adolescent experience. And a man in his sixties, also drawing on the norm of indexing a German context with German, said, "but when we're in Germany we say 'w *GESCHÄFCIE*.'"

These results indicate that it is the space/time map which makes German acceptable within a matrix of Silesian and/or Polish. When presented with prompt sentences without a clear link to Germany, in time or space, respondents rejected the codeswitch as not sounding realistic. German is perfectly acceptable within Silesian speech when the connection of the referent to Germany is clear to the participants. It is then appropriate the way the word "decant" is appropriate when talking about wine, but sounds strange when referring to milk. This is a register phenomenon at the level of phrases.

To summarize: when different linguistic forms are applied predictably to different contexts, they belong to different registers; enregisterment is an ordering of community experience. Registers are culturally specific because community experience is culturally specific. In the case of autochthonous Opole Silesia, the culture of register is based on the experience of life between two states. We saw this in choices of words for objects in pictures, and we saw it in the way that German words and phrases are used in speech.

LANGUAGE LOYALTY CLASHES WITH LINGUISTIC TOLERANCE

Autochthonous Opole Silesians definitely maintain a loyalty to Silesian per se. I found this in listening to autochthonous Opole Silesians in their daily lives; I found it when I surveyed language attitudes; and, as I mentioned in passing, I found it in my sentence contrast elicitation technique, in responses to sentences designed to elicit the acceptability of Silesian within a Polish matrix and vice-versa. I expected that if respondents found a switch too strange to accept, they would pay attention to other clues in the prompt sentence—if most of the sentence was in Polish and there was a strange switch to Silesian in it, I expected that they would choose a Polish alternate for that word or phrase, or vice versa. Instead, if one word was in Silesian, they chose that word and then translated the rest of the sentence into Silesian to match it. They may have thought I wanted such translation, despite my directions, or they may have simply been reluctant to replace Silesian with Polish.

On the other hand, as we have seen, linguistic tolerance is a community value. These are not people who examine their own speech, or that of their fellows, for the extent to which it diverges linguistically from standard Polish, and find that the more highly divergent, the better. They do not examine their own speech for the extent that it conforms to some ideal of standard Silesian; no one has imagined such an ideal. An important face of their brand of cultural loyalty is loyalty to the idea of a linguistic tolerance sorely lacking in the former totalitarian ideologies of Germany and Poland.

These two values exist in tension with one another. The logic of total tolerance could leave the community without a language to be loyal to. That being the case, to what extent can a community practice linguistic tolerance and still maintain a sense of itself as Silesian-speaking?

We have a partial answer in the culture of register; one that we will continue to examine: material taken from German and Polish, *if used in a way ideologically defined as appropriate*, need not disrupt speakers' sense that they are speaking Silesian. Indeed, it may even enhance it. Good Silesian speakers codeswitch skillfully, like Franz. Yet Franz, and one other respondent, hated the registers from picture exercises, told me that it made no sense, interfered with his wife Brigitte's responses, and had very interesting things to say about why. His loyalty trumped his tolerance.

Loyalty and tolerance are aspects of linguistic ideology, of how people think about language. Register and reference are terms we use in the analysis of language itself, of speech, of linguistic choices such as those elicited in structured elicitation exercises. Yet in the final analysis, of both language and of ideology, there is a tension between loyalty to reference and tolerance of register. To understand this, we need to understand that register and reference do not exist in simple contrast: the one a matter of picking something out of a field of material reality (reference), the other a matter of placing it into a field of social experience (register). Rather, they have a historical, evolutionary relationship to one another: differences of register can become differences of reference. And in a linguistically complex social field, that fact can mean the end of a language. That ultimately is why Franz resisted the registers from pictures exercise.

To understand how this is so, consider the data of figure 3. Focus on which prompts elicited what frequency of Silesian-origin, Polish-origin, or "either" responses. If we consider only nouns, we see that "cups," "poker," and "shovel" elicited the highest frequency of Silesian-origin choices (indeed, I made sure to include "poker" because Magda had had to stop and think hard when I asked her what the Polish word for it was). In a world of birthday-parties and coal stoves, these are all items of intensely frequent domestic use, and seldom encountered outside the home. In contrast, several of the words which received fewer choices of the Silesian alternate are things caught up in frequent, Polish-speaking, purchase encounters, having a dimension of exteriority and experienced, often, as named in Polish: "button," "chocolate," "coffee," "train," and "ceiling/floor." (Trains are not themselves purchased, but tickets for them are; one would not think that "ceiling" and "floor" are frequently purchased, but as it happens there was a storm of house renovations in the 1990s). This is consonant with the interpretation that if the context in which the thing is found is socially German or Polish, then the word may be as well. This would explain why Polish words are being actively loaned into Silesian now, whereas German words—currently—are not, while German words were being actively incorporated when Silesia was in Germany. What has been stable over history, then, are the principles by which lexical items from other languages may be used in Silesian. This is the space/time map—linguistic ideology—at work in linguistic change.

The "Registers from Pictures" exercise turned up a similar process of linguistic change—as well as some respondents' objections to the enregisterment that facilitates it. I focused particularly on the "space/time map" because it is an ethnographically specific order of cultural experience, but it bears noting that autochthonous Opole Silesians share other registers with other Europeans, with other members of the global economy. In this exercise, respondents sometimes made reference to "elegance," or "impressiveness" in justifying their responses. Familiarity with the realm of marketing, an order of cultural experience of very wide currency, also with its own register, justified a choice of "ROWER" because, the respondent said, "you can see that it's ROWER GÓRSKI"— a mountain bike. In the same way, the respondent who cited SKANSEN as appropriate to the museum house said she'd heard that word on the radio for such museum houses; this is a register distinction of Polish society at large.

Regardless of the specifics of what register is in play, these are register distinctions which partition the world according to orders of experience, rather than semantic distinctions which partition the world according to orders of perception. Yet the one easily becomes the other.

Take one of the classic examples of English historical linguistics: the distinction between "cow" and "beef," "pig" and "pork," "sheep" and "mutton." As the commonly told story goes, these distinctions originated after the Norman invasion of 1066, when downtrodden Anglo-Saxon peasants, forced to tend the animals for their Norman French overlords, called the animals "pigs" in the sty, or "sheep" and "cows" in the fields (or rather the etymological ancestors of these forms). But when required to serve them up at table to their French-speaking masters, they had to call them by the twelfth-century antecedents of "pork," "mutton," and "beef." Originally, this contrast would have neatly coincided with the division of social domains in which the bilingual peasants used their two languages (cf. Fishman 1972). One can even imagine a twelfth-century linguistic anthropologist showing these bilinguals a picture of meat being served in a banquet hall together with a picture of meat being served in a peasant's hut, and, to the question "Which of the words you know do you think goes with each of the pictures?" they would answer that some form of "beef," goes with the great hall, and some form of "cow flesh" goes

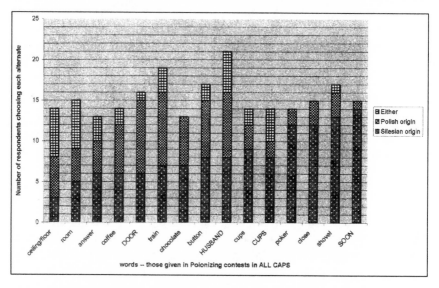

Figure 3. Autochthonous Opole Silesians' choices of words of different language origin, presented in context sentences that emphasized either Polish or Silesian.

with the hut. This would be a register distinction based on lived experience. But, as we all know, this contrast of context was eventually reinterpreted as a contrast of perceptible characteristics: on the hoof vs. on the plate is a semantic distinction. A picture of the most lowly dining room imaginable would not, in a modern English-speaking environment, draw the word "cow" instead of "beef." The semantics of English distinguish the two. You don't eat cow, or herd beef. The words simply mean different things.

Precisely the same process of semanticization is underway in Silesia today; it turned up in both "Registers from Pictures" and the sentence contrast exercise. Here, finally, we get to the pictures of "gates." These pictures did not work out for me in terms of eliciting registers, because I didn't know that I was showing people pictures of different things. I conflated a pedestrian-sized gate with a vehicle-sized gate; for me, they're both "gate," but not for my respondents. The confusion this caused turned out to be very useful, because it spurred a thorough exploration of these words with Franz and his wife, Brigitte. They explained:

> The museum picture was *pot* [fence] with *furtka* [pedestrian gate]. The local snapshot was *furtka* with BRAMA [vehicle gate]. They also have *furtka* with BRAMA, whereas Brigitte's mother has *furtka* with *wrota*. The difference is that *wrota* is made of wood. The picture in the magazine cannot be *wrota*, because it's metal.

Here, the difference is not one of register, but one of reference. The Silesian and Polish origin words have come simply to mean slightly different things for these speakers. Here are some other opinions that people offered that are properly of reference, rather than of register:

> *dylufka* [floor] is made out of boards; PODŁOGA is of vinyl or tile.
> BLACHA [baking dish] is a baking dish; PŁYTA (<PŁYTA) [platter, baking sheet] is a serving dish only.
> SIOŁLKA [cup] is a mug; FILIŻANKA (<FILIŻANKA) [cup] is a teacup.
> CUG [train] is a steam train; POCIĄG is an electric train.

Take note of the fonts, here: it's the words loaned from Polish, THESE WORDS, that always name the thing that is modern or elegant. Yet they specify different things. A mug is no more a teacup than a cow is a plate of food.

When linguists tell the story of how English formed a semantic distinction between "cow" and "beef," they are usually celebrating the lexical enrichment of English, renowned for its immense vocabulary. Yet the happy end could have been a worse one. When languages die, it is often because the language of a ruling elite replaces that of a socially subordinated group. Upwardly mobile members of the underdog group adopt the social habits, including the language, of the group they are striving to identify themselves with. In this trajectory, families become first bilingual, and then monolingual in the prestige language, and this process gradually widens to include more and more of the population until the language of the subordinated group goes out of usage entirely. After the Norman invasion of England in 1066, French became the language of the ruling elite. English, as Hoenigswald has pointed out, "could have died in the Middle Ages but didn't"—in England, as it turned out, French died (Hoenigswald 1989: 347). In this way, similarly, seventeenth-century German was threatened, also, by French (Waterman 1966: 138); Finnish, by Swedish (Ellis and mac a'Ghobhainn 1971); Hungarian, by German (Inglehart and Woodward 1967–68: 34; Gal 1979, 1989); and Gaelic, by English (Dorian 1981: esp. 2, 15, 27, 38). It is a very common process, and it is underway, also, in Silesia—though we can't know what the final results will be. After all, despite the threats, people still speak German, Finnish, Hungarian, Gaelic, and English.

Just as French words replaced many Anglo-Saxon ones, in Silesian too, many words have simply been replaced. We no longer know the word for "button" that circulated before everyone started using *KNEFLIK*, and the same can be said for essentially the entire huge realm of Germanicized lexicon. The Silesian words that were replaced are simply gone. And *KNEFLIK* seems to be on its way out, a usage of the elderly, while younger speakers say "guzik"— *GUZIK*, if you will. And so, the use of foreign-origin words within a subordinate language, register or no, can be a step down the plank that ends with a leap into the cold sea of language death. If all English words had been replaced by French ones, that would have been the end, not the enrichment, of English.

The matter turns on the concept of "domain." In the "Registers from Pictures" exercise, many respondents thought about what kind of people would be associated with the object and what language they would be likely to speak with such people. A sensitive appreciation of this can be seen in the response to "chair," by a woman in her twenties: the two kitchen chairs were *STOLIK*, while she would call the modern library chair and the fancy carved one something different according to whom she was talking to. One infers that if she were talking about a modern kitchen chair, she would be in somebody's kitchen, and she doesn't ever go into Poles' kitchens. The museum chair is *STOLIK* because it's old, and besides, outings to this museum are something that autochthonous Opole Silesians do together, in groups (though plenty of groups of Poles go too). However, if she were to encounter the other two chairs, she might be talking to Silesians or talking to Poles; hard to say. The two *STOLIKI* unambiguously reminded her of situations in which she uses

Silesian. Similarly, two respondents said that the eggs in the store should be JAJKA because, "in a store, you say JAJKO for *jajco*." If the egg is in the nest in your own barn, why would you refer to it in Polish? Eggs in nests don't lie within the linguistic domain of Polish. These considerations—setting, interlocutors—constitute linguistic domains.

A few respondents, however, told me that the task was senseless, since domain was the only consideration that mattered. Of the six respondents who refused in this manner, five—a couple in their forties, a woman and a man in their sixties, and a woman in her seventies—were very strongly German identified, and, except for the man in his sixties, active in the German Minority. I believe that what is relevant about that is that these are people who look outward from the ethnic group, and who are therefore more aware of linguistic and cultural boundaries. This intuition is supported by the fact that the sixth refuser was Franz Skorupka, who is, as we will continue to see, not less but much more linguistically sensitive than most people. In addition, he works in a Polish-speaking context outside the village. And he got into an eloquent argument with Brigitte who rarely leaves a Silesian-speaking environment and was perfectly happy to enregister for me. So did his neighbor, Karl Sattler; we met his wife in chapter 3, in the discussion of personal names. He also works in a Polish-speaking context, and his wife also rarely leaves the Silesian-speaking environment.

We will start with the Sattlers. Note that they were interviewed separately from Franz and Brigitte, and at a different time.

Mrs. Sattler identified the suit as having GUZIKI, while the vest had *knefliki* because "it looks like a TRACHTENKLEID." Mr. Sattler argued, saying, "Look, in German you have one word, KNOPF, for both of these. It's the same for us. What there is, is, there's *KNEFLIK, REISSVERSCHLUSS*, and *DRUCKKNOPF* [a button, a zipper, a snap]." (In other words, only different things deserve different words in Silesian, as in German.)

Mrs. Sattler identified the teenage gymnasts as *dziołchy* because they look folklorey. The snapshot, she said, is DZIEWCZYNA, and the little girl, DZIECKO. Mr. Sattler said, "All *dziołchy*—small, medium-sized, and large."

Franz, who insisted that the only thing that mattered was "who I'm talking to" at every prompt, articulated his position with reference to "chair": "If someone comes to whom I speak Silesian, I'm going to say, '*siednij sie* na *stolik*' [sit down on the chair] whether it's an ordinary chair or some fine upholstered one."

Both men showed some awareness of the enregisterment of Silesian with respect to Polish, and resisted it. This is especially evident in Franz's reference to whether the chair was an "ordinary" or "fine upholstered" one. And in fact,

Franz is keenly sensitive to the ways in which the difference between Silesian and Polish is a difference of register, as we will shortly see. His insistence, and that of Mr. Sattler, on interlocutor as the only criterion for word choice can be seen as a way of loyally establishing defensive boundaries around Silesian: this is our word for it, period, no replacements regardless of register. It is a claim for the integrity of Silesian, and for the domain of its use. You should use the Silesian word for shovel if you're speaking Silesian. Kasia was right to get upset at the news that she was habitually using a Polish word, and her grandfather was wrong to reprimand her about it. Loyalty over tolerance.

It seems that that claim is where some speakers draw the line: in the choice between, on the one hand, segregating languages in a multilingual repertoire and, on the other, accepting an ideology of enregisterment that allows for linguistic importation. It was Franz and Brigitte who told me that the vehicle gate in their front fence is BRAMA, because it is metal, and they didn't argue about that; for Franz, that is fully a Silesian word, making a useful semantic distinction; he didn't tell me that it's not a Silesian word. But its incorporation (a good thing) would have been impossible without enregisterment, which can lead, also, to loss of Silesian words (a bad thing). Those more aware of the sea of Polish surrounding the Silesian-speaking enclave react defensively when confronted with enregisterment. They seem to say, "I speak Polish where it's appropriate, but Silesian is Silesian: leave the Polish out of it!"

So the tension between loyalty and tolerance is ultimately unresolved. The minority status of autochthonous Opole Silesians in the Polish state determines that. And that situation—a sea of Polish around an island of Silesian, a Silesian enclave deep within Poland, a borderland culture far from the border—reminds us of unequal power relations.

This is the chapter that, in its discussion of the space/time map, has made the strongest claim so far that autochthonous Opole Silesian culture is distinctive and autonomous. Yet even here, in the culture of register, we see that autochthonous Opole Silesian culture is a matter of what the community has done with what lies beyond itself. Now we shift focus: we cannot fully understand what autochthonous Opole Silesian culture has done with what lies beyond itself until we understand the inverse: what the states that lie beyond have done to Opole Silesia.

Chapter 6
LANGUAGE, POWER, AND THE TWO STATES

That which lies beyond—the two states—what have they done with autochthonous Opole Silesia? The Nazis suppressed Slavic culture. Soviet forces invaded. The borders were revised. The Polish Communists took over. The
Stalinists suppressed German culture. Many were expelled. Cataclysmic
changes faced those left behind, as well as decades of the grim daily life of
the Soviet bloc. In this chapter, we further fine-tune our view of autochthonous
Opole Silesian linguistic culture, continuing to look at it through the lens of
register; but looking also at the harsh power dynamics out of which that culture
has, remarkably, been forged.

We begin with a look back at how German is enregistered by the
space/time map, but this time, we look also at the state of German-Polish relations in 1993. From there, the chapter turns back to the Silesian culture of
language by examining, first, how autochthonous Opole Silesians conceptualize the differences between their Silesian and their Polish. That conceptual-
ization shows that Silesian and Polish function as registers with respect to one
another, within speakers' multilingual repertoire, and understanding that en-
ables us, further, to understand how Polish functions as a register within speech
that Silesians consider Silesian. It is possible for a person to speak in a way
that is linguistically almost indistinguishable from standard Polish for extended stretches, without anyone, speaker or listeners, thinking that the language being spoken is Polish. But it has to be done right; it has to accord with
cultural ideas about register.

These ideas, then, "tame" the associations of the Polish language with the
oppressive power of the Polish state, and with the bad experiences that many
autochthonous Opole Silesians have had in interactions with Poles. But those
associations are never quite vanquished, and it is a powerful, potentially
volatile act to use Polish in a way that makes people recognize it as Polish.
The same is true of German: there are norms that govern the use of German

and make using it acceptable within Silesian. When those norms are violated, its use is offensive.

The chapter, then, begins with a reminder about the dynamics of oppressive power, then turns back toward cultural autonomy; then slowly follows a trajectory from autonomy to power, from autochthonous Opole Silesian culture back out to its context.

THE DYNAMICS OF POWER: FEAR UNDERGIRDS AESTHETICS

When the last chapter focused on mapping space and time in language, I described this mapping as a cultural aesthetic, and as an aspect of an autonomous Opole Silesian culture. I presented cultural autonomy as neutralizing the power dynamics of life between Poland and Germany. I did that by suppressing—silencing—some of my fieldnotes. There is more than aesthetics at stake in the idea that different languages are appropriate to different national-political spaces.

When we went to Germany in March 1993, Marta's nephew and Magda's son Łukaś was five years old. His adult kin prepared him in advance by teaching him a variety of basic German phrases, and he was the one called on to symbolize linguistically our passage into a different space of linguistic appropriateness. When we crossed the Oder-Neisse line, his mother told, him, "Speak German!" Łukaś said, "WAS IST DAS?" and a few other phrases. It was a purely ritual gesture, and talk immediately reverted to Polish. Łukaś, however, had taken it much to heart. A little while later, we found ourselves driving behind a vehicle with only one taillight. When we caught up with it, we saw that its registration was Polish. "Of course!" Marta exclaimed, implicitly referring to the stereotype of Poles as disorderly scofflaws.

"What?" inquired Łukaś.

"He's not supposed to be driving like that!" his aunt replied.

"Why not?" asked Łukaś. "Doesn't he know how to speak German?"

Łukaś, at five, had gotten the point about appropriate social behavior that he had been meant to get. And at one level, this sense of linguistic aesthetics truly is the driving force. Marta, who resists using German in Poland, amazed me by addressing me in German in a private context, and by consistently addressing me as "Elisabeth" instead of "Elżbieta." On another level, however, it became increasingly evident that the fear that drove families to speak only German to their small children during the Nazi period was not completely dead in the 1990s.

As we were leaving the house a few days later, Łukaś said something loudly in Polish. Marta showed him the palm of her hand, an autochthonous

152

Opole Silesian equivalent of a shaken index finger, indexing the imminent possibility of being slapped. Marta said, "You are in Germany and here you speak German, and if you can't, then speak quietly." When I asked her and Magda why, she just said, "It's better that he should speak quietly." But a few days later, I received a more revealing explanation. Coming back from a walk, we passed a kiosk. Marta called ahead about fifteen yards to her nephew in German, "Henryk? Do you want an ice-cream?" When I asked her why she had used German, she shrugged defensively and said, "Because. Because there's no need to broadcast to the entire neighborhood where we are from. We will leave but Henryk stays, you know. I was thinking of him."

Recent incidents of AUSLÄNDERHAß (hate crimes directed at foreigners) were on everyone's mind, and found their way into conversation. When, on the way back, we stopped for lunch on the Polish side of the border, I heard Magda tell Łukaś, "Yes, you may." He had asked, too quietly for me to hear, whether he could speak Polish out loud again now.

It is not that the appropriateness of language to space is *not* aesthetic. It is; we know that because autochthonous Opole Silesians follow the norm when there is no threat. But there is an underlay of threat, both contemporary and historical. The aesthetics that Łukaś was explicitly taught can be seen as a choice of repression, in Billig's terms: they didn't tell him that they were afraid to be recognized as foreigners. Aesthetics silences fear.

In this chapter, I want to further my argument that the openness of Silesian speech to both Polish and German is culturally structured through a shared sense of register. It is this shared sense of register that allows autochthonous Opole Silesians to see themselves as speaking Silesian without having to restrict themselves to the use of linguistic material which they, themselves, would recognize as contrastively Silesian. Speaking Silesian is a cultural practice, and the norms of that culture are more important than whether one says *s*koła or szkoła, KNEFLIK or *GUZIK*, and so on. This shared sense of register is something established within the autochthonous Opole Silesian community, passed on to children: an expression of cultural autonomy.

It does not do to forget, however, that it has been forged partly out of experience that has been deeply disturbing. In the sense that the choices in response to the "registers from pictures" exercise were not fraught with a sense of threat; in the sense that it can be merely aesthetically pleasing to say, 'A COUNT USED TO LIVE THERE," or 'In Poland it's snowing, and here it's raining, RAINING AND RAINING"; in the sense that there can be a beautiful resonance between the appropriateness of a white shirt for the first day of school in Germany and the appropriateness of quoting the principal's insistence on it in the original German; in all these instances, the way that German and Polish function as registers within the multilingual Silesian language constitutes a transformation of power dynamics. Using languages that were imposed under duress, with threats, has been stripped of fear, and transformed into a valued aspect of aesthetic culture. It has been a process of taming.

HOW SILESIANS DIFFERENTIATE POLISH FROM SILESIAN

In the "Registers from Pictures" exercise, I specifically did not tell people which language to use; nor did I comment on which language they used. That was what I wanted simply to emerge. In the next exercise to be discussed, "Stories from Pictures," on the other hand, I did ask for "Polish" or "Silesian" because I wanted to see what people would do to turn a story in Polish into a story in Silesian, or vice-versa. It was, then, respondents' own sense of what the linguistic difference between the languages is, that I was after. I asked respondents to look at xeroxed pictures, some of which were single pictures presenting a situation, and some of which were series of pictures which present a simple story. I asked each respondent to tell the story of the pictures first in one language, then in the other (or others—some respondents gave a German version). I varied the order of languages. It sometimes happened that the respondent began before I specified a language, and I asked afterward whether s/he had been speaking Polish or Silesian. I found that when I asked people specifically to speak "Polish" or to speak "Silesian," what I got was not what we conventionally think of as different languages, but rather what linguists call different registers.

I usually recorded in people's homes, and there were usually other family members present. Much, then, was in play: the connotations of a research event complete with tape recorder and microphone, the dynamics of my relationships with the respondents, and those of their family relationships. A father's frustration at his son's performance in this elicitation technique, for example, gave me material on how German is used for intensification. Furthermore, to ask people to speak Silesian in a self-conscious manner into a tape recorder, or to "describe what's happening in these pictures in Silesian," was culturally out of step. The fact of the tape recorder and the nature of the exercise introduced "performance criteria" which would elicit as nearly standard Polish as possible from most people, in any situation *other* than being explicitly asked to "speak Silesian."

One of the respondents, Angelika Stanik (sister of Diana Osa), initially insisted that what I had asked *could not be done* (October 29, 1994). A plausible English telling of the series of three pictures would be: "In the first picture, a boy is sitting by the bank of a river, fishing. In the second, he stands up, smiling, because the rod and line have gone taut. He starts to pull, and in the third, he sees that he's pulled out a heap of weeds." Angelika, in response to my request that she tell this story in Silesian, said, "This is the way a Polish teacher would do it," and then did it in her best schoolroom Polish. Then she babbled about other things before catching herself and returning to the task. Finally she offered a Silesian version, but her footing was completely different. Whereas the Polish had started, "In the first picture a boy is sitting and fishing. In the second, his line is moving, so he probably has caught something," the Silesian was, "Oh, look, there's a boy sitting by the river fishing. Look at his cute little pants! He's going to get all wet, isn't he? Oh, I see he has them rolled up. Oh, look, his line's moving!" The Silesian word *łobejrz*, "look," recurred frequently. In other words, she presented the picture as if it were real, for she could imagine speaking Silesian to describe a boy fishing in a river, but she could not imagine using Silesian to describe a set of pictures of a boy fishing in a river. The exercise was too academic for Silesian.

My explicit request for a version "in Silesian" sometimes did not override the power of the tape recorder to elicit standard Polish. Magda, Marta's sister, working with a picture I call "The Pig in the Store," gave me a first rendition which sounded very Polish to me despite my request that it be in Silesian. So I asked her how it would be if it were as Silesian as it could possibly be? She laughed and said, "It was already pretty Silesian." She did it again: While the first attempt was characterized by a lot of self-interruptive questioning ("There's a piglet . . . or is it a bear? No, it's a bear . . .") and helpful interjections from Łukaś, (who was six, by that time), her second is "clean," and, despite the fact that it follows a request for Silesian, Silesian forms are almost absent:

speaker	line	text
Magda	1	Na tyM obRAZku widze sklep. Jedna kobIEta
		In this picture I see a store. One [i.e., a] woman
	2	kupuje . . . bardzo duże marzylonce . . .
		is buying . . . a lot of ??
	3	mo*ł* koszyk . . . *no* . . .a PROSIAK, a PROSIAK zadowolony
		has a basket . . . and the piglet, and piglet happily
	4	WYCHODZI. Chyba coś fajnego kupił i WYCHODZI.
		leaves. Probably something nice he bought and leaves.

Cont. on Page 156

speaker	line	text	*Cont. from Page 155*

Magda   5   (laughs) WYCHODZI, zaglądA, a tam wszyscy do cyrku
                  He leaves, he looks, and there everyone to the circus
         6   lalą, on tyś.
                  are going, he also.

What is striking about this is not only the relative density of Polish forms, but the intonation patterns of the segment, which are schoolroom Polish: the sentences and phrases sound almost like a slide straight down a musical scale. This is the pattern I've watched drilled into children in first grade. It is an exaggeration of what Polish sounds like. And the drilling is probably necessary, because the typical intonation of Silesian is very different—so much so that, even if you can't hear the words, the melody of speech will tell you whether somebody is autochthonous Opole Silesian. For example, in the post office, where the public telephones were, I wasn't near enough to hear the linguistic features that I italicize in transcripts. What I could hear was the different intonation. In essence, while typical Polish intonation consists of sets of downward slides, Silesian intonation has a lilt. A simple sentence like

A *wasa dziołcha* jus taka *sroga*!
And your (form.) daughter already so big!
My, isn't your daughter getting big!

has ups and downs, with peaks on the syllables "*wa*," "*dzioł*," and "*sro*." That particular lilt is the intonational stereotype.

    Magda, a second time, responded to my request to describe a different series of pictures "a second time but this time as Silesian as possible," by saying, "It was already in Silesian. Because our speech it's like, we speak a little in Polish, Silesian, in it, it's already mixed." Yet her speech in that story, too, was characterized by a high density of Polish alternates.

    This is the voice of fear. For Magda, Silesian is what she speaks. She's not confident that she has a repertoire of styles. She won't presume to present herself as speaking Polish.

    Yet, her asides have a much higher density of Silesian forms, for example:

Łaj!! *Ino* . . . nie *tyn* mi puści!
Oh! Only . . . not this me let out!
Oh! Just don't let anyone hear this!

LANGUAGE, POWER, AND THE TWO STATES

It is well to remember Angelika's confusion and Magda's fear as we consider the responses of more confident respondents. We will consider three transcripts. Two come from girls, one age seventeen and the other twelve, and the other (and most clearly illustrative) comes from Franz Skorupka, age thirty. All, then, were schooled in Poland. What is most important to keep in mind in reading these is the classroom culture of language I've described.

Lucyna Kowolik, age twelve (whose grandfather figures in chapter 9), started by offering me a Silesian version of the story of the girl in the meadow. In English, and in detail, this story would go something as follows: "A little girl is sitting next to a fence in a meadow playing with a bucket and spade. There's a bird on the fence. It flies away and she watches it; then she gets up and chases after it. She stops looking where she's going, trips over a stone, falls on her head, and then she sits there with a headache and cries." In Lucyna's Silesian version, the italicized zero marker in square brackets, *[Ø]*, indicates that a sound is missing in Silesian that would be present in Polish:

Silesian (given first)   Polish (given second)

1 Na p*[Ø]*ocie, uh, *sie dziołcha* siedzi   Na łące obok pʟotu siedzi . . .
    On fence, uh, [refl] girl sits   On meadow by fence sits . . .
2 koła p*[Ø]*ota, na tym p*[Ø]*ocie siedzi,   PTASZEK i [hesitations] ptAK
    next to fence, on this fence sits,   bird [dim.] and [hesitations] bird
3 uh, pt*o*k. I tEn pt*o*k odlecio*ł* i ta   odleciał ona patrzi gdzie on, uh,
    uh, bird. And this bird flies off and the   flies away she looks where he, uh,
4 *dziołcha* zaglądo*ł* za nim, gdzie on leci   leci.
    girl looks after him, where he flies   flies.
5 No i, pot*y*n ona staniła i   I ta DZIEWCZYNKA
    So and, then she stood and   And the girl
6 chciała go *chycić*.   chciała go ZŁAPAĆ.
    wanted him to catch   wanted him to catch
7 nie widziała że tam jes*[Ø]*   nie widziała że tam jesT
    [neg] she saw that there is   [neg] she saw that there is
8   na tej łʌce
      on this meadow
9 kamien sie przewrociła   kamien jakiś i sie przewrociła.
    a stone [ref] she fell down.   stone some and she fell down.
10 I potEM myśli co *joł* zrobiła*[Ø]*   I potEM myśli. . . co zrobiłam,
    And then she thinks what I did   And then she thinks, what I did,

Cont. on Page 158

157

Silesian (given first)	Polish (given second) *Cont. from Page 157*
11 g*[Ø]* owa mi boli *ni?*	eh, czemu nie patrzyłam
12 head me hurts no?	eh, why [neg] I looked
	gdzie JA BIEGNIĘ.
	where I run.

Let's consider, first, features that we conventionally think of as distinguishing different languages: phonology and lexicon. In her Silesian version, for the most part, where Silesian phonology differs from Polish, Lucyna uses the Silesian: "p*[Ø]*ocie" vs. "pLocie," (lines 1 and 2); "g*[Ø]*owa" (line 11). There are some phonological issues subtle enough to be difficult for me to judge: I confidently hear the difference between "t*y*n" and "tEn," (line 3), "pot*y*n" and "potEM," (lines 5 and 10). But "łące" (line 1), "siedzi" (lines 1 and 2), and "gdzie" (lines 3 and 4) have Silesian pronounciations which are beyond me to hear. (Dobra is among the villages that natively uses "*kaj*" for "where," but there are plenty of people around who use the Silesian variant of "gdzie.") Lexically, Lucyna uses contrasts between "*dziołcha*" and "DZIEWCZYNKA," (lines 1 and 5), and "pt*ok*" vs. "PTASZEK" and "PTAK" (lines 2 and 3—actually a contrast of both phonology and lexicon). But she does not use the Silesian alternates for "odleciał," and "zagłąda" (line 5). Yet these words, Silesianized phonologically, seem to fit in Lucyna's comfortable Silesian—which is why I did not put them in small capitals. As usual, most of the transcript is in the normal serif font, representing speech that is both Polish and Silesian. What, then, in Lucyna's mind, constitutes the difference between Silesian and Polish? It's the way she organizes the story, and organization is a feature of register.

There are features in this transcript which remind me of Angelika's initial resistance to this exercise and the compromise that then allowed her to do it. Consider the difference between the two versions of line 5, which serves as a transition in the story: "So and then she stood and," compared to the Polish "And the girl . . ." The Silesian is colloquial, giving the story an air of casual interactive talk. Similarly, in line 5, the presence of the conjunction "and" in the Polish version makes explicit something left to the listener to fill in in the Silesian version: this is a mark of a more carefully grammatical and logical discourse.

But what I find most dramatic is the Silesian "*ni*" at the very end (line 11). This kind of element in discourse serves what is called "phatic function," that is, it's there to ensure that the channel of communication between interlocutors is open. Like "you know," in American English, it doesn't help create the message but rather invites the listener to indicate, with a nod or a word, that the message is being received. In this case, there is a neat overlap between the story that Lucyna is telling and the situation in which she is telling it. Whose phatic is this? Is it addressed by the little girl to her imagined interlocutor, or by Lucyna to me, or both? However we understand it, it serves to emphasize, as did Angelika Stanik's Silesian version, that the mode of communication is "I am talking to you," and not "I am describing a set of pictures for you." The Polish version lacks any such phatic.

That Polish is associated with the speech genre of formally telling a story, rather than informally talking about what's happening, is evident again in the responses of Anna Krysiak, who was seventeen at the time of this exercise.

	Silesian (given second)	Polish (given first)
1	Siedział *sie synek*	Pewnego razu CHŁOPCIK
	Sat [ref] boy	Certain time boy
2		siedział SOBIE
		sat [ref]
3	nad, eh, jeziorem, i . . . łowi ryby	uh, nad jeziorem i ŁOWIŁ ryby
	by, eh, lake, and . . . caught fish	uh, by lake and caught fish
4	*Naroz*	NAGLE,
	Suddenly,	Suddenly,
5		po jakimś tam czasie, NAGLE
		after some there time, suddenly
6	poczuł że ryba mu *biere*	poczuł że ryba mu BIERZE
	he felt that the fish to him took	felt that the fish to him took
7	i ciągnie ciągnie aż tu	i zaczył nawyać na wendke, [. . .] i
	and pulls pulls until here	and starts to pull on the rod [?] and
8	NAGLE *obejrzoł* że	w tym momencie ZAUWAŻA że
	suddenly he sees that	in that moment he notices that
9	to nie ryba *ino* um, uh,	to nie jes*[∅]* ryba TYLKO, uh, jakiś . . .
	it not fish but um, uh,	it [neg] is fish only, uh, some
10	*gors* trowy.	CUPEŁ trAwy.
	heap of grass	heap of grass

Consider "pewnego razu," "a certain time," or "once," or "one day"—this is a phrase of introducing a story however you translate it. "After some time," in line 5, reinforces the work of "suddenly" in marking a transition. The Polish of line 7 is both syntactically more complex ("starts to pull" vs. "pulls pulls") and more referentially specific ("on the rod"). "In that moment" (line 8) once again elaborately marks the progress of the action. The Polish version is conceived as a formally told story.

But it is Franz Skorupka, then in his thirties, and, as I said, the most linguistically sensitive person I worked with, whose responses illustrate what is going on here with the most beautiful clarity:

	Silesian (given first)	Polish (given second)
1	Na tym pierwszym obrozku	Pierwszy obrAzek przedstawia
	In this first picture	First picture presents
2	widza jak taki mały *synek*	małego CHŁOPCA
	I see how such small boy	small boy
3	siedzi na trowie i	siedziącego na brzegu rzeki
	sits on grass and	sitting on the bank of river
4	*chytoł* ryby w wantku.	ŁOWIĄCEGO ryby.
	catches fish on rod.	catching fish.
5	Na drugim, *ni,*	I drugi obrAzek przedstawia
	In second, no,	And second picture presents
6	stan*oł*, bo zaczyn*oł* brać.	że, eh, CHŁOPIEC poczuł, że
	stands, because begins to take.	that, eh, boy felt, that
7		zaczyna, zaczyna, ehn,
		begins, begins, ehn,
8		zaczyna sie branie!
		begins [refl] taking!
9		Oh, zaczyna sie branie!
		Oh, begins [refl] taking!
10	*Po lekku* ciągnie i zamias*[Ø]*	I wyciąga zamias*[Ø]* ryb,
	Slowly pulls and instead of	And pulls instead of fi,
11	ryby, i zamias ryby	zamias*[Ø]* rybki, wyciąga
	fish, and instead of fish	instead of fish [dim] pulls out
12	wyciąg*oł* jakiś *zielsko.* No.	. . .jak to po polsku *pedeć?*
	pulls out some weed. Yes	. . how that in Polish say?
13	Tak miało być	Zamias*[Ø]* ryby wyciąga
	So it had to be?	instead of fish pulls out
14		GLONY, ni? Bo to są GLONY
		weed, no? Because those are weeds
15		to po polsku są GLONY, ni?
		those in Polish are weeds, no?

"The first picture presents a small boy sitting on the bank of a river catching fish." "In the first picture I see how some little boy is sitting on the grass catching fish on a rod." We see here the difference between a stance of objective description and one of personal experience, as well as relative syntactic complexity (more powerfully obvious in case-rich Polish: "małego chłopca siedziącego . . . łowiącego"). Franz's Silesian uses the phatic function, reminding listeners of the channel of communication, in line 5 ("*ni*") and again at the end (line 13), when he comments, satisfied, on his own performance ("Yes") and speaks to me ("So it had to be?" or, perhaps, "That's what you wanted?"). His Polish version only does this at the end, (lines 14 and 15) when his search for a Polish lexical alternate has caused him, essentially, to break off the performance. And, in lines 6 through 9, Franz searches, and finds what he wants, in a syntactic form considered a mark of formal, written, impersonal discourse in both English and Polish: a nominalization ("branie," "the taking"—a noun formed from a verb). The University of Chicago's undergraduate composition course spends its first week poking fun at the common conception that gerunds lend the weight of formal authority to writing; it *is* a common conception, one that Franz has apparently also picked up somewhere.

Where? Precisely the same place that the hapless undergraduates get it: school. All three of these speakers, schooled in Polish, draw on their experience of school in creating a juxtaposition between Silesian and Polish versions of the same story. The objective descriptive stance, the complicated syntax, and the referential specificity, in addition to the phonological and lexical contrasts, allow us to identify the versions labeled "Polish" as differing from those labeled "Silesian" in the ways that registers differ from one another. "Register," as I have defined it, refers to a cultural ordering of community experience, and the experience ordered here is that of school. That's what accounts for Angelika's immediate reaction: "This is the way a Polish teacher would do it." That's what accounts for Magda's fearful school-imitating Polish even when asked for Silesian. "Polish" and "Silesian," then, function as registers with respect to one another, because by using them, a speaker can invoke contrasts among orders of experience, regardless of the semantics of what is being said.

In a sense, Angelika was right: the whole exercise was inherently contradictory. You wouldn't ever describe a set of wordless pictures that tell a story in Silesian. That's a schoolroom exercise; something you would do in Polish. But, respondents were imaginative, and when asked to do this, they responded by making Silesian versions that pretended that that's not what they were doing, that actually they were really talking about a little boy sitting on the grass catching fish on a rod. In this way, they used linguistic indices to place what they were talking about into the proper context of the Silesian-speaking realm of their experience.

Again, these indices, taken together, constitute a register, the use of which infuses speech with cultural meaning.

So, if Polish and Silesian function as registers with respect to one another within the multilingual repertoires of autochthonous Opole Silesians, what does this tell us about the openness of speech that speakers define as Silesian to massive importation from Polish? What about natural discourse, when no linguistic anthropologist is asking for something silly? What can we make of stretches of natural discourse in which, when transcribed, the density of markers of Polish—phonological, lexical, and intonational—suddenly increases dramatically, only to drop off again farther along? Such stretches are considered "code-switches" in some literature. I avoid that appellation because having been there along with the tape recorder, I know that nobody reacted as if the language of interaction had been changed to Polish. Use of Polish as identified linguistically is acceptable within speech socially identified as Silesian. But it is ideologically regulated.

Consider the following, advantageously succinct, example: I taped Angelika Stanik expounding the virtues of cows (we were using a book called *Secrets of Village Animals* to give her something to talk about in Silesian). She says: "This is a cow. A cow is a very good animal because it gives milk, and from the milk there's butter, and cream, right, so many good things there are from a cow, and a cow has a calf, right? a small one. And you can slaughter the calf and then there's the meat. There are very many advantages to cows. . ." (she goes on; it's a thirty second stretch). When I transcribed, and examined the intonation, I found that the introductory words stood out, and so did a summarizing sentence a few seconds later:

To jes[Ø] krowa. Krowa to jes[Ø] bardzo zwierze dobre . . .
That is cow. Cow that is very animal good

The second sentence has the typical Silesian lilt.

In contrast, consider the concluding words, "There are very many advantages to cows:"

Bardzo dużo korzyści jes[Ø] z krowy, WIESZ?
Very many advantages is from cow, you know?

The intonation of this sentence is typically Polish. Furthermore, practically speaking, there is nothing that distinguishes it from Polish, since although Silesian drops the final "t" of "jest" (is), it would be careful Polish indeed that would articulate it between an "s" and a "z." In this sentence only, Angelika uses the standard form of "you know."

Note that this sentence, "There are very many advantages to cows," is an organizer, and the fact that it is in Polish accords with the use to which Lucyna, Anna, and Franz put the standard language. At the same time, though, the sentence is Angelika's most declarative statement. Seconds before, and seconds later, in describing her own family's dependence on their cow, she uses a high density of Silesian forms:

2   można zabić i *zajś* mięso je*[∅]*. Bardzo dużo
     one can slaughter and again meat is. Very many
3   korzyści jes*[∅]* z krowy, WIESZ? My momy krowa
     advantages is from cow, you know? We have cow
4   i wiemy co to je*[∅]*, momy mleko momy
     and we know what it is, we have milk we have
5   *masełkoł*, momy serek, wszystko momy, *wes*?
     buttermilk, we have cheese, everything we have, you know?

The shift from declarative statement back to description of personal experience is accompanied by Silesian forms. Examples of this conjunction of Polish phonology, forms and intonation with such explanatory moments in discourse occur regularly in my tapes.

The key is that autochthonous Opole Silesians use the linguistic resources of Polish when they focus on speech as transmitting information. Again, the key is in the classroom. "Kasia, please tell me the names of the major cities on the river Vistula?" 'Please madam, the names of the major cities on the river Vistula are: Gdańsk, Toruń, Warsaw, and Cracow." In other words: "Let me tell you about the major cities on the river Vistula."

It is important to understand that transmitting information is, itself, not simply about whatever the subject of the information is about. Transmitting information—explicating—is, in itself, a particular kind of speech event, which creates a particular kind of relationship between interlocutors. It's not just "major cities on the river Vistula." Importantly, it's "Let me tell you." It is a form of talk which makes a claim on the listener's focused attention. It is, as Kipling put it in his children's stories, "Hear and attend and listen; for this befell and behappened and became and was." (Kipling 1912: 69).

163

Chapter 6

Let's consider then, a transcript of natural discourse in which objectively, one could perhaps identify "code-switches," or stretches of speech in which the resources of Polish are more densely employed. The speech in question took place during a birthday party for Franz Skorupka's son, which happens to be also St. Nicholas Day (December 6, 1994). One of the guests is describing her daughter's ill health to me, the only person present who didn't already know the story. Franz's father-in-law introduces the topic by commenting that the child, Klaudia, is now better. In brief, Klaudia had come down with mumps and ever since then, she'd gotten every cold and bronchial infection to pass through the neighborhood. I identified: reversing the usual fieldworker's pattern, I had gotten a bad viral infection of the kidneys while in Chicago between field trips, and had subsequently been ill repeatedly until, I assert, the good Silesian climate healed me. It's this assertion that prompts the explication, and disagreement: according to Klaudia's mother, the climate right around Dobra is not healthy.

speaker	line	utterance
f-in-law	1	Ta Klaudia jes*[Ø]* zdrow*oł*. That Klaudia is healthy.
mother, to EV	2	*Ł*ona miała w tym wrześniu ta świnka, *ni*? I po tej She had in this September those mumps, no? And after those
	3	szwince ta*n* wystrachiła ta oporność organismu, *ni*? mumps there she lost the immunity of organism, no?
	4	I już czwarty *ro*z jes*[Ø]* przeżębiona co albo gardło and already fourth time is infected what either throat
	5	albo oksrzele czwarty *ro*z. Nu i te*s* [. . .] zbad*oł* or bronchus fourth time. So and also [. . .] he examined
	6	na razie nie do antybiotyków TYLKO bańki i takie krople for the time not to antibiotics only cups and such drops
	7	*co* zmagajĄ działanie tych, uh, na oskrzelach są takie what overcome the activity of those, uh, on the bronchi are such
	8	żenskie, na, takie, oskrzele, *ni*? [interjection from EV] [. . .], on, such, bronchus, no?

Cont. on Page 165

speaker	line	utterance	Cont. from Page 164

9 *Nu*! Bo to *nieby* zmagoł działanie tego że to,
Yes! Because that sort of overcomes the activity of that so that it,

10 bronisz
you defend

11 No, i nie *wia* jak to ta*n*. Piątek m*o*m jechać do
So, and I don't know how that there. Friday I have to go to

12 kontroly, to *obejrzymy* co tam.
control, so we'll see what there.

She had mumps this September, right? mumps, she lost
the immunity of her organism. And now she's gotten sick
four times, either in the throat or bronchitis, four times. So
they've given her for now not antibiotics but only cups
[glass cups applied hot to the skin to form a vacuum] and
these drops which strengthen the activity, uh, on the
bronchi there are these [. . .], on the bronchi, right? [inter-
jection] Yes! So that sort of strengthens the activity of that
so that it fights things off, right? So I don't know what's
going on, on Friday I have to go for a check-up, so we'll
see what's going on.

Topic switch:
13 A tu u lekarz to *ino* antybiotyk, antybiotyk i . . .
And here at the doctor it only antibiotics, antibiotics, and

14 niedziela skończy[∅] brać a w czwartek *ty zajś jes* choroł
Sunday stop to take and on Thursday you again are sick.

15 To jak to tak? *Jakby* ten organ już wcale nie broni
So how that so? If that organ already at all does not defend

16 *ino DURCH*, NAOKRĄGŁU chory.
only through, by circle sick.

And here all doctors do is give out antibiotics, antibiotics,
and if you stop taking them on Sunday on Thursday you're

Cont. on Page 166

sick again. What's the good of that? If the organism stops
fighting things off completely then you're sick constantly.
[I reply, saying:] Yeah, I had a similar experience, except
this good Silesian climate has strengthened me. But I got
sick last February, a bad influenza in the kidneys, and then I
got every cold that came through the area. Through the
whole summer, too, until I came here to Silesia. But here
I've been healthy.

mother   17   Przecież tu, właśnie w okolicy Barkowa, NIE?
                 But here, just in the area of Barkowo, no?

            18   To, nie ma takiego dobrego klimatu.
                 Then, there isn't such a good climate.

                 But here, right around Barkowo, right? This isn't such a great climate.

EV   19   Lepiej jak w Chicago, mi sie wydaje
                 Better than in Chicago, to me [refl] it seems!

mother   20   Nu, możliwe bo to jest duże miasto [stoi], ale tu my
                 Well, possible because that is a big city [stands], but here we

            21   *som* na jakiś takich skałach magmowych, KTÓRE
                 are on some such igneous formations, which

            22   promenują. Jeszcze na dodatek ta hołda, *ni*? z tej huty
                 wander. Yet on addition that refuse pile , no? of that steelworks

            23   to, dodatkowe i tu właśnie Borkowo, Falenty do Opola, to
                 then, additionally and here just Borkowo, Falenty to Opole , it

            24   jes*[Ø]* właśnie taki rejon gdzie dzieci bardzo dużo chorują
                 is exactly such a region where children very much sicken.

                 Well, that's possible because that is a big city. But here we are
                 on these kind of igneous formations, which wander [send out
                 malign physical influences]. And in addition, the refuse pile,
                 right? From the steelworks then, that additionally and here

Cont. on Page 167

Cont. from Page 166

> from Borkowo to Falenty to Opole is precisely a region
> where children get sick a great deal. [The refuse pile is a
> mountain of metallic waste and ash. The speaker is sug-
> gesting that the messed up magnetic forces of the area
> cause sickness.]

Klaudia's mother's discourse divides into two parts, and the point of division is my contribution to the conversation. What comes afterward is more Polish in relative lack of Silesian lexical, phonological and syntactic alternates, as well as in intonation. Yet the reason cannot be that she suddenly felt herself to be speaking to me; she knew she was doing that from the beginning. Let's examine this shift more closely.

Lines 2 through 12 serve to bring me up to date on the story of Klaudia's health. The story is a blend: Klaudia's mother, here, is clearly drawing on what she has been told by the doctor. She is not disagreeing with it, but rather representing it: the doctor has prescribed interventions intended not to attack the infections directly, but rather to strengthen Klaudia's immune system. That she is representing is reflected in the repeated nonliteral use of deictic words that indicate distance from the speaker: "those mumps" (line 2), "those mumps there" (lines 2–3), "that immunity" (line 3), "such drops" or "these drops" (line 6, i.e., "I personally wouldn't know exactly what kind of drops"), "such [. . .]" (line 8— I haven't been able to figure out what "żenskie" means in English here), and "there" (lines 11 and 12). Every line has at least one Silesianizing element, except line 6, where the speaker says TYLKO instead of *ino* for "only," in contrast to lines 14 and 16. Again, this alternate comes in the middle of a stretch of speech which represents the Polish-speaking doctor's point of view. Yet, with the exception of the choice of TYLKO, Klaudia's mother is translating into her own speech.

In lines 13 through 16, the speaker criticizes doctors in Poland for over-prescribing antibiotics and thereby undermining patients' immune systems (though presumably this particular doctor knows better). Again, where Polish/Silesian alternates exist, in these lines the Silesian alternates occur. The repetition, "*DURCH*, NA OKRĄGLU" in line 16 is an intensification switch, as discussed in chapter 5; they happen both from Silesian to German and Silesian to Polish.

Lines 17 through 24 form a contrast. There are Silesian elements in these lines: *som*, "we are" in line 21 and *ni* in line 22. But these lines stand out in that there are Polish elements. In line 17, we see the only instance of the Polish phatic, NIE. KTÓRE, "which," in line 21 is very striking. In line 7, the speaker used invariant *co*, "what" to relativize the following clause; KTÓRE, which declines by case, number, and gender, is the standard Polish mechanism. "Gdzie," in line 24 also makes an impression of standardness, but without another example from this speaker of the use of the word for "where," it's not possible to judge whether, in her Silesian, she says *kaj*.

Beyond these alternates, there are several words which mark an expository register in a way similar to Lucyna's repetition of information ('and she saw that there is on this meadow . . ."), and the use of "and" ("a stone and she fell down . . .") and to Anna's "one day," and "suddenly, after some time." I am referring to "przecież" ("yet, still, after all, on the contrary") in line 17, and "na dodatek" ("in addition") and "dodatkowe" ("additionally") in lines 22 and 23. These, too, lay out transition and logical progression in an explicit way.

And finally, intonation plays an important role. If we consider the intonation of speech, the segments which respond to my contributions, lines 17–18 and 20–24, display a pattern different from that of lines 2–16. These first, more Silesian lines appear flat in comparison. But the more marked intonation of lines 17–18 and 20–24 is not characteristically Silesian. For that, we need to look at line 1, spoken by Franz's father-in-law. This has the characteristic rise in intonation in the middle of the sentence, a more extreme one than any that occurs in the younger speaker's speech. Rather, the steady falling intonation of line 18 is reminiscent of the Polish intonation that children practice in choral reading in first grade. It is repeated at the end of line 24.

In short, in lines 17–18 and 20–24 we have, indeed, a stretch of discourse in transcripts when the density of markers of standard—phonological, lexical, and intonational—suddenly increases dramatically, but without, apparently, being noticed by any of the participants as a change in the language of interaction. What allows for this is a shared sense that it is appropriate to call upon the linguistic resources of Polish when the main purpose is the explication of something. It was appropriate, then, to use Polish to explicate to me the unhealthy nature of the immediate environment. This kind of use of Polish—always socially unremarked—was something I noted frequently:

> Mr. Kaczmarcik, in a conversation in the tavern that ranged over many topics, spoke Silesian while joshing with Marta, and switched to Polish to discuss the politics of garbage removal and population loss, and then switched back to Silesian when the conversation again took a more playful turn (October 9, 1994).

At the annual school field day (June 1, 1995), there was a complicated hopping game. One had to hop to a pole with a ball between one's legs, and then there was another ball which had a strap attached to it; one put that around one's ankle and then kicked the free ball in front of one and zig-zagged between poles. I heard a boy explain all that to another in Polish. A few minutes later a girl came by, walking with a girlfriend, and called out, "Michał, co ty *bajes* robił?" [Michael, what are you going to do?]

Mr. Joszko, the head of the volunteer fire department in Dobra, had invited some firemen from Opole to the same event to give a demonstration for the children. Explaining what the firemen were doing, from behind a microphone, he spoke to them in Polish. But after the demonstration was over, when calling out to them without the microphone from the side, inviting them to come see what the fire truck looked like from the inside, he spoke Silesian.

The third example in particular begins to give a sense of the conjunction of several elements which make the use of Polish socially appropriate: not only was the communication expository, but the demonstration was being explicated in an explicit performance context, through a microphone (remember the dissonance between speaking Silesian and *my* microphone). We can further clarify this conjunction by distinguishing aspects of the ideology of Polish in play. Consider, as one aspect, that Polish is conceived as being "clearer," a more effective vehicle for information:

A girl called out to her friend riding by on a bicycle, "*kaj* ty je*dżieś*?" [Where are you going?] "Co?" [What?] the cyclist called over her shoulder. "GDZIE ty jEDZIESZ?" her friend called out. (January 17, 1993).

Here, distance and wind were interfering with communication; the speaker responded, seemingly, in the belief that Polish would compensate for that. That is one aspect of the ideology of Polish. But the associations of Polish with contexts in which focused attention is paid to the speaker (school, media, microphones), furthermore, allow speakers to use Polish performatively to make a claim on attention:

A four-year-old child, playing at the counter in the tavern, said a sentence in which the word "obro*ł*zek" [picture] appeared. When nobody paid any attention to her, she repeated herself, saying "obrAzek," instead. (January 19, 1993).

At the spring Field Day at school, there was a game of "hot and cold" where a blindfolded child had to find an object within a roped-off space by following directions called out from the sidelines. One of the parents called out, "*na zold, na zold*" [backwards] but when the child didn't respond, added, "z POWROTEM." (June 1, 1995).

Again, when a speaker focuses on getting information across, and uses Polish to do so, the conception of the nature of Polish is invoked in two ways. Polish is conceived as being "clearer," a more effective vehicle for information. But Polish also is conceived as the vehicle of making a claim on the listener's focused attention. These two examples well illustrate that: both the small child and the parent were saying, by their use of Polish, "Pay attention to me!"

And that's OK. For there is room in social life for explication, and for focused attention. That is a feature of communication everywhere, in all linguistic environments. If Silesians have been exposed to oppressively negative evaluations of their speech, as in the joke about the Silesian girl who wants chocolate and cookies, and if these evaluations have found their primary stage in that place where attention is most adamantly demanded, school, they nevertheless have room for it in interactions within their own community, not overlaid by the tensions of relations with a dominant ethnic Other. That they use Polish in such situations, and that such usage is entirely socially acceptable within norms of "speaking Silesian," is an example of creating autochthonous Opole Silesian culture out of what lies beyond it.

Yet this usage remains ambivalent; it remains somewhat socially dangerous, because demanding somebody's focused attention remains an act of power. The use of what is linguistically Polish between social equals such as in the following example is entirely normative:

At a birthday party, Roman used Polish to explain something financial. As he spoke all attention was on him. Later, on a different topic, he said, "JA CI MOWIĘ moje zdanie na temat twojego centralnego." [I'll tell you my opinion on the subject of your central heating.] Again, Polish; again, all attention on him (December 13, 1992).

But its use between people whose power is not equal is also entirely normative:

Marta's brother Józef and his family visited Dobra in late November 1992. One afternoon (November 28), Łukaś headed out to join his cousin Henryk. Józef stopped him. In standard Polish, he told Łukaś to tell Henryk to come home. He had already been gone for two hours and he had been told to return after one. "Tell Henryk to come back immediately or I will come get him!" Józef said.

If we consider the child's point of view, the power dynamics in play in using Polish are self-evident in this example, even though they are not interethnic dynamics, but rather intrafamilial ones.

And the interethnic dynamics involved lurk; Polish power to control Silesian speech, in school, in the workplace, everywhere except "here." Polish may be accepted as a register of explanation, the need to call on others' focused attention acknowledged, but the origins of that register remain. Brigitte's perception that I had misused a single word helped clarify this for me:

> Brigitte works in one of the grocery stores in Dobra. One morning in the store, as Brigitte gave me two breasts of chicken, I asked, "Are they frozen?"
>
> "Yes," she said, "but they're sure to thaw by the time you're ready to cook them." (It was still several hours until lunchtime.)
>
> "Of course," I said.
>
> The word I used was "Oczywiście," which I thought was appropriate to a casual conversation between friends and a word both in Polish and Silesian. But Brigitte repeated that word and laughed, and it was the sort of laugh that gently pokes fun at a slight mistake. So, guessing the problem, I reached for a synonym that I thought was more Silesian, though Poles use it too, and said, "Pewno." Just to make sure, I gave the word the intonation that is characteristically Silesian, i.e., a rising higher pitch on the first syllable than the last. At that, Brigitte smiled.

Later (September 23, 1995), I asked a group of people in the tavern which word they thought was more Polish: "oczywiście" or "pewno." They all agreed, instinctively, that the former was, but they noted that both are used. Angelika Stanik's comments had been more reflective. I had asked her, initially without telling her the context, whether she thought "oczywiście" was more Polish, and "pewno" more Silesian. She thought about it for a minute, then said yes. Then I told her what had happened, and she said, "She probably understood you like this: 'oczywiście,' as if you'd already known that, as if you were saying, 'Why did you tell me that? I know that.' Whereas 'pewno,' it's more like you're agreeing, 'Oh yes, of course, I see that they will thaw.' It's like, when I'm in school and the teacher examines me on something, and I'm telling her what I know, and she'll say, 'OCZYWIŚCIE, OCZYWIŚCIE.' She already knows it, and I'm just telling her what she already knows" (April 8, 1995).

It was not an egalitarian thing to say, "oczywiście," and there was no accessible social reason not to behave in an egalitarian way. There was nothing to explicate, and I already had Brigitte's focused attention. If I had needed even more of it, if it had been a matter of my saying, "Of course, but look, Brigitte . . ." and going on to tell her something specific about the chicken, or my lunch

171

plans, or anything else pertinent to its frozen state, I suspect that she would have found "oczywiście" an entirely appropriate word for "of course." But my actual usage of the word was untamed by commonly understood autochthonous Opole Silesian norms of language use which allow the use of Polish. It grated on her, a little.

WHEN SILESIANS USE POLISH TO "TALK ABOUT" POWER

Given Brigitte's reaction to one word, it is no surprise that when Silesians use the linguistic resources of Polish in a way that others interpret as, in fact, speaking Polish, the context is some sort of bad behavior. Consider the following happening in the tavern, between about 8 p.m. and 1:30 a.m., November 26, 1994, with enough alcohol flowing that I note having been seriously hung over the next day. There were seven people present, between the ages of about twenty and about thirty-five.

> I don't know quite why, but when Bartek entered the tavern there was a reaction—a vocalization from all that seemed to express that Bartek was for some reason notorious, at least for the evening. Mariola particularly hammed this up. She was sitting at the end of the bench, so it seemed likely that Bartek would sit in a chair next to her. She took this chair and turned it with its back to Bartek. He found another chair and pointedly sat next to her. She began to tease him, to the delighted attention of all present. At one point Bartek turned to her and said, "Ci GADAM, JA wcale z tobą nie rozmawiAM." [I tell you, I'm not talking with you at all.] This elicited another "Ooooh!" from the others, and Artur commented, "In Polish!"

This was a conversation, I noted, in which the usual patterns of the use of Polish prevailed: not always were contrastively Silesian alternates to Polish linguistic elements used. Words which are contrastively Silesian and words drawn from, or also occurring in, Polish, both occur, and the latter, as usual, occur without provoking any reaction. Mariola said to Bartek at one point, "Daj mi spokoj" ["Give me peace," or "Leave me alone!"] There exists a Silesian alternate to this—"D*ej* mi *[Ø]*pokoj," for example. And I heard Artur use the word "ubrane" (dressed) at one point in the evening, and its contrastively Silesian equivalent, "*loblecone*" later. Everyone was using enough linguistic cues of Silesianness that everyone understood each other to be speaking Silesian. Except when Bartek came out with the utterance quoted above. What made that different?

It is not just the Polish phonology. It is that this utterance, literally, said, "I am not talking to you." It was presented as a rejection of the conversation. The Polish phonology re-inforced the literal meaning.

It would be a very serious breach of solidarity to be seen as doing that sincerely. In fact, I never saw it happen. On this evening, talk had been socially defined as humorous. Everyone knew that Bartek didn't really mean it. It was not a real rejection. It wasn't really him talking.

To summarize the uses of the linguistic resources of Polish we've discussed so far: Polish because "different people speak Silesian differently," which can be observed to mean that young people speak a Silesian much closer to Standard than older people. Polish because such speakers, especially, tend to incorporate words and phrasings taken from Polish: "My grandmother says *kneflik*, but I myself say *GUZIK*." Polish—like German—to symbolize the temporal and political/spatial context. Polish as an expository register. Polish to demand attention, whether to explanation or to authority. None of these uses requires speakers to signal that they are distancing themselves from their own speech, or to be understood to be so doing.

But untamed by these ideological parameters, Polish will place its user outside a Silesian-speaking interactional context, and be seen as a rejection. Recall that the language attitude survey reveals quite a bit of agreement with the statement that a Silesian who stops speaking Silesian stops being 100 percent Silesian. Beyond the pale of the limits summarized above, literally, you've got to be joking—or understood to be a foreigner, as Brigitte understood me. Otherwise, the risk is that you will be seen as having made yourself a foreigner. No, the only other use of Polish that I saw was this: Polish used to mimic the speech of actual Poles, particularly schoolteachers. For example, Mrs. Sattler, now in her sixties, recollected for me what happened when her son had his first science lessons in school (April 22, 1993). The children were asked to write down the names of domestic plants, so her son wrote the names he used domestically: *BLUMENKOHL* (cauliflower), *BOHNEN* (beans). . . . Immediately, she was called in for a conversation with the teacher, who said, as she recollected and mimicked:

> Przeciew, JA NIE wieM co pisze pani dziecko!
> But, I don't know what writes your child!
> Co to jest, "*BLUMENKOHL*"? Co to jest, "*BOHNEN*"?
> What is that, "*BLUMENKOHL*"? What is that, "*BOHNEN*"?

Not only was this reaction repressive with regard to Silesian linguistic practices, but, by the lights of a culture that highly values multilingualism, the teacher was, in essence, stupidly boasting about her own ignorance. Still, this event had happened long before its telling in 1993; Mrs. Sattler's son is almost exactly my age. It was told with a bit of a smile.

Chapter 6

But such tensions persist to the present day. At the same December 6, 1994, gathering at which Klaudia's health was discussed, Franz spoke bitterly about how his younger son, Michał, was being treated in preschool. The teachers were blatantly favoring other children; he was so insulted that he had returned the St. Nicholas Day packet of goodies given to his son unopened, informing them that it wasn't wanted; he would buy something similar for Michał himself. He then claimed that they never allow Michał a chance to recite, and to complain about the favoritism of Santa (one of the teachers dressed up). Franz satirized the teachers' Polish speech in the same way that Mrs. Sattler did. The segment of conversation ended ominously with the arousal of Brigitte's father's long-standing fears that teachers deliberately behave in provoking ways, and then retaliate if Silesians fail to suppress their angry reactions:

speaker	line	utterance
Franz	1	Ale *zech* to zauważ*ol*, je*[Ø]* *c*ysty klan! Klan jest! But [1st person past marker] it noticed, it is pure clan! Clan it is!
	2	Nauczycielki mają swoich popiłków. Pawałek, Rafałełek, Teachers have their dolls. Paul [dim.], Rafael [dim.]
	3	dziewczynki i koniec. Reszta, to s*on*, to nie s*on* dzieci little girls and end. Rest, those are, those not are children
	4	nie *wia* to jes*[Ø]* internat albo to jes*[Ø]* dom dziecka I not know it is boarding school or it is orphanage
	5	albo to j' przedszkoła. or it is preschool.

But I have seen that it's a pure clan! A clan! The teachers have their dolls. Little Paul, little Rafael, the little girls and that's it. The rest aren't treated like children, I don't know if it's a boarding school or an orphanage or a preschool!

| | 6 | Wierszyk: ĸto ᴍówi, chodż, chodż, też chciaʟeś ty, [. . .]
verse [dim.]: who speaks, come, come, also wanted you |
| | 7 | też chciaʟeś ty, to chodż, chodż, ty!
also wanted you, so come, come, you! |

Cont. on Page 175

174

Cont. from Page 174

speaker	line	utterance

8 Cz*a*mu sie nie zapytała, Michał, umie*s*? Nie podoba mi sie!
   Why [refl] did not ask, Michael, can you? It does not please me [refl]!

   Verse: "who will recite, come, come, you also wanted to do it,
   you also wanted to, so come, come, you." [the inclusion of the
   teacher's "ty," in addition to the person-marked verb, emphasizes her inclusion of the child—some other child than Michał.]
   Why didn't she ask, 'Michał, can you?' I don't like it!"

9 Nu. *Joł* dziesi*ej* wedzi*oł*, do Mikołaja przychodzi [. . .]
   Yes. I today saw, to Santa Claus comes [. . .]

10 Jolanta Pason. Ta *dziołcha* idzie *sie* [. . .] Nu, fakt że
   Jolanta Pason. The girl goes [refl] [. . .] Well, fact that

11 jest najmniejsza z tych wszystkich ta*n* dzieci, przy*s*ła
   she is the smallest of those all there children, she went

12 dostała paczk*a, ni*? Pasonka, ta *dziołska* chciała iś*[Ø]*
   she got a package, no? Pasonka, the little girl wanted to go

13 zar*o*z, *ni*? Je*s*ce jedna paczka! Albo *łod* rodziców albo
   at once, no? Still one package! Either from parents or

14 kogoś, *ni*? No, to jeszcze jedna paczka, *ni*? Chciała
   somebody, no? Well, so still one package, no? She wanted

15 iś*[Ø] siednonć, ni*? Ona BĘDZIE SIEDZIEĆ przy Mikołaju!
   to go sit, no? She is going to sit next to Santa Claus!

16 bo ten, Mikołaj musi mieć *ino* t*e*dziecko, *ni*?
   because that, Santa Claus must have only that child, no?

17 Nie mo*z*e mieć inne, t*e* [. . .]
   Not can have other, that one [. . .]

   "Well. I saw today how Jolanta Pason went up to Santa
   Claus. The girl goes up—it's a fact that she's the smallest

Cont. on Page 176

of all the children there—she goes up, she went up, she got a
package, no? The little girl wanted to leave right away, no?
Yet another package! Either from parents or from somebody,
no? Well, so yet another package, no? She wanted to go sit
down, no? But she's going to sit by Santa! 'Cause this
Santa's got to have this particular child, no? He can't have
any other, it's got to be that one."

18 Ale *joł* cekom a*s* Michał *wyledzie* z przedszkoła. To je*[Ø]*
But I wait until Michael goes out from preschool. That is

19 *niedugo*. A jak *joł* jon spotk*om* na drodze, [to jej dam] zdan*a*
not long. And when I her meet on the street, [then I will give] opinion.

"But I'm going to wait until Michal leaves preschool. It's not long now.
And when I see her on the street, I will give her a piece of my mind!"

f-in-law   20 Nic nie zrobi*s* to s*on* . . .
Nothing you won't do those are . . .

Franz   21 Tera*[Ø]* nie zrobi*a* nic, bo one sie w ogole [interrupted]
Now I won't do anything, because they [refl] anyway

f-in-law   22 *Łone ino* czekaj*on* na *taki coś*! *Ino* czekaj*on*!
They only wait for such a thing! Only they wait!

Note that in lines 6 and 7, the intonation has the characteristic falling lilt of
Polish; line 8, "MiCHAŁ, umiE*S*?" has the characteristic lilt of Silesian. There
can be no question of the connotations of the use of Polish here: it is firmly
associated with Polish-speaking teachers behaving badly. Franz is quoting, in
lines 6–7, and the contrast of what the teachers said with what they should
have said is depicted as a contrast of the Polish words that were said with the
Silesian words that weren't. The only other contrastively Polish words, in line
15, are also, indirectly, a quote. When Franz speaks Polish, here, he is not
speaking in his own voice.

However, Klaudia's mother did speak Polish in her own voice in telling me
about the climate. That's how it works: it's permissable to use a high density of

Polish alternates in a stretch of speech that is expository and that particularly calls on the focused attention of the listener. Other than that, there has to be some ongoing signaling that speech is in Silesian, even if it's only a sprinkling of *ni*'s. And besides that, a high density of Polish alternates is used in discourse contexts that establish that the speaker is not speaking as him or herself, but joking, or quoting. Let me be clear: in two years of fieldwork I *never* heard Polish used among autochthonous Opole Silesians in any other ways than those I have described.

Franz used Polish in an acceptable way, yet in a way that firmly calls to mind the the harsh power dynamics which have pertained between the autochthonous Opole Silesian and Polish societies. Franz's speech, so to speak, looks toward the boundary, the edge where that contrast between identities is salient, because beneath the explicit criticism of his son's teachers runs a subtextual articulation of that criticism in ethnic terms. His solidary position is not in question: he is using Polish only in quotes. His using Polish to quote them places *their* solidary position in question. The quoting of the teachers in Polish brings in a host interethnic hostility and stereotype, reminds listeners of stories such as Mrs. Sattler's. So the oppressively asymmetric origins of this shared sense of register are very near the surface in Franz's speech.

It is, subtly, a "behaving like" critique. Autochthonous Opole Silesians, as Urszula Krysiak told us, don't see any problem with Poles speaking Polish. But Franz's son's teacher—the only one he complained of by name, at least— is not Polish. Franz's son's teacher is Mrs. Sattler's daughter-in-law. She lives about a kilometer away; Mrs. Sattler lives across the street.

Mrs. Sattler considers herself staunchly Silesian; Franz considers himself staunchly Silesian. She believes strongly that it's right to pass on the Silesian dialect to the next generation, because "you have to hold to what your parents gave you;" Franz thinks similarly. Unaware of any criticism of her daughter-in-law's teaching, she volunteered to me her approval of it: she teaches the children to speak Polish, and speaks to them in the classroom context in Polish, but she speaks to her own children in Silesian and also to the preschoolers in Silesian, in unofficial contexts (August 29, 1995). Franz, who also values his ability to speak standard Polish, would agree that it is the school's job to teach it. And yet, wherever people share responsibility for something, whether for a child, as here, or for property, as in the next chapter, there is the potential for conflict. The relationship between teachers and parents can be difficult anywhere. And in this case, there is a conflict between Franz, factory worker and Silesian storyteller, and the younger Mrs. Sattler, Polish-teaching preschool teacher. To approve of teachers teaching Polish is one thing; to make one's living actually doing it, another. The contrast of languages, with its origin in difficult interethnic relations, is a metaphor for this division, this conflict.

In a community where the question of "who do you consider yourself to be?" is highly fraught, the multilingual repertoire of autochthonous Opole Silesians is also a language of divisions. These divisions do not amount, in a simple way, to a division of ethnic or national identity. It is more accurate to say that the contrast of languages is a site where multiply overlaid conflicts related to class, status, and interpersonal negotiations find articulation. At this point, it is enough to understand the way that contrast of languages works to articulate conflict. As we continue on, we will need to broaden our understanding: in the next chapter, it's not just contrast of languages in speech ("code-switching"), it's also how people ascribe identity to others; and in the following chapter, it's not just how people ascribe identity to others, it's also how they ascribe identity to themselves, who they feel themselves to be. It is, in short, an entire social discourse of identity. And identity, it turns out, is all about morality.

To conclude this chapter, we consider one more example of the relation of language and power, one more instance in which switching languages serves as a metaphor for conflictual relations. It is an extremely clear example; readers can hardly miss the symbolism of the German here. It does raise a question, though: I never heard Polish used, in all seriousness, to create, or intensify, a conflict: Bartek was kidding; Franz was quoting; Józef was just being a dad. But when it came to the contrast between Silesian and German, it was a different story. So what's different about German, then, that German is used explicitly to assert power? That's the question that will begin the next chapter.

WHEN GERMAN IS USED TO ASSERT POWER

At the beginning of my third stint of fieldwork (March to October 1995), I was looking for a place to live. Marta, who knows everything that goes on in Dobra, found out that Bernard, who had emigrated to Germany some years previously and who owned a house not far from her parents', was visiting, and that his tenants, a Dobra couple with young children, had just moved out. She convinced him, over a half liter of vodka, to offer to rent his house to me. She was very excited about the house, which (Bernard had told her) was fully furnished, had a washing machine, and was only going to cost half a million złoty a month. This was about $30, while I was prepared to pay up to $60. Bernard decided to go over to the house; Marta told him she would go get me and meet him there. She appeared at the house where I was temporarily staying and we drove over to his house, parked Marta's several-year-old Opel behind the owner's black Mercedes, and entered the yard through the gate.

Inside the house, we found the owner, his uncle, and the local couple who had been renting the house. The owner had not taken off his long coat, but one could see a very fine white shirt with what could only be called a "cravat"—neither a tie nor a bow tie, but a little triangle of tie material at the collar. The house's appearance contrasted with that of its owner: it was very dirty and very empty. Everything the owner thought was there—furniture, washing machine, dishes, and so on—was gone. He was in the process of loudly accusing the tenants of stealing it. The tenants, for their part, were shouting back. They had been paying the taxes on the property! They had put a lot of work into the house for which they had not been reimbursed! The owner's mother-in-law had given them permission to throw out what they didn't want or need! The landlord countered that the tenants owed rent from August to December as well as electricity, and that he would take the matter to a judge. Drawing himself up and facing the woman from a distance of several feet, he said threateningly in German: "DAS IST NOCH NICHT DAS ENDE!" ("This is not yet the end!" or, colloquially, "You haven't heard the last of this!") The woman answered in Silesian, "*Gołdej* po polsku!" (Speak Polish!) (In this context, the tenant fell back on the historic linguistic contrast where, opposed to German, "Polish" means Silesian Polish.) The landlord translated, and the woman retorted, "What 'end'?!" The argument continued and eventually the landlord told the tenants to "get out or get thrown out" ("*bez p[Ø]ot bajes leceć!*" "Over the fence you will fly!") The tenants moved into the yard, the man making some reply to which the landlord responded by coming out of the house, grabbing him by the front of the jacket and shirt, and forcing him backward to the gate (he was considerably larger than the tenant). "DU AR-SCHLOCH!" (you asshole!), the landlord yelled, to which the tenant replied with a near translation: "Do dupy! Głęboko!" (Up your ass! Deep!) The couple left, the man saying something about "po polsku" as they stalked off.

Bernard's switch to German was an escalation that was quite a bit more intense than that of the customer who wanted milk in his coffee. That was merely a complaint; what Bernard said was a threat. His tenants immediately called him on it, and countered his next use of German with words just as strong in Polish. His use of German seemed to remain an issue as the encounter ended, although I didn't quite hear what they said as they stalked off. Here was German as a language of threatening power, used by landlord in relationship with his tenants—a relationship of unequal power.

And yet, the German was used in this way among autochthonous Opole Silesians. Bernard was born and grew up in Dobra; his wife is also from Dobra. This was not an encounter across a line of ethnicity, only across a line of power. A line that I never heard anyone cross by using Polish. So what's different about German?

Chapter 7

IDENTITY ASCRIPTIONS AS A LANGUAGE OF MORALITY

We have spent several chapters understanding Silesian culture. At this point, we need to understand more precisely what it means not to identify with that culture.

In chapter 4, I began with a description of Silesian houses, and with the sociological data about self-identification that Berlińska and Jonderko gathered in 1990 and 1993. This shed light on the question of how the German Minority was able to organize itself so effectively and so quickly: the leaders tapped the authority structure of the autochthonous household. The story of Bernard and his tenants appeared in chapter 6 to emphasize the linguistic aspect of Bernard's using German to threaten and the way the tenants reacted to that; German was used as a language of conflict, in a way that Polish is not used. In this chapter, we draw on the ethnography of houses, kinship structure, and the sociology of self-identification to consider why it was that, although Bernard's house had been emptied, people in Dobra sided with the tenants; they disapproved of Bernard. This was expressed, among other ways, by saying that Bernard was "playing the great Herr;" an explicit reference to German identity used to express moral opprobrium. In order to understand how and why ascriptions of identity are used in Dobra as statements of moral disapproval, we need to get back to both the meaning of the sociological data, and to the meaning of the houses.

This chapter will provide a more detailed understanding of the divisions and conflicts in play: those between autochthonous Opole Silesians and Poles, and those between autochthonous Opole Silesians and Germans. We have, at this point, a clear picture of language and power. What we need is a clearer picture of people's social positions, how they got there, and how language and power relate to that: in short, a picture of the ethnographic and historical context. It is this that will lead us, first, to an understanding of how *identity ascriptions*—people talking about others in ethnic terms—function as moral evaluations. Chapter 8 explores how *identity assertions*—people talking about

180

themselves in ethnic terms—function also as moral statements. This leads us ultimately, in chapter 9, to the psychological issue of why, for some, identity can be so vehement. In the conclusion, a connection is suggested: vehemence can turn to violence.

SILESIAN IDENTITY, NATIONAL IDENTITY, AND PERCEPTIONS OF THE STATES

Look again at figure 1. As I said above, the tower in the middle of the figure represents the fact that, in both 1990 and 1993, almost 50 percent of respondents said that they considered themselves to be simply "Silesian." In terms of national identity, age correlated strongly: 72.2 percent of those who considered themselves German were born before 1937, while 57.1 percent of those who considered themselves Polish were born after 1953. This makes sense in that it is age that justifies the trio of reasons that people claim German identity: I was born in Germany, I went to German school, the language here was German. What we need to focus on here is not so much the correlates, but the claim.

If we compare the right side of the figure, that is, respondents who asserted some degree of German identity, with the left side, respondents who claimed some degree of Polish identity, we see a valley to the right, and a cliff to the left. The least popular response of all was, "more a Pole than a Silesian." And the reason that that is so is also the reason that I observed German, never Polish, used in sharp social conflict.

Recall that almost 40 percent of respondents who considered themselves simply Polish had a Polish spouse, and observe that there were more of them than of respondents who considered themselves simply German, without acknowledging any degree of Silesian identity. Just as there is something about age which is connected to how people formulate statements of who they are, there is something about marrying a person whose family came from central or eastern Poland that encourages people to formulate their identity as Polish, which their siblings who married autochthonous Opole Silesians are less likely to do. What is it?

The clue is in the "claim." Recall that the discussion of the League of Expellee group's visit to Ostrów revolved around the Ostrovians claim to German identity. Yet identity is not supposed to be a claim. According to the hegemonic ideology of identity, people inherit their identity. You're not supposed to have to "claim" to be a member of your ethnic national group any more than I have to "claim" to have brown eyes. But in reality, it is not so simple: group affiliations are social constructs, not natural ones.

Berlińska and Jonderko did not ask people whether they felt themselves to be "more a Pole than a German" or "more a German than a Pole," because those identities are mutually exclusive. National identity subsumes regional identity (both Londoners and Liverpudlians are English) but excludes other national identities (neither are French), just as regional identities exclude one another (a Londoner is not a Liverpudlian). In the borderland situation, it is the national identity which is not straightforward. That means that this placement of "Silesian" as the logically central response option expresses the social fact that Silesian identity is an *origo*, a place from which one moves.

That movement is not neutral. The history of Silesia is a history of internal colonialism which has stigmatized and "otherized" autochthonous Opole Silesians. Both officials of the German and the Polish states and ordinary citizens have been the agents of this. Being born into the indigenous population means inheriting a lesser status. To claim a national identity is to claim something better than what one was born into. Silesian identity is something individuals may, or may not, move out of. Whether they do or do not is a morally complicated matter.

National identity is a "higher order" not just logically, but socially. Upward mobility, with its connotations of escape, is a more apt image for it than lateral mobility. Notice, then, that more people who identify predominantly as Silesian can accommodate some degree of national identity than the reverse. They can make a bit of a claim. It is not as easy for people who identify predominantly as Polish or German to accommodate some degree of Silesian identity. This suggests that people who see themselves as having primarily national identity do not want to "claim" Silesian identity. There is, then, a threshold of identity which seems to constitute a Rubicon: once a person "steps over" into a predominantly national identity, "being Silesian" gets "left behind."

Now, why is this more sharply true for the contrast between Silesian and Polish identity than for that between Silesian and German identity? It seems that crossing the threshold of identity more irrevocably commits one when crossed in the direction of "being Polish," than in the direction of "being German." And that offers some insight into the low intermarriage rate of less than 10%, and the fact that almost 40% of respondents who considered themselves Polish had a Polish spouse. Consider how the dynamics of mobility would work out for the Silesian and Polish partners of a couple. The trip to the altar could easily take the Silesian partner across that Rubicon into Polish identity; by the same token, the fact that marrying a Pole seems so easily to entail a reformulation of identity may shed light on the fact that fewer than 10% of autochthonous Opole Silesians do it (Berlińska 1990: 111).[1] Becoming Polish is a drastic step.

IDENTITY ASCRIPTIONS AS A LANGUAGE OF MORALITY

That the chasm between "Silesian" and "Polish" is more pronounced than the one between "Silesian" and "German" reflects the fact that, as Berlińska states,

> Currently there exists a state of ethnic tension in Opole Silesia. Its source is the feeling of social distance between the groups and the feeling, common among Silesians, of being the objects of prejudice, discrimination, and persecution. Close to 80% of Silesians stated that Silesian culture is not valued in Poland and that the Silesian dialect is derided. This phenomenon was also perceived by 44.7% of immigrant [Polish] respondents. 60% of Silesians responded that they are entitled to feel resentful because they have not been admitted to managerial positions. One in five immigrant Poles corroborated these symptoms of discrimination. (Berlińska 1992: 120)

Berlińska could find only a few interviewees who declared themselves "Poles" or "Pole-Silesians," and,

> expressions of doubt preceded all these responses. Only [one] 33-year-old . . . described his national feeling thus: "Well, I am certainly not a German, because how can I be one when I didn't even go to their school? [One of the three oft-cited groundings of German identity, note.] First of all I am a Pole. If the Kashubs and the Poznanians can be Poles, then I can too. First I'm a Pole, then a Silesian, but not a German, as those who came here after the war would like to believe." It was an exceptional response, demanding recognition of the regional distinctiveness of Silesians and the acknowledgment of their *right to Polishness.* (Berlińska 1989: 7; emphasis mine)

To demand acknowledgment of a right is, as I stated above, to make a claim. From the autochthonous point of view, it is difficult to identify as Polish for two reasons. One, Poles treat Silesians scornfully. Two, the Polish Communist government failed to establish its state as a positive object of identification for anyone, regardless of ethnicity. Few enough were the Poles who identified with it. But Poles had access to a counter–national culture, defined historically, in opposition to Communism. Identification with this Polish counterculture was blocked for most autochthonous Opole Silesians by their perception of being oppressed not only by the Polish state (like everyone else), but by the Polish people. All these factors undermined the possibility of seeing Silesian regional identity as subsumed in Polish nationality, of identifying with Polish literature and history or with a Polish "heritage" acquired and learned in school, and of investing Polish citizenship with the significance of personal identity.

Attitudes toward Germany are much more complex, ambivalent, and varied than those toward Poland. It is not infrequent to hear autochthonous Opole Silesians complain that when they go to work in Germany, they are treated like "white niggers." On the other hand, such attitudes are balanced by positive ones. Some of the nuances of people's feelings about the two states are expressed in the following anecdote, set in the 1980s, that circulated in Opole Silesia:

> A man, schooled before 1945, went to a government office to fill out some forms. The clerk, on hearing that he needed help with writing the requested information in Polish, said scornfully, "How many years have you been living in Poland, and you still don't know how to write Polish?" The man retorted, "How many years have you been governing our lands, and you're still rationing butter?" (Berlińska: personal communication)

That autochthonous Opole Silesians may be considered Germans is a function of German constitutional law. That they may, for their part, consider themselves Germans is a function not only of an ideology of nationalism whereby national identity subsumes regional identity, but also a function of desire. Frederick II wrested Silesia from Maria Theresa of Austria, in the mid-eighteenth century, because he saw the economic potential of Upper Silesian coal, the industrial potential of the Katowice region. Silesia became an internal colony, a form of inclusion inherently incomplete. (Americans may want to compare Appalachia, a coal-rich region stereotyped as linguistically and culturally not quite fully American.) Yet the oldest autochthonous Opole Silesians remember the 1920s, the time when, as Matuschek put it, "the Silesian village awakened from lethargy and threw off many traditions" (Matuschek 1994: 60), a time when assimilating to German culture seemed possible and attractive. What those who were children after 1933 remember is, as Anton Fischer told me, "We were always taught that we were a 'VOLKSSTAMM,'" a branch of the race; in other words, that they really were Germans (January 30, 1993). Some people believed this; some think in those terms and believe it still. This inclusion erased the historical fact that previous German governments had repeatedly classified autochthonous Opole Silesians as "Poles," but again, for many, it presented an attractive ideal; a repression to be embraced. And then, in the postwar period, the German economic boom, the "WIRTSCHAFTSWUNDER," did nothing to ease this desire in a population stranded in the grim economy of Communism.

The political oppression of Communism, the sense of interpersonal oppression autochthonous Opole Silesians feel from Poles, and the economic grimness of Poland compared to West Germany from the 1960s forward have all combined to create a certain clarity of hostility between autochthonous Opole Silesians and Poles. That is why people don't use Polish to create or intensify conflict. It would be a very serious social breach to do so. On the other hand, every society has a certain number of insensitive jerks who would not care about committing serious breaches of social solidarity. In Dobra in the 1990s, however, individuals like the landlord Bernard were unlikely to identify with the Polish state. They would be more likely to identify power with Germany—to use German to threaten and insult people.

So for all the positive associations autochthonous Opole Silesians have with Germany and German identity, in Dobra, being seen as German can be a bad thing, can be seen as "playing the great Herr," as becoming the oppressor. The German language, as we have seen, has to be handled within the enregistering norms of the community; other tokens of Germanness have to be handled within the community's social and moral norms. In Bernard's case, the norms he ignored were those concerning what a house means, culturally, and what the proper way is to manage the relationships that revolve around it. Understanding the cultural meaning of houses makes it clear why Bernard's neighbors would think that, despite the fact that he owned the house, he had claimed something that he had no right to.

"PLAYING THE GREAT HERR": WHAT THE LANDLORD DID WRONG

Bernard was the owner of the house, but his attitude toward it was reprehensible in terms of autochthonous Opole Silesian cultural norms. The owner is not the only stakeholder in a Silesian house.

Consider the cast of characters: when Marta and I arrived at the house, we found Bernard, his tenants, and his uncle. This uncle, as I was told later, was the brother of the owner's wife's mother. Consider the position this uncle was in, then, with regard to this house: houses are usually inherited by daughters, so in this case Bernard's wife had inherited it as had her mother, the uncle's sister, before her. In autochthonous Silesian terms, this made the house the uncle's *ojczyzna*,[2] or ELTERNHAUS, in German; that is, the house of his parents in which he had grown up. The tenant, for her part, had an older sister living at home with her child, leaving no room for her and her husband and children in her own *ojczyzna*. That being the case, the mother had responsibility for her younger daughter's housing; it was she, as I was repeatedly told, who had arranged the rental with Bernard's wife's uncle (i.e., "I see that your *ojczyzna* is empty and there's no room for my daughter in hers, so . . ..").

Recently, prior to Bernard's visit, the tenants had moved from his house to an apartment in Barkowo, a nearby town. This was a cast of characters having various different rights in the house in which we were standing: the owner had the rights of ownership, but the tenants' investment of labor in the house deserved respect, as did the tenant's mother's agreement with the uncle. The uncle, especially, had culturally recognized rights to make decisions concerning his own *ojczyzna*. Autochthonous Opole Silesians consider that people have a continuing legitimate interest in what happens to their own *ojczyzna*, not only after ownership changes hands, but even after death: Marta, for example, in making plans for the house she has inherited, often tries to imagine the wishes of her deceased father-in-law (who, exceptionally, is the one who grew up there, as opposed to having moved in with his wife). When she muses in this manner, she often comments, "After all, it is not my *ojczyzna*."

Furthermore, a house is not considered an asset in the same way as in the West. The many autochthonous Opole Silesians who have emigrated to Germany, leaving empty houses, are reluctant to rent, and still more reluctant to sell. Instead, they come back to their houses on vacations, and try to get kin to look after them. This attachment to houses was succinctly expressed by one emigrant who, when I sought her out at her home, answered the door in work clothes of a smock and triangular scarf, and gruffly informed me that she didn't have time to talk and had nothing to say, other than, "This is my house. As long as I live I'll keep coming back here." I asked her if she'd ever consider selling the house. Her answer was a flat no (April 14, 1995). The attitudes expressed are widespread.

Yet Bernard rented, and he seems to have considered the rent an actual source of revenue, rather than a token arrangement; he was also quite willing to contemplate selling. Once the confrontation was over, Bernard returned with us to the tavern, where he unwound over a drink. He said that all his work here in Poland had been stolen, had come to naught. At this point he could just sell the house. Marta argued: it's a nice house, and there's so much space there! After a bit he cheered up and returned to his plans to renovate it. But he kept repeating how shocked he had been at the sight of the empty, dirty house.

Consider, now, the norms invoked by the many commentators, for between the tenants, the tavernkeeper, and its decibel level, the incident got around fast. As I said, those who heard about it and talked to me about it sided with the tenants. Izabela, who, as we will see, has had her own troubles with absentee homeowners, told me that Bernard had abandoned that house when he emigrated. The reason for the arrangement between the woman tenant's mother and Bernard's wife's mother's brother (the uncle who was present) was that the house was going to fall in on itself if not attended to. So, implicitly, Izabela invoked the norm that people retain some rights of interest in their own *ojczyzna*, especially if it's not being properly cared for. The tenants, therefore, were caretakers as well as rent payers, and furthermore, according to Izabela, "they had their own furniture." So Bernard was at fault in not respecting his uncle's rights in his *ojczyzna* and his and the tenants' concern for its condition.

Or, as Iwona and her mother, Maria Rataja (whom we met briefly in chapter 3), explained it:

> Bernard as a youth was the leader of the [Communist] Youth League around here. Very active. Then he left Poland and now he comes back playing the great Herr, with his black Mercedes and all. He, the idiot, forgot that at one point pipes burst in that house, and everything got ruined, and the tenants put a great deal of work into that house. The tenant's mother is not the kind of person who would allow her daughter to steal furniture from a landlord. And besides, that house is not insulated and they had to buy five or six tons of coal in winter, and pay for electricity, and a very high rent. They had to pay 500,000 złoty! And only one of them working, and them with two children. Bernard's entire family is in Germany, and his parents, when they left, signed the deed of their house over to *strangers*!

So Bernard was seen as at fault in not respecting the tenants' work on the house, their circumstances, and the arrangements made by his elders: his wife's mother's brother and the mother of the woman tenant. Everyone who commented on the situation invoked this norm of respect by making reference to what Bernard's mother-in-law and her brother had said at the time the house was rented. Furthermore, consider his attitude: "All my work in Poland has come to naught, I might as well sell the house." *Sell* his wife's and mother-in-law's *ojczyzna*?! What would his next-door neighbor, the woman who told me she would return to her house as long as she lived and never sell it, think? Would she think this was par for the course for a family who, upon emigrating during the Communist era, when selling houses was not possible, would do something so culturally disapproved as signing a house over to non-kin?

Maria and Iwona seem to see Bernard not only as having behaved badly in one incident but also as simply not a good person, and they also see his parents in the same way. Bernard is beyond the pale. He is a formerly active Communist, whereas most Silesians, like most Poles, did not approve of people who actively aligned themselves with that regime. Now, he aligns himself with German, rather than Silesian, identity (becoming, it seems, an all-too-active capitalist). He is, in addition, an idiot, an exploitative landlord, and the son of parents who have turned their backs on a vitally important moral imperative of Silesian society, which is that houses stay within families. It all seems to go together. And the summary of it all, for Iwona and her mother, is that he "plays the great Herr." And he most powerfully played that role by yelling at his tenants in German, a misuse of the power of that language. Identity emerges as a summation of morality.

Because of the close historical connections of Silesia with Germany, because positive associations with Germany are salient for autochthonous Opole Silesians, they are more likely to identify in whole or in part as German rather than as Polish. But whether they do, and how they manage that, implicates their standing in their own community. Autochthonous Opole Silesians, and most especially those who have emigrated to Germany, run the risk of being considered to "play the great Herr." They are easily considered to have gotten above themselves. The most commonly cited manifestation of this is linguistic: people known from birth, after a few years in Germany, suddenly claim to have forgotten all their Polish and Silesian. Villagers, borrowing from German in irony, call them "*ANGEBRY*" or say that they "*ANGEBUJĄ*," from German SICH ANGEBEN, to show off. This is not a necessary outcome of emigration. It is possible to emigrate and maintain a good reputation in the village. But it requires managing relationships in careful conformity to autochthonous Opole Silesian norms.

HOW TO DO IT RIGHT: NORMS OF EXCHANGE AND SILESIAN IDENTITY

Of the norms that must be considered, besides those concerning houses, the most important concern exchange, the passing of goods, services, and money from person to person (though these also implicate houses, in that building a house is a communal project in autochthonous Opole Silesia). It was Marcel Mauss, writing in 1908, who first pointed out that what he called "The Gift" can establish and maintain social relationships, and that the exchange of gifts can be an important expression of living a moral life. Mauss called the kind of exchange that serves the continuation of positive social relationships "delayed reciprocal exchange," because the recipient of the gift gives back to the giver (reciprocally, then), not immediately, but at some unspecified future point (after some delay). It is the delay that most distinguishes the transaction from one of, say, buying, that is, exchanging money for goods; in that situation, the participants are finished with it, and with one another, immediately; they need never see one another again. In a community that operates according to delayed reciprocal exchange, on the other hand, people continue their relationships, because waiting follows giving, and waiting for the appropriate moment to reciprocate follows receiving.

IDENTITY ASCRIPTIONS AS A LANGUAGE OF MORALITY

In the context of autochthonous Opole Silesia, each successive exchange can affirm that the participants all adhere to a set of norms. It is people who breach those norms who get tagged with an epithet of some sort of outsiderhood, some sort of "having gotten above themselves." Thus, while in classic analyses of delayed reciprocal exchange, the community was assumed to be confined to this form of economy by isolation from a cash market economy, this is not the case for Opole Silesians. Economically, they are merely encouraged in it by their relative lack of cash. But I argue here that delayed reciprocal exchange has cultural meaning that transcends purely economic motives. Recall that Silesian houses are designed and built within the community; men work for one another in the tasks of building and maintaining houses, and their wives can arrange this work, telling their husbands whom they are going to help, and when. This saves everybody the cost of employing workers, but it also literally builds the community into the house itself. Similarly, autochthonous Silesians domestically produce such food as beef, rabbit, duck, potatoes, vegetables, fruit, fruit juice, jam, mushrooms, pickles, and dairy products, and exchange these things within kin and neighbor networks. Such exchange is economically important, for it saves them the cost of buying these products. The disappointing potato harvest of 1994 provoked widespread disgusted comment: "We're going to have to *buy* potatoes!" Yet exchanging products also affirms relationships in an ongoing way.

Managing one's position with respect to delayed reciprocal exchange can be tricky. This is because, as the comment about the potato harvest reflected, all the domestically produced food can be bought, as can the services of plumbers, carpenters, bricklayers, electricians, farmers, and laborers. And there is a place for buying in autochthonous Opole Silesian life. Not only do Silesians buy things in stores, they buy and sell among themselves. Deciding when and with whom to engage in exchange can be a fraught decision, precisely because there is an alternative: what Mauss called "a tradesman's morality," which focuses on asking the fair market value of the goods (not cheating people), rather than on establishing and/or maintaining a social relationship per se. And inflected into this contrast is an entire set of social contrasts that ultimately come down to social closeness vs. social distance:

relationships of exchange   family vs. nonfamily   friends vs. others
vs. relationships of
buying and selling

The cost of doing it badly can be one's good reputation in the village. And it is a short step from the contrast between "friends" and "others" to that between "us autochthonous Opole Silesians" and "those others, Germans or Poles."

189

As an illustration, consider the following incident, in which Marta, the young widow, stresses the social distance of her relationship to her late husband's father in order to justify refusing a request from his in-laws to give them a cart that he had bought. Given her relationship with him, she argues, it is appropriate to sell the cart, not to mobilize it in exchange relations. But, on the sly, she does mobilize it anyway.

> Marta had an old cart which had belonged to her late husband's father, the former owner of the property she has now inherited. Marta sold it to Karol, a bachelor neighbor for a million złoty [about $50, or 40 euros] on the understanding that he would prepare one of her fields to be planted with potatoes. But they agreed that its "real" price was a million and a half złoty, and that should anyone ask, that is what the neighbor would tell them he had paid.
>
> Marta was upset because her husband's maternal aunt had asked if her brother (his maternal uncle) could have it for free. She had said that if it was hers she would have given it but that she wasn't going to give away something that her father-in-law had worked for. So she sold it instead. (Notes, July 16, 1993)

Various tensions are evident in this report. For a start, while Marta was engaging in goods for labor exchange with her neighbor, she didn't want this widely known. Since such exchange requires negotiation, it may be that Marta feared questions: Was it fair? Was it equitable? And what are this young widow and this bachelor to one another, anyway? For whatever reason, she did not want their relationship to be perceived as close, and the way to accomplish that was to make people think it was simply a sale, to hide the element of exchange within it.

She might have especial reason to fear questions from her husband's maternal kin. She does not like this aunt, and I have it independently from Marta and Iwona that her husband did not either. To them, she presented the cart, the object, as one which she had no right to exchange. The cart had been bought with money earned by her father-in-law. While he could have mobilized it in exchange transactions, she, a mere daughter-in-law, did not have such full rights to the cart. Marta played on subtleties of kinship norms which hold that ties to in-laws are less strong than those to families of origin. She was less than his fully entitled heir, the house not her *ojczyzna* but that of her deceased husband. By bringing forth this logic she also implied that they, mere sister- and brother-in-law to her father-in-law and no blood kin to her, had a weak claim to the cart. Thus, she argued, it was appropriate to sell it, not to give it away.

Yet, on the sly, she only partly sold it. Instead, she put the cart forth in exchange for something she concretely needed from her male neighbor, that is, to have her field prepared for planting. If this had been known, it would have been seen, correctly, as a slight to her in-laws. She was trying to bring the neighbor closer to her, and to push her father-in-law's in-laws away. Relations of exchange between her and her husband's maternal kin had atrophied, while Marta was actively fostering such a relationship with her neighbor.

The place of money within exchange relationships is always sensitive. Dobrans display their sensitivity, for example, when they receive a gift or service from friends or neighbors, but not their own close family. In this case, it is standard for the recipient to say, "How much should I pay you?" It is also standard for the reply to be, "Nothing, because you did such-and-such for me." Reference to prior exchange seems to be mandatory; I've been in situations where interlocutors would not let the topic rest until I have cited some concrete instance of their prior gift to me. This is Silesian politeness: the recipient gives the giver the chance to reaffirm that they are on good, neighborly, friendly terms. To actually suggest monetary payment would suggest a reevaluation of the entire relationship in market-based terms. It would be rude and then some. So engaging in exchange relationships, and deciding when to use money, is sensitive even within Dobra. It is vastly more so when one of the participants has access to the German cash economy; that is, when one of them is an emigrant. This is so because, in short, emigrants have too much money, and not enough opportunity to engage in exchange. They have already left the community in a literal sense, by moving to Germany. They are, as I said, easily considered to have "gotten above themselves." So it takes great sensitivity for them to keep their exchange relationships in good repair.

In his discussion of exchange, Bourdieu makes a point beautifully apropos to this dilemma. Maintaining one's relationships is all a matter of style:

> In every society it may be observed that, if it is not to constitute an insult, the counter-gift must be deferred and different, because the immediate return of an exactly identical object clearly amounts to a refusal (i.e., the return of the same object). Thus gift exchange is opposed on the one hand to swapping, which . . . telescopes gift and counter-gift into the same instant, and on the other hand, to lending, in which the return of the loan is explicitly guaranteed by a juridical act and is thus already accomplished at the very moment of the drawing up of a contract capable of ensuring that the acts it prescribes are predictable and calculable. ["Buying" and "employing," I would add, also work in this same manner.] The difference and delay must be brought into the model . . . because the operation of gift exchange presupposes (individual and collective) misrecognition (*méconnaissance*) of the reality of the objective mechanism of the exchange, a reality which an immediate response brutally exposes. . . . It is all a question of style, which means in this case timing and choice of occasion, for the same act—giving, giving in return, offering one's services, paying a visit, etc.—can have completely different meanings at different

times, coming as it may at the right or the wrong moment . . . ; the reason is that the lapse of time separating the gift from the counter-gift is what authorizes the deliberate oversight, the collectively maintained and approved self-deception without which symbolic exchange . . . could not operate. (Bourdieu 1977: 5–7)

Put another way, emigrants have too much access to gifts that cost money (to money itself, for that matter) and not enough access to gifts that cost time. And the former kind of gift can eclipse the latter, because both emigrants and autochthonous Opole Silesians who still live in Silesia attach prestige to gifts that cost money. Consider the following: on the day after my birthday in 1994, Kasia and Eva turned up at my house (during my second trip to Dobra, I was no longer living with Marta). They brought a gift from their mother, Magda. Magda had sent a large jar of preserved mushrooms, picked that fall in the woods around Dobra, and another of garden-grown dill pickles. She also had sent a Polish-produced small circular hanger intended for drying socks. And she had sent a bar of German chocolate and a kilogram of German coffee. Those were the only two items that she had wrapped. For her, it was the purchased, German items that warranted that honor.

There is a place in autochthonous life for both purchase and for the exchange of goods produced outside the system of formal purchase, but their valences are different. Here, purchased German goods deserved to be wrapped; home produced ones deserved to be given, but not wrapped. German goods are prestige goods, here assimilated into an autochthonous cultural pattern of giving. Yet prestige can be a dangerous force.

It is a disadvantage, in terms of staying with that "collectively maintained and approved self-deception," to be absent from ongoing interaction, not to participate on a regular basis in an economic life that produces pickled mushrooms and other ordinary, staple, and appropriate gifts, to have too easy access to gifts that carry potentially overshadowing prestige. So how should one do it? Well, not like this:

Suzanna and her husband have been living in Germany for several years, but, like most emigrants, they still own a house in Silesia. Izabela is the wife of Suzanna's second cousin. She lives across the street from the house, and she takes care of it by cleaning occasionally, airing it, draining the pipes, and keeping an eye on it; she also gets it ready for their visits. Around New Year's, 1995, Izabela was infuriated when she received a letter from Suzanna which read, in part:

> I've sent a box of candy for the kids. I must say, I'm a little surprised by your long silence. I haven't heard anything from you since I came for Justyna's First

Communion. Perhaps you thought my gifts were not appropriate, I don't know, or that they were inadequate. . . .

Tell me, Izabela, what kind of state [has the house been in]? Have you been going over there every so often to dust, and have you been opening the windows from time to time, and letting the water run? Please be honest with me.

Have you gotten to feel that you're doing too much, that is with our house? Perhaps you no longer have time for it. It would be good to reach some agreement about it. Why don't you write to me and tell me how much you think you ought to be paid for looking after the house for us, OK? (Notes, January 13, 1995)

Above, I said that autochthonous Opole Silesians regularly ask one another, "How much should I pay you?" The question acknowledges the monetary value of a gift; its ritual reply, "Nothing, because you did such-and-such for me," reaffirms the relationship as one of good, neighborly, friendly terms grounded in delayed reciprocal exchange. People are supposed to ask this, when they have received something. But not like this. The problem here is that, in two ways, Suzanna gave the impression that she didn't want the ritual answer, she wanted a real answer. Izabela was enraged.

If Suzanna had been practicing proper style, according to local norms, then this letter might perhaps have served to realign an exchange relationship which had begun to deteriorate. Izabela, a little guiltily, would have written back to the effect, "No, it's all right, I've been going over there fairly often, and it's not too much; you've certainly done enough for me in the past; certainly there can be no question of payment."

Unfortunately, Suzanna had not put Izabela in a position to say this. She had not done enough for Izabela in the past. When they had last left the house after a visit they had left it a wreck; Izabela had cleaned it up. Izabela had paid the summer's electricity bill, and Suzanna had not yet reimbursed her. Her daughter had, indeed, properly thanked her for the First Communion presents. Suzanna had received, and received, and received, and received: thanks, and electricity money, and house cleaning, and ongoing care of the house. Izabela considered her implication that she, Izabela, owed her something at this point, outrageous. A positive reading of her question, "How much should I pay you?" would see Suzanna as acting the role of the recipient who actually doesn't owe anything—who had actually prepaid the latest gift in ongoing delayed reciprocal exchange. But she had not set her own stage this way. That is the first way Suzanna gave the impression that she wanted a real answer. Secondly, the question is supposed to come after one has received something. One does not precede this question with a reference to what one has given. Because of these missteps, Izabela took Suzanna to mean that she seriously wanted to turn her into an employee, after years of treating her as family, according to the norms of delayed reciprocal exchange.

To me, Izabela fumed:

> You know, Ela, I won't stand for being treated this way . . . ! She doesn't pay me to look after that house; I do it from my own good will. And now she has the nerve to interrogate me about what I'm doing or not doing, and to throw it up to me? . . . Just because she's "pani Magister"! [The title of a woman having a master's degree] Uneducated people deserve to be treated with respect too! . . . They emigrated four years ago. Four years, and now she asks me how much I want to be paid for looking after the house? I ask you, is that normal? (January 13, 1995)

Izabela pointed to Suzanna as an outsider: she emigrated four years ago, and she's behaving this way "Just because she's 'pani Magister!'" Suzanna is one of very few villagers to have left Opole Silesia for university study. And if anyone in Dobra had ever called me "pani Magister" (I did not yet have a doctorate, of course), I would have done some serious soul-searching as to what I had done to offend that person. Emigrants do well to protect villagers' pride, if they wish to stay on good terms. Having removed themselves physically from the village, they must work especially hard, and sensitively, at the graceful management of social relationships. The price for failure, as discussed above, may be alienation, for though emigrants may have money, it is the villagers who retain control of the village, its houses, and its social relationships. If emigrants ever want to go home again, they need to stay on good terms.

It is possible for emigrants to manage their position in a way that brings no such censure down on them. When they are the recipient of a gift, as Suzanna was the recipient of Izabela's work on her house, they must make sure that they have been giving enough in return. When they are the giver, themselves asked, "How much should I pay you?" they must make sure that they have been gracious recipients. It is especially important for a giver whose economic clout is disproportionate to be able to cite a prior gift. The alternative would be to imply, "Nothing, because who needs you anyway? I can afford to give without receiving in return."

Now for an example of how one *should* do it:

> Marcin, a friend of Marta's late husband, on a visit from Germany, gave Marta ten bars of marzipan in chocolate (Sarotti brand) and another five of milk chocolate (same brand), a box of assorted chocolate costing 24 German marks, ten marks for each of her parents ("for Sunday dinner") and 100 marks for Marta. She protested, saying, "you need this money, you have four children." But he refused to hear her objections. So she gave him half a liter of vodka and a duck.

IDENTITY ASCRIPTIONS AS A LANGUAGE OF MORALITY

She commented to me, "He's been in Germany for five years and hasn't eaten duck there; it's expensive there. Since we have it, why not give it, no?" (Notes, January 2, 1993)

Duck or rabbit is the meat of the autochthonous Sunday dinner. They are eaten after chicken noodle soup, accompanied by red cabbage and dumplings made of mashed potatoes, egg, potato starch, and salt. It is the dumplings that are most explicitly mobilized as symbols, and they clearly illustrate the extension of kinship to ethnicity. They serve, first of all, as a metonym of dinner. To be "*po kluskach*" (after dumplings), means that one has already eaten dinner. Yet they are also a symbol of familial togetherness. Marta, returning to the house on a Saturday after a quarrel with her father, declared, "We will make our own dumplings tomorrow!" meaning that we would not join her parents' Sunday dinner as customary (Notes, December 19, 1992). By the operation of extension of kinship to ethnicity, they are also a symbol of Silesianness. At my very first Sunday dinner, she had made a formal introduction: "These are dumplings that Silesian families eat on Sundays." And when I returned to the field after a year's absence and her mother saw me eating the dumplings, she said, 'We'll make a Silesian of you yet." They are listed, too, as "Silesian dumplings" in Polish restaurants—in Poland, and in Chicago.

The ingredients for dumplings are available in Germany, but it is hard to raise ducks in an industrial housing complex. In Marta's giving Marcin the main dish of a Sunday dinner, we see that what was being offered was a symbol of belonging—in Silesia—in exchange for prestige goods and cash. It is common that what travels west to relations in Germany are, indeed, domestically produced foodstuffs, while what travels east is cash, chocolate, coffee, household appliances, and other manufactured items. And yet, the discrepancy in market value between Marcin's gift and Marta's did not pass unnoticed. While Marta remarked that duck is expensive in Germany, it cannot have been lost on anyone that a half a liter of vodka and a duck are not worth nearly two hundred marks.[3]

Note, then, that if handled appropriately, money itself can be a "gift" in the Maussian sense, as long as its giving is not explicitly negotiated, as long as, like the goods, it comes as a surprise. This is particularly evident in the custom of giving, for some special occasion such as a First Communion, a bouquet of flowers in which paper money is literally hidden: folded into crisp accordians and placed here and there within the bouquet, so that the amount of money—perhaps even its presence—is surprising. One way of describing

Suzanna's failure at delayed reciprocal exchange is that she failed to realize that it is of the very essence *not* to "reach some agreement about it."

As Bourdieu states, it's all a matter of style, and this is intensely so for emigrants, for their situation puts them on the outside of the common experience of the community in a significant way. People's behavior in exchange relationships is thus critical. The difference between generosity and showing off—being one of the *ANGEBRY*—can be a matter of method. Marcin gave a great deal, but he placed much of the gift in stereotyped goods, he spread the money around within the family receiving it, and, perhaps most importantly, he accepted the duck and the vodka with good grace, appreciating their symbolic value.

Bernard, of course, did everything wrong, and while Suzanna seems on some level to have wanted to maintain her relationship with Izabela, there doesn't seem to be much evidence that Bernard cared what anyone thought of him. His conspicuous display of consumption in driving a black Mercedes and wearing such fine clothes runs counter to protecting the pride of the villagers. And villagers are easily disposed to seize on ethnicity as the type of outsiderhood they see manifested in nonconformance. Bernard earned the epithet of ethnic outsiderhood by a combination of adopting the status symbols of German identity and violating the norms of kinship and neighborliness that are, by symbolic extension, the stuff of ethnic solidarity. But if identity can emerge as a summary of morality (Bernard "plays the great Herr"), it can also stay backstage; no one accused Marcin of any such thing. And, as we will see, what is true for the contrast between being Silesian and being German is also true for the contrast between being Silesian and being Polish.

APPROVING SILENCE VS. WORDS OF CONDEMNATION: NEIGHBORLY RELATIONS BETWEEN SILESIANS AND POLES

I have not used the phrase, "Silesian-German Relations," because great ambiguity surrounds the question of whether Bernard, or any other autochthonous Opole Silesian, actually is "German" or not. Autochthonous Opole Silesians can consider themselves German, to some degree, in some measure, and they are subject to being so considered. This is a question they explicitly discuss, personally with regard to their own identity, and with regard to the group as a whole. In Dobra, that is not true of the divide between being Silesian and being Polish; I never met anyone who considered him or herself a Pole, and the closest Polish attitude to considering autochthonous Opole Silesians as Poles could be paraphrased, "Those Silesians, they ARE really Poles, why can't they admit it?" So while the question of German identity is on the surface of social life, the question of possible Polish identity, in Dobra, was shrouded in silence.

Similarly, I never heard an equivalent of someone being accused of "playing the great Herr" on the Polish side of the identity spread. I never heard anyone assert that some other person was "behaving like a Pole" (or worse, like a *chadziaj*), or that someone else thought of him or herself as a Pole. As I've said, I never saw Polish used seriously to create social distance between a speaker and interlocutors, the way that Bernard used German. It is not technically impossible: we see the possibility of such things in subtle readings of, for example, Franz's comments on Michał's situation. But that is as far as it goes. These things were never overtly expressed. If I were to voice my interpretation that Franz's comments, implicitly, accused his son's teachers of acting like or being *chadziajki*, to Franz, I am confident that he would protest that he meant nothing so appalling.

We have seen that identity can emerge as a summary of morality on the German side, within the community of autochthonous Opole Silesians: it can emerge into discourse, as it did in the case of Bernard, or not, as with Marcin. The same is true on the Polish side, except that it concerns people who are not "from here," that is, it concerns Poles. It is not the case that immigrant Poles get called *chadziaje* as a matter of course. Only immigrant Poles who violate autochthonous Opole Silesian norms of behavior get called *chadziaje*. That is what really counts.

Of the two families to be compared here (and while there are not many Poles living in Dobra, there are some), the family I call the Malinowskis[4] has been very happy; so happy that they have bought a plot of land in Dobra and hope to build a house of their own. In the case of the Malinowskis, it was months before I found out that they were Poles; Iwona told me when I commented that their little girl, who was in the first grade class that I'd been observing, spoke remarkably good Polish for a child so young. The Kowalskis, on the other hand, have been miserable, isolated from their neighbors, experiencing a sense that they are shunned as *chadziaje*, an interethnic hostility that they return. In the case of the Kowalskis, the first thing that I heard about them was that they were Poles. The difference has nothing to do with their ethnicity. In fact the Kowalskis actually *are* partly Silesian, according to the dominant ideology of inherited identity. The husband of the family has a Silesian mother. The Malinowskis, on the other hand, are, as autochthonous Opole Silesians say, "pure Poles," with no kinship connections to autochthonous Opole Silesia whatsoever.

Both the Kowalskis and the Malinowskis were pressed into looking for a house to rent in Dobra by the shortage of housing in towns and cities. It is not

easy for an outsider to the community to find a place to live in an autochthonous Opole Silesian village (I, myself, simply lucked out in my first fieldwork
stint; during my second and third trips, Marta and other friends helped me).
As we have seen, this is not because there are no empty houses; it is because
houses are the focus of such culturally specific attachment. As Marta once put
it, "Everyone knows about plenty of houses that are empty, but when someone
comes looking for a house to rent, there are none." These two families' re-
spective stories of house hunting are of a piece with their experiences once
they found the houses.

It was very important to Mrs. Kowalska that I include the story of her experience looking for housing in this book. I take the strength of that desire itself an indication of her sense of rejection by her autochthonous Opole Silesian
neighbors. And, she is right; while autochthonous Opole Silesians feel discriminated against in the wider Polish society, they retain control of the villages, their houses, and their social relationships. That is a form of power, and
they use it. Out of respect for her wishes, I start with her story and observations
on her situation. Following that, I'll compare her family's experiences to the
happier ones of the Malinowski family, and analyze why both families' experiences show that in autochthonous Opole Silesia, the discourse of ethnicity
is a discourse of morality.

Mr. Kowalski's mother comes from Dobra, but she married a Pole, and he
grew up in a nearby city. When the family failed to find housing in any of the
larger towns, it was through his mother's kin that they were finally able to find a
house in Dobra to live in.

As Mrs. Kowalska made clear, the search for the house had not been a happy
one, and the house that they ultimately found was not in good condition. It had become run-down as a result of standing empty and unattended to for several years
before the Kowalskis moved in. How well it was attended to before that is also open
to question, for the wife of its owner had emigrated, leaving her alcoholic husband,
who eventually threw himself under a train. The house was thus formally owned by
the suicide's widow, but essentially abandoned by her. It had been left to the Kowalskis to make the house habitable. They had thus had to put much time and money
into renovations, including installing an indoor bathroom. It should also be noted
that very few houses at the time had central heating, and the coal stoves people relied
on require regular maintenance to work well; draughts from broken or ill-fitting
windows seriously impact their heating capacity. The Kowalskis were living there
without any written agreement, having no legal status as tenants, and could thus be
evicted without warning. They certainly expected no reimbursement for their efforts
and expense. Their situation was only a little better than that of squatters.

But the most bitter point for Mrs. Kowalska is that when the family failed to find housing in Opole or one of the other towns, and were forced to look in the villages, she encountered outright ethnic discrimination. "I had a belly out to here, pregnant with Marysia, and I was going door-to-door asking people if they knew of any housing for rent. But because I spoke to them in Polish— because I am a *chadziajka*—no one knew of anything. And it was only when an aunt stepped in, and said that I, too, am a Silesian because I was born in Opole Province, that something happened."

Mrs. Kowalska's loneliness and isolation are intensified by the fact that her husband is a truck driver, frequently away from home for days at a time. She feels rejected by her neighbors, her only friend (and a somewhat reluctant one) being her next-door neighbor, Diana Osa. The Kowalskis have provoked tensions with the entire Osa family not only by expressing negative attitudes towards Silesians but by punishing their daughter for picking up Silesian turns of phrase from the Osas' daughter. And, on the other side, Diana Osa reported that Mr. Kowalski had approached a neighbor for help in cutting up some boards and was refused. She wondered aloud: did the neighbor have some legitimate reason, or did he refuse Kowalski simply because Kowalski had spoken Polish when asking for help? (Notes, November 11, 1994).

Accidentally, but given the density of kin relationships, not too surprisingly, Diana Osa is Mr. Kowalski's second cousin once removed. Yet it was Diana Osa who instantly told me that they were Poles, and the first time I met the Kowalskis, at her house, she looked Mr. Kowalski straight in the eye and told him, "Maybe I could consider myself Polish, if it weren't for people like you."

I pointed out at the beginning of the chapter that in sociological research, the least popular ways for autochthonous Opole Silesians to report their sense of identity were "more a Silesian than a Pole," and, dead last, "more a Pole than a Silesian." I argued that people of autochthonous background who ascribe to Polish identity tend to do it completely, that Polish and Silesian identities do not coexist as easily for individuals as German and Silesian identities. In particular, I surmised that this had something to do with the low intermarriage rate, that "the trip to the altar could easily take the Silesian partner across that Rubicon into Polish identity." In Mr. Kowalski's mother, we seem to have had a Rubicon crosser, and the results are evident in her son.

In a later conversation at the Osa home, Mr. Kowalski reported that as a child, he did occasionally visit his mother's relatives, but considered the train ride to the village a trip into an alien world in which he could barely understand what was being said. When Diana Osa pulled out a family photograph album to show Mr. Kowalski pictures of the relatives they have in common, it emerged that he had never seen pictures of these relatives before, did not know who they were, and was shocked to realize that they had served in the German army in the First and Second World Wars. His parents had told him nothing about his mother's side of the family. He was ill prepared to find his family forced into dependence on them by the housing shortage in the towns and cities. I wonder, also, whether the aunt who intervened, late and rather ineffectively, considering the condition of the house that resulted, bore a grudge against Mr. Kowalski's mother for marrying outside the group, or, once she had, for failing to teach her children anything about autochthonous Opole Silesian culture.

Social networks are the only way to find rental housing among autochthonous Opole Silesians. My own success in my first fieldwork stint—meeting by chance a recent widow facing a winter alone in a big house—is so exceptional that Dobrans regularly ascribe it to heavenly intervention. You cannot do it by going door to door. That Mrs. Kowalska spoke Polish to whomever answered the door simply underlines the fact that no Silesian would ever do it for any reason (and as a fieldworker, I should know; the brusque interaction with the emigrant houseowner quoted above was one of the few times I tried it, and you see the result.) Yet apparently, the Kowalskis neither had "acquaintances" to go through, nor, perhaps, fully understood the importance of having them.

It was the Malinowskis, who arrived in the region with no prior connections, who more easily established the kind of network necessary to find a place to live in Dobra. Here is their house-hunting story:

The Malinowski family comes from a village in Małopolska, north of Cracow. Mr. Malinowski comes from a farming family, Mrs. Malinowska from a family of factory workers. Mr. Malinowski's brother inherited the farm, leaving him to find his way in the world. Shortly after his marriage, he found his way to Toronto, where he worked for several months as a plumber, shortly before the fall of Communism in 1989. After his return, Mrs. Malinowska's sister, who had moved to a city in Opole Province, wrote and told them that there was a shop for sale in her neighborhood. Partly afraid of rising unemployment in state-run enterprises, they used the savings from Toronto to buy it.

Now they faced the problem of finding housing. Housing guarantees had ended with Communism; besides, they were no longer employed by the state. So Mr. Malinowski drove all over the place looking for a place to live. Finally, through acquaintances, they found their way to the family who is now their next-door neighbor, relatives of Franz Skorupka, who are related to their landlords. They put them in contact with the owner of the house, and they were able to rent it. The house was empty, but had been well looked after by its owners' relatives, who continue to live in Dobra.

Again, the key phrase of this narrative is *through acquaintances*. Mr. Malinowski, now the proprietor of a small store, had, either through contacts with customers or in some other way, succeeded in establishing friendly contacts with people across the ethnic divide. Their intervention was critical in the Malinowskis' finding the house to rent.

Just as I took Mrs. Kowalska's insistence that her negative story be included in this book as reflecting the strength of her sense of rejection in Dobra, I took Mrs. Malinowska's sadness at facing the prospect of moving away as reflecting the strength of her sense of acceptance. For, at the time they told me all this (April 12, 1995), it had emerged that blood is thicker than water. A young male relative of the owner had married, and the owner had decided that he and his wife should rent the house. Mrs. Malinowska was visibly sad as she told me this; she said that it was difficult. They had assumed that they would be in Dobra for the few years it would take to build a house on a plot of land they had bought in Dobra. But because the apartment in a nearby city they had found is more expensive than living in a house in a village, the plan to build would have to be put on hold. She noted that you can do what you want in a village house, without worrying about disturbing the neighbors. There's not much room in city apartments. Her nieces and nephews, who live in one, are always very happy to be able to play outside in the open spaces of Dobra. Her children had been very happy in the Dobra elementary school; now they would have to change schools. All in all, she did not welcome the coming move back to a town inhabited largely by her "own" ethnic group and hoped that the family would be able to move back to Dobra quickly.

CONFORMITY AS KEY TO ETHNIC HARMONY

So what accounts for the Malinowskis' ability to gain acceptance in Dobra and feel comfortable there, where the Kowalskis continue to feel rejected and isolated? It is not simply, I think, a matter of revenge on the part of Silesians with long memories for Mr. Kowalski's mother's marital escape into the society of the *chadziaje*. Other factors intervene. These appear to be of two natures, and both relate to the fact that the Kowalskis are both from Opole Province—but from a city, while the Malinowskis, in contrast, are from Małopolska—and from a village.

The first implication of this relates to the contrast between Opole Province and Małopolska. The Kowalskis grew up in a situation of actual interethnic tension. Not many autochthonous Opole Silesians live in cities in Opole Province but by report, cities are places where they often try to hide their identities. In Małopolska, in contrast, the Malinowskis would not have been exposed to negative attitudes toward autochthonous Opole Silesians. Second, it means that the Kowalskis don't have the practical skills of life in a village. When I asked the Malinowskis, on the other hand, to compare life in Dobra with life where they came from, they told me there were no great differences. They, too, were from a village, and "we're used to this kind of life."

In a society where social ties are maintained partly through delayed reciprocal exchange of labor, this is an important matter. The Kowalskis, according to Diana Osa, are actually quite dependent on their neighbors. Mr. Kowalski lives in an exceptionally run-down house requiring a lot of work, yet, brought up in an urban environment, he lacks the tools and some of the skills necessary to work on his house. He is a truck driver, and his work takes him away from the village frequently for stretches of several days. Because of his job, his lack of tools, lack of technical skill, and possibly lack of social skill, Mr. Kowalski is prevented from participating in this exchange. The Malinowskis, in contrast, who grew up with the skills of village living, can exchange labor with their neighbors as they wish.

Another point in Mr. Malinowski's favor: he's not in his own place for a reason that autochthonous Opole Silesians can sympathize with. His brother inherited the farm. His wife doesn't come from a farming family. So they had no choice but to move away from their native village. This account signals that they came to Dobra from a place which is culturally imaginable to autochthonous Silesians, and, unlike nearby cities, it is not imagined as "enemy territory."

The Malinowskis drew other important parallels between Dobra and their native village. When I asked about the dialect, they said that there's a dialect where they're from, too, and some of the words are similar. Mrs. Malinowska had German in school, and that helps with the German loan words. I asked whether their children had started picking up Silesianisms from the other children. Mr. Malinowski said, "Yes, a few things, but we don't allow it. We're not going to pretend that we're Silesians. Why should we alter our speech?" So rather than denigrating the Silesian dialect, as the Kowalskis did, their attitude toward Polish can be recognized as a mirror of Silesians' attitudes toward Silesian. They are Poles, so it's appropriate that they speak Polish; the respondents to my survey on language attitudes affirmed that.

The Malinowskis fit in. In an ongoing way, they participate. Their rural background is imaginable to autochthonous Opole Silesians. In short, in terms of background, skills, lifestyle preferences, and (allowing for differing native language) language use, they conform.

Note that, primarily, I knew that the Kowalskis are not doing well in Dobra from two sources: Mr. and Mrs. Kowalski themselves, and Diana Osa, who bitterly complains of them in ethnic terms, although she is too polite to use the term *chadziaj*. Diana Osa has a kin relationship to Mr. Kowalski which is recognized locally: they are distant cousins. So when Diana Osa complains about her Polish neighbors, she's not thinking about ethnicity in terms of kinship. She's thinking about how she perceives them to act. Hers is a commentary of moral opprobrium.

The contrast we have, then, is one of approving silence vs. words of condemnation. The discourse of identity ascriptions is a discourse of moral disapproval. Poles who gain acceptance don't get talked about as Poles. Silesians who behave appropriately, even if they live in Germany, don't get talked about as Germans.

That being the case, why would some people in Dobra ascribe German identity to themselves? In the next chapter we turn from identity ascriptions to identity assertions.

Chapter 8

IDENTITY ASSERTIONS AS A LANGUAGE OF ASPIRATION

The last chapter laid out a pretty good argument for avoiding being seen as German at all costs. Who would want to come across as an arrogant jerk, like Bernard? Who wants to be seen, at best, as socially incompetent, like Suzanna? And yet, Dobra has an active German Friendship Circle (or DEUTSCHER FREUNDSCHAFTSKREIS), an active branch of the organization that is, as I said, at once a political party and a social club. It is the historical complexity of the relationship between Silesia and Germany that accounts for that, and the key to that aspect of identity is the answer to the following question: why is it that the active members of the German minority speak the best Polish in Dobra?

Urszula Krysiak, whose daughter Anna gave us Silesian and Polish versions of the story of the boy fishing in chapter 6, organized the petition to the German government which resulted in a teacher of German arriving in Dobra in the fall of 1992. Urszula, remember, was also the person who followed out the logic of my agree/disagree statement, "People who stop speaking Silesian stop being 100% Silesian." She said that if Silesians who stopped speaking Silesian also stopped *being* Silesian, there would be no problem with their not speaking Silesian, since not speaking Silesian is perfectly appropriate for people who aren't Silesian. Urszula's account of the campaign that brought the German teacher to Dobra was among the most eloquent narratives I have ever heard in Polish.

Mrs. Krysiak, when talking to me informally, spoke a typical Silesian for someone of her age, characterized by phonology, the phatic *ni*, an occasional German loan word, and an occasional intensification switch to German. But when it came time to switch to expository register and explain to me how it had been to bring the German teacher, the distinguishing characteristics of her speech were contrastively Polish, and her control of them was flawless. But the most revealing element was not anything that can be represented by a change of font in a transcript. It was the rhetorical figure that she used.

IDENTITY ASSERTIONS AS A LANGUAGE OF ASPIRATION

The part of the narrative that I want to focus on occured in mid-story, so let me give some background first. As the organizer of this campaign, Urszula Krysiak had not only to work closely within the local and regional organization of the German Minority, but also with Polish educational officials in Opole. The program which has brought German teachers into many Opole Silesian village elementary schools is administered by the BUNDESVERWAL-TUNGSAMT, under the rubric of service to ethnic Germans abroad, and defined as "supplementary instruction in German as a native language." (A ludicrously inappropriate formulation for Opole Silesia, as for most other situations of societal multilingualism. "Heritage language" would be much more accurate.) Teachers are recruited from schools in Germany, and while they are paid through the same channels as local teachers, their pay is supplemented by the German government to the level of the position they left. A job in Germany is also guaranteed to them upon their return. They are, as one of them explained to me: "legally employees of the local educational authority, officially representatives of the federal German government, and present at the behest of the German Minority—and this is the sphere of tense relations (SPANNUNGSRAUM) in which we have to move." (Notes, March 31, 1993).

This is how Mrs. Krysiak explained the process by which the German Friendship Circle requested that a German teacher be sent to the village: One of the early steps was to ask parents to sign a statement affirming that they wished their children to be taught German. Eighty percent signed. However, after the teacher had been assigned and had arrived, the principal asked parents to sign a statement that they understood that German was to be an academic subject, that their children would receive grades, and that they agreed to their children's participation in it. This time, only 30 percent signed.

She explained this phenomenon as follows:

1   . . . jak już był tEn nauczyciel to sie ludzie wystracili
    . . . when already was this teacher then [refl] people feared

2   że to już jest BEZPOŚREDNIE w szkole, że oni teraz
    that that already is unmediatedly in school, that they now

3   AUTENTICZNIE muszą zadecydować. Do mnie
    authentically must decide. To me

4   zaczeli przychodzić tu też ludzie co teraz mają robić? JA
    began to come here also people what now they have to do? I

Cont. on Page 206

5   MÓWIĘ DLACZEGO? Czemu nie chcĄ podpisać, NIE, PRZECIEZ *Cont. from Page 205*
say why? Why [neg] want to sign, no, since

6   JA znAm, wiEM DOSKONALE że to też tak samo sĄ
I know, know excellently that that also the same they are

7   pochodzenia niemieckiego. Przychodzi jedna mama,
of heritage German. Comes one mama,

8   i MÓWI, JA sie boję o moje dziecko. JA MÓWIĘ czemu?
and says, I [refl] fear for my child. I say, why?

9   No, bo inne nauczyciele—bo tutAJ nauczyciele sĄ wszyscy
Well, because other teacher—because here teachers are all

10   *RICHTIG* Polacy, NIE—Że bĘdĄ moje dziecko szikanować.
true Poles, no— that they will my child cheat.

11   NIE? Że sie bĘdĄ na nich, na tych dzieciach, tak jak by
No? That [refl] will to them, to these children, as if

12   odgrywać muscici [?], bĘdĄ im złe stopnie stawać i coś
play the part of [........], they will them bad grades give and something

13   takiego.
of that [sort].

So when the teacher was already there, then people became afraid, that it's right there in school, that now they really have to decide. People began coming to me here asking what they should do? And I said why? Why don't they want to sign? Since I know perfectly well that they are also of German heritage. One mother came to me and said, I am afraid for my child. I said, why? Well, because the other teachers—because the teachers here are all real Poles—they will take it out on my child. You see? That they will play the part of [....], give them, these children, bad grades and things like that.

Just to resolve the story, a discussion was held one evening at the school at which parents were encouraged to air their anxieties. Although all the teachers in the school are, indeed, "real Poles" except for one Upper Silesian who might be thought of differently, the principal is an autochthon from an Opole Silesian village, who is widely respected for living up to his oft-stated goal that "everybody should be able to feel at home in school." His insistence on parents' signing this statement of intent was meant to protect academic standards. This was explained, and reassurances were given that "those times are past," that their children were not going to be treated in the way that they remembered being treated themselves. The presence of the teacher also allowed for reassurance concerning the other major anxiety of the parents: "Our children have enough trouble with Polish. How are they going to handle German?" The teacher promised not to overtax them and to use relaxed, playful, pedagogical methods—for which, indeed, she soon became notorious among her much stricter Polish colleagues.

These are the characteristics that make this passage seem Polish: There is no distinctively Silesian phonology. The phatic used is NIE. There is, true, one Silesian German loan, *RICHTIG*, "true" or "real" in line 10. But in this context, it is difficult to imagine the use of the Polish lexical equivalent. PRAWDZIWI POLACY ("true Poles") sounds like the title of a nationalist pamphlet extolling heroes of Poland's troubled history. It could hardly convey the sense, "true Poles as opposed to us, people who use words like *RICHTIG*."

Consider, also, the modifiers "BEZPOŚREDNIE," in line 2, "AUTENTICZNIE," in line 3, and "DOSKONALE," in line 6. I put them in small capitals not because I know of alternate Silesian lexical equivalents, but because "unmediatedly," "authentically," and "excellently" all serve to intensify the force of what she is saying, and Silesian tends to intensify by using German elements. These are highly idiomatic words, which I needed to modify to render a normal sounding translation: "it's *right there* in school," "they *really* have to decide," "I know *perfectly well* . . ." Perhaps the mechanism of intensification shares a cultural logic with what one would expect from Silesian speech: to intensify, switch to, or import from standard. But German is valorized as Silesian in people's evaluations of speech; Polish is not. The effect of these words is to make the passage sound more Polish. In general, the overwhelming impression is of fluent control of standard Polish, and this is intensified when we consider Mrs. Krysiak's rhetoric.

In line 4, Mrs. Krysiak moves into a rhetorical device which, during the twenty months I spent listening to autochthonous Silesians tell stories, joke, explain, describe, instruct, and otherwise talk, I never heard from anyone else. I did, however, hear it in the following stories:

"When I left to come here I was driven to the railway station by a cousin. She said to me, 'I wish that I, too, had been deported to Siberia.' I asked her, 'Why?' She said, 'So that I could go to the gathering at Jasna Góra as well!'" (Notes, May 8, 1993)

"A fourteen-year-old girl came to me and said, '. . . I feel like killing myself.' A fourteen-year-old girl! I asked, 'but why?' And she said, 'because nobody is ever at home, and nobody has time to listen to me, and my sister is away at university now and I've even been forbidden to invite my friends over.'"

"(Someone) came to me and said (something surprising or shocking), and I said why?" . . . and that's how I introduce my story. Except that nobody ever did introduce a story that way except Mrs. Krysiak and those residents, one per village, who are most closely tied to standardized, national Polish culture. Jasna Góra is the name of the monastery which houses the Black Madonna of Częstochowa. The context was a sermon to a congregation of survivors of Soviet deportations to Siberia given in front of the high altar of the heavenly Queen of Poland. In the second story, the ellipsis which I inserted, in order to maintain suspense, replaces the word, "Father." This context was a Lenten instructional service on "Christian family life" (the previous example had concerned the evils of divorce, while this one was identified as "a family which, although intact, is lacking in the warmth of family love"), given in the Dobra church. This device is a feature of Polish *sermon* style. In describing the process by which she, an activist of the German Minority, reintroduced instruction in the German language to her village after forty-seven years, Mrs. Krysiak not only spoke in a very standard style, but she spoke to an outsider (me) in the voice of an outsider.

It is her ability to inhabit that voice, and to do so easily and unconsciously, that we should notice. It shows an exceptional level of control of standard Polish. Franz, for example, once told me that he recognized that Poles could do things with the Polish language that he could not do; tell stories, make people laugh. So Mrs. Krysiak can be distinguished from her neighbors linguistically, and the observation that people active in the German Minority speak better Polish can be generalized. Recall that, for example, the chair of the local German Friendship Circle and his wife reported that they prefer speaking Polish, sometimes speak German, and confine Silesian to neighborly contacts where it would be insulting to speak Polish. They were the only respondents to the sentence contrast exercise whose response consistently favored Polish over Silesian. In every sentence where the switch was syntactically permissable, they chose the Polish alternate. In one sentence where the switch occurred within a syntactically highly cohesive verb phrase, they said the Polish element was acceptable; that it could be either way. Everybody else rejected the Polish alternate, but these two just didn't want to reject a Polish element.

So there is a division among Dobrans that inheres in linguistic practice. But the particularly Polish rhetorical device that Mrs. Krysiak used to express herself has division embedded in it in another way. For in using it, our activist, although she is presenting her community to me as a German one, draws a coherent set of distinctions between herself and her fellow Dobrans.

In all examples of this device, it conveys solidarity brought up short; expresses the speaker's surprise at discovering difference where similarity is expected. What a surprising thing, the priests seem to be saying, to hear such a comment from a teenage girl who should be having fun, from a cousin who should shudder at the thought of deportation, from a human being, and Roman Catholic like myself. What a surprising thing, Mrs. Krysiak seems to be saying, to perceive such anxiety among people who, she knows, "are also of German heritage."

It is a figure which belongs to relationships of strange solidarity, of solidarity across an unbridgable fissure. The relationship between priest and people is such a relationship, one of common humanity, Roman Catholicism, and good will, but also vast difference in power, privilege, and experience. I found this strange solidarity exemplified at its most weird in priests addressing women gathered for instruction in the following manner: "Dear sisters in Christ, we have come together today to consider our duties as Christian wives and mothers." Hello? The celibate male priest has duties as a Christian wife and mother? Yet I recognize that such relationships exist in my own culture, too, and so does this use of "we." It as the same device that I use in this book when I say, "We must understand more precisely . . ." or when, as a teacher, I say, "We're going to learn . . ." I already understand precisely; I have already learned. I say "we" precisely to obscure the differences between myself and you, my readers: to be polite, to bring you in. As I said, it expresses solidarity across a chasm.

Using it, Mrs. Krysiak indexed a set of contrasts between herself and others: she is the dispenser of advice; they are the seekers. She is bold; they are fearful. She is well-informed about the current political situation; they are in need of information and reassurance. She, in short, is the leader; they the followers. And what remains even more implicit: she is able to move in administrative networks beyond the village—able to deal with the educational authorities in Opole, for example—which requires fluent control of standard Polish; they move within village networks.

The "Germans" we met in the last chapter were people who, by their behavior, set themselves apart from other Dobrans. For some Dobrans who assert German identity, on the other hand, what is in play is the fact that they have been set apart from others over the course of several generations. The division in autochthonous Opole Silesian society is not only a matter of who conforms to local norms and who does not, not only of what identity people assert themselves as having, and not only a division of linguistic practice and capability. It is a division of social class that has developed over time. Further, social class has implications for identification with the state. And identification with the state is a morally fraught issue—in a totalitarian state.

THE CLASS DYNAMICS OF IDENTITY: THE BEST AND WORST HOUSES IN DOBRA

We can begin to understand the class dynamics of identity in autochthonous Opole Silesia by looking, yet again, at houses in Dobra, this time not only at how they are constructed, but how they differ. The best houses in Dobra are closely associated with German identity; there are reasons for that that have to do with identity and wealth. But the worst houses in Dobra, it emerges, are also closely associated with German identity, for the same reasons.

The Krysiak house is one of the best. It is near the village center and is attached to the Krysiak carpentry shop, which specializes in windows and doors. The shop's market is a regional one, primarily in Opole Province, with customers from all over the autochthonous ethnic enclave, including many emigrants to Germany who maintain houses in Silesia. Mr. Krysiak trains apprentices according to Polish professional requirements and does business, of course, within the wider Polish environment.

In some respects his is a typical house: a high fence fronts the street, and moving to open it spurs the barking of a dog; the house has a side entrance. It is no longer a three-generational household, for Mr. Krysiak's parents are deceased. Mrs. Krysiak moved in with him, and his older sister had moved out, to the household of her husband. At the time of the interview, then, the household consists of parents and two adolescent children, living in much more space than most Silesian families have. They have single function rooms: a living room and a TV room, a kitchen and a dining room, and three bedrooms. The floors are finished in tile, rather than linoleum, the walls recently papered, and the furniture is nice. In these ways, the house represents exceptional wealth.

This house is different from the more modest "typical" house described in chapter 4 in terms of the sum total of money that has evidently been spent on it. But, as we saw in the last chapter, economic issues in Silesia are cultural as well. The appearance of this house is an appearance that was purchased. Its owner, with his windows and doors, helps create the purchased look of other houses. His networks are not those of labor exchange within Dobra. He makes windows and doors for the regional market, for *sale*. And, he does a lot of business with emigrants who maintain houses in Silesia. These emigrants, as we have seen, generally have more money than autochthonous Opole Silesians who have stayed behind.

Consider the contrast: I was visiting the Kowolik family in their home. Their household consists of the senior Kowolik couple, in their sixties, their son, his wife, and their four daughters (one of whom is Lucyna, whose Silesian and Polish versions of the story of the girl in the meadow were analyzed in chapter 6). Their house was built by the senior Mr. Kowolik on land given to him and his wife by her parents, after several years of living with them. When the junior Mr. Kowolik married, he expanded the upstairs of the house to accommodate his family. Recently, they had put in new windows, made from German-produced materials. The cost of materials for each window was 2,000,000 złoty (about $100, or 80 euros), so in all the project had cost over 10,000,000 złoty (about $500, or 400 euros). The senior Mr. Kowolik had worked in Germany for two months to pay for it.

"Who did the work?" I asked. They told me they had hired a mason and worked alongside him. Disingenuously, I asked, "Oh, you didn't hire Mr. Krysiak to make the windows?"

"Oh, no!" I was told. "If we had had Mr. Krysiak do it, it would have been even more expensive. And besides, Krysiak makes windows to standard sizes. We made these windows ourselves; they are not of standard size."

Yes. Krysiak's business is not a local business. It looks out from the world of village networks to a wider world, a world of standard sizes. Standard sizes, and standard speech; the windows he makes go hand in hand with the Polish his family speaks. So theirs is one of the best houses in Dobra, and we can see the connection between wider networks, standard-sized windows, standard language, and wealth. But we still don't know how some Dobrans have been set apart from others, in terms of class, over the course of several generations, or what that has to do with German identity. For that, we need to look at some of the worst houses in Dobra.

Before she renovated it in the late 1990s, Marta's house was one of the worst in Dobra. And the building where she had had her tavern during my research, down the block from her house, until she moved it into her newly renovated house, is another one of the worst. What's interesting is that the fact that she identifies so strongly as Silesian has something to do with living where she does now, having grown up in a house that's neither among the best nor among the worst. It has to do with her social position, literally, on the map, as well as in terms of social class.

What had become the worst by the 1990s had once been the best.

Marta's married name is Schraft. She lives in the village center; her tavern, in the 1990s, was in another building in the village center. Hers is the house that I described in chapter 2 as having a very large room, two smaller rooms, a kitchen, and a small bathroom on the first floor; five rooms including a kitchen on the second floor; and at least four finished attic rooms on the third floor. And hers is the house that engineers said was in such bad condition that it would be cheaper to raze it than to renovate it. The building that housed the tavern is the one that had been up for sale in the 1980s, but the sale fell through when the buyers saw the state of the property and the fungi growing in many of the long-abandoned rooms. It is time to explore why these impressive buildings had so little upkeep during Communist times, and what that has to do with the German connection of the village center, and the differing identities of people like Urszula Krysiak and Marta Schraft.

Let us start by reviewing the German connection of Marta's own tavern. As I described it in chapter 3, Marta had filled it with German products: German-produced juices, chips, candy, and ice cream; an electronic game of chance, labeled entirely in German except for a few words, like "fun!" and "happy!" in English. The tavern was a sales point for bus tickets to various German cities where many emigrant autochthonous Opole Silesians live, and where many who live in Silesia were travelling to work. She played, almost entirely, German popular music. The bulk of her business was in the sale of German products, which she had been selling since 1983. Her personal connections with autochthonous Opole Silesians in Germany allowed her to drive to West Germany, buy, and return, something that Poles could not do until the fall of the Berlin Wall in 1989. Yet Marta is vehement about her personal identity as Silesian. In the years after my research the Polish market for products developed. Specifically Silesian music and decorations came onto the market. Marta had removed all the German stuff from her tavern by the time I visited in 2000.

We saw in the last chapter how ascriptions of identity function as moral statements; we saw in Urszula Krysiak's story that there are those who identify as German, and we saw a rift between Urszula and her fellow Dobrans. For Marta that rift is acute, and it is intimate. Marta's unusual social position as the widow of Stefan Schraft and a female small-business owner means that she has to confront the very real differences in attitudes and moral values that separate those who consider themselves Germans from those who consider themselves Silesians, both within her family-by-marriage and within Dobra at large, as represented by other entrepreneurs (many of whom identify as German), and by her clientele. The difficulties of this confrontation account, in large measure, for her vehemence. This is the first time, but not the last, that we will link vehement identity assertions with difficult personal experiences.

A "Silesian" and a "German" Attempt to Decide the Fate of a House

What happens when a son who has emigrated to Germany and the widow of his brother, who remained in Silesia, coinherit the family property? Johann Schraft is the older brother of Marta's deceased husband, and he had emigrated soon after his marriage in 1979, by obtaining a tourist exit visa and applying for citizenship once in Germany. His wife, Anna, joined him two years later, and in 1984, a son was born.

As the first stop on our March 1993 trip to Germany, before going on to Marta's and Magda's brother's house (where everyone was happy), Marta, Magda, Łukaś and I spent three days at the home of Marta's brother-in-law, Johann, Anna, and their nine-year-old son. It was a tense visit for all of us. Marta and Johann, joint heirs of the Schraft house and land, had quickly found themselves in serious conflict over what to do with it. The descent into conflict had not only been quick but probably inevitable: two personalities less suited to conducting any sort of business with one another could scarcely be imagined. Beyond the personality issues, however, lurked a social and cultural dimension: implicitly, Marta's desires for the house seem consonant with what it means to her to "be Silesian," while Johann's seemed consonant with his own sense of himself as "a German." Less than six months after Marta's husband's death, their eventual agreement as to how to divide the property was far in the future.

Marta wanted to move her tavern to the the house, a plan which required considerable investment in its renovation. The building in which Marta's tavern was located until 1997 (when she achieved her goal) was, as I said, in dreadful shape. Marta had no formal lease or agreement with the owner, who could not sell but did not want to invest in renovations and upkeep. He had emigrated to Germany in the mid 1980s, and his alcoholism was complicating Marta's attempts to reach a more stable agreement with him. The storefront she was using for the tavern, which had once been a grocery store, was very small; that building had, once, also housed a large tavern, but that part of the building was uninhabitable. The Schraft house is also in the village center; it too, once housed a tavern in more prosperous days. Eventually, Marta and Johann resolved their conflict: she took ownership of the house, and he got the land. But at this point in time, Johann wanted only to sell the property. He saw no point in keeping a house, or anything else of value, in Poland.

Johann found himself under an avalanche of Marta's disapproval of his abandonment of his parents, his brother, his property, and of Silesia itself, an abandonment epitomized, for Marta, in the fact that his son had been raised monolingually in German. Johann is a person who tends to avoid conflictual conversations; Marta is not. Stalemated, on this visit they did not discuss the disposition of the property until the morning of our departure.

In the house, then, were two children who did not share a language; Johann, who strongly preferred to speak German;[1] and four women differently positioned with respect to him. Magda, whose German is minimal, did not converse with Johann. Marta, whose German is somewhat better, and who would have had, at any rate, no compunction about forcing him to speak Silesian, did not converse with him because she was temporarily prevented by Johann's avoidance and by the intensity of her own anger at him. Anna was busy translating for the children, planning meals and activities, and generally hosting. So who ever talked to him? I did. I spent a lot of time in "informal interview" with Johann. He and I sat in the living-room speaking German, while the other three women, who consistently refused my help, spoke Silesian as they worked in the kitchen. There were divisions in play at many levels: a gender line, a professional line, a linguistic line, and a line of Silesian vs. German identity.

I began to understand how these lines overlay each other when I asked Johann why he had emigrated. He said, "That's easy. At work they kept saying to me, 'You lousy German, you lousy German,' so finally I said, 'OK, I'm a German, am I? Fine, AUF WIEDERSEHEN.'" As a young man in the 1970s, he felt, in other words, discriminated against as a German. His parents were of strong German national identity. His father had refused to emigrate, saying (as Marta repeatedly pointed out to me, drawing the sad contrast with Johann), "My place is here." But Johann's father believed that the borders would be revised, that Silesia would return to Germany. Johann told me this, and Marta at one point let me read his correspondence, which indicates the same. So, for Johann to feel that his place, after all, was in Germany was not a real change from his father's position. Johann accepted, correctly, that the German-Polish border is permanent. We cannot know whether his father would still have felt that his place was in Silesia if he had done the same.

Johann and his family live in predominantly Protestant northern Germany, and as is typical for this region, the Roman Catholic parish they go to is attended primarily by postwar expellees from German-speaking Lower Silesia and their families. Johann and his family live in a neighborhood of duplexes which is entirely German. When, on a walk, neighbors of Johann's commented, "I see you have visitors from Poland," he quickly corrected, "From *Silesia*." Left to themselves, Johann and his family speak only German. I never asked him straight out, but I would be surprised if Johann were to claim to identify as anything other than German. The tensions of the visit concerned the property, but attitudes toward the property were structured by the fact that its two owners had a very different sense of identity and of where each of their "place" was.

Yet one evening, tensions eased. The children were asleep, and photo albums had been brought out, discussed, and left closed on the coffee table. The five adults were settled on couches, pleasantly intoxicated, and in this environment, once explication of the photos was finished, Johann spoke Silesian. Magda, then, was not shut out. Gender receded; all the women's work had been done. Everyone was taking turns talking, and taking about equal turns, myself included. And in the midst of this pleasing symmetry, Marta sighed and said (perhaps strategically), "If only we could get something going in the center [of Dobra], the center was just wiped out [i.e., by emigration]."

I was suddenly alert. If Marta was trying to take advantage of the relaxed atmosphere to push her agenda for the Schraft house, her strategy was foiled by her housemate, who saw other potentialities in the comment. Visions of the sociology of spatial organization had begun to dance in my head.

"The peripheries weren't?"

"C'mon, think about how many people live in Mama's house." (Seven: Marta's parents, her sister Magda, her sister's husband, and their three children.)

Magda and Anna shrugged, looked at each other, said it was coincidence. Marta said the biggest farms were always in the center, and the people were gone. She went down the main street of Dobra naming names. Then Johann said, in German, "It was like this." In German, he explained that the younger generation didn't want to work the fields, and the older generation couldn't manage it alone. Then the conversation went back to other subjects, in Silesian.

I had broken the mood, reacting to the mention of something so sociologically significant that I simply had to ask pointed questions about it. The pattern that ensued, a series of very short dialogs of the other women with me, was tied up when the man present took it upon himself to explain to me what had happened. German entered this Silesian conversation in the same way that

Polish often does: as an expository register. Yet its way was paved by the sudden reemergence of an asymmetrical form of talk. After I reinvoked the division between researcher and informant, the other divisions suddenly also came back into play: between informants who claim to know and those who don't, and between male and female. With them came German, in the voice of the man who knew.

Johann's use of German looks like uses of Polish we've examined: an appropriate language to use to lay out "how things are." In the sense that standard languages are used to make a claim on people's focused attention, they are languages that dominate: there is an echo of state domination of Silesia in the way that people speaking German or Polish dominate interaction, even when this domination is socially acceptable. But in this situation, the fact that Johann felt himself to be in a position to lay out "how things are" for me, ironically, sprang directly from the fact that, during this visit, he was being contested. Besides being expository, Johann's use of German referenced his role as my informant. He wound up in that role because the other women conspired to make me his interlocutor. They did so because they couldn't deal with him for various reasons. Of those reasons, the most intense were Marta's. The intensity of Marta's reasons sprang from the fact that, although she was reluctant to ask him for anything, she needed something of significance from him: his signature on legal documents that would give her the authority to invest heavily in a house in Silesia that Johann wished only to abandon. The conflict was only exacerbated by her sense of Johann's emigration as, in essence, disloyal—disloyal to Silesia.

After all, the Schraft house is not her *ojczyzna*. She married in. Exceptionally, but in a way patterned by class, as we shall see, she moved in with her husband and his parents, rather than her husband moving in with her and her parents. When the engineers advised her to raze the house, she told me that she couldn't do that. She chose to renovate, and she continued the renovation even when, in 1995, the central chimney collapsed, almost bringing the roof down with it. It is what she thinks her father-in-law would have wanted. But if she had grown up in the house, or in any house in the village center, she might see things differently—as Johann does. Ironically, then, there is something about Johann's upbringing in that house—his *ojczyzna*—that allowed him psychologically to "move away" from the moral compulsion to invest in it and take care of it. Whereas Marta, who grew up on the village periphery, remains more grounded in Silesian norms that require one to invest, to take care of, houses.

It's a family conflict, an intimate conflict, but then, that's just the point. The fact that this is a community in which some people consider themselves to be Germans and others don't is an intimate, intracommunity, intra*familial* problem. It is a problem near the surface of social life, not easily denied. And this particular family conflict, as we shall see, happens to shed light on the whole historical development of the village center: indeed, on the way that class intersects with identity in Dobra at large.

"Our Village, Dobra, Has Come Way Down in the World": The Rise and Fall of a German, Bourgeois Village Center

The buildings of the village center date from the first decades of the twentieth century, the oldest of them from 1890. They represent fundamental change in Dobra. This stretch of main street, between the church and the railway tracks, physically reorganized the village; its center had been the church itself, with roads radiating outward from it. Once the railway arrived in 1860, there was a new, important space to be filled. Not only were all the buildings between the church and the tracks built in the decades following the arrival of the railroad, but entire new streets, running parallel and perpendicular to the tracks and the new main street, were also laid during this time. In terms of building, it was a fundamental modernization of the village. The center itself was built to be a business district. It was rich, bourgeois, and German. The building was complete by about the turn of the twentieth century.

We know that the village center was rich, bourgeois, and German both because we have the memories of older residents and because we have an eyewitness: Georg Garant, born 1875, the staunchly German-identifying school principal with the indefinable last name, lived in Dobra from 1924 to 1945. The school, at that time, was in the village center; his house was next to it. Several years after fleeing advancing Soviet forces in January 1945, he dictated his memoirs to his daughters, a grandson typed them up in booklet form, and in 1988 they were copied and distributed to the family and, thereafter, to the Dobra German Friendship Circle. I was given a copy by Mrs. Pilawa, wife of the chair of that organization.

"Principal" was a high social position. Its occupants were civil servants (BEAMTE), and as such community leaders. Garant observed his environment from an elite position. It is interesting to note that an elite position is a German-identified position. Consider the way he described a village in which he lived as a child: '. . . was a little hole, a desert. The teacher and our father were the only German speakers" (p. 8). It is unlikely that Garant's father, that Garant himself, did not speak Silesian. How would they have gotten along with all those people who spoke no German? No, what he probably meant was that, in these last decades of the nineteenth century, there were only two bilinguals in this village. Or, consider a village in which he worked:

> ... is a miserable, sleepy hole offering no possibility for advancement. The village is surrounded by forest, the ground nothing but sand. The people work on the estate, in the forest, in the brick works and in the two sawmills. In the winter logs were brought to the sawmills. There was a brewery, but it closed. The Jew Adler was the only merchant. The butcher, Daniel, came every Saturday with maggoty meat. We rarely bought meat. (13)

The great contrast with Dobra concerns the possibility for advancement, economic life, and German identity:

> On January 4, 1924 we moved into Dobra, with all our baggage and [son] Günther in a baby carriage. Now we began a new life. The position was ideal. The church, the rectory, and the post office were across the street, it was a three-minute walk to the train station. Three bakers, three butchers, three taverns, next to them a general goods store, [for the family] a pretty garden . . . a big yard, stalls, a barn. . . . Children took the train . . . to school. From the church I had a good income [as organist], I was made a civil servant. (32)

> ... The inhabitants were, with few exceptions, German-oriented. . . . The people greeted politely and spoke German. Newborns were christened with German names. (47)

Implicit in these remarks is an organization of class, social space, and identity of which language is the accessible sign. Garant phrases his approval of his village center environment in Dobra in terms of its economic activity, but also in terms of its being a German-speaking environment. He looks to christenings as a reflection of people's "orientation."

Yet we cannot, in fact, be sure that the people who "greeted politely and spoke German," also spoke German on the streets they lived on, in the village peripheries, or whether their greetings to people of less exalted position were in German. The 1921 plebiscite results for Dobra, as the standing exhibit in the school tells us, were 443 for Poland, 454 for Germany, which suggests a more complicated picture than widespread, unambivalent German national identity with "a few exceptions." Garant saw the village from a high social position and from the village center. He saw it at its most German.

We can, however, assume that in those other villages where Garant lived before he was lucky enough to move to Dobra, in the "miserable, sleepy little holes," people spoke Silesian Polish even to him. Garant's comments reflect a relatively recent sociolinguistics of social space. The train tracks were laid in Dobra in about 1860; before then, the village center was quite different, not bourgeois, and was in all likelihood not German-speaking. Opole Silesia, then, was undergoing a process of language shift. It was a process of language shift classic in its outline: expansion of German, the language of a socially and politically dominant part of the population, at the expense of Silesian, as upwardly mobile native speakers of Silesian adopted social habits "po pańsku," as Matuschek reports that they sometimes put it: after the fashion of the state. Dobra had traveled farther along this path than the other villages where Garant had lived. By 1924 it had progressed to the point that a German-speaking social space had emerged.

So Garant moved into Dobra, as I suggested, in the heyday of its economic activity and growth. The center had been built; its buildings were, at most, half a century old, and in them were lively businesses and social concourse of a cosmopolitan, German nature. But, as Marta bemoaned above, matters have changed much for the worse since then.

Garant and his family fled west as Soviet forces approached Silesia in January 1945, and this flight heralded the beginning of the process by which the village center was, as Marta put it, "wiped out." Emigration from Silesia to western Germany is nothing new; it began long before 1945 and has continued since. But the flight of refugees in 1945 and the expulsions that followed were unprecedented in scale.

In villages like Dobra, most immediately affected were the richest people, those also most likely to have been, by choice or coercion, Nazi party members. Garant and his family were among these. Although it is clear from his memoirs that his family left before the Soviet army arrived, as a civil servant, a STANDESBEAMTE of the Nazi state, he was a prime candidate for expulsion, or even imprisonment, by the Soviet army and the subordinate Polish authorities they quickly installed. Garant was responsible, for example, for approving the genealogical surveys that families had to complete, in order for the state to establish whether they were, or were not, Slavic, or were, or were not, Jewish; these surveys threatened punishment for incomplete or false answers. Kurt Lasok, also, the owner of a large brickwork in Dobra, left quickly: he had been employing Polish forced labor. A family headed by a man whose signature appears in the old Schraft tavern records as approving its purchases also left immediately. In none of these cases is it known whether they fled ahead of the invading forces, or were forced to leave by them. Other families, about whose relationship with the Nazi state I know nothing, also left.[2]

Chapter 8

The Schrafts did not. At that point, the extended family centered on Johann's father and his father's brother. Both men were married. Johann's father was a Soviet prisoner of war, and Johann and his brother, Marta's deceased husband, had not yet been born. Johann's father's brother remained in Dobra during the war, with his wife and children. Johann's parents lived in the house he and Marta inherited, and his father's brother's family lived across the street. It was that branch that saved the entire family from expulsion. According to Johann's cousins, their father had been manipulating records in favor of local farmers when it came time for state expropriations, and they returned the favor by telling the relevant military authorities that they were certainly Poles (interview, June 12, 1993). Two years after war's end, Johann's father, still a Soviet POW, signed the loyalty oath to the Polish state, promising "to break off forever all connection with Germans and Germandom, to uproot thoroughly feelings for Germandom," and so on, as described in chapter 2. He did this while a prisoner, and under threat of expropriation and expulsion from his home. Johann made it very clear to me that his father had felt coerced, and that it was because his father had succumbed to the pressure to sign this oath or lose his home that the identity of the family must be protected in this book (letter from Johann, October 9, 1993).

But not all German-identified Dobrans left immediately after the war. Some stayed, and many others fled initially, but returned. The entire village center was not at once and immediately abandoned, as if the plague had hit a medieval town. Many families remained, or returned, but as we will see, they did not fare well, nor did the enterprises which remained. As the chairman of the German Minority, Roland Pilawa, put it (in July 1992, on the occasion of the celebration of the seven-hundredth anniversary of the first written mention of the name of the village), in hesitant and grammatically inaccurate German, "Our village was once an administrative center with a civil office, had three mills, a sawmill, a brickwork, a post office, and three butchers. The village is now so poor than nothing of the abovementioned enterprises remains. The mills and the sawmill were torn down, the brickwork burned down and so on. A great many young inhabitants have emigrated to Germany. Our village Dobra has come way down in the world." So the process was not immediate but it was thorough. The ultimate result was well-expressed by a man who had been a teenager when the war ended: "It used to be that the villages around Dobra were poor, and Dobra, rich. Now it's the other way around. If you go to Grabina, you see painted houses, well-kept up fences, a satellite dish or even two on every house. And Dobra? Totally run-down. Especially the village center. When I was young, and we used to go to dances in those villages, I tell you, mothers used to lead their daughters out by the hand, saying, 'Take her, take her!' Anyone from Dobra would have been a good match" (Notes December 17, 1992).

The reason for this reversal of village fortunes is that Dobra, with its more developed class structure, presented more of a target for Communist attempts to create a classless—or more accurately, one-class—society, compared with Garant's little, miserable, sleepy, desert hole villages. The civil office was moved to a nearby industrial town. The butchers and millers were expelled after the war, or later gave their properties to the state in return for an exit visa, or were forced by high taxes to divide and sell them. As for the brickyard, it was made a state enterprise after its owner was expelled. It is widely believed in Dobra that the Communists burned down the brickyard on purpose because they wanted to consolidate that industry in one of the nearby cities. Clay is still quarried in Dobra and taken to that brickyard.

The nostalgia which has developed for the village center that once was is intense, and widespread especially among those who remember it, or some of it, or who have particular interest in the village center (like Marta). But it is also complicated by the fact that for the last twelve years of its existence, the village center that thrived in Dobra, with its life after the fashion of the state, was the part of Dobra most closely identified with the Nazi state. This is true because in both Nazi Germany and Communist Poland, it was people in economically and socially higher positions who were under the most pressure to join the Party, to carry out the policies, and otherwise show themselves to be good citizens of the totalitarian state. Nostalgia for better times, then, is problematically equivalent to nostalgia for Nazi Germany.

In a sense closely tied to the observation that identity statements are moral statements, what Marta meant by telling me that she considered herself to be Silesian was that her family had kept its distance from the Nazi regime, and that she was not nostalgic for that era. And yet, and yet . . . "If only we could get something going in the center, the center was just wiped out." How can one not be nostalgic for what came before the defeat of Naziism, before the Soviet invasion? For there is really something wrong in this village. The village center is, indeed, totally run-down. Paint has faded to oblivion; facades have cracked, especially under windows. But the deterioration seems to involve more than infrastructure, and more than the space of the village center. Consider this: on October 16, 1994, the priest, during parish announcements, thanked the people of the neighboring village, Nowa Studnia, for their collection of potatoes, apples, and other harvest fruits, given as alms to the Franciscan monastery in Opole. "As for Dobra," he continued, "there is nothing for me to say thank you for, since nobody gave anything."

"Lack of organization," the priest told me later, when I asked him to what he attributed Dobra's negligence. Simply, people would have had to talk about the task; somebody would have had to go around with a cart, and people would have had to be ready to load their contributions onto it. No one did this. There was a certain lack of enthusiasm, or social apathy.

Gathering potatoes is not the only matter in which I, and Dobrans themselves, observe a lack of organization. Harvest customs, for example, which require a collectivity of people to carry out, are generally observed in Nowa Studnia, but not in Dobra. The children of Nowa Studnia come to the Dobra school for seventh and eighth grade, and Kasia, then a sixth grader, told me that they are the ones with all the good ideas for class skits, they are the ones who have the creativity to write funny poems, they have more energy. In the early post-Communist years, Dobra did not attract the kind of investment which had given other villages a renovated, well-equipped hall in which to hold discos and other parties, as teenagers noticed. A Franciscan priest from Opole, charged with preparing the congregation for Easter in 1995, told the parents and later repeated to me, when I introduced myself to him as a sociologist, that in comparison to other villages, Dobra children behave badly in church. In other villages, as people bemoan (and as I have observed), people decorate their houses for summer festivals, so that the entire village looks festive; in Dobra they don't.

Why so much inadequacy? Why this malaise? Why don't people decorate for summer festivals?

This is a key question because answering it answers other important questions: Are the concurrent leaders of the German Minority the sociological descendants of the families of the village center? (No.) What else informs the vehemence of Marta's Silesian identification? (She's seen as a kind of interloper.) What is the nature of relationships within Dobra which leads people of, broadly, the same demographic origin to claim so vehemently two different identities? (They're stuck in a historically grounded conflict.) In accounting for Dobra's drab appearance during village festivals, we can draw definitive connections not only to what had developed by 1924, and to what happened right after the war, but also to the shape of the social structure—and culture of identity—left behind.

THE DEVELOPMENT OF CLASS-LINKED GERMAN IDENTITY

Some Dobrans have been set apart from others over the course of several generations. They have been set apart by the terms of social, economic class.

Many members of that class were forced to leave Dobra immediately after the war. Some of the concurrent active membership of the German Minority are, indeed, relatives of the village center families of the 1920s, but not many. The rest are members of families who were not quite in that group, but who aspired to be. It was a group that had social boundaries around it, but it could be joined. You could get in. Upward mobility was possible, in German times. You had to get rich, in culturally specific Silesian terms.

In Opole Silesian terms of the pre-Nazi era, "making it," meant not just having money, but having enough money to do one specific socially important thing: to provide your daughters with a substantial marital dowry in cash. That was what allowed a family to be a member of the bounded society of the German-identified bourgeoisie. Wealth enabled your children to marry people who also dowered their daughters in cash. Here's how it worked.

In Opole Silesia, for many decades and in the 1990's, every married couple's ambition, regardless of class or wealth, has been to build and own a house, with accompanying land. Before 1945, success in farming was a primary road to wealth, so families wanted as much land as possible, and various government incentives existed at different times to encourage people to claim it by clearing the forests. Now, there is land in excess of what can be worked, and people covet it less. But they still want the house, and they still want enough land to allow for some farming. This ideal is still robust in Silesia; it has generated an intricate complex of cultural norms of ownership, as we saw in the last chapter. Importantly, people want one of their children to inherit the property. As I said in chapter 4, the height of power in the life cycle is to be the parents of a grown married child with growing children, the heads of a three-generation household. This is the key wound, for the older generation, of the second massive emigration wave of the postwar era, that of the 1980s. It was an emigration predominantly of young people, so parents lost their heirs, their continuity.

This continuing emphasis on house ownership and inheritance has constituted a common set of cultural ideals throughout autochthonous society for the approximately 150 years that constitute the broadest scope of this study. However, how inheritance works out in practice has depended on social position. Remember that when I described the "typical" autochthonous Opole Silesian house, I mentioned that in many houses, one enters and faces a stairway and two internal doors on either side, and that these doors often carry metal plaques inscribed with the surname of the family residing on that side. There's a difference of surname between the two related families living in the house because typically, it is a daughter who stays, and she takes her husband's name.

223

But that was not true in all families. Rich families were able to realize the ultimate dream of property staying within the family, which is that it stay within the family *name*.

This is because the best dowry most parents could offer was inheritance rights to the family property. As numerous family histories reveal, in the early decades of the century, a family of moderate means with three daughters and two sons would be likely to dower one of them by giving her husband inheritance rights, and the other two, if possible, by giving them and their husbands land on which to build their own houses. If there was not enough land, a daughter could be given money and goods, but unless the value were high (and the first spending priority was to buy more land), this was very much a third and worst choice. Maria Rataja told me, "It used to be like India, here, for women in that position." The family's sons, then, would get land or the inheritance rights to a house through their own marriages. If they did not, life in Germany usually offered enough opportunity that they could make a living beyond the confines of this system.

So, the autochthonous Silesian norm for postmarital residence, both stated and statistical, is uxorilocality: husbands move in with the family of their wives. Family histories reveal many couples moving in with the wife's parents, and then, after several years, building a house on land given to them by her parents. But one daughter remained. She and her husband inherited; the property stayed within the family. But most families could not aspire to the ultimate ideal, which was for the property to stay not only within the family, but within the family name, since women take their husbands' surnames on marriage. In order to allow a male to inherit the house, a family had to be able to afford to dower its daughters in other ways. Only rich families could do this.

So how could a late-nineteenth-century family get rich? They could, if they commanded enough labor, in the form of children or relatives, hope to take advantage of government-incentive programs to turn forest into arable land. Farming that land could yield profits enough to change their position vis-à-vis the dowry system, allowing what anthropologists call patrilocal, patrilineal inheritance of the primary property and assuring the family a place among others whose sons, rather than whose daughters, inherited. The histories of the families who inhabited the village center are replete with postmarital patrilocality. And until 1945, they were replete with people marrying within their own class. After the war, in those families who remained, everything fell apart.

With the help of Maria Rataja and Hans Drabik, two unrelated people in their sixties, I surveyed the histories of the thirteen family properties which occupy the center of Dobra. The histories start in the later half of the nineteenth century, and most of them start with a man coming to Dobra from some other, unknown, place. They built the center, over the course of some fifty years, between about 1860 and about 1910. They were strangers, people who had come to Dobra from somewhere else, but in Dobra, they built a new social space together. And their children married each other, their daughters, by and large, moving half a block away to the home of their husband's parents.

I present here, in detail, the histories of the four village properties which best illustrate the processes I've been describing. Again, what these family histories show is, before the end of the Second World War, patrilocality (newly married couples living with the husband's parents) and class endogamy (marriage within the group defined by patrilocality, which implies wealth). Since 1945, the histories are replete with alcoholism, suicide, early death (before having children), marriage without issue (no children), hypogamous marriage (marriage "down," i.e., to someone from a poorer class), emigration, and, in the immediate postwar period, displacement (people who fled the advancing Soviet forces and became refugees) and expulsion (people who were forced to leave once those Soviet forces had arrived.) All in all, it constitutes what can only be called a demographic collapse—simply put, the all but total disappearance of an entire segment of society.

It will become evident that the reason that Dobra's village center does not get decorated for summer festivals is essentially that there's nobody there to do it.

That said, this history leads on to other questions. Our concern is not so much who these people were, as they are, for the most part, gone. Rather, the question is who they were in relationship to who the concurrent leadership of the German Minority is, and how that relationship, in turn, informs the asserted identities of its inhabitants. Using the sociological concept of class, we can connect the concurrent active membership of the German Minority to the village center that was. Those sociological relationships begin to shed light on why some people assert an identity that others use as a summary of moral criticism. It springs from the sociology of how people are positioned, but, on a deeper level, from the fact that for all persons, managing their positions—navigating the social terrain in which they find themselves—poses moral dilemmas. In totalitarian states, these dilemmas can be acute.

BRAUER AND TYL: THE PLACE OF THE GERMAN MINORITY CHAIR

Eduard Brauer moved to Dobra from a small, nearby village, and, in 1895, built a property consisting of a large house with fields and outbuildings, and three large ground-floor halls suitable for retail space. (We know the exact date because he had it carved into a cornerstone.) He opened a tavern, one of the three

225

operating in the village center in the early decades of the century. It is remembered as the "working man's tavern," as the three taverns served customers stratified by class.

From the 1910s to the 1920s, two children were born: an older daughter, Maria, and a younger son, Erhart. In the 1930s Maria married a man named Pilawa, from a neighboring village, who moved onto the Brauer property. Erhart also married, and his wife joined him on the property. It was big enough to divide between the two couples. This couple, then, managed to keep both their son and their daughter on the property.

In the early 1940s, Maria and her husband had their only child, a son, Roland Pilawa. The family moved further west within Germany, but returned after the war, and continued to live on the property. In the late 1940s, two sons, Karol and Eugen, were born to Erhart and his wife. Roland and Karol and Eugen are thus first cousins, and grew up in the same large property. I never observed them talking to one another, though. Roland is the concurrent chair of the German Friendship Circle.

In the 1960s, Roland Pilawa married Teresa, from across the street (class endogamy), and they started a family. They built a house on his inherited land near the village center (patrilineal inheritance—in our interview, he made sure I understood that the land came from his parents, not hers—this was a way of signaling class membership to me), and ultimately had five children.

This is the situation as of 1995: Eduard Brauer's children, Maria and Erhart, have died. His daughter Maria's husband has also died; only his son's wife survives. Neither of their two sons, Karol and Eugen, ever married; they still live at home with their now aged mother and make a living by contracting their services as farmers and hauling coal. (Karol is the recipient of Marta's cart, as described in the last chapter.)

The first Tyl of this property was the son of a man from a local city. He built a large house at the corner of the main street and the railway tract. He married a local woman who joined him on the property (postmarital patrilocality).

In the 1920s, two children were born: an older son, Kurt, and a younger daughter, Judith.

In the 1940s, Kurt married a woman from the nearby, large village of Rybna; his wife moved in with him (patrilocality). He rebuilt the house, inherited it (patrilineally), and they live there still. Three children were born. Two of them died young without issue. A daughter lives patrilocally with her husband in another village; their son, now an adult, will inherit the property. Why does the daughter not inherit? Presumably she carried a substantial monetary dowry into her marriage in the place of offering her husband inheritance rights. And her husband inherited his parents' property.

IDENTITY ASSERTIONS AS A LANGUAGE OF ASPIRATION

Judith married a man who came from money but had none; his father had been disinherited because he married a household servant (what anthropologists would call a drastically hypogamous marriage). The couple was given land by her parents near the village center on which they built a house (matrilocality; a land dowry). It is their daughter, Teresa, who later married Roland Pilawa (class endogamy).

The brother of the elder Mrs. Tyl, from Rybna, is concurrently the chairman of the Rybna German Friendship Circle.

The Tyl property is thus inhabited only by a couple in their seventies.

LASOK AND SCHRAFT, OR, MARTA, THE OUTSIDER WITHIN

I do not know whether, in the latter nineteenth century, the father of Kurt and Józef Lasok established a huge property which he later divided for his sons to develop, or whether Kurt and Józef came to Dobra together but separately developed their enterprises. Suffice it to say that by 1930, Kurt Lasok was the owner of the brickyard, and Józef had the village center property including a very large tavern, serving "the intelligensia," a grocery store (in the room where the tavern was), and a dance hall with a stage, and two upstairs "bed and breakfast" rooms.

If Kurt Lasok married and had children, they shared his fate of expulsion after the war on account of his having used Polish forced labor in his brickyard.

This family's genealogy exhibits a dense form of class endogamy, marital sibling exchange: "My son marries your daughter and my daughter marries your son." Józef Lasok married a local woman named Edith Emmerling; she moved in with him (patrilocality). Her brother married her husband Józef Lasok's sister. Józef Lasok and his wife had two sons in the 1930s to 1940s. One married and moved to Opole, and died young (early death without issue). The second is the current owner of the property.

No one currently lives on the property. The last inhabitant, a former household servant of the family who own the property, died in his eighties in 1995. The owner emigrated to Germany in the second half of the 1980s, after his parents' death. He never married and is an alcoholic. Marta's tavern was in operation in the building from 1983 to 1997. The only other ongoing use of the building is a state-run grocery store that occupies what was once the dance hall. (This is where Brigitte works.)

In 1997, Marta moved the tavern to the house she had (by agreement with Johann), inherited from her husband: the Schraft house, which had been a tavern before. The man who told me about how mothers from other villages

227

would lead their daughters out by the hand when young men from Dobra were around: he was talking to me in the yard of the Schraft house. Talk turned to the fate of the village center, and he gestured toward the house: "Schraft! One of the biggest! And now . . ." he shrugged.

In the early years of the twentieth century, the Schraft family owned a huge expanse of farmland; this house, as well as a large red brick house across the street from it; and a house on a side street of Dobra. Johann Schraft (the grandfather of Marta's brother-in-law, for whom he is named) came to Dobra during the latter half of the nineteenth century. In the early years of the century, Johann Schraft had five children: three girls followed by two boys. The two older girls died without marrying. The third daughter married a man named Doss, and was given land on which to build near the village center (matrilocality). That house was turned over to a Polish family when its inhabitants fled after the war (displacement).

The rest of the property was divided between the two sons, Johann Jr. and Ulrich. Most of the farmland and the large red brick house went to Johann, while Ulrich (the father of Marta's deceased husband and brother-in-law) was to make his living through a tavern. To this end, Johann Sr. bought the house opposite (now Marta's house) from a man named Lysschek (whose aging son when last heard from was living in New Jersey).

He gave inheritance rights to his own house (the red brick one) to Johann Jr., who was joined by a wife from a neighboring village (patrilocality). They had two sons who survived beyond infancy, born in 1937 and 1939. These are the cousins of Marta's brother-in-law who told me that their family had escaped expulsion due to the intervention of "Polish" farmer neighbors. Neither of them married. After repeated attempts to emigrate, they turned their entire property over to the state in return for an exit visa in the 1970s. Most of their farmland was turned into a park of cottage gardens for the industrial workers from Barkowo; this forms an expanse on one side of the village. Their house was made into housing for people being supported by the state because they cannot work. Some inhabitants stay a short time; others, longer. The most severely alcoholic and, as people recognize, most mentally ill person, lives in that house with his wife and adolescent daughter. The house is visibly neglected; for example, an attic window was left open throughout the winter months of 1994–95.

While the fate of the Doss house illustrates one common mechanism by which Poles entered Silesian villages to stay, the fate of the Schraft house illustrates another. The Polish inhabitants of the Doss house are, I sense, respected for their education and accepted in the village, though the Dosses are remembered by some older people. But the transfer of the Schraft house to the state made the home of the most successful of German society into that of the least successful of Polish society.

In Dobra, there are other houses which were transferred to the ownership of individual Polish families after the war. There are also two other large houses, just beyond the church, whose owners fled in 1945 and which were, likewise, made into state-owned housing cooperatives (though not, I believe, assigned to those unable to work). The same thing happened throughout Opole Silesia. In order to understand the hostility between the autochthonous Silesian and immigrant Polish communities, it is important to realize that intimate interethnic contact was established by acts of expropriation by the Communist state on behalf of Poles—whose country had just been devastated by the German occupation.

Ulrich Schraft's first son, Marta's brother-in-law, was named Jan only because Johann, its German equivalent, had been outlawed. Ulrich, as I mentioned above, adamantly refused to emigrate, holding that "my place is here," and believing that Silesia would one day be returned to Germany. Johann, essentially, stayed long enough to get married to a woman from a small—and much poorer—neighboring village (hypogamous marriage), then emigrated knowing that, as his wife, Anna would eventually be allowed to leave. It took two years to work out her emigration.

Ulrich's second son, Stefan, was born in 1963. He died, childless, of the effects of alcoholism at the age of twenty-nine, in 1992. His brother Johann had married down in terms of social class, and Stefan too, had married hypogamously: he married Marta.

Marta, as it happens, grew up on the other side of the tracks, that is, outside the village center. Her family are not owners of businesses. Her father is a skilled worker in the nearby steelworks. Her sister, who lives with her husband and children in the same house with her parents, is married to a plumber. Marta is the only member of the family ever to have studied for *matura*, the Polish pre-university secondary school diploma, and she is the only entrepreneur. Her social position, then, as tavernkeeper in the village center, is not one she inherited from her parents. To a large extent, she attained it through the exercise of her own talents and drive. To a certain extent, however, she attained it by marrying and outliving the last nonemigrant survivor of one of the richest families in Dobra. She is now, by marriage, the only representative of the entire Schraft family living in Poland.

So why does nobody decorate for German Minority festivals? Well, who would do the decorating? The Brauer property is inhabited by two uninterested middle-aged bachelors and their aged mother. The Tyl property is inhabited by a couple in their seventies. One Schraft house is inhabited by emigrant Polish wards of the state, the other, by Marta alone. And of all the other properties not considered here in detail, only one houses a family with growing children who are the descendants of the people who built the house. The sum totals: in my survey of the village center of thirteen family properties since mid-century, there were three cases of alcoholism (one fatal) and a suicide. The class endogamy has been succeeded by twelve cases of failure to marry, death before marriage, marriage without progeny, and two cases of hypogamous marriage. There have been fourteen cases of emigration away from the property. Three properties have completely passed out of the hands of the family into that of the state (two of these are completely abandoned), one is without an heir, and three have been, or stand to be, inherited atypically for the Silesian system (that is, by a too distant relative). Lack of decoration is the outward sign of demographic collapse.

If the village center were to be decorated for summer festivals, it would have to be done by the leadership of the German Minority themselves, coming into the village center, decorating property that does not belong to them. And this is practically unthinkable in autochthonous Opole Silesian conceptions of ownership. In Rybna, where Mrs. Tyl's brother is chair of the German Friendship Circle, the decorations for the 1995 seven-hundredth birthday of the village festival (August 12, 1995) were much more impressive. This was achieved by individual families working on their own property. For example, families made straw-stuffed figures, dressed them in old clothes, and displayed them by the street along with old farming and household implements, placing them in scenes associated with Silesian and German life. When I asked where this idea had come from, Mr. Tyl told me that he didn't know, but people had been around to other village festivals picking up ideas. After a while, he said, people started making their preparations in semi-secrecy, hiding their work from their neighbors in order to compete with them in making original, interesting, and pretty displays. That is the kind of thing that people will do with their own property. Rybna is a village with a less firmly defined village center, and the area of the village which visitors see, coming from the bus or train, has evidently not been "wiped out." This kind of community effort through attention to one's own property is precisely the kind of thing that cannot happen in the center of Dobra.

For even Roland Pilawa does not live in the village center, and he is the *only* leader, or active member, of the German Minority who comes from one of its families. As I mentioned above, the social position of all the rest is, in one sense, like that of Marta: they all come from families which live beyond the tracks, or beyond the church. But most of them are people of some means, and they come from families that have had some wealth since before 1945. Some are also entrepreneurs, who were able to keep private businesses through the Communist era, like Anton Fischer, who owns an electrical workshop, or Józef Krysiak, who owns a carpentry shop. Others have held managerial positions in the nearby steelworks, like Roland Pilawa. They are people somewhat higher in the social hierarchy than Marta, or Franz Skorupka. But not as high as Garant and his ilk once were. These were the people just slightly down in the social hierarchy. The people best positioned to look up, and see what they stood to gain, if they could just become slightly richer.

Theirs, then, is a nostalgia for a class they identified with but did not quite belong to. When Roland Pilawa said, "Our village Dobra has come way down in the world," he was looking back in time, but also holding out a vision that, for most of his German Minority–identified hearers, constitutes looking up. They are looking up, as well as back, at the place, sociological and sociospatial, to which they would have aspired to move. It was an aspiration that encompassed the economic, cultural, linguistic, and political realms: an aspiration to have money, live a metropolitan life, speak the national language, and identify with the nation-state. And Communist Poland destroyed their dreams.

Even in Communist Poland, they tried. That's why it's the active members of the German Minority who speak the best standard Polish in Dobra. This is not unique to Silesia: for professionals in the United States as well, an aspiration to "speak well" by the standards of the state is part and parcel of aspirations to upward mobility (Silverstein 1987). Those of strongest German identity at the time of the transfer of Silesia to Poland were those in whom this "longing for standard" had taken firmest hold. Mrs. Krysiak's grandparents, and her husband's grandparents, did not speak only German at home until 1945 because of Nazi coercion, but, as her father emphasized to me, by choice. After 1945, they reintroduced Silesian, under coercion, but their educational, social, and economic aspirations remained. They were among those whose dissatisfactions with the new order prominently included the fact that, as in Garant's sleepy little hole, there was no possibility for advancement—in a state that was rationing butter and other basic commodities in the 1980s. (By comparison, the rationing of food in Britain ended, never to return, in 1954.) Frustration notwithstanding, by virtue of class membership, they held certain attitudes toward professional life and the education needed for it, and these this did not change when Silesia became Polish: their children went to strongly academic high schools and learned excellent standard Polish.

Painfully. Later in our acquaintanceship Urszula Krysiak, with visible anger, shared the way the "longing for standard" worked itself out in her life, as she looked forward to raising children of her own, and how her attitudes had changed:

When I was in high school in Opole, the person sitting to my right said their opinion and the person sitting on my left said what was on their mind, and the Silesians only nodded. We said nothing in Silesian, nothing! And I decided that when I had children, I would speak to them only in Polish, so that they would never have to go through what I went through! But when the time came for them to go to pre-school, when they started to be with other children, they immediately began to speak Silesian! And even children from families from elsewhere [i.e., immigrant Poles] start speaking Silesian. The dialect is not dying! And that's a good thing. I think that Poles have become more tolerant of Silesians than they used to be in Communist times. I'm not afraid, anymore, to speak Silesian where I can be heard by Poles, and it used to be completely different. (Notes, March 19, 1995)[3]

This is an entirely different, and less studied, expression of solidarity. Here, she acknowledges that her fellow villagers essentially saved her from what she now sees as the folly of abandoning Silesian. And indeed, despite the fact that in her first interview, she presented her fellow villagers as her fellow Germans, she later told me that she herself feels that Silesia is the only place she truly identifies with.

So ultimately, Urszula, also, identifies as do most autochthonous Opole Silesians: as Silesian, perhaps with some degree of Germanness. Yet the division between her and her fellow Dobrans remains: both her expressions of solidarity were of the type where someone saves someone else, and that implies a kind of division. Whoever is in the role of savior, it is clear that Mrs. Krysiak stands on one side of a social division within autochthonous Silesian society. It is a division at once of ethnic and ethnic national identity, of language, of class, and of social practice. In terms of identity, it divides "Germans" from "Silesians." Linguistically, it is a division of competence, of practice, and of where loyalties are placed: within the cultural norms of speaking Silesian, or in the aspiration to speak good Standard. In terms of class, it divides the more rich from the not-so-rich. And in terms of social practice, the division is a function of whether or not one is grounded in the norms of belonging, of delayed reciprocal exchange of goods and labor, and of the cultural construction of house ownership, or in the "tradesman's morality" of buying and selling.

TOTALITARIAN STATES AND THE MORALITY OF ASPIRATION

So what's wrong with wanting upward mobility, with aspirations, with adopting a national language and a national identity, with identifying with the state? Well, in 1925, in the democratic Weimar Republic, nothing. But from 1933, when the Nazis came to power in Germany, to 1989, when the Polish Communist government fell, potentially quite a bit. In my discussion of identity ascriptions as a language of morality, and of silent approval vs. words of condemnation, it should be noted, I was not working with people who are active in the German Minority. I was working with people on the Silesian-identity/Silesian-language/not-so-rich/delayed-reciprocal-exchange side of the division. They use identity ascriptions when people violate their norms; the identity of people they get on well with remains unspoken. But there's another kind of silence reserved for people perceived as cozying up to the totalitarian states. And there's an absence of social practice that, in analysis, speaks loudly.

SINGING AND DANCING AS ACTS OF COLLABORATION

A totalitarian state is one that lays claim to the totality of its citizens' lives: to their identities, yes, but also, simply, to their activities. Participation comes at a price of collaboration. Even a party—a social gathering of people—is under the purview of the Party, in a state with no freedom of assembly. In the two totalitarian states, even singing and dancing took on a moral valence.

In the summer of 2007, eighteen years post-Communism, I discovered that Silesians had learned to dance.

Kasia got married. During the twelve-hour party that followed the wedding mass, I was amazed at the skill I saw on the dance floor. Everyone came with a dance partner, for many, a spouse or boyfriend or girlfriend, but for some, simply a member of the opposite sex with whom one intended to dance. The uniformity of the German popular music that had been the only kind in Marta's tavern, in the 1990s, was gone, replaced by a grand variety of European and American popular styles. With partners, people danced tango, cha-cha, waltz, rock-and-roll, and several other styles that I don't even know the names of. Magda and Roman's footwork burned holes in the floor. In groups, they did line and circle dances, some reminiscent of traditional Slavic dances. In the middle of one such circle, Henryk did break dancing, spinning on his shoulders, undulating from feet to hands, walking on them, bouncing back to his feet.

"People have been taking lessons," Marta told me, happily. It seems that once again, autochthonous Opole Silesians have been taking in customs from the outside and making them their own.

I used to think that autochthonous Opole Silesians were the most unmusical people I had ever encountered. They sang nowhere except in church, and at German Minority gatherings, where only those who had gone to German school sang the songs they had learned fifty years prior. They never sang in harmony, usually glided into initial notes rather than hitting them cleanly, and often sang flat. In church, their minimally skilled organist was no help; they did marginally better when she konked out completely, leaving them to their own devices. They did dance, sometimes, at parties, but never in a way that demonstrated much ability. In fact, they couldn't even keep time. In Ostrów, after the lectures and official pronouncements, there were a variety of entertainments, including a Polish folk dance troupe, dancing traditionally to highly rhythmic music. The audience, several hundred autochthonous Opole Silesians, seemed to enjoy it very much, and frequently clapped along with the music—always out of time. At the time, I saw it as just a cultural trait, I had no explanation for it, and I didn't think it much worth searching for one. Now, I see it as a form of passive resistance that had worked itself into the status of a trait passed on to new generations.

I was, however, curious enough to ask about it during the dissertation fieldwork period. Tactfully, and toward the end of my fieldwork (June 1995), I asked the Kowoliks why Silesians don't sing. In answer, I got silence. They gave me a look that I found difficult to interpret (stony? blank?) and Mr. Kowolik, Jr., suggested that I talk to Gertruda Jaskula. He looked up her address for me.

I knew who she was. She was the leader of the German Minority cabaret that my sociologist colleague, Danuta Berlińska, had seen and enjoyed—the cabaret that had made her think that Dobra might be a lively place for me to do fieldwork, the one that I had tried to talk to Marta about on that October afternoon when we met for the first time, when she told me she didn't know anything about any cabaret, that she's Silesian and stays away from that kind of thing. So, I went to Mrs. Jaskula's house (no telephones until 1996, remember) and invited her to come to mine. After our visit (June 21, 1995), I understood the look better, and had some new insight into Marta's vehemence.

Mrs. Jaskula, who was in her late sixties, told me that she had been singing all her life. First, she told, me, she had sung with the BUND DEUTSCHER MÄDEL, the "League of German Girls," and at the time of the invasion, even though (she emphasized) the BUND was not the Party (in fact it was the girls' branch of the Hitler Youth), she was arrested, taken to Opole and brought up before a tribunal of Soviet military authorities. So, she told them, "Well, if you want to start a Stalin Youth, I'll sing with that too." And they applauded her, and let her go. And later, after things settled down, there had been the KOŁO GOSPODYNI WIEJSKIEJ, the "Circle of Village Housewives," and she had sung with that. And then that had broken up (she said she didn't know why, when I asked—people just stopped going), and the German Friendship Circle had been organized, and now she sings with that. She just likes to sing. The KOŁO GOSPODYNI WIEJSKIEJ was created by the Polish Communist Party when they began to fear that the rural populace would simply retreat into their family lives, live at a very small-scale local level, without any public life at all—and that, then, the Roman Catholic Church would fill the gap. It was designed to be ideologically neutral; it was not part of the party. But people who belonged to it had privileged access to goods, a better chance of getting, for example, a new washing machine (Zdzisław Mach: personal communication). I was interested to see how the Kowoliks would remember that organization.

Mrs. Kowolik, who is about ten years younger than Gertruda Jaskula, and her daughter-in-law were not particularly eager to talk about it. They remembered quite a few things that the KGW had done: organized informational lectures, sold goslings and chicks more cheaply than one could get them privately, sponsored coffee and cake get-togethers, and organized various fieldtrips. Both of them had occasionally gone to these, but they weren't very involved, were not organizers, and had never gone on the excursions. Mrs. Kowolik remembered specifically that her parents had not allowed her to go. They always told her that there was too much work on the farm for her to go gallavanting off on some field trip.

And the organizers, I asked, did they get something from the Party for organizing all this?

They equivocated; they didn't know, probably not—though it was work for them, so they should have gotten something, surely—but, as the proverb says, "the ones closest to the trough get the most food" (July 3, 1995).

Mrs. Kowolik's parents are long deceased. Recall that in my first conversation with the Dobra school principal (and quite unelicited), I was told, "You will never hear about what happened here after the war. That generation has died without talking about it to their own children." That's the generation of Mrs. Kowolik's parents. If they had political reasons to keep their daughter at home, close to the trough of their own farm, far from the trough of the government, they did not tell her.

Hans Drabik, on the other hand, can speak for himself. He is Urszula Krysiak's father; he helped me with the history of the village center; he told me that he had both stayed out of the Communist party and kept his children out of the scouts, and he told me why:

They tried to get me to join more than once. But I wouldn't. I was in the Hitler Youth, I know how it was. It was a coercive organization. I stayed out of the Party, but that meant I couldn't advance. The factory directors, they were all Party members. And yet they sent all the apprentices to me, because I knew what I was doing and they didn't. I stated my opinion more than they liked, perhaps, but they needed my skills. There are people who went straight into the Party after the war. They forgot what it was like under Hitler; they forgot what happened here after the war. Straight in. And then, when the letters went around for people to sign declaring that they were Germans, they didn't sign them. . . . Now the ones who . . . are leading the German Minority are the former Communist Party members who didn't sign the letters. And it was the Party members who could visit Germany, and did, during Communist times, while I was not allowed to leave the country. (June 11, 1995)

Couldn't advance at work, couldn't sing or dance outside of it. As far as I know, there were no dance lessons being offered in Silesia in the 1990s. Before that, if there were, they were under the auspices of the state; everything was. Gertruda Jaskula had no moral compunction about affiliating herself with whatever party-sponsored singing group came along. It didn't bother her that two of them were organized by brutal dictatorships. But many of her fellow Dobrans talk with disapproval about "elastic people," or those who "sway with the wind." They talk about those who are willing to identify themselves with anything, whether it's just in order to sing or in order to gain advantage in other ways—the new washing machine, the exit visa, the promotion at work, or any of myriad other advantages that party membership conferred. In other words, as Bucholtz and Hall put it, identities may indeed shift and recombine to meet new circumstances. In certain circumstances, however, this "shifting" may be seen, not as "dynamic," but as betraying a lack of moral integrity.

Poles under Communism had a counterculture sheltered by the Roman Catholic Church, eventually giving rise to Solidarity. For Silesians, their counterculture was their own "very small-scale local level," autochthonous Opole Silesian society. Holding to it provided some insulation from the coercion of the state. In Communist times, their economy was based on a mix of household agriculture and wage work; they were "peasant-workers," and that was good:

Perhaps the best-placed class [in Communist Poland] are the so-called CHŁOPCY-ROBOTNICY, the "peasant-workers" who contrive to keep the family plot whilst holding down a job in a factory. Many such families living on the fringe of the great industrial regions, have the best of both worlds—a high cash income all the year round, a cheap supply of home-grown food, and an independent [i.e., privately owned] base. They are prosperous and relatively secure. (Davies 1984: 56)

As we saw in chapter 7, maintaining "good standing" in a Silesian community requires negotiating the problems of life in accordance with local cultural norms. Marta and Marcin both had to think through the complexities of various claims and counterclaims, and various possible interpretations of others who would evaluate their actions according to local cultural norms. For those who could do that, and do it well, the economic position of the community offered a "relatively secure" life, such as it was in Communist Poland. For example, one could eat the butter provided by the neighbor's cow, when butter in the stores was rationed. But one had to stay within the parameters of those norms; one could not depart from them; one could not "advance."

Recall that one of Garant's comments on Dobra was that it, unlike the other villages in which he had lived, offered opportunity for "advancement." In the Communist era, what this meant was that in smaller, more entirely agriculturally based villages, Communist Party membership remained essentially a nonissue, while in Dobra, it was an issue. As the chair of the Dobra village council explained to me:

> People who had no chance of advancement could afford to be principled about not joining the Party. Those slightly higher up had a decision to make. And those who were well-educated really were under pressure to join. But this by a long shot does not mean that they believed the stuff. There were people who believed; people who'd fought with the Underground during the war, for example, fanatics. And during the fifties and sixties, being a party member really carried with it having to toe the Party line. However, by the seventies and eighties, it didn't mean much. I didn't join; I was wise enough not to, but people joined for purely practical reasons. I don't really hold it against them. (September 8, 1995)

In Dobra, as opposed to a more isolated village like Grabina, where Mr. Kowolik Sr. grew up, there were many people who did stand in a position to advance. They could, then, refuse to join the Communist Party, and live a "relatively secure" life—although, as Magda once told me, during the crises of the 1980s, those well-connected to the West and Communist Party members were considerably better off (May 4, 1993). Those who did join the Party ultimately received some understanding about their choice from people like the chair of the Dobra village council, but a condemnatory attitude from others, like Marta.

Whether to identify, by participating, with the state that controlled all aspects of life beyond the very small scale level of families and their networks, was a moral issue.

It was totalitarianism that made identity a moral issue, that made assertions of identity into moral statements. Like the reticence about names discussed in chapter 3, identity as a language of morality is a cultural practice that has a history. And the most acute moment of this "making" was the close of the Second World War, when enemies were defined in ethnic-national terms.

Chapter 8

Remember the Schraft family. They did not flee Dobra as Soviet forces approached, and they were not expelled because, despite the fact that they belonged to the German-identified bourgeois class, their neighbors interceded for them, telling the relevant military authorities that they were certainly Poles (interview, June 12, 1993). It was not possible in 1945 for the farmers of Dobra to say, "Let them stay because they were good to us; they subverted the expropriations of the Nazi state." They had to say, in Silesian, "Let them stay. They are Poles, like us." Johann's father, for his part, was forced to choose between returning from the Soviet Union to his home in Dobra, or to an uncertain future in still-occupied Germany; to return to his home, he had to declare himself a Pole. He lied; he never considered himself Polish, and Johann is sensitive about his father's moral compromise. He insisted that I emphasize the coercion his father experienced, and protect the family's identity. An identity ascription—moral praise; an identity assertion—moral compromise: both the one and the other coerced by the state.

In Silesia, identity is a moral discourse intimately connected to the dilemmas of living in two totalitarian states. Nothing dramatized that for me more vividly than a tense encounter in the tavern. Readers may remember it as one of the incidents cited in chapter 2 as one of my examples of the culturally specific use of the word "here":

> I came into the tavern to find a stranger in his late forties sitting across from my housemate, disheveled and clearly drunk. A neighbor of ours came in, and the stranger began a conversation with the three of us which quickly became heated; he was set on determining "how German" Dobra was. At one point he asked who the head of the local German Minority was, and on being told the name, asked "Is he a German?" Our neighbor replied impatiently, "He was born in Germany and he stayed here." ["Germany" moved; "here" is ambiguously contrasted with it.] (March 26, 1993)

That something was amiss, on that late afternoon, was evident in several ways. I had come to the tavern so that Marta could go home and feed the calf. She did not go. Customers are rarely so forward as to sit at the same table with her, and there were plenty of empty tables in the tavern. Marta's legs and arms were crossed, and she did not look happy. The man made a couple of conversational remarks to Marta in rather indistinct German; he seemed to be having some trouble finding the words.

The neighbor who came in was Mr. Kowolik Sr.; he was with a friend. He commented in German that this person was "UNBEKANNT," unknown.

IDENTITY ASSERTIONS AS A LANGUAGE OF ASPIRATION

That was when the stranger, pursuing the conversation in Silesian and Polish, started asking questions about the Germanness of Dobra. He asked Marta and Mr. Kowolik what the German name of the village had been, and was told the name that most people remember: the name given to it by the Nazi regime when the names of all Slavic-sounding villages were changed. ("GUTDORF," one could imagine, since "Dobra" means "good.") He asked how many Germans there were in the village.

It is a taboo question. One inquires about the demographics, if at all, by saying: "How many people are there from around here, here?" Better not at all.

Mr. Kowolik replied, "Germans, everybody, but in German?" He shrugged. In this reply, he played on an ambiguity difficult to translate: "po niemiecku," "in German" refers either to a linguistic sense or the sense expressed in the phrase, "po pańsku," after the fashion of the state. Menus in city restaurants translate "po polsku" as "à la polonaise/nach Polnischer Art/Polish style." The stranger persisted, "But German blood, DEUTSCHES BLUT. How many people are there here from eastern Poland?"

Marta said, "Ten percent." By this time the emotional temperature was beginning to rise.

"Oh, that's nothing." (Many villages have become more mixed than this.)

"It's 10 percent."

"That's nothing!"

"There are not many of them living here, but they are here," Marta retorted.

That was when the stranger asked about the local branch of the German Minority and who was in charge of it. In response to his question, "Is he a German?" Marta dodged: "That I don't know. I can't say."

Mr. Kowolik interjected, "He was born in Germany and he stayed here!" And the stranger, at every possible moment, kept repeating, NIEMIECKI KREW, DEUTSCHES BLUT: German blood. Finally he finished his beer and left. Marta and Mr. Kowolik exploded. Marta said, "Where does he get off, playing the big German when he doesn't even speak German well? If my husband were still alive he would have given him what for! Last summer a man came in talking like that and he said, 'You asshole!' (I said, 'Honey! Watch your language,' but he said) 'You asshole. You don't even speak German well! How dare you?!' And the guy apologized."

Mr. Kowolik said, "He wants to be high? Shove a pitchfork up his ass and hoist him up! During the war there was a man whose name was Liś, and he decided his name was Linder, and when my mother said to him, 'DZIEN DOBRY, PANIE LIŚ,' [Good day, Mr. Liś] he said, 'ICH HEISSE LINDER, AND HIER WIRD DEUTSCH GESPROCHEN!' [My name is Linder, and German is spoken here!] But after the war these fanatics were the first with the red armbands!"

> MARTA: And there were people here in Dobra who hung signs in front of their doors that said "We speak Polish!" Weren't there?
> MR. KOWOLIK: The Minority, he wants to know? Full of Party people! I was born Silesian and I'll die Silesian! I'll have nothing to do with the likes of them!
> MARTA: I heard a few names like [she listed the surnames of several of the local German Minority leaders], and that was enough for me!

Mr. Kowolik picked up on one of the names, asking if that man had been a Communist Party member. Marta replied, "What do you think? He was the one who signed people's permission to go to Germany! And them first to Communion on Sunday!"

Mr. Kowolik's friend spoke for the first time: "How can such people even take Communion?" There is no more severe expression of moral disapproval in a Catholic society than to question a person's fitness to take Communion. Given that Polish Catholicism at the time had not implemented many Vatican II reforms, it implied that the person had made a flawed private confession.

The first time I was ever invited to the Kowolik home, the first time I met Mrs. Kowolik, she told me: "I will never forget—in the grocery store that used to be where Marta's tavern is now, there was a sign that said, 'WER ALS DEUTSCHE POLNISCH SPRICHT IST EIN VERRÄTER SEINES VOLKES' [A German who speaks Polish is a traitor to his race]" (January 23, 1993). The stranger had hit a nerve.

This was an encounter that evoked a strong identity assertion: "I was born Silesian, and Silesian I'll die." That statement articulated a position in a social conflict. One dimension of the conflict in the tavern touches the contrast between the ideal of national identity as learned ("civilization") vs. the ideal of it as racial. The stranger didn't speak German very well, but, in the ideology he was espousing, that matters and then again doesn't matter. What matters most fundamentally is "blood," and after that, people of "German blood" are seen as having a moral obligation to behave appropriately to their race, including linguistically, as expressed in the Nazi-era sign in the grocery store. The stranger, after all, did present himself in German, even though the conversation immediately evolved into a predominantly Silesian and Polish speaking one. And, after all (he might say), the German language was suppressed under Communism. People had no choice but to let their German get rusty, not to transmit it to the next generation. Many leaders and active members of the German Minority said this. But in the second ideology, if Germanness is something learned, something aspired to, something achieved, then speaking German well does matter, and anyone presenting himself as German should speak German well or put in the work to learn it. These are moral issues: a moral obligation, a moral excuse, a moral evaluation.

The second dimension of the conflict was voiced only after the man left. He was talking within the terms of Nazi ideology, which Marta and Mr. Kowolik objected to because they see it as fanaticism, and they see fanatics of one brand morphing easily into fanatics of the next brand, because what they are fundamentally after is the power to bully others. When Mr. Kowolik said that he was born Silesian and would die Silesian, he was condemning the behavior of the Mr. Liś's of the world. In Silesia, identity assertions summarize and articulate moral positions. The moral dimension of that conflict was made explicit by the connection to the citadel of morality of this community: the Roman Catholic Church.

Part of what it means to identify as Silesian is a matter of form of relationship with the state. It is a matter of a particular stance in relation to two totalitarianisms. It is a matter of being trapped between the Scylla of Nazi Germany and the Charybdis of Communist Poland.

Marta sees identifying as Silesian as the moral high ground. Earlier in the chapter, we explored the fact that, by virtue of family background, Marta not only does not belong to the formerly established German-identified bourgeoisie (who are almost entirely gone now), but also does not belong to the group of families which experienced Communism as the destruction of the group they aspired to join, who now constitute the backbone of the German Minority. That group might be unlikely to accept an entrepreneur who is of peasant-worker background and a woman to boot. But Marta has made no effort whatsoever to gain their acceptance.

This constitutes a moral position which she has sacrificed to maintain. The mutual lack of acceptance between Marta and the German Minority has had very practical and deleterious implications for her business. Faced with the task of renovating the run-down Schraft house, Marta confronted prohibitively high interest rates in Poland. German investment in businesses in Opole Silesia, while widespread, is channeled through the Silesian Development Foundation, which favors larger, better established enterprises; Mr. Krysiak's carpentry shop got a grant from this source, for example. More to the point, by the Foundation's rules, applications must be approved by the local German Friendship Circles (presumably to insure that the money is really going to "Germans in Poland"). When I accompanied Marta on a visit to its administrator in Opole, he stated explicitly that the money was for "our people" and asked outright whether Marta had applied for the German citizenship to which she is entitled as the progeny of citizens of the German Reich in its 1937 borders (July 2, 1995). She has not. She sees this kind of requirement, I believe, as a post Communist coercion by the powerful: identify with us, and we will help you advance. Same old story. She stays away from this kind of thing.

Marta's father was among those who did not join the Party. But some made that moral compromise. Many of those who chose not to join continued to resent those who did; Marta heard Communist Party members condemned in the privacy of her home throughout her childhood. Yet when, during the 1989 drive to organize the German Minority, it was those same Communist Party members who came by with a declaration stating the signators to consider themselves of German nationality, her father signed at once. He did not take the position, "Thank you, no: I was born Silesian, and I'll die Silesian. If being German means being German in the kind of sell-out terms your ilk represents, I'll pass on it, thank-you." Marta was appalled.

I don't know for sure, but it is quite possible that Mr. Kowolik also signed that declaration. His sister, who must have shared many of the early life experiences that ground Mr. Kowolik's Silesian identity, is the chair of the German Friendship Circle in Grabina. Perhaps later experience made a difference for her: Grabina is a smaller, more agriculturally based village, where the carrots of Party membership grew much less thick. Mr. Kowolik answered my astonished question, "Your *sister* is chair of the German Friendship Circle?!" by telling me that he hadn't known this; they didn't stay in close touch, and "she has always liked being involved in things" (April 29, 1993).

Why did Marta's father sign that declaration? We know that perhaps 92,000 signatures represented young people whose names were signed by their parents or grandparents. We know that a subgroup of the Dobra population—and in other, "sleepy little hole" villages it would be a smaller subset yet—considers itself German for sociological reasons of class that have developed over several generations. Mr. Drabik belongs to this group; so does his son-in-law Mr. Krysiak, who told me simply that his family had always considered itself German. So it's not difficult to see why that group signed the declaration of German identity.

But because that subgroup had been most state-identified in German times, because they were well off and wanted to remain that way, because they were invested in education and getting the kinds of positions that educated people get, they had been under the most pressure to join the Nazi party, and had been under most pressure to join the Communist party, and some of them

242

did. That put them in conflict with others of their own generation. That being the case, why was this signature campaign so successful? Why were people like Marta's father willing to put their differences aside, at that historical moment, to help present the community to the newly attentive outside world as, quite simply, German? What flipped this situation of conflict and division into one of vocal solidarity?

Nobody, I was told without asking, would ever talk to me about what happened in Silesia as the Second World War ended. The Kowoliks were silent when I asked why autochthonous Opole Silesians don't sing. Twelve years later, I came to see their lack of musicality not as a cultural quirk, but as active nonsinging, and nondancing. In other words, I encountered a pattern of silences. It was in the breaking of this pattern that I came to understand, specifically, the vehemence of identity.

Chapter 9
VEHEMENT IDENTITY AS A LANGUAGE OF SILENCE

The organized, vehement, vocal assertion of German identity of the immediate post-Communist era arose out of the silencing of the very experience that gave rise to it. In other words, for the generation that lived through the war as adolescents and young adults, it was the experience of the end of the war that forged their German identity, and expressing that identity is their indirect way of talking about that experience. Identity assertions, for them, are a language of silence: the language of their losses.

Four narratives of wartime trauma will help us understand this. Each of the four people whose stories we consider poured out the tales of trauma they had suffered as young people to me the very first time they met me, and three of them repeated those stories to me later in our acquaintanceship. One was the aunt of Marta's late husband, the one who wanted the cart in chapter 7. One was Mr. Kowolik, whom we have also met. Another was Renata Janta, who survived the carpet bombing of Dresden in February 1945. And the fourth was Anton Fischer, who had worked as an electrical apprentice in the IG Farben plant in Auschwitz—and who locally organized the signature campaign in Dobra.

The brief story of Marta's aunt will help to set the stage:

> And then came the front. The Russians and the Poles. And then you couldn't speak German! Informers crept under the windows! But now it's better. People speak whatever they want.
>
> When the front came a Russian officer came into our house. "DEUTSCH ODER POLNISCH?" [German or Polish?], he asked. My mother said nothing. Neither did my sister.
>
> "DEUTSCH ODER POLNISCH?" he asked again.
>
> Finally I said, "HALB UND HALB! ICH VERSTEHE DAS ODER DAS!" [Half and half! I understand both!]

VEHEMENT IDENTITY AS A LANGUAGE OF SILENCE

"GUT," said the officer. "ICH SPRECHE BESSER DEUTSCH." [Good. I speak German better.]

That there is a subtext of threat to this story is clear in the fact that without some sense of what the teller and her mother and sister had to fear from this question, "German or Polish?" it has no power as an anecdote. This story would have no dramatic tension to a listener who does not know that the German population of eastern Germany was being subjected to looting, expulsion, incarceration, violence, and rape, and that an answer of "Polish" constituted a claim to be considered, as one poster advised Soviet and Polish soldiers, as "comrades" rather than "enemies." It read, "Soldiers of the Soviet Red Army, remember: the inhabitants of this Polish land have German passports. You can distinguish them: Poles speak Polish, Germans don't! On the Oder Poles are your comrades! Germans, your enemies! Death to the German occupiers!" (Osmańczyk 1980: 46).

Marta's aunt became only a little more explicit about this:

> He wanted to lodge his troops with us. We said OK, for one person, but not for everyone. So the officer slept in a room to himself and the soldiers piled up in another room.
> When I got pawed I hit back, and went to the officer and said if it happened again I would throw them all out. He backed me up, called the soldier over and told him he'd shoot him on the spot if he did it again. But my sister went and hid in the hayloft whenever they were around. (December 19, 1992)

It's an extreme threat, to shoot someone on the spot. It makes sense in context: rape was perpetrated, on a massive scale, assuming its all-too-common role as a tool of vengeance in warfare. It would take an extreme threat from an officer to discourage it. But that that is the case remains implicit in this narrative.

At this point, it is time to consider more explicitly the way a story creates a silence, or, as Billig put it, the way that "in conversing, we also create silences" (1999: 261). The particular moment—December 1992—when this woman told me her story formed an unusual vantage point, because the silence—the repression—was about to change. Telling the stories of the Soviet invasion or not telling them had long been a highly sensitive issue in central Europe, and a politicized one. It had been a situation in which telling created glaring silences, inexcusable silences. Why? In the ethnic-national context of the Second World War and the Holocaust, people suffered *as*: they suffered as Jews, they suffered as Poles, they suffered as gays, they suffered as Germans— the vast majority suffered on account of an identity that they in no way chose.

Chapter 9

Some, of course, suffered as Socialists or resistance fighters or political prisoners, on account of an identity that they did choose, but that was not the situation of most. No single individual has a story to tell that illustrates the sufferings of members of all of these groups. Because of this, the tellings recapitulate the divisions.

The problem is acute in a unique way for the victims who belonged to the same group as the perpetrators. Take as a comparison the problem between Polish survivors and Jewish survivors: when the Poles tell their stories, they're not telling the stories of the Jews; when the Jews tell their stories, they're not telling the stories of the Poles. Yet German survivors, when they tell their stories, are in addition not telling the stories of the atrocities committed by other Germans. What about the Nazi occupation of Poland? Of western Europe? What about the Holocaust? Since people suffered as Germans while others committed atrocities also as Germans, how do German survivors tell their stories? In the first decades that followed the war, they quite simply didn't: at least, not in the media.

In the mid-1990s, German society grappled more openly with that problem. The Third Reich surrendered unconditionally on May 8, 1945. In its coverage of the fiftieth anniversary, broadcast by satellite to Silesia, the German media included interviews with women raped by Soviet soldiers. In Opole Silesia, two months prior to that, Radio Opole aired a special program in which three Silesians talked about their experiences of rape, the camp at Łambinowice, and discrimination after the war. And, also in 1995, the bilingual publication of *Ujrzałem Twarz Człowieka* (I Saw a Human Face) presented reminiscences, with historical contextualization and scholarly commentary, by Poles who were aided by Germans during the war and Germans who were aided by Poles after it. In this book, both Germans and Poles appear as victims, as persecutors, and as rescuers. The book not only provides balance, but suggests that the place for those who suffered as Germans and those who suffered as Poles to find common ground is in the fact that all, indeed, *suffered as . . .* something (Bach and Lesiuk 1995).

What is most interesting here is the way that suffering as Germans, in the instance, seems to have psychologically super-glued German identity for some Silesians. It is in this specific form of identity that we gain insight into the difference between the kind of "labile, nominalistic" identity that Berlińska described for autochthonous Opole Silesians of the early twentieth century and the vocal German identity of the 1990s. Here, too, is the heart of the difference between the form of national identity found by Brubaker et al. in Transylvania, where nationalist politics largely left the Romanian and Hungarian hearts of

246

ordinary people unmoved, and the heartfelt emotion of the German Minority in Opole Silesia. And, finally, it is here that we can raise the question about these historically constituted, politically inscribed, but not terribly forcefully felt identities: what happens to them when ethnic-national warfare breaks out, as it did in Yugoslavia?

Here, we compare the story of Mrs. Janta, who vehemently asserts her German identity, and Mr. Kowolik, who vehemently asserts his Silesian identity, examining what each of them brought from their childhoods into the experience of trauma, what each of them took from that experience into adulthood, and, ultimately, how we can account for the vehemence.

"What I Went Through as a German": Renata Janta's Story

I first met Renata Janta in August 1993, when I was planning my return in 1994 by looking for a house to rent. Mr. Krysiak brought me to the house owned by his older sister, who lives in Germany, and when we arrived, there was a social gathering in progress. She presented Mrs. Janta, a neighbor, as an added attraction for me of living there: born in Dobra, knowledgeable about the whole area, retired, and having time should I want to interview her. I got the more complete narrative two years later, on June 9, 1995. I had interviewed her, but linguistically: I had asked her to do my "registers from pictures" and "stories from pictures" exercises. The trauma narrative came on their heels, uninvited. This is what she told me.

Her mother fled with her, her two sisters, and her brother, as the front approached, and, before the Oder-Neisse line was established, they found themselves in Dresden. They were there in February 1945, when the city was carpet bombed. An aunt they'd been traveling with died in the bombing; they don't know where. She remembered vividly hiding in a cellar, and when the time came that they had to escape, that there was a bathtub full of water. Many people dipped their heavy winter coats in the water, because on the street, hail-sized balls of burning material were flying everywhere; the water was intended as a protection. However, it was February and cold, and the people who had soaked their coats were soaked themselves, to the skin. She was glad that she, with her two sisters and brother and mother, did not soak their coats. She held a blanket up as a shield as they ran, and the fireballs bounced off of them. The entire center of the city was reduced to a sort of maze of destroyed walls: a wall here, a wall there, filled to a height of more than a story with rubble.

After this their mother found a place for them in a village. They were hungry; it was hard to get food; she decided their chances were better at home.

Chapter 9

They returned to Görlitz, which was now a border town. Though her four children were monolingual speakers of German, she was bilingual: in Silesian she told the border guard that she was returning from forced labor in Germany, and they let her into Poland.

Traveling atop a load of grain in a cargo train, they reached Leignitz, soon to be Legnica. There they encountered a train of expellees from the area of Neisse, soon to be Nysa. They were filthy, hungry, traveling without sanitary facilities and with little food. She remembers young women whose skirts were entirely covered with menstrual blood; people stinking of excrement. Their mother was told that Neisse had been depopulated; it was empty. Neisse is not very far from Dobra, maybe 40 kilometers, and their mother seems to have been unaware of two crucial facts about it: it is west of the post–World War I plebiscite line, and no bilingual Silesian/German speakers lived there. She thought that if Neisse had been emptied, then she would find no one in Dobra either. The family returned to the village in Germany. She remembered seeing mountains of luggage that expellees had been forced to abandon on the Polish side of the Neisse.

Meanwhile, their father had been on the western front. He ended up in the British zone in a POW camp. He asked the British authorities whether he could return to his home in Poland, and he was told that if he spoke Polish, he could. However, when he tried to cross the border at Frankfurt an der Oder, he was turned back despite the fact that he spoke Polish. He was trying to find his family during all this time, and eventually a letter caught up with them. His wife sent word back, and they arranged to meet. On his way to meet them, he went to the Polish Consulate, and made arrangements for their admission to Poland. They arrived back about a year after they had fled, in spring 1946. By that time, Lower Silesia had been emptied of its its entire—and entirely German—population.

What we need to consider is not only the facts of violence but also its meaning. The meaning that Renata Janta attributes to this experience is that she suffered innocently for no reason other than that she is a German. She expressed this most powerfully in an argument with her seventeen-year-old daughter, Sylvia. Sylvia, in true adolescent get-a-life-Mom manner, was giving Mrs. Janta a hard time about her sense of ethnic-national identity. She, Sylvia, considered herself neither German nor Polish nor Silesian, but rather a citizen of the world. All these divisions are meaningless: Europe is uniting, borders becoming obsolete. Mrs. Janta exploded: "What do you expect from me?! How can I think of myself as anything but German, after what I went through because of who I am, and what I always have been, and what I was born to be?" (July 30, 1995).

VEHEMENT IDENTITY AS A LANGUAGE OF SILENCE

This is an expression of ethnic-national identity forged partly, as we shall see, in the kind of class-related social experience we have been discussing, but forged also, importantly, in the personal experience of trauma as an adolescent. It is noteworthy in its intensity.

"THERE ARE ALWAYS FANATICS": FRANZ KOWOLIK'S STORY

Mr. Kowolik is equally intense, but as we have seen, he is not intense about being German. The first time that I met him (November 30, 1992) he told me at length and in German about what he had experienced during the Soviet invasion: seven children, the family displaced, his mother incarcerated in a camp, his father disappeared, that if it had been known that he spoke German, he would have been beaten. "But," he concluded fiercely, "No one can ever take from me the German language that I learned in school!" A few months later, he elaborated. My notes for April 9, 1993 (near the anniversary of an important date for him) render a narrative that moves from what school was like under the Nazis, to what it was like to be in the Polish army, to the experience of being displaced after the war. The order is not chronological, but thematic.

> There was such discipline! After break the children lined up by class, girls in one line, boys in another, and that's how we went into the building, there was such discipline. One time I whistled in line, and the principal was on me in a minute: "You! Come to me after break!" But I didn't go. Soon an older student came in: "Kowolik, report to the principal." I went. "You! Why didn't you come?" "I forgot." "And why did you whistle?" "I don't know." "Here, give me your paw! Here's for forgetting and here's for whistling!" There was such discipline, I will never forget, and when somebody ratted: So-and-so was speaking Polish, then forget it. But when the war started, it all fell apart. Most of the teachers were drafted. And what the children get away with these days. . . . [he shook his head disapprovingly]

> When I was drafted, the other soldiers ridiculed my Polish, but I went to the officer and he backed me up and told me to come straight to him if I had any more problems. There are always fanatics. And my German was useful—the officers came to me when they needed to know something in German, and that just goes to show that the more languages you know, the better off you are.

> After the war we were displaced. Someone came to me and told me to escape into the woods. That was October 18, 1945 [about ten months after the front reached Silesia]. I said, "Why? I wasn't in the Party. I've never done anything to anybody!" That was October 18, 1945, and I got back on April 6, 1946. And on the

Chapter 9

18th my mother was transported [to an internment camp] to Oppeln, her and my youngest sister. She was three, and they set her out between Grabina and Raschau. After two weeks I found out that people had taken her in, and I went to get her. We stayed with our grandma.

There were two families of *chadziaje* living in our house—we couldn't go back. When we got back on the 6th of April the house had been cleared out. Later we found out that the house had also been looted by people from our own village. We had to start over from scratch, with seven children, with one cow. Not easy, not easy.

If we had the task of accounting for the difference between Mr. Kowolik's sense of himself as Silesian and Mrs. Janta's sense of herself as German on the basis of their trauma narratives alone, one difference would stand out: in Mrs. Janta's narrative the roles are all clear, whereas in Mr. Kowolik's narrative they are not. In Mrs. Janta's narrative the enemies are the military enemies of the Third Reich: the western Allies who destroyed Dresden, the Soviet Union which invaded from the east, and who ethnically cleansed Lower Silesia with the explicit, formal approval of the western Allies. These are the enemies, and the victims are Germans. She sees herself as one of these German victims. The ethnic-national divisions of the time, as categories, appear in the roles of the protagonists of the narrative: as persecutors and victims.

But who are the enemies in Mr. Kowolik's story? Who caused his suffering? Fanatical Nazi schoolteachers who beat children for speaking Silesian Polish, Polish soldiers who ridiculed his Silesian Polish because it was not Polish enough, the occupying authorities (Soviet and Polish), two displaced Polish families, and his family's own neighbors. The statement that sums it all up for Mrs. Janta is this: "This is what I went through as a German." But what kinds of statements does Mr. Kowolik bring forth? "No one can ever take from me the German language that I learned in school." "I was born Silesian and I'll die Silesian." "It just goes to show that the more languages you know, the better off you are." Kowalik has a sense of Silesian identity, prominently grounded in multilingualism.

Yet there is more to it than that. I believe that we can find in these kinds of traumatic experiences, and in the way people process and narrate them, an explanation of the *vehemence* of the discourse of identity in this central European context. We can understand that ethnic identity is, indeed, constructed (socially, historically, and also psychologically), and, in understanding that construction, also, perhaps, understand why ethnic-national identity can be so salient that people die and kill for it. It is not because people *are* whatever

250

they are, but because of what actually lies behind the statement, "I am [insert appropriate ethnonym]." The explanation for the differing conclusions of Mr. Kowolik and Mrs. Janta resides not only in what they got out of their experiences after the war, but what they took to them. And an examination of that, in turn, sheds light on how a particular form of postwar suffering, the suppression of the German language, became so powerful a force in constructing a common German identity in the generation that came of age in the late forties.

Furthermore, I believe that this point is particularly salient in understanding the German identity of Anton Fischer, the man who, in all of Dobra, was most given to reciting formulae of right-wing German ethnic-nationalist ideology—the man whose trauma narrative is so intense that I ultimately put it first in this book, for fear that otherwise, it might disrupt *my* narrative.

A LOSS OF LANGUAGE AND A LANGUAGE OF LOSS

There are indications that Mrs. Janta comes from a family highly identified, by mid-century, with the Dobra German bourgeoisie. She is not the only person in her narrative who identifies unquestioningly with Germans. Her mother does too. She fled with her children as soon as the front approached. When she learned that Neisse had been cleared of its inhabitants, she assumed that Dobra, too, would have been cleared. She and her husband had not transmitted any Silesian to any of their four children. And the family of her daughter, Renata, is closely associated with active members of the German Minority; I met Renata through Mr Krysiak. Her daughter, Sylvia, has grown up speaking only standard Polish at home.

All this contrasts with Mr. Kowolik. His family attempted to stay on their farm. When urged to flee, his response was, "Why? I wasn't in the Party. I've never done anything to anybody!" He was not expecting to become an object of revenge on account of his Germanness. He and his siblings spoke Silesian at home. His family are not socially close to the active members of the German Minority. His children and grandchildren have grown up speaking Silesian at home.

Trauma aside, these two individuals fit the sociological profiles of "German" vs. "Silesian" identity that I've outlined. They occupy two sides of what I've described, in this and the last two chapters, as a chasm within autochthonous Opole Silesian society. The interesting point is that Mr. Kowolik's sister also occupies the Silesian side of that divide. Yet she, like so many others of her generation, was more than ready to sign a declaration that she is German.

Chapter 9

Mr. Kowolik's sister is Julia Kunitsch. She described the process by which the German Minority leadership in Gogolin gave instructions as to how, specifically, people should canvass their villages for people willing to declare their German identity; we met her in chapter 4, in the context of considering the role that generation and household authority structure played in the organization of the German Minority. She had a more emotional story to relate, as well:

Once we had the names, we got in the car and took the letter to Gogolin.

And in the meantime, there'd been a whole lot of meetings. The police and fire department watched the cars, so that no one would vandalize them, because that was the very beginning. At these meetings there was always coffee and cake, which we liked, but someone always said,

Teraz sobie siedziemy, i schodzomy się i śpiewomy i gołdomy!

[Now we sit, and we meet and we sing and we talk!]

Ale potyn trza bandzie robić!

[But after necessary it will be to work!]

We didn't know the organizers personally then, but we knew that they were the ones who were helping us, so we trusted them. In one place, we met in a private hall that was across from an apartment complex, where mainly Polish families lived. We were especially quiet there, only talked inside, because they were afraid that the Poles would start something, break the windows or whatever. And then, slowly, we started to learn what rights we had, what the laws were, until we got to the point of the registration.

One time we went to St. Anne's Mountain. And we were outside, not in the cloister, and in front of us there were people with video cameras. We started to sing, and some cried with joy that we could sing in German.

And we didn't have long to wait before we went to Gogolin, to hand in the letters. And Mr. Kroll kept saying, quietly, quietly, we don't have long to wait, we're just waiting for guests. After a while, the guests arrived, the same ones that had been at St. Anne's Mountain, the ones with the video cameras and everything. And then they told us we should sit down, they brought us into this big hall, and we got started. We sang, we recited poems, and they recorded everything. That was something.

And then the councils were elected, first for groups of villages and then for individual villages. We got money from Gogolin, and we put on various cultural performances and events, and we started to get sponsorships. And then after two years I was elected. And there's a lot to do!"

There is further insight to be gained about how savvy the German Minority leadership were: they not only understood the authority structure of the

Silesian household, but they spoke to their people in Silesian, and they knew how to stage a media event. They were skilled cultural brokers, moving easily between the requirements of the village and those of the wider European scene. Yet all the organizing and cultural brokerage in the world would not have made a success of this signature campaign if people of that generation had not been ready to "cry with joy that we could sing in German."

There is something very particular about the generation that came of age at the time the Second World War ended. Those are the experiences that lie behind that readiness to cry with joy that they could, at last, and publicly, sing in German. They form a common bond within that generational cohort which—at least during the heady times after the fall of Communism—overrode the internal divisions of the autochthonous Opole Silesian community.

If we look in preexisting social conditions for a common bond of German identity between the leaders of the German Minority and the bulk of the heads of household who signed, it's not there. If we look for it in the specifics of trauma after the war, we have to conclude the same. Immediate postwar experience in Opole Silesia was, in part, a matter of luck; there wasn't the horribly uniform fate of the Lower Silesians. Mr. Kowolik's mother was incarcerated, his sister left to her toddler fate; that was Grabina. Another nearby village, inhabited by Hussites who had come from the Czech lands in Frederick II's time, was cleared, the people sent to Czechoslovakia. In Nowa Studnia, Diana Osa's grandmother had to flee and hide from the Russians for fear of rape; but she escaped. Nevertheless, one of her close kin witnessed a family massacred. In Dobra expulsion was carried out according to a list; families were targeted individually. Mrs. Janta's sister, Mrs. Kania, told me that a man known to have supported the Silesian Uprisings was greatly celebrated by the arriving Polish troops and had it in his hands to determine people's fate. The Schraft brothers told me that they had been saved by "more Polish" villagers who remembered with gratitude that their father had cooked the books when recording how much farmers gave up in Nazi expropriations. And those "more Polish" Dobrans themselves? Rape was experienced by many women, pillage by all; all were threatened with expulsion, but few, beyond the German bourgeois village center, were actually forcibly expelled. There are really only three things that everyone had in common: everyone suffered in some respect, everyone suffered because they were German citizens, and, most saliently, everyone lost the German language.

Consider the comments of Mrs. Kania: "If it hadn't been for Silesia's transfer to Poland, nobody would speak Silesian any more at all. Old grandmothers, they still spoke it. But we didn't. My father still knew it; he taught it to us after the war" (July 30, 1995). Maybe it is true that Silesian would have died out; it is especially possible that it is true of Dobra. In 1924, when Garant arrived, Dobra was farther along in the process of shifting from Silesian to German than were other, more isolated villages (like Grabina), and it is now farther along in the process of shifting from Silesian to Polish. The immediate linguistic effect of the Soviet invasion was that it interrupted this process of language shift. In extirpating the German language, it occasioned a shift *back*.

Not all monolingual speakers of German were so because their families had felt coerced by the Nazi regime. Some families may have revived Silesian gladly, but families who had chosen some decades before Nazism to abandon Silesian also revived it, feeling coerced by the Stalinist regime. The whole village was suddenly monolingually Silesian-speaking, for no one spoke standard Polish yet, and people remember being afraid to speak German. Monolingual adult German speakers whose parents had not transmitted it as they grew up in the early 1900s learned Silesian from friends and neighbors. Those more assimilated or advanced with respect to the process suddenly became the pupils of people they might previously have looked down on. So were they divided, pupils and teachers? Or united, having all lost one of their languages, even if, for many, German was not their only language?

There was certainly division. Even after decades, the linguistic divide between those who spoke Silesian before 1945 and those who didn't persists and is recognized. "You can always tell the people who learned only German as children," a man in his forties told me. "They don't make a distinction between 'sz' and 'ś.' It's all the same sound to them." The degree of palatalization of this affricate (spelled "sh" in English) is phonemic in Polish and Silesian, but not in German (or English). Those who did not learn to produce it in childhood have trouble with it. (I certainly have trouble with it.) Or, as Diana Osa told me, "My neighbor doesn't distinguish between 'oni,' and 'one.' She says 'oni' to everything." In Polish and Silesian, there are two genders of third person plural pronoun, 'oni' (virile, referring only to a group that includes a male human) and 'one' (nonvirile, referring to all other groups). German, like English, has only one word for "they"—as does this woman, socialized entirely in German. The radical, enforced change, then, did not erase the German/Silesian division even linguistically. Yet all these comments come from my third research trip; it took over a year for me to become a person to whom one would say such things. And only once did I hear the speech of such a monolingual German speaker, forced to learn Silesian after the war (although she managed to emigrate within about ten years after it), ridiculed. The dominant historical consciousness of the prohibition of German minimizes this division. It's not something you talk about. What people vocally remember is the shared loss.

VEHEMENT IDENTITY AS A LANGUAGE OF SILENCE

The prohibition of German had a profound impact on people regardless of their position vis-á-vis the ongoing language shift. Athough not deprived of their only language, Silesian-German bilinguals found that Poles considered their Silesian Polish inferior. It was only after the war that people started to refer to their local speech as "Silesian," rather than as "Polish," for only after the war were people forcefully made to understand that what they were speaking was not, after all, Polish, or as good as Polish. Mrs. Kania told me that even the daughter of Dobra's most famous Upriser experienced this denigration of Silesian: she went to a government office to take care of some bureaucratic matter and was asked to write something. She told them that she couldn't write Polish. They told her that after all the time she'd been in Poland, she should be able to write Polish. She said, "You should be glad we kept the Polish language alive through all this time" (June 2, 1995). It must have been a disappointment. Ironically, for autochthonous Opole Silesians who favored Silesian Polish, the coming of Poland was the loss of Polish.

For some, then, the loss of German was the simultaneous loss of Polish, as the linguistic political situation shifted. Others, German monolinguals, had no Polish to lose. Everyone in the community lost German, but beyond the spoken language, there was another loss that everyone shared. Even sounds that German and Polish share are spelled very differently in the two languages. Because the German and Polish orthographies are so different, autochthonous Opole Silesians could not write Polish. And that meant that the loss of German was the loss of literacy. Further because Silesian lacks technical vocabulary and Silesians had fulfilled that need using German technical terms, they all found themselves unable to discuss matters as simple as bicycle repair beyond their own community: they did not have Silesian Polish terms to use and did not know the standard Polish terms. The loss of German was the loss of technical and vocational competence. And because their background knowledge of history and literary tradition was a German one, the loss of German was the loss of intellectual and artistic culture.

It was also the loss of music. By 1945, there was no longer much Silesian Polish folk music being actively transmitted in Opole Silesia. People sang in clubs (which had, of course, been brought into Nazi organizational structures), in schools (of which the same is true), and in church. After the war, all German lyrics were outlawed. Propagandistic Nazi doggerel was outlawed along with Schubert. Critically, for the connection between music and what autochthonous Opole Silesians would call "heart," the Polish Roman Catholic Church also introduced an entirely Polish musical liturgy.

I believe that it is this common experience of suffering that has lent itself to articulation as German identity. "I was born in Germany. I learned German.

The language here was German." So many people of Marta's father's generation expressed it that way that it seemed a kind of mantra of identity. People of that generation emphasize what they lost. The brilliant organization of the leaders of the German Minority can only have helped, but again, their organization would have had nothing to mobilize if people like Marta's father had not been willing to put their differences aside in order to proclaim themselves Germans.

Language itself is the language by which everyone who experienced the trauma of the invasion is able to articulate a sense of shared victimhood. Innocent victimhood, too, is a stance of humans as moral beings. This is especially true in a Roman Catholic environment where the moral imperative to follow Christ regardless of the suffering this may entail is extended to the glorification of innocent suffering in its own right. And here, as elsewhere in Europe, language is a primary emblem of identity. It is the suppression of German that the generation that experienced the loss as adolescents found to give voice to "What we went through as Germans."

So literally, they all lost the German language. They were also left with traumatic experiences. These are difficult to talk about; they are difficult to listen to. In a situation where everyone had suffered violence, who would want to listen? People were unable to speak of their trauma directly. Instead, the loss of the German language became the metanym and emblem of all the losses. And because language is a primary symbol of identity in Europe, losing German meant being German. When it became politically possible, they gave voice to their generation's experience by in solidarity declaring themselves and their families to be German. The loss of language became the language of loss, and what that language said was, "We are Germans."

It was a very simple expression of very complex experiences.

COGNITIVE DISSONANCE, REPRESSION, AND IDENTITY

What we have so far is an explanation of identity assertions grounded in discourse, and drawing on the idea that conversation necessarily entails silences. But there is more to Billig's reformulation of Freud's repression concept than that. And in his discussion of repression as a key concept of depth psychology, we find an explanation for identity as, precisely, "enduring psychological states" (the characterization that Bucholtz and Hall reject): as lasting, deeply felt, and vehement.

Add to this the proposition of Erik Erikson that the specific psychosocial task of adolescence is the formation of ego identity. What would it be like to undertake that task in the face of conditions as violent and oppressive as those in the immediate aftermath of the Second World War and ongoing conditions in the newly transferred territories?

It is in the stories of Renata Janta and, especially, Anton Fischer that the theory of cognitive dissonance meets Billig's reformulation of repression. It is here that Anton Fischer's experience as an adolescent at IG Farben, Auschwitz branch, meets his handing me a business card of the gothic-print "government in exile" of the "East German territories of the German Reich" forty-nine years, eleven months and one week after that experience ended.

Recall from Chapter 1, that Mook related the experimental results of research into cognitive dissonance theory to the situation of an individual caught in the position of perpetrator in a totalitarian situation. Once a person has hurt another, a dissonance emerges between the act of violence and a self-image as "a kind and humane person." At that point, the perpetrator can either revise his or her self-image, which is painful, repent and refuse to do further harm, which, in a totalitarian situation, is heroically dangerous, or "buy in" and accept the proposition that the victim deserved the treatment: "I hurt this person, but he deserved it! In which case my hurting him was not such a bad thing after all. Maybe I ought to hurt him some more!" (Mook 2004: 237). That's the position of the perpetrator, of what I would call the "innocent perpetrator," since the acts of harm, especially the first one, are coerced.

That's not quite the way that vehement national identity took root in Renata Janta, though. For her, it's more closely the kind of cognitive dissonance described specifically with regard to initiation. The experimental research involved subjects being "offered" membership in a group—a discussion group, as it happened—varying the severity of the "initiation," or what they were told was required in order to join the group, and then gauging the subjects' attitudes toward the group. "The results clearly verified the hypothesis. Subjects who underwent a severe initiation perceived the group as being significantly more attractive than did those who underwent a mild initiation or no initiation" (Aronson and Mills 1959: 180).

Now, nobody exactly "offered" Renata Janta membership in the German VOLK. Autochthonous Opole Silesians were told that they had it and that they had better not do anything to make the authorities think otherwise. Previous German regimes, however, had in a sense made an offer: upward socioeconomic mobility, and, accompanying that, national identity. Renata Janta was the daughter of parents who had chosen to take that offer. And here's where we have to return to Erikson as well as to the anthropological origins of what we know about initiation, that is, to van Gennep's *Rites of Passage*. Initiation, cross-culturally, makes an adolescent into an adult. Psychologically, it does not matter whether that experience is ritualized and intended to serve that function. If Erikson is right, intense experience in adolescence will serve to form ego identity. The carpet bombing of Dresden was a severe initiation for Renata Janta. How can you expect, as Renata asked her daughter, someone who has gone through that atrocity in the process of becoming an adult, to distance herself psychologically from German identity? The group she was joining was the group of adult Germans. She had no choice about it. We all join the group of the adults of the societies that raise us. Her daughter's comparatively mild initiation allows her to see beyond her local society, to see herself as "a citizen of the world," but for Mrs. Janta, even to acknowledge that "Europe is uniting, borders becoming obsolete," is psychologically impossible for her, let alone distancing herself from German identity itself. The dissonance would be too painful. Whatever is negative about German identity has to be repressed.

Yet Renata Janta, in my experience, did not insert right-wing quasi-Nazi nationalist polemics into every conversation. For that, we have to look at the very mechanism of repression itself, in Billig's terms. We have to look not so much at Mr. Fischer's story itself, but at the way he told it.

ANTON FISCHER'S STORY REVISITED

I want to focus attention on the way that Anton Fischer's interviews were a bizarre mix of memory, denial, justification, insight, and, most centrally for our purposes, repression. The first instance of this emerges when he remembers his curious adolescent self asking about the colored triangles on the prison garb of the prisoners in the electrical workshop: "I asked about it, and the guy said, 'Yeah, that's because we're political prisoners, you see?' They had to be distinguished, the different kinds—the political prisoners were in a separate camp. Or criminals, or deserters, or black marketeers. Well, I had no idea about the camp, I just worked there." Here we have a hint of justification in "they had to be distinguished," followed almost immediately by denial: "I had no idea." This is a denial that echoed through Germany and beyond for decades: we didn't know.

How true might that have been? It is a key question because Anton's position is much easier if it is true than if it is not true, or only partially true. If Anton was "innocent," not only in the sense of not being at moral fault, but also in the sense of knowing nothing about what was going on around him, his trauma springs from later revelation, after the war, when he went to the Auschwitz museum with his brother-in-law, as he told me he had done in response to my gentle question the first time I met him, at the Christmas party, when indeed it was closely followed by the "we didn't know" formulation. As either he or his sister was already married at that point, I assume that Mr. Fischer was already an adult at the time of the visit. Because I argue that Anton Fischer's German identity hinges on one moment, the moment when he found himself looking into a drawer filled with weapons, it matters what knowledge he brought to that moment. This is the moment about which he asked me, "What would you have done, as a German?"

We will look at what he may have seen, the complex role of the camp orchestra, the food situation, and finally, at what he said about the air. It is his reply to my direct question as to whether he could smell the burning bodies of Holocaust victims that most clearly reveal how nationalist polemic, for Anton Fischer, accomplishes repression.

What Anton Fischer May Have Seen

Recall that Anton Fischer drew me a sketch map of Auschwitz that included a shortcut into town that he used to take. He said that the shortcut passed by fields where he saw women working, guarded by women. He told me—that is, he knew—that these women lived in a separate camp.

In an effort to understand what Anton saw as he took that shortcut, as well as what knowledge he could and could not have had as an apprentice, I peered at many published photographs of Auschwitz, trying to see in their blurred black-and-white images what Anton Fischer saw in three-dimensional color memory. Crowded lines of exhausted prisoners waiting for death? Did he see that? No: those are SS photos, taken where no civilian was allowed to go. Living skeletons, mountains of corpses? Did he see that? No: those are the images of the camp's liberation. IG Farben itself looks like any grim industrial complex of the time. A photo taken inside one of the workshops shows men working, and, as Mr. Fischer asserted, they do not look like they're starving to death. But the photographic image of women working, guarded by women, could only have looked worse in real life. Two of the "separate camps" at Birkenau were women's camps, and it is Birkenau that gave us our most horrific images: selection, crematorium, death camp. This photograph shows hard, forced labor. So it is probable that Anton Fischer did see that, on his way to and from town and the railway station that took him home for the weekends.

But when he told me about it, there was no emotion in his voice, no break with the assertion he made at the Christmas party as part of his self-presentation as having known nothing: "We saw what was to the right and to the left."

What was to the right or to the left of the shortcut, however, must have shown him something of the reality he would later deny knowing anything about.

THE COMPLEX ROLE OF THE CAMP ORCHESTRA

Historically, the role of the camp orchestra was complex enough, before we even consider how it functions in a conversation that spans decades and stretches from Anton Fischer's Jewish electrical mentors to me in the 1990s. As described by Guido Fackler (2007), camp orchestras had cultural antecedents in the German military, they existed in many concentration camps as early as 1933, and their purposes in the camps were many. An early use was frankly propagandistic:

> Among the main tasks of the ensemble was to perform concerts in the camp square for fellow prisoners, although guards were also part of the audience. However, while the apparent or ostensible purpose of these concerts was to entertain and edify the prisoners, they were, in fact, designed for a different purpose. When a delegation from the International Red Cross visited the camp in October 1935, the commander used the ensemble for propaganda: musical performances were used to make things seem better than they were; and the outside world was deceived as to the real purpose of the camps.

Beyond this, the motives for camp administrators setting up orchestras included their use in regulating the daily life of the camp (including accompanying the daily march to and from forced labor), prestige among camp commanders, a role in a privilege system among prisoners, and gruesomely, to provide background music to punitive torture and executions. "An ambitious camp commander with cultural pretensions might also use the orchestras to advertise the 'orderly' conditions within 'his' camp when it was being inspected, or when visitors were shown around. The ensembles also gave concerts for the entertainment of the SS, or with their permission for the inmates, generally in connection with the 'privileges' already mentioned" (Fackler 2007). They occasionally lulled "newly-arriving prisoners into thinking that they did not face immediate death" (Fackler 2007). They entertained the guards. And as for the SS, Helena Dunicz-Niwinska reported of her experience in Birkenau: "Works by Grieg, Schumann and Mozart [were played] for the connoisseurs among the ranks of the SS who came to 'relax' after the process known as selection" (Fackler 2007).

According to Anton Fischer's narrative, none of this, not even the daily accompaniment of the prisoners' march to and from forced labor, was something he saw for himself. When he told me about the orchestra—the moment when it dawned on me that he was telling the truth—he was smiling and his tone was celebratory: ". . . and when they went out in the mornings to work, there was an orchestra playing! And they were greeted with music when they came back in the evenings!" It was as if he were in some way responsible for the camp and I were the International Red Cross in 1935. In a Bahktinian sense, he was voicing the propaganda of the time.

But in the extended interview, he told me that Jop Jupiter, his teacher, had told him about the orchestra. Recall that as he guided me along his sketch map, he pointed to the iron gate inscribed with "Arbeit Macht Frei," and behind it, he pointed out a camp in which there were, "How many was it? What did Jop Jupiter tell me? I've looked for him, we wanted to find each other after the war, for certain reasons, because we became real friends. . . . Oh, yes! Ten thousand! There were ten thousand Jews in that camp. And they told me that they had an orchestra, which played in the mornings when they went out to work, and in the evenings when they came back."

In the first conversation, the mention of the orchestra had another function besides the propagandistic one. It was insider knowledge. It was part of Mr. Fischer's claim to have been there, that "he knew what things had been like there." It changed the course of our conversations because it worked on me: in that pre-internet age, it was a detail that could not have been common knowledge in Silesia. Although I immediately, and once again, rejected the propagandistic aspect, this detail made me consider the possibility that Anton Fischer had in truth been there. But this second telling brought in other inter-locutors, Jop Jupiter and Prinz Eugene. I followed up, rather amazed, "They told you that?"

The firm reply, "Yes. Prinz Eugene and Jop Jupiter used to tell me things." The questions that this raises, it seems to me, are these: Why would they tell him anything? Why would they tell him that? And what does their having done so have to do with Anton Fischer's handing me the Gothic, recidivist business card fifty years later?

Why would they tell him anything? It seems that these two inmates of Auschwitz developed a relationship with the young Anton Fischer beyond the bare essential communication of how to fix wiring—a relationship of human beings, of teachers and student. They told him things because human relation-ships entail telling. Why would they tell him that? Here I think of what Marta told her five-year-old nephew when he spoke loudly in Polish outside the house in Germany: "You are in Germany and here you speak German, and if you can't, then speak quietly." What do you say to a child? Do you say, "Don't let yourself be heard speaking Polish because we could all be attacked by neo-

Nazi skinheads"? It is a matter of masking. What good could have come of telling Anton the unvarnished truth? They handed him this piece of Nazi propaganda because it was something that they could hand him in relative safety—for themselves, and for him.

What does it have to do with Mr. Fischer and his business card? Remember that according to a discursive psychological approach to repression, speech accomplishes repression. Recall that in the theory of cognitive dissonance, it's what we tell ourselves about our experiences that reduces cognitive dissonance to a manageable level of discomfort. Anton Fischer faced that moment, "What would you have done, as a German?" from a context of relationship with teachers who were Jews. There was something about that which required a lot of talking about how great Nazi Germany was.

THE FOOD SITUATION

He knew. He did know. It was the food that brought him around, shall we say, to accessing that knowledge. He started with justification, but he turned in mid-sentence:

> As for food, he said, "We didn't have it any better than the Jews, we were living in a camp just like they were, and we got cabbage soup, different things, we did not get great food, right? We got camp food!"
>
> "So," I said, "You're fourteen years old, you've never been away from home, you're used to your mother's cooking, and here you are eating this camp food. What was that like for you?"
>
> He replied, "I used to take care of myself a little with stuff from home. When I came home, I ate a good dinner, and my mother would pack some food for me, some bacon, onions, garlic, because the, the [he stammered] because that's what the Jews wanted! I would ask them what I should bring them from home, and they always said, 'Onions and garlic!' And so I had some extra food, and then, and, I'll tell you, I'm going to tell you what happened that made us friends!"

Later in the interview, I followed up: "When you found these weapons, was that the first time it occurred to you that the Jews might want to stage an uprising?"

He said immediately, "No. They wanted to defend themselves. But in the camp where they were, they couldn't have [the weapons], no? But in the workshop, nobody was paying close attention to what they had in their drawers."
I said, "What did you think, why did they want to stage an uprising?"

"I knew, I was still maybe, I just knew that there was something not real about the whole thing." He laughed uneasily, saying this. "I knew that if I reported it, it would have been curtains for them." He drew his finger across his neck.

VEHEMENT IDENTITY AS A LANGUAGE OF SILENCE

So why all the justification and denial mixed up in the memory? Mr. Fischer had an amazing story to tell. It's a story in which he is a hero. He's not a Klebold or a Harris. It could have been a source of pride.

But the problem, the problem that forces the repression, is that he's a German. He was a German even by the sociological terms I outlined in chapter 8; the evidence of his network in Dobra, his parents' expectations that he have a career beyond farm work, and the pattern of postmarital residence in his family, as well as his assertion that he spoke only German until 1945 and that his parents seldom spoke Silesian, all point to an established German identity in his family. All that is over and beyond his having been taught his identity in school in the Nazi era. He faced that moment as a German.

THE AIR, AND THE SPEECH THAT ACCOMPLISHES REPRESSION

Consider the way he handled the following question, a few seconds after the exchange above:

EV: How was the air? I've heard that it stank. [i.e., of burning bodies]
MF: No, not at all. There were, well, in Auschwitz two big smokestacks, right? But not in the factory. Emissions, gases, smoke, that all went through a smokestack 30 meters high, or higher. . . . It was a chemical factory, normal, right, that there was a crematorium that there was another camp I didn't know it, I had nothing, we had simply train station, go home, to work, only at the train station there were patrols, you had to show papers, well, the whole world was like that then, today too, whoever was a Communist was God, and now they're telling us what really happened, the Communists . . . in Germany . . . in Katyn . . . there was also, there, the war was started by Hitler *and* Stalin, only Hitler invaded fourteen days earlier, and Stalin from the other side, but that's not what history says, they said only Hitler started it.

There are so many ellipses because he was muttering; what he said is partially inaudible on the tape. Nor was he maintaining eye contact with me at that point. He seemed to be going over oft-repeated lines of thought out loud. He was no longer talking to me; he was talking to himself. What he was saying—another defense of the Fatherland—was serving to stop his thinking about the reality of Auschwitz, about the stench of burning bodies. He was repressing. And the emotional force of what he was repressing was the guilt of his identification with Germany.

Unlike with Renata Janta, it was impossible for me to have a conversation with Anton Fischer in which he did not volunteer one or several justifications of Nazi Germany. If the cognitive dissonance of "what I went through as a German" made it impossible for Renata Janta to identify in any other way than as a German, for Anton Fischer the work of reducing cognitive dissonance—of repression—seems never to have ended. It's true that I was a sympathetic outsider; I was a researcher and a writer. I was born nineteen years after he started his apprenticeship. I may well have been the Eyes of History in Anton Fischer's eyes. But he was the only one who related to me in this manner from the beginning of my research to the end. If he chose me to occupy that role, it is because I filled his need to have someone in it. Just as the others needed to be listened to, in a context in which young people did not want to listen. But specifically what Anton Fischer needed me to listen to went beyond the trauma narrative. He needed me to listen to him repress the trauma narrative.

VEHEMENCE AS A RESULT OF TRAUMA

When people are traumatized because they are members of ethnic-national groups, their identification with that group is strengthened. Commentators have been right to consider the ethnic nationalism of Europe as irrational, but it is a mistake to assume it is inherited, "primordial," or "tribal." It is grounded in personal experience. Anton Fischer may identify as German because of his family background, but he identifies as German in this particular, intense way, because of his experiences. He is rigidly and vehemently German because he experienced the most important moral dilemma of his life, and the deepest traumas, as a German. He constantly defends Nazi Germany because the cognitive dissonance he was left with is so severe that it takes constant narrative work to contain it.

I would emphasize again, in closing, that the phenomena I've described are not specific to people's experience as Germans. When I attended the pilgrimage of Poles who had survived the Soviet deportations to Siberia, I found them just as intense, just as rigid, as the Germans I was used to talking to. In the sermon that gave me the figure of speech quoted in chapter 8, the deportations were interpreted as "our fate as Poles." But, the priest continued, we shouldn't be unhappy about that fate because it brings us nearer to the Way of the Cross. Later, a Polish choir from Grodno, Belarus (formerly Poland), sang in the hall of Pope John Paul II. They sang and recited in Polish with strong Russian accents and brought the house to tears with a poem that ended: "Beloved homeland, return to Poland! Let it be as it once was!" Following that, several priests spoke. One talked of meeting a young Pole in the former Polish territories, and how beautifully she spoke Polish. More than one priest emphasized the choir's work in preserving the Polish language. The chaplain in his speech worked up to pointing at the enormous picture of John Paul II, arms outstretched, which forms the backdrop to the stage: "Look how he embraces you . . . and he is a Pole! Flesh of your flesh, blood of your blood, bone of your bone." There was much emotion among the audience.

Extreme trauma in adolescence, cast in ethnic-nationalist terms, creates the initiation effect noted by cognitive dissonance theorists. It does not make for great flexibility of thinking later in life. When we look at people who seem rigidly and irrationally assertive of identity, asserting it vehemently, or even violently, we need to look deeper at what this discourse is *not* saying. What experiences have given, or are giving, rise to this vehemence? How is this identity, in whichever situation, a language of silence?

Conclusion

In the introduction, I encouraged readers to look at this book as at a computer map, operating at two levels, one comparatively "zoomed out"—that would be the level of "anthropology among the social sciences"—and the other comparatively "zoomed in"—"this book within anthropology." I offered a guiding question for each level; for the first, a question about the worth of the culture concept, and for the second, a question about ethnic and national identity. In the final analysis, it's important to emphasize that the two levels really are only different views of the same map.

That is true because the question of vehement identity is only a specifically anthropological question insofar as anthropology is what the word claims to be: the study of humans. And in that sense anthropology encompasses (encompass-es) all the humanistic social sciences anyway. So the question of vehement identity points outward from Dobra and cultural/linguistic anthropology at psychology and history at the least, and is, thus, just as much a question about anthropology among the social sciences. The quest for a revitalized, neo-Boasian culture concept, for its part, rather than bounding the view to what's under the magnifying glass, places Dobra on a conceptual grid defined by the intersections of conscious lives with lived events, and is thus likewise a question about anthropology among the social sciences.

I offer two last observations in conclusion. One is a sketch of comparability. The other is a postcard from an anthropology in the midst of its own dynamic cultural change. I wouldn't divide them according to levels of map scale, but rather according to a slight shift in primary audience. Professionals, the sketch of comparability is your invitation. You may or may not find my sketch compelling in light of other research, and I invite you to respond as you see fit. As for the postcard, that is for you readers for whom this book is among your first encounters with ethnography. You don't reply to a postcard, of course. Postcards are for looking at and talking about. I wish you the best of conversations.

A SKETCH OF COMPARABILITY: TONE BRINGA'S *WE ARE ALL NEIGHBOURS*

We Are All Neighbours is an ethnographic film by anthropologist Tone Bringa, who conducted fieldwork in a village in Bosnia of mixed Catholic and Muslim population prior to, then during, the violent ethnic-national war that broke up the former Yugoslavia. The film was aired as part of the "Disappearing Worlds" series by Granada Television, filmed and aired in 1993. It was actually finished before the front lines reached the village; for us, it is the short addendum covering the return trip, after almost all the Muslims had fled the village, and their houses "shelled, burnt, or vandalized," that most speaks to comparison with this book.

The first part of the film sets out a view of identity in the village where the differences are similar to those found by Brubaker et al. in Cluj, Romania: people are aware of them, but they are not terribly salient in everyday life. In Janina Fenigsen's words, "they were aware of identity differences among them, yet were tolerant and often genuinely friendly toward each other. They were confident that they would never get drawn into the conflict as people in other places did. It took a particular set of circumstances and outside political militancy that selectively privileged some and penalized others to invest these identities with the kind of vehement antagonism that led to destruction and bloodshed" (Fenigsen: personal communication).

What changed, in the trauma of war? As the fighting came closer, Bringa reports, people felt pressure to declare whether they were Muslim or Croat. "To be a Catholic increasingly means describing yourself as a Croat. The church is becoming a focus for that Croatian identity." More than anyone else, it is a Bosnian woman named Nusreta whose point of view guides the film: her point of view and that of her family. She, too, began to feel the importance of expressing her sense of herself as a Bosnian Muslim. By that point, she felt it would be difficult for her to visit her Catholic friend Slavka: "Listen, we had expected it from the Chetniks. But not from our Croat neighbors! And this is why I feel offended." (If her form of expression is cognate to the Polish, the translator aimed too low. "This is what hurts me," might be better.)

It is interesting to note that at this point, Bringa is able to cross the divide in a way that seems to become impossible for her, the anthropologist, after the war engulfed the village. She joins Slavka and her family for coffee and asks her the same question. After describing the strain in her relations with Muslim neighbors, she says, "Suddenly people can change their face! With me, the change happened in a day. I can't describe it." It is not entirely clear what it is that has changed, but it seems to have to do with identity.

Bringa and the film crew leave Nusreta and her husband waiting, expecting the worst. One assumes that not only have they finished the work, but the area has become too dangerous for outsider civilians. There are places in the world where anthropologists cannot go or stay. Bringa picks up the story eight weeks later. A change that happened in a day, it turns out, is the attack of the Croat army on the village. Nusreta and her husband have fled; they are "at their daughter's house, over the mountains." Access to the village is now tightly controlled by the Croat army. Bringa and the camera crew are able to go in only with the protection of an armed UN escort.

267

CONCLUSION

What is striking at this point is an extreme contrast in Bringa's encounters with Nusreta and her family as opposed to with Slavka. For the Muslims, this is fresh trauma; there is nothing repressed or silenced about it. Lives have been on the line. Tragedies have occurred. Description risks trivializing the emotions involved: they are intense (minute 48:30).

Bringa herself seems to have been deeply affected. What she found in the village was that "The Catholic houses were intact. But almost every Muslim house had been shelled, burnt, or vandalized." She talks to Slavka over her fence this time; the footage starts with Slavka's shrug in response to the question "Why?" Bringa follows up with "What have you done to them?" Slavka replies, "We didn't do it." When Bringa points out that no Catholic houses were damaged, Slavka agrees, factually. When Bringa asks "What happened?" she gives an account of the events of the attack. Neither she nor Bringa express any emotion directly.

Back among refugees, Bringa listens to the grief of an old woman's betrayal by a Catholic friend of forty years who failed to so much as warn her that combatants were approaching. Another refugee reports that of her two brothers killed, one was killed by his next-door neighbor. About the possibility of future coexistence, Nusreta's husband says he doesn't have the will for it, "I saw what they did. They wanted to destroy us completely. . . . From the moment we fled to save our lives, we no longer wanted to live with them." Nusreta, asked if she could live with them, added, "Now? Impossible. We can't live with them anymore. How can I live with them when they destroyed all I have? How can my nephew? They shot his wife and burnt his home. How can that woman, left a widow with three children? Her neighbor told her, I killed your husband! There can be no more living together."

The film closes with brief film snapshots of daily life—baking, chickens, a hug—in houses of Muslims, followed by images of the same settings, destroyed.

Of all persons in the film, only Slavka maintains a distinction between civilians and combatants. For the Muslims, the expression of the trauma aligns precisely with the inability to maintain that distinction. It's about the friend who didn't warn, the neighbors who killed neighbors. It's them and us.

Vehement identity? No, actually. Bringa doesn't record any identity assertions. Everyone understands that "they" are Catholic Croats, but in this film, they are not named; neither are "we." A possibility for comparison, though? Yes.

The question for researchers is no longer whether identities are constructed, contextual, and situational. Bringa's film, this book, and many other works tell us that they are. Nor need we observe that from the point of view of an individual, identities are "inhabitable" or not for reasons grounded in social construction. The question, rather, is that of psychological superglue. Sometimes identities associated with ethnic and national groups do endure. The "German Minority in Poland" shows us identities that endured across situations and through decades. But the sociology of German identity in Opole Silesia also shows this happening under very specific circumstances.

How could we know that when those specific circumstances occur, whether in Silesia or elsewhere, the result is likely to be vehement identity? How can we compare "identity" in one culture with "identity" in another? Consider the following analogy: When we locate a place on a map, we use a grid of latitude and longitude. These agreed upon concepts allow us to compare locations. To compare social and cultural phenomena, we also relie on agreed upon concepts. The concepts analogous to latitude and longitude that this argument relies on are generation, adolescence, and trauma. Comparison, then, depends first on those three being similar to the current case. If they are, then we can ask whether ethnic or national identity is similarly rigid. If they are not, and yet we see vehement identity, we can ask what differences in specific circumstances are leading to the same result.

How, then, do we even establish that the three concepts that provide the means of comparison work? Remember that moving beyond a view of culture as "stable and bounded 'islands' of cultural distinctiveness" (Bashkow 2004:443) depends on finding difference that is *relevant* to a particular analytic concern. Relevant difference is distorted when we examine it through concepts which, themselves, are different in the cultural context under consideration than they are in ours. What I would like to suggest, however, is a certain "good enough" approach to this dilemma. Generation, adolescence and trauma may not mean exactly the same things in Opole Silesia that they do for the readers of this book, but I argue that what they mean is similar enough. I'll develop the thought most thoroughly with reference to "generation."

In early July 1993, my parents visited me in Dobra. I arranged for a July 4 party in Marta's backyard, with watermelon, hamburgers, and "hot dogs," that is, kielbasa and bratwurst. This was my chance to smooth over the fact that as an only daughter, I was not living with my parents, by asking my father, "Just use your German to tell everyone it's OK with you both that I'm here, OK?" I arranged the chairs in groups of four or five, as Americans do, to facilitate small group conversation. The guests arrived and immediately re-arranged them into three large circles, one for each generation.

In 2009, I had another interview with the soon-to-retire parish priest of Dobra. When I asked him about German identity this time, he shrugged and said, "That generation is dying out."

CONCLUSION

There are two points to be made about the concept of "generation." One, it doesn't mean the same thing everywhere. My guests' view of appropriate chair arrangement suggests that it is more, not less, salient in Silesia than in my native culture. And, on the other hand, we cannot assume that it even exists as an organizing principle everywhere. But, there's no reason, if we are careful, not to use it in comparative analyses of other conceptual phenomena, like identity. And what holds for generation holds also, I believe, for "trauma" and "adolescence."

Or, another concept: let's return to what Kulick and Schieffelin had to say about the concept of an inner self, a person's "true colors": "This concern with surface and depth is a profoundly Western problematic, one that has arisen from a long history of meditation on supposedly fundamental binaries (presence versus absence, body versus soul, mind versus body, conscious versus unconscious, etc.)" (2004: 352) Because such binaries are not universal, Bucholtz and Hall represent the view of identity as "enduring psychological states" as inadequate, and for a globally encompassing theory of identity, it is. But it is equally inadequate to rule out a concept being analytically cogent in several sets of situations, *situations that, when compared, can teach us much*, just because we recognize that the concept cannot be applied universally. Kulick and Schieffelin are right, but Silesia happens to be in the West. Bucholtz and Hall are right, but our inadequate concept happens to be one that we share with a large number of humans. We can proceed to compare within and between these sets of contexts, where certain concepts hold, and are useful. In fact, we used to call such sets of contexts "ethnographic areas." We can jettison the geographical aspect, in this "ever-changing world of transnational cultural 'flows'" (Bashkow 2004:443), but revitalize the analytic concept.

And it is really important to understand how identities become psychologically superglued. People kill and die, and say that it's about identity.

A POSTCARD FROM THE NEW ETHNOGRAPHALAND

One of Bashkow's major points is that boundaries are drawn by all analysts, whether they be anthropologists of the professional variety or the kind of students of humanity that all of us have to be, since human living seems to entail a certain amount of analyzing our social situations. The kind of "gridding" I sketched above nods to that; all locations are specified and all maps drawn with respect to some decision about boundaries, however taken-for-granted the boundaries may be. A telling example is a coastline: try to find the coastline of New England on a topographic map that shows the depths of the ocean wa-

270

ters in exactly the same way that it shows the heights of the landforms. The actual coastline looks just like the other contour lines; it's really difficult to see where it is. The exercise makes it clear that even marking the coastline is a decision about what boundaries count.

How, then, are we to think about culture now that we've gotten past our "bounded island" phase?

Boundedness, as Bashkow and Bunzl between them point out, is a visual metaphor that functions both as an image and as an anthropological autobiography. Metaphors, on the face of it, are useful and necessary things in ethnography, as in any form of written representation.

Andrew Orta has already given this book one extremely useful metaphor, as I discussed in the introduction: describing the Aymara as "capillary endpoints of global processes." This metaphor allowed for comparison in that Opole Silesia can be described as "at the arteries." Arteries in the sense of blood vessels met arteries in the sense of transportation infrastructure, and set up a discussion of Opole Silesia as a place that people travel through but not to. At this point, I want to consider, briefly, the other salient metaphor that Orta employs: weaving.

He got it from the Aymara, who are weavers. They use it as a metaphor too. Orta uses it to convey the five-century-long and troubled relationship of the Aymara with the Roman Catholic Church. When he wants to invoke the negative aspects of the postcolonial position of the Aymara, he talks about "porous entanglement." More positively, he uses words like "inter-twining" and "braiding": "Aymara are immersed in their own ongoing simulation of coherence, braiding meaningful order out of a complex world" (Orta 2004: 22).

It's another metaphor for culture that doesn't rely on a conception of boundaries seen either as a "blank space" or as a "thick line."

I used a metaphor to organize this book. Here it is: A tree, backlit by strong sunlight, is like autochthonous Opole Silesian culture. The tree is complicated, fractal; what you see depends on where you look. The light, which comes from outside, is an integral part of the image, not to mention an integral part of the photosynthesizing tree. We navigated a journey of looking at autochthonous Opole Silesian culture from various perspectives. In chapter 2, our perspective was finding out where this tree is. In chapter 3, our perspective was all about edges. There is tree, and there is sky, and they are different. In reticence about names, in managing impressions, outsiders are directed to focus on that edge beyond which not much detail is in evidence. When leaves are dense and the sunlight behind them strong, they appear to be simply one dark mass.

CONCLUSION

But we can see the details. In chapters 4 and 5, let's say, our gaze shifted away from the edge where the sunlight is strong, more to the center of the tree. Our eyes adjusted, and we could see the details of the leaves. The tree—culture—can be imagined as a "filter" (a metaphor suggested by Rosenblatt: personal communication). Looking at the dark leaves, the lighter ones, the branches, we can even speak of "patterns," Ruth Benedict's 1934 metaphor for culture. The light—which exists beyond the edges of the tree, and in one sense is certainly not part of it—becomes part of the pattern.

In chapters 6 and 7, it's as if the sun were behind very thick leaves. We can look at the sun only because the tree is there; otherwise, it would blind us. The sunlight plays gently in the leaves, but it doesn't do to forget that it's harsh. So, also, has been the power of the states. In moving from aesthetics to fear, from norms of identity to their violation, we move from a space of autonomous culture to a place of oppression; metaphorically, from looking at leaves to glimpsing unfiltered sunlight. By the end of chapter 8, and in chapter 9, we're looking straight at the sun.

The end of the "islands" is not the end of either culture or metaphors for it. Anthropologists are challenged to expand the repertoire.

For the ethnographic experience—the fieldwork experience—has changed as a result of globalization. Let's return, at this point, to the introduction's consideration of the "Malinowskian fieldwork tradition":

> [It] privileges direct observation and links it to a radical separation between "home" and the "field," which, in turn, creates a "hierarchy of purity of field sites." In this framework, "real" fieldwork is conducted in a remote site, a notion that—along with the colonially veiled constitution of center and periphery—constructs the archetypal fieldworker as a "Euro-American, white, middle-class male." . . . Fieldwork thus becomes synonymous with a "heroized journey into Otherness," the trope that engendered and cemented Malinowski's mythopoetic charter of modern ethnography. . . . (Bunzl 2004: 435)

Americans have all sorts of myths of a solitary individual, usually white, usually male, going off into Otherness to act the hero: the Wild West; the inner-city classroom. They don't align with reality well: they are myths. In the case of fieldwork, they have come to align with reality startlingly less well than they did during the mid-twentieth-century decades when anthropology consolidated its position as a academic discipline. That journey is decidedly not what it once was. Consider the following twist.

In one of the autochthonous villages, there is a small museum in a large room above the volunteer fire department. As it was the kind of thing an ethnographer could be expected to find interesting, the volunteer curator invited me to come and see it. It was mainly old farm and farmhouse implements, old iron and steel. It made a rather drab impression. In one corner, however, there was a display of hand-woven textiles in bright colors. They were not Silesian, obviously. In fact, they looked Andean. So where were they from and why were they there?

They were indeed Andean. They were Aymara, made by one of the indigenous peoples of the highland Andes, in Bolivia. "We have a priest from this village," explained the curator, "who is working there as a missionary."

"Really?" I said, my mind reeling. "I have a university classmate who is doing research with the Aymara and the missionary priests who work with them."

This is not how my culture—the culture of the anthropologists—has traditionally operated. Among the anthropologists, you see, each member develops a relationship with a specific other people, the ones who used to be called "the Capitalized Ethnonym," a.k.a "informants," a.k.a. "my people." Anthropologists have generally not shared this relationship; a few husband-wife or other teams aside, it has generally been a relationship between a set of people and an individual anthropologist. Then we anthropologists compare, swap stories, share analyses. But we felt alone in our remote, far-flung fieldsites. And the world was not a place that presented us with this kind of crossover. We're not used to finding the stuff of another anthropologist's relationship mixed into our relationships. I was trained to "take notes on everything," but I had not anticipated taking notes on Aymara textiles.

Also, Andrew Orta and I both thought that we were going to work with people who were in some sense the underdog. In his case, the primary representative of the global system is the Roman Catholic Church. In mine, it's the two nation-states, Germany and Poland. But my underdog Silesian turns out to be his representative of the global system. Ironic.

But this missionary priest did not send those textiles halfway around the world in order to be ironic. Why were they there?

Neither Orta nor I got beyond, "Ironic," until I read his book. Here's the ethnography that made it make sense:

> The global phenomenon of missionization is inseparable from its concrete local manifestation: missionaries whose personal trajectories span—say—childhoods in rural Poland, training at an urban seminary, a year of study in Chicago, three years of work with migrant laborers in North Carolina, and an ongoing pastoral stint on the Bolivian altiplano. (2004: 9)

One of these Polish priests went through a crisis in the early years of his work in Bolivia that Orta considers as reflecting the "entangled history of Aymara

CONCLUSION

and missionary" (103). Father Miguel—I'll call him Father Michał—initially had difficulty "relating" to the Aymara, a difficulty that was resolved in what Father Michał calls "a personal transformation" (101). Part of it was the following realization:

> And I discovered my own roots. I come from the peasantry. . . . I discovered my own deep roots in that we also, in spite of all of these things, as Polish campesinos and under *minifundia*—another correspondence with them—we had to defend our identity before communist power, and especially during Stalinist times. (110)

In other words, as Orta comments, Father Michał learned to "align" himself with the Aymara:

> Miguel's conversion and comparable narratives are conditions of the possibility for establishing meaningful frameworks of missionization, *aligning transcendent frames of meaning and action* with the localized fields of missionary practice through the translocal biographies of missionary selves. (111, emphasis mine)

Stating it another way, missionaries must achieve plausibility for the Aymara and the Aymara must be plausible to the missionaries:

> The self-contextualizing character of missionary conversion involves the missionary positing and positioning himself as a plausible evangelical subject within the mission field. The plausible subjectivity turns in part on the possibility of intersubjectivity. It is this intersubjectivity, I think, that is asserted in the reciprocal self-consciousness of missionaries. (115)

Bear in mind the discussion of the cultural importance of house building in autochthonous Opole Silesia (chapter 8) as you read the following. It emerges that one instance of "aligning trandscendent frames of meaning and action" involved a "frame" in a literal sense, the frame of a house:

> [L]et me return indirectly to the case of Miguel, through experiences recounted to me by other members of his order. In the early 1980s they expanded their missionary activity among the Aymara, inheriting an altiplano parish from another pastoral team. During their first years in the parish, the priests built a new parish house. They recounted this to me as a significant step in their process of being "accepted" within the parish. The construction of the house was a self-conscious performance on the part of the missionaries of their capacity to work. For some this sense of themselves as laborers was tied to their sense of their Polish identity. (Orta 2004: 116)

CONCLUSION

OK, so that's it. One of these priests is an autochthonous Opole Silesian. He sent the Aymara textiles back to the curator of his village's museum, so they could be displayed alongside implements of traditional Silesian life, as an act of reciprocal self-consciousness, and as a symbolic act of alignment of their Aymara culture with his Silesian culture. For what does such a museum do but display culture? And how better to align two distant cultures, connected in the life of one priest, than by literally lining up their work, placing them next to one another, in a museum?

It was also a symbolic act of self-alignment. As if to say: I, the priest, am here with the Aymara, with them in a profound way, and in an expression of that, I will place their textiles in a room in my native village, alongside the artifacts of MY tradition. His doing so, I would further surmise, expressed his sincerity, in the terms of that Western duality: his self-alignment with the Aymara is not just something that he's "performing" in Bolivia; it goes as deep in his soul as his own rural Silesian heritage.

Note that the exact, specific meaning of house construction and house ownership does not have to be the same in order to constitute framing a house as "aligning a transcendent frame of meaning and action." The point is, the missionaries figured out that it *has meaning* for the Aymara, as for them. The specifics—the differences that would emerge on close examination—are unimportant and, indeed, irrelevant. In the same way, theautochthonous Opole Silesians' concept of generation need not be exactly the same as ours in order for it to be useful. It is relevant difference, not difference per se, that is interesting for anthropology; and there is such a thing, in anthropology as elsewhere, as relevant similarity. These priests found a useful relevant similarity.

Where in Poland are the other priests from? Are there a number of autochthonous Opole Silesians or only one? Do other areas of rural Poland have "cultures of house building" that are similar to that in autochthonous Opole Silesia? I don't know. The easy experience of the Malinowskis in Dobra suggests that the answer could well be yes. On the other hand, Franciszek Jonderko's work (2007) might suggest that it's no. This is perhaps a topic for further research.

But that's the point of ethnography. It solves the cross-cultural mysteries of human living and raises more questions to be curious about.

CHAPTER ONE
MAPS FOR THE BOOK

1. For making this clear to me, I am grateful to geographers Tomasz Komornicki, Piotr Rosik, and Kevin Sutton for their presentations and conversations at the conference, "Networks of Infrastructure and the Phantom Borders in East Central Europe," (2012) a conference of the Centre Marc Bloch in Berlin, funded by the German Federal Ministry for Education and Research, in cooperation with the European University Viadrina, the University of Basel, and the International Association for Railway History.

CHAPTER TWO
OPOLE SILESIA, BETWIXT AND BETWEEN

1. That Silesia had had no political connection with Poland since the twelfth century is debatable only insofar as, between 1163 and 1339, there was no Poland with which to be politically connected. When Casimir the Great recreated a Kingdom of Poland in 1339, he was, however, its sovereign; that's why he was in a position to cede it. Also, that the region's development was due to German work is undeniable, though again, during the time in question there was no Poland that could have done the work. It is also clear that both states needed Silesia's resources. Whether there were "Polish national traditions" in Silesia depends on definition. I also found that there is no folk memory of medieval Polish history. There was some agitation on behalf of the Polish cause in Silesia during the time of the Partitions. I agree that the Silesian dialect "constituted no characteristic of nationality and was not incompatible with German national consciousness." These arguments continue to be brought forth in political discourse about Silesia.

2. The "informant" is Franz Skorupka, whose linguistic insights figure importantly in chapters 5 and 6. The name is a pseudonym; I discuss my reasons for using pseudonyms in chapter 3.

3. Nysa (German Neisse) is situated on the Glatzer Neisse. Neisse is a common river name in Silesia; there are at least three of them. When Stalin first suggested a Polish western border "on the Oder and Neisse," it was widely assumed that he meant the Glatzer Neisse, only a few kilometers east of the western plebiscite line, not the Lausitzer Neisse, 350 kilometers west of it.

4. Hannan (1996: 5) notes exactly the same phenomenon of identification of self and place in neighboring Teschen Silesia, which remained with Austria when the rest of Silesia became Prussian.

NOTES FOR CHAPTER SEVEN

CHAPTER THREE
SILENT MEMORY AND IDENTITY TALK

1. Polish and Silesian are indicated as usual; normal typeface indicates translation from German.

2. In German usage, such as in this woman's comment, the term "Upper Silesian" includes Opole Silesians.

CHAPTER FOUR
FINDING CULTURE

1. The part of this paragraph regarding seating patterns in church has changed completely in the intervening years; I left the entire passage in the "ethnographic present" because I do not have the basis to assert whether the entire complex has changed or not.

2. Cf. Shapiro (1991), who argues that in many systems, upward mobility within a stratified system is open to cultural rationalization, while "those who intentionally move down in the system are more threatening to its values than those seeking to move up. The latter may constitute a threat to the group concerned with maintaining its privileges, but the former constitute a threat to the principles on which the hierarchy itself is based" (270).

CHAPTER FIVE
A CULTURE OF LANGUAGE

1. A reasonable Silesian equivalent would be: "*joł* jes*[0]* ciekawy *ile* godzina jes*[0]*" [I am curious how many hours it is]. The formulation, in Polish, can be more casual than the one offered.

2. *Ździebko* consists of a /z/ with tongue held high against the palate followed by a /j/ with tongue held high against the palate followed by a high vowel, followed by a nominal ending. For the mouth, it is a very small word.

3. A village's soccer field is used for its big parties. "Village green," minus the archaic connotations, might translate the sense of the term in this context.

CHAPTER SEVEN
IDENTITY ASCRIPTIONS AS A LANGUAGE OF MORALITY

1. We are, here, again in the "ethnographic present." It is likely that the rate of intermarriage has increased, with interethnic tensions having subsided

and with EU membership, with its open labor migration market, simply giving young people more opportunities to meet people of the other group.

2. In light of the discussion on the community's having "closed in on itself" after the war, in chapter 4, it is particularly interesting that in Polish usage, this word designates a different object of personal loyalty, one of much broader scope. It means "fatherland."

3. Note the discrepancy: Marcin's gift was worth about 200 marks, yet about 50 German marks, or 500,000 złoty, was considered a high monthly rent for Bernard's tenants.

4. Readers familiar with the work of founding anthropologist Bronisław Malinowski may be interested to know that Malinowski, like Kowalski, is an extremely common Polish surname, common enough to appear in elementary textbooks of the language. This is why I chose it as a pseudonym. "Malina" means raspberry; a "kowal" is a smith.

<h2 style="text-align:center">CHAPTER EIGHT</h2>

IDENTITY ASSERTIONS AS A LANGUAGE OF ASPIRATION

1. This has changed. More recently Johann has more frequently preferred Silesian.

2. I was shown such a genealogy by Mrs. Pilawa, see below, filled out by her mother (September 7, 1995). I was told about Kurt Lasok by the woman who gave me most of my information about the families who owned property in the village center, Maria Rataja. Marta showed me the records of the Schraft tavern. The name is the same as that of the concurrent German Minority chair, and she thinks that it is the same family. When I took their genealogy, and asked, strategically, "Pilawa, that's a pretty unusual name, isn't it? Are there any other families in Dobra with that name?" Mrs. Pilawa said, "There was one, unrelated to us, but they left right after the war. Other than that, no." She might have been lying, but I don't think she had any reason to think I knew anything about Nazis named Pilawa.

3. Urszula may be somewhat too optimistic, at least for the immediate post-Communist period. Her daughter Anna and a friend from Dobra who was going to the same high school in Opole both reported ongoing interethnic tension. Angelika Stanik, at a different high school, reported that when a teacher had spoken about an example of Silesian speech which had confused her when she arrived in the area after the war, and then asked, "Now who here would know what this means?" all the autochthonous Opole Silesians in the class unobtrusively looked around at one another and silently decided, as a group,

that no-one would raise a hand (Notes, December 16, 1994). The school system keeps young children in village schools for primary school and, at that time, middle school, so high school was often the first significant interethnic experience for autochthonous Opole Silesians.

Agha, Asif. 2004. "Registers of Language." In Duranti 2004.

Ahonen, Pertti, et al. 2008. *People on the Move: Forced Population Movements in Europe in the Second World War and Its Aftermath.* Oxford: Berg.

Anderson, Benedict. 1983. *Imagined Communities: Reflections on the Origin and Spread of Nationalism.* London: Verso.

Aronson, Elliot, and Judson Mills. 1959. "The Effect of Severe Initiation on Liking for a Group." *Journal of Abnormal and Social Psychology* 59 (2): 177–81.

Bach, Dieter, and Wiesław Lesiuk. 1995. *Ujrzałem twarz człowieka: niemiecko-polskie kontakty przed 1945 rokiem i po wojnie.* Wuppertal: Peter Hammer Verlag; Opole: PIN Instytut Śląski.

Balikci, Asen. 1970. *The Netsilik Eskimo.* Garden City, NY: Natural History Press.

Barth, Fredrik. 1969. Introduction to *Ethnic Groups and Boundaries*, ed. Fredrik Barth. Boston: Little, Brown and Company.

Bashkow, Ira. 2004. "A Neo-Boasian Conception of Cultural Boundaries." *American Anthropologist* 106 (3): 443–58.

———. 2006. *The Meaning of Whitemen : Race and Modernity in the Orokaiva Cultural World.* Chicago: University of Chicago Press.

Basso, Keith. 1979. *Portraits of "The Whiteman": Linguistic Play and Cultural Symbols among the Western Apache.* Cambridge: Cambridge University Press.

Benedict, Ruth. 1934. "Anthropology and the Abnormal." *Journal of General Psychology* 10 (2): 59–82.

Berlińska, Danuta. 1989. *Społeczne uwarunkowania ruchu mniejszości niemieckiej na Śląskim Opolskim.* Opole: Instytut Śląski.

———. 1990. "Die sozialen Strukturen in Oberschlesien." In *Oberschlesien als Brücke zwischen Polen und Deutschen*, ed. Dieter Bach and Janusz Kroszel. Mülhelm: Evangelische Akademie.

———. 1992. "Odrębność kulturowo-społeczna województwa opolskiego." In *Śląsk Opolski: Region i jego struktura*, ed. S. Malarski, 116–24. Opole: Instytut Śląski.

Berlińska, Danuta, and Franciszek Jonderko. 1993. *Postawy polityczne stosunki etniczniej mieszkańców Śląska Opolskiego.* Opole: Instytut Śląski w Opolu.

Billig, Michael. 1999. *Freudian Repression: Conversation Creating the Unconscious.* Cambridge: Cambridge University Press.

Bjork, James E. 2008. *Neither German Nor Pole: Catholicism and National Indifference in a Central European Borderland.* Ann Arbor: University of Michigan Press.

Blommaert, Jan, and Jef Verschueren. 1998. "The Role of Language in European Nationalist Ideologies." *In Language Ideologies: Practice and Theory*, ed.

BIBLIOGRAPHY

Bambi B. Schieffelin, Kathryn A. Woolard, and Paul V. Kroskrity, 189–210. New York: Oxford University Press.

Bourdieu, Pierre. 1977. *Outline of a Theory of Practice*. Stanford, CA: Stanford University Press.

Brubaker, Rogers. 2004. *Ethnicity Without Groups*. Cambridge, MA: Harvard University Press.

Brubaker, Rogers, Margit Feischmidt, Jon Fox, and Liana Grancea. 2006. *Nationalist Politics and Everyday Ethnicity in a Transylvanian Town*. Princeton, NJ: Princeton University Press.

Bucholtz, Mary, and Kira Hall. 2004. "Language and Identity." In Duranti 2004: 369–94.

Bunzl, Matti. 2004. "Boas, Foucault, and the 'Native Anthropologist': Notes toward a Neo-Boasian Anthropology." *American Anthropologist* 106 (3): 435–42.

Butturini, Paula. 1989. "German-Polish Mass Is Latent Sign of Change." *Chicago Tribune*, 13 November.

Bżdziach, Klaus, ed. 1995a. *"Wach auf mein Herz und denke": Zur Geschichte der Beziehungen zwischen Schlesien und Berlin-Brandenburg von 1740 bis heute / "Przebudź się, serce moje, i pomyśl": Przyczynek do historii stosunków między Śląskiem a Berlinem-Brandenburgią od 1740 roku do dziś*. Berlin: Gesellschaft für interregionalen Kulturaustausch; Opole: Stowarzyszenie Instytut Śląski.

Bżdziach, Klaus. 1995b. "Einführung/Wprowadzenie." In Bżdziach 1995a: 12-18.

Choroś, Monika, and Łucja Jarczak. 1995. "Veränderungen von Orts- und Personennamen in Schlesien vor und nach dem Zweiten Weltkrieg" / "Zmiany nazw miejscowości i nazwisk na Śląsku przed II wojną światową i po 1945 r." In Bżdziach 1995.

Coulmas, Florian. 1985. *Sprache und Staat: Studien zu Sprachplanung und Sprachpolitik*. Berlin: Walter de Gruyter.

Davies, Norman. 1982. *God's Playground: A History of Poland*. New York: Columbia University Press.

———. 1984. *Heart of Europe: A History of Poland*. Oxford: Oxford University Press.

deZayas, Alfred M. 1977. *Nemesis at Potsdam: The Expulsion of the Germans from the East*. Lincoln: University of Nebraska Press.

Dorian, Nancy. 1981. *Language Death*. Philadelphia: University of Pennsylvania Press.

———. 1985. *Tyranny of Tide*. Ann Arbor, MI: Karoma.

———, ed. 1989. *Investigating Obsolescence: Studies in Language Contraction and Death*. Cambridge: Cambridge University Press.

BIBLIOGRAPHY

———. 2010. *Investigating Variation: The Effects of Social Organization and Social Setting*. Oxford: Oxford University Press.

Dorren, Gaston. 2014. *Lingo: A Language Spotter's Guide to Europe*. London: Profile Books.

Dotts Paul, Barbara. 1994. *The Polish-German Borderlands: An Annotated Bibliography*. Westport, CT: Greenwood Press.

Duranti, Allesandro, ed. 2004. *A Companion to Linguistic Anthropology*. Malden, MA: Blackwell.

Dwórk, Deborah, and Robert Jan van Pelt. 1996. *Auschwitz 1270 to the Present*. New York: W.W. Norton.

Ellis, Peter Berresford, and Seumas mac a'Ghobhainn. 1971. *The Problem of Language Revival: Examples of Language Survival*. Inverness: Club Leabhar.

Erikson, Erik. 1980. *Identity and the Life Cycle*. New York: Norton.

Evans-Pritchard, E. E. 1940. *The Nuer*. New York: Oxford University Press.

Fackler, Guido. 2007. "Music in Concentration Camps, 1933–1945." *Music and Politics* 1 (1): http://quod.lib.umich.edu/m/mp/9460447.0001.102/--music-in-concentration-camps-1933-1945?rgn=main;view=fulltext.

Festinger, Leon. 1963. "The Theory of Cognitive Dissonance." In *The Science of Human Communication*, ed. Wilbur Schramm. New York: Basic Books.

Festinger, Leon, and J. Merrill Carlsmith. 1959. "Cognitive Consequences of Forced Compliance." *Journal of Abnormal and Social Psychology* 58:203–10.

Fishman, Joshua Aaron. 1972. "Domains and the Relationship between Micro- and Macrosociolinguistics." In *Directions in Sociolinguistics*, ed. John J. Gumperz and Hymes Dell. New York: Holt, Rhinehart and Winston.

Gal, Susan. 1979. *Language Shift: Social Determinants of Linguistic Change in Bilingual Austria*. New York: Academic Press.

———. 1989. "Language and Political Economy." *Annual Review of Anthropology* 18.

Geertz, Clifford. 1973. *The Interpretation of Cultures: Selected Essays*. New York: Basic Books.

Hannan, Kevin. 1996. *Borders of Language and Identity in Teschen Silesia*. New York: Peter Lang.

Harden, Elaine. 1990. "Polish Ethnic Tension Roils Campaign." *Washington Post*, 17 February.

Hechter, Michael. 1975. *Internal Colonialism: The Celtic Fringe in British National Development, 1536 1966*. Berkeley : University of California Press.

BIBLIOGRAPHY

Heffner, Krystian. 1993. *Oppelner Schlesien: Der Bevölkerungs- und Raumumgestaltungsverlauf des Dorfbesiedlungssystems.* Opole: Instytut Śląski.

Hill, Jane H. 1985. "The Grammar of Consciousness and the Consciousness of Grammar." *American Ethnologist* 12 (4): 725–37.

Hoenigswald, Henry M. 1989. "Language Obsolescence and Language History: Matters of Linearity, Leveling, Loss and the Like." In Dorian 1989: 347–54.

Inglehart, Ronald F., and Margaret Woodward. 1967. "Language Conflicts and Political Community." *Comparative Studies in Society and History* 10 (1): 27–45.

Jonderko, Franciszek. 2007. *Społeczne uwarunkowania budownictwa mieszkaniowego na wsi na Śląsku Opolskim.* Opole: Wydawnictwo Instytut Śląski.

Kaeckenbeeck, G. 1942. *The International Experiment of Upper Silesia.* London: Oxford University Press.

Kaps, Johannes. 1952–53. *The Tragedy of Silesia.* Munich: Christ Unterwegs.

Kempowski, Walter. 1975. *Ein Kapitel für sich.* Munich: C. Hanse.

Kifner, John. 1990. "Fondness for Germany Endures in Polish Silesia." *New York Times*, 9 March.

Kipling, Rudyard. 1912. 'The Cat That Walked by Himself.' In *Just So Stories*, 69–76. Garden City, NY: Doubleday & Company.

Kluckhohn, Clyde, and Dorothea Leighton. 1946. *The Navaho.* Cambridge, MA: Harvard University Press; London: Oxford University Press.

Koehn, Ilse. 1977. *Mischling, Second Degree: My Childhood in Nazi Germany.* New York: Puffin Books.

Kulick, Don, and Bambi Schieffelin. 2004. "Language Socialization." In Duranti. 2004.

"Lasy Opolszczyzny." 1995. *Trybuna Opolska,* 4 June.

Lowie, Robert. 1934. *An Introduction to Cultural Anthropology.* New York: Farrar & Rinehart.

Mach, Zdzisław. 1989. *Symbols, Conflict and Identity.* Krakow: Uniwersytet Jagielloński.

Marks, Sally. 1976. *The Illusion of Peace: International Relations in Europe, 1918–1933.* New York: St. Martin's Press.

Matuschek, Herbert. 1994. "Zapożyczenia i interferencje językowe w kontekscie dwujęzyczności na Śląsku Opolskim." In *Śląsk—Pogranicze Kultur: Materials from a Popular Scientific Session.* Opole: Wojewódzka Biblioteka Publiczna im. E. Smolki.

BIBLIOGRAPHY

Mauss, Marcel. 1967. *The Gift: Forms and Functions of Exchange in Archaic Societies*. New York : W. W. Norton & Company.

Mazower, Mark, Jessica Reinish, and David Feldman. 2011. *Post-war Reconstruction in Europe: International Perspectives, 1945 1949*. Oxford: Oxford University Press.

Milczarczyk, Maciej, and Andrzej Szolc. 1993. *Historia 7: W imię wolności*. Warsaw: Wydawnictwa Szkolne i Pedagogiczne.

Mook, Douglas. 2004. *Classic Experiments in Psychology*. Westport, CT: Greenwood Press.

Nowak, Edmund. 1995. "Schatten über Lamsdorf" / "Cień Łambinowic." In Bżdziach 1995a: 452–53.

Orta, Andrew. 2004. *Catechizing Culture: Missionaries, Aymara, and the "New Evangelization."* New York: Columbia University Press.

Osmańczyk, Edmund Jan. 1980. *Był rok 1945*. Warsaw: Państwowy Instytut Wydawniczy.

Pogonowski, Iwo. 1996. *Historyczny atlas Polski*. Krakow: Wydawnictwo Baran i Suszczyński.

Poplack, Shana. 1980. "'Sometimes I'll start a sentence in English *y termino en español*': Toward a Typology of Code-switching." *Linguistics* 18: 581–18.

———. 1988. "Contrasting Patterns of Codeswitching in Two Communities." In *Codeswitching: Anthropological and Sociolinguistic Perspectives*, ed. Monica Heller. Berlin: Mouton de Gruyter.

Powdermaker, Hortense. 1933. *Life in Lesu: The Study of a Melanesian Society in New Ireland*. New York : W.W. Norton & Company

———. 1966. *Stranger and Friend: The Way of an Anthropologist*. New York: W.W. Norton & Company.

Rauziński, Robert. 1992. "Charakterystyka demograficzna miast i gmin opolszczyzny w latach 1945–1990." In *Śląsk Opolski: region i jego struktura*, ed. Stanisław Malarski. Opole: Instytut Śląski.

Rauziński, Robert, and Kazimierz Szczygielski. 1992. *Współczesna sytuacja demograficzna w województwie opolskim*. Opole: Państwowy Instytut Naukowy and Instytut Śląski w Opolu.

Romaine, Suzanne. 1994. *Language in Society : An Introduction to Sociolinguistics*. Oxford: Oxford University Press.

Rose, William. 1935. *The Drama of Upper Silesia*. Brattleboro, VT: Stephen Daye Press.

Rosenblatt, Daniel. 2004. "An Anthropology Made Safe for Culture: Patterns of Practice and the Politics of Difference in Ruth Benedict." *American Anthropologist* 106 (3): 459–72.

BIBLIOGRAPHY

Rospond, Stanisław. 1959. *Dzieje polszczyzny śląskiej*. Katowice: Wydawnictwo "Śląsk."

Sahlins, Peter. 1989. *Boundaries: The Making of France and Spain in the Pyrenées*. Berkeley: University of California Press.

Schneider, Peter. 1990. "Is Anyone German Here?" *New York Times Magazine*, 15 April

Seizer, Susan. 1997. "Jokes, Gender, and Discursive Distance on the Tamil Popular Stage." *American Ethnologist* 24 (1): 62–90.

Shapiro, Judith. 1991. "Transsexualism: Reflections on the Persistence of Gender and the Mutability of Sex." In *Body Guards: The Cultural Politics of Gender Ambiguity*, ed. Julia Epstein and Kristina Straub, 248–80. New York: Routledge.

Silverstein, Michael. 1987. "Monoglot 'Standard' in America." Working Papers and Proceedings of the Center for Psychosocial Studies, no. 13.

Stocking, George W. 1992. *The Ethnographer's Magic and Other Essays in the History of Anthropology*. Madison: University of Wisconsin Press.

Tooley, T. Hunt. 1997. *National Identity and Weimar Germany: Upper Silesia and the Eastern Border, 1918–1922*. Lincoln: University of Nebraska Press.

Urban, Thomas. 1994. *Deutsche in Polen: Geschichte und Gegenwart einer Minderheit*. Munich: C.H. Beck.

———. 1995. "Klärungsversuche" / "Próby wyjaśnienia." In Bżdziach 1995a: 453–57.

Urciuoli, Bonnie. 1996. *Exposing Prejudice: Puerto Rican Experiences of Language, Race and Class*. Boulder, CO: Westview Press.

Van Gennep, Arnold. 1961. *The Rites of Passage*. Chicago: University of Chicago Press.

Várdy, Steven Béla, and T. Hunt Tooley. 2003. *Ethnic Cleansing in Twentieth-century Europe*. Boulder: Social Science Monographs.

Verdery, Katherine. 1985. "The Unmaking of an Ethnic Collectivity: Transylvania's Germans." *American Ethnologist* 12 (1): 62–84.

Waterman, John T. 1966. *A History of the German Language, with Special Reference to the Cultural and Social Forces That Shaped the Standard Literary Language*. Seattle: University of Washington Press.

Weber, Eugen. 1976. *Peasants into Frenchmen*. Stanford, CA: Stanford University Press.

Woolard, Kathryn. 2004. "Codeswitching." In *A Companion to Linguistic Anthropology*, ed. Alessandro Duranti. Malden, MA: Blackwell.

Index

*The pseudonyms of autochthonous Opole Silesians
who appear repeatedly are indexed by their first names.*

INDEX

domain: linguistic, 106, 148–50; social, 146
Dorian, Nancy, 10–12, 35, 117, 148
Dotts Paul, Barbara, 41
Drabik, Hans. *See* Hans Drabik
Dwórk, Deborah, xviii

Ellis, Peter Berresford, 148
emigration: of Franz Boas, 4; from Opole Silesia, 33, 188, 215–16, 219, 223, 225, 229–30
Erikson, Erik, 256–58
ethnic identity, 15, 70, 88, 250
ethnicity: and boundaries, 14; and cognitive psychology, 18; and conformance/nonconformance to social norms, 196–98, 203; as extension of kinship, 195; and German citizenship, 43, 72; linked to native language, 41, 72; and Nazi classification, 43; and social construction, 16, 39
ethnographic area, 6, 270
ethnonyms, 26, 29, 36, 275, 297
Eva (Magda's daughter, Marta's niece), 108–9, 118, 127, 192
Evans-Pritchard, E. E., 37
exchange. *See* delayed reciprocal exchange

Fackler, Guido, 26
Feldman, David, 44
Festinger, Leon, 19
first grade, language socialization in, 104–7, 156, 168
Fishman, Joshua Aaron, 106, 146
fonts, how to read, 24
Franz Kowolik (survivor of ethnic cleansing), 237–44, 247, 249–53
Franz Skorupka: intensification codeswitch of, 138; and jokes, 110, 118–19; on Poles speaking Polish, 208; and registers from pictures, 144–45, 149–50; Silesian identity of, 119, 177; and stories from pictures, 157, 160–61; use of Polish to express disapproval of, 174–78, 197; use of standard Polish of, 163; on words for "fence," 147

Gal, Susan, 137, 148
Geertz, Clifford, 5
German Friendship Circle, 52, 54–55, 111, 118, 217, 226, 227, 234
German identity, x, 15, 22, 51, 197; ascription of, 88; assertion of, 89, 93, 101, 210, 244, 252; associated with age, 92, 101; boundaries of, 85, 182, 214; claim to, 73, 92, 181, 183; and class, 242; fear of admitting to, 88; houses associated with, 210–11; sociology of, 269; status symbols of, 196; and suffering, 251, 255, 258; "super-glued," 246; and upward mobility, 218, 231
German Minority: active membership of, 17, 223, 225, 230–31, 233, 240–41, 247, 251; activists

of, 114, 208; cabaret of, 48, 57, 34; gatherings of, 233; and household structure, 91, 253; leaders of, 117, 220, 222, 225, 230, 236, 238–40, 252–53, 256; and its "party line" xvi, 83, 74; process of organization of, 22, 34–35, 57, 86–87, 90, 93, 180, 242, 252; and standard language, 204, 208; and summer festival decorations, 229–30; and upward mobility, 231. *See also* Social and Cultural Society of the German Minority; German Friendship Circle
gerontocracy, 90
Gertruda Jaskula (singer), 234–36

Hall, Kira, 17, 72, 236, 256, 270
Hannan, Kevin, 43, 277n4
Hans Drabik, 224; on Hitler Youth and the Polish Communist Party, 235
Harden, Elaine, 35
Hechter, Michael, 29
Heffner, Krystian, 52
Henryk (Józef's son, Marta's nephew), 140, 153, 170, 233
Hill, Jane H, 137
Hitler Youth, 234–35
Hoenigswald, Henry M, 148
Holocaust, x, xiv–xvi, 29, 245–46, 259
humor, genre of, 109–10, 112. *See also* speech genre

identity: ascriptions of, 14, 21, 180, 203, 233; assertions of, 21, 85, 180, 203, 213, 241, 244, 256, 268; discursively created, 106; enduring, 17, 256, 269–70; harnessed by German Minority, 16; social discourse of, 178; sociology of, 180. *See also* ethnic identity; German identity; national identity; Silesian identity; vehement identity
ideology: linguistic, 116, 120, 144–45; nationalist linguistic, 76–77; totalitarian, 120
ideology of linguistic tolerance, 23, 116–18, 120–21, 143–44, 150
index, linguistic. *See* linguistic index
Inglehart, Ronald F., 148
intonation, 122, 156, 162–63, 167–168, 171, 176
ius sanguinis, 43
Iwona (daughter of Maria Rataja, second cousin of Marta Schraft), 60, 119, 187–88, 197
Izabela (wife of Suzanna's second cousin), 186–87, 192–94, 193

Jarczak, Łucja, 63–67
Johann Schraft, 9, 213–16, 220, 227, 229, 238, 279ch8n1
jokes, 102–3, 108–12, 114–15, 118–19, 170; derogatory toward Poles, 46; as socially acceptable use of Polish, 173, 177
Jonderko, Franciszek, 54, 86–89, 91, 180, 182, 275

288

INDEX

INDEX

76, 79, 81; and local identity, 88, 182, 184; and the nation-state, 80; of previous generations, 92; as related to trauma, ix; social space of, 76; and upward mobility, 182, 257; and Wilsonian ideals, 41. *See also* ethnic identity; German identity; identity; Silesian identity

Nazi Germany, x, xiv, 221, 262, 264; and Communist Poland, 7, 221, 241

Neo-Nazis, 53, 261–62

Norbert Nicholaus (father of Marta, grandfather of Kasia), 66, 68, 92, 242–43, 256, 115, 117, 150

Nowak, Edmund, 47

occupation, German, 253; Nazi, 246; Polish, 17

Oder-Neisse line, 61, 176, 247

Oder-Neisse territories, 95

Oder Rver, 52, 61–62, 73, 75, 92, 269, 271. *See also* Oder-Neisse line; Oder-Neisse territories

Opole, city of, x, 41, 51, 250. *See also* Oppeln

Opole Regency, 45

Oppeln, 45

Orta, Andrew, xxi, 3, 31, 37, 271, 273–75, 277

Osmańczyk, Edmund Jan, 245

parts of speech: directional verbs, 139; gerunds, 161; relativizers, 168

patrilocality, 224–28. *See also* marriage

peasant workers, autochthonous Opole Silesians as, 236

phatic function, 158, 161

phonology, 158; Polish, 163, 172; Silesian, 63, 204, 207

Pilawa, Roland. *See* Roland Pilawa

Pilawa, Teresa. *See* Teresa Pilawa

place names, 62–66, 77

Pogonowski, Iwo, 28–29

Poplack, Shana, 141

Powdermaker, Hortense, 2–3, 10, 15, 114

priests: 55, 95, 209, 222, 264, 273–75; parish priest of Dobra, 56–57, 73–74, 84, 221, 269

psychology: cognitive, 18; depth, 256; discursive, 21. *See also* cognitive dissonance

race, x–xi, xxi, 9, 40,39, 61, 67, 72, 184, 240

railways, 25, 29–30, 32, 41, 48–49, 51–52, 55, 217, 226, 259

Rauziński, Robert, 32–33

reference (linguistic), 120–22, 144–45, 147

register (linguistic): culture of, cultural meaning of, or shared sense of, 124, 138, 143–44, 150, 153, 161–62, 177; defined and contrasted with reference, 120–23, 144–46; expository, 168, 171, 173, 204, 216; and language death, 148, 150; and loyalty vs. tolerance, 144, 150; narrative organization as, 158; and "registers

from pictures," 124–38, 144, 145, 147, 148, 149, 153, 154; semanticization of distinctions of, 145–47, 150; Silesian, German, and/or Polish as, 150, 151, 154, 161–62, 185; and the space/time map, 138–39, 143

registration: of personal names, 69; of villages, 51

Reinish, Jessica, 44

Renate Janta (survivor of the carpet bombing of Dresden), 244, 247–48, 250–51, 253, 257–58, 263–64

repertoire, multilingual. *See* multilingual repertoire

rite of passage, fieldwork as anthropologists', 5; discursively created in school, 106

Roland Pilawa (German Minority leader), 220, 226, 230–31

Romaine, Suzanne, 116

Roman (husband of Magda), 170, 233

Romanticism, German, 72

Rose, William, 28, 35, 42, 51

Rosenblatt, Daniel, xxi, 3, 13, 272

Rospond, Stanisław, 75

Sahlins, Peter, 41

Sattler, Mr., 149, 150

Sattler, Mrs., 60, 149, 173–74, 177

Schieffelin, Bambi, xviii–xvix, 2, 17–18, 20–21, 270

Schiller, Friedrich, 79, 81

Schneider, Peter, 35

Schraft, Anna. *See* Anna Schraft

Schraft, Johann. *See* Johann Schraft

Schraft, Marta. *See* Marta Schraft

Schraft, Stefan. *See* Stefan Schraft

Seizer, Susan, 102

semantic distinction, 124, 146–47, 150

semantics, 121, 161

Shapiro, Judith, 278n2

silence: approving, 196, 203; conspiracy of, x, 22; as creative culture, 62, 70; disapproving, 233–34; and identity, 21, 265; and identity assertions, 244; as object of analysis, xiv, xviii, 21; and Polish identity, 197; and repression, xviii–xvix, 20, 65–66, 79, 158, 243, 245, 268; and reticence about sharing names, 59

Silesia, Upper. *See* Upper Silesia

Silesian identity: assertions of, 58, 85, 97, 181–82, 247; of Franz Kowolik, 250; of Marta

Silverstein, Michael, 231

Skorupka, Franz. *See* Franz Skorupka

Skorupka, Brigitte. *See* Brigitte Skorupka

Social and Cultural Society of the German Minority, xiv, xvi, 16–17, 35, 48, 51, 53, 70–71, 74, 80, 83

social space, 225; of class, 52; of class and identity, 218; of German national identity, 52;

290

INDEX

German-speaking, 219; of the Roman Catholic Church, 95; sociolinguistics of, 219; for the use of Polish, 106
speech genre, 159
Stalin, 56, 89, 234, 263
Stalinist Communist government or regime, 45, 151, 254
Stalinist era, 73, 92, 99, 274
standard language: contrast with Silesian of, 126–27; development of, 79; as language that dominates, 216; and participation in the nation, 79, 211; sense of ownership of, 116; used as narrative organizer, 163; used to express specificity, 130, 135, 140
Stefan Schraft, 212, 229
Stocking, George W, xxi, 8, 10
Sudetenland, region of (Czech lands), xiii, 38, 71
suicide, 198, 225, 230
summer festivals in Opole Silesian villages, 48, 71, 93, 97, 222, 229, 230
Suzanna (emigrant homeowner), 192–94, 196, 204
syntax, 161; and language mixing (code-switching), 141–42
Szczygielski, Kazimierz, 33
Szolc, Andrzej

Teresa Pilawa, 217, 227, 279ch8n2
tolerance. *See* ideology of linguistic tolerance
Tooley, T. Hunt, 41–42, 44
totalitarianism, 13, 62, 69, 237, 241. *See also* Communist Poland; Nazi Germany; Stalinist Communist government
treaties, xvii; post–World War I, 40; Treaty between the Federal Republic of Germany and the Republic of Poland on the confirmation of the borders existing between them, 71; Treaty of Good Neighborliness and Friendly Cooperation between Poland and Germany, 22, 84

Upper Silesia: autonomy of, 53, 74; borders of during Nazi occupation, 42; cityscape of, 39;

dialects of, 40, 46; and the division of Silesia into three parts, 28, 45; and German citizenship, 43; industry of, 32; and the post–World War I peace treaty, 40; and the railway, 29, 31, 38, 51
Upper Silesians: as different from Opole Silesians, 43, 45–46; and German citizenship, 43, 78; as speakers of standard German, 82
Urban, Thomas, 45–46
Urciuoli, Bonnie, 61
Urszula Krysiak: on bringing a German teacher to Dobra, 204–210; identity of, 212; on Poles' attitudes toward Silesians, 231–232; pronunciation of name of, 70; on Silesians speaking Polish, 118, 177; uxorilocality, 9, 87, 224. *See also* marriage

van Pelt, Robert Jan, xviii
Várdy, Steven Béla, 44
variation. *See* linguistic variation
vehemence: and violence, 181, 265, 267; of identity assertions, xix, 13, 15, 21, 70, 213, 222, 234, 243, 247; of the discourse of identity, 250, 265. *See also* vehement identity
vehement identity, 16, 18, 22, 58, 86, 212–13, 244, 256–57, 264, 266, 268–69
Verdery, Katherine, 43
Verschueren, Jef, 16
village center: demographic collapse in, 219, 220; description of, 49–50; historical development of, 219; map of, 49, nostalgia for, 221, 228; and post-marital patrilocality, 224, as rich, bourgeois, and German, 52, 217–218; run-down condition of buildings of, 212, 220–21; social problems among the families of, 225–30

Waterman, John T., 148
Weber, Eugen, 51
Woodward, Margaret, 148
Woolard, Kathryn, 24, 121, 137

Yugoslavia, 52, 56, 247, 266

CPSIA information can be obtained
at www.ICGtesting.com
Printed in the USA
FFOW04n0024080317
33143FF